TRISTRAM KENNEDY AND THE REVIVAL OF IRISH LEGAL TRAINING

IN THIS SERIES

1   *Brehons, Serjeants and Attorneys: Studies in the History of the Irish Legal Profession* (1990)

2   Colum Kenny, *King's Inns and the Kingdom of Ireland: The Irish 'Inn of Court', 1541–1800* (1992)

3   Jon G. Crawford, *Anglicizing the Government of Ireland: The Irish Privy Council and the Expansion of Tudor Rule, 1556–1578* (1993)

4   *Explorations in Law and History: Irish Legal History Society Discourses, 1988–1994* (1995)

5   W.N. Osborough, *Law and the Emergence of Modern Dublin: A Litigation Topography for a Capital City* (1996)

6   Colum Kenny, *Tristram Kennedy and the Revival of Irish Legal Training, 1835–1885* (1996)

ALSO AVAILABLE

The Irish Legal History Society (1989)

Tristram Kennedy
and the
Revival of Irish Legal Training
1835–1885

COLUM KENNY

IRISH ACADEMIC PRESS
in association with
THE IRISH LEGAL HISTORY SOCIETY

This book was typeset
in 11 pt on 12 pt Plantin by
Carrigboy Typesetting Services, Durrus, for
IRISH ACADEMIC PRESS
Kill Lane, Blackrock, Co. Dublin, Ireland,
and in North America for
IRISH ACADEMIC PRESS
c/o ISBS, 5804 NE Hassalo Street,
Portland, OR 97213.

© Colum Kenny 1996

A catalogue record for this book
is available from the British Library.

ISBN 0–7165–2591–7

All rights reserved.
Without limiting the rights under copyright
reserved alone, no part of this publication may be
reproduced, stored in or introduced into a retrieval system,
or transmitted, in any form or by any means (electronic, mechanical,
photocopying, recording or otherwise), without the prior
written permission of both the copyright owner and
the above publisher of this book.

Printed by
ßetaprint, Dublin

To my mother

and

in memory of my father

Gabh mo chomhairle a mheic mhín

Lean dot fhoghlaim – béara bhuaidh!
ná déana doghraing dod dheoin,
gach ní ná tuigfe, tuig féin,
agus bu léir duid fa dheoidh.

Meabhraigh gach seanfhásach sunn,
giodh seanfhásach nocha searbh,
is as is fhearr bhéara breith
dá bhféagha gach leith, dar leam.

Ní rosgadh ná ráidhe a fhior,
ó losgadh is aille an t-ór,
dá ndéana an corp is a chiall,
do-bhéara sgiamh ort gun ól.

Take my advice, gentle youth

Persevere in your study – victory will be yours!
Do not create difficulty of your own design;
Pay attention to everything that you will not understand
And it will be clear to you eventually.

Learn every old precedent here;
Though it be an old precedent it is not objectionable;
It is on its premise you will best give judgement
If you consider every aspect, I believe.

That which does not tell the truth therein is no maxim,
Gold is more beautiful for [its testing in] fire;
Should you relate both the text and its significance,
It will confer dignity on you at the drinking feast.

From an address to an Irish law student, c.AD 1290,
composed by Giolla na Naomh mac Duinn Shléibhe Mhic Aodhagáin, jurist;
translated by Dr Máirín Ní Dhonnchadha.

Preface

BEFORE THE COMMON LAW was introduced into Ireland, there had long existed on the island an indigenous juridical system which included provisions for legal training. The training was provided by brehon lawyers and their educational apparatus was of greater antiquity than that of the English inns of court. The last vestiges of the brehon system were finally submerged only when Gaelic Ireland was suppressed from the end of the sixteenth century. Those who represented the culture of the conquerors did not put in place in Ireland an alternative to the law schools which had been lost. Instead, they obliged young men to travel to London to complete their legal training. It was not until the nineteenth century, with the emergence of a new era of professionalisation and with the rise of nationalism, that Irish people began again to enjoy the benefits of a system of legal education which was provided for them within their own country.

This book tells the story of that revival of legal training in the nineteenth century, a revival which is intimately connected with the fortunes and ambitions of one particular individual, namely Tristram Kennedy. While it is not suggested that he alone was responsible for the events which are considered in some detail below, his words and actions played a significant role in the reform of legal education in Ireland and England.

The years between Kennedy's call to the bar and his death were eventful ones, not only for his country in general but for the legal profession in particular. It was then that the earliest practical attempts to revive the formal training of lawyers in Ireland were made. A campaign for reform finally culminated in the provision of approved law courses locally and the repeal of the Statute of Jeofailles. For over three hundred years, that statute had required the Irish to attend one of the inns of court in London, regardless of the quality of training provided there.

An account of the eventful life of Tristram Kennedy acts to remind us of the great political and social movements of the period and sets the scene for a consideration of the various factors which determined the shape of legal education in the United Kingdom of Great Britain and Ireland. Particular attention is paid to the Dublin Law Institute which Kennedy founded and which he ran with the support of that great educational reformer, Thomas Wyse MP. The institute was a catalyst for further developments and these are examined in relation both to the universities and to the inns of court. Special chapters are also devoted to the absence of a chamber system in Ireland and to the experiences of those who finally succeeded in having repealed the requirement that they eat, as Daniel O'Connell is said to have put it, 'so many legs of mutton' at the English inns.

The original motivation to write this book was provided by the personal experiences of its author who, a quarter of a century ago, first had reason to ask how Ireland came to have the system of legal training which it does.

On a warm summer afternoon in 1971, two young law students took their ease in the dappled shade of an old tree in the garden of King's Inns. The author and his friend, Jimmy Heron, were discussing their experiences and perceptions of the educational system through which they found themselves passing. The relationship between the benchers and the universities defied common sense, and the mixture of supposedly 'academic' and 'practical' subjects was unsatisfactory and confusing. Men and women were being called to the bar who were not adequately prepared for practice: family and political connections seemed to provide special advantages when it came to professional advancement. The system of education also failed to satisfy the contemporary taste for intellectual and social engagement with events in the world at large. To the two earnest, if languid, students reclining on the benchers' lawns, this state of affairs called forth a critical response.

In the short term, the pair decided to stimulate debate about legal issues by founding with some others two small ginger groups within the community of law students. They were particularly interested in aspects of prison reform, and so they called their first association 'The Phoenix Society', as an acknowledgement of the suffering endured in jail by the leading Fenian, O'Donovan Rossa. Later came 'The Law Students' Union for Action'. In the slight publications of these transient associations, this author first turned his hand to Irish legal history. Once again, as when Kennedy opened his institute, law students held strong opinions on reform.

Although shortly after that sunny conversation of twenty-five years ago an outline of Kennedy's ambitions and achievements became known to the author, many questions remained unanswered. Why had such a radical experiment as the Dublin Law Institute been tried and why, since it seemed so reasonable, had it been abandoned? It was only much later, during my research into the history of King's Inns itself, that I came to realise that

Kennedy's actions were ahead of their time. Then Daire Hogan, whose book on the legal profession in the nineteenth century is of great value to historians, drew to my attention a reference to Kennedy's work as a compassionate land agent and this further stimulated my interest. It soon became evident that Kennedy, the son of a staunchly protestant family from Derry, was a remarkable man. Although most of his own life was ultimately not spent as a practising lawyer, he serves nonetheless as a symbol of the Irish legal body's efforts to assert its independence and its professionalism.

Qualified first as an attorney and then as a barrister, in which capacity he practised for some years, Kennedy's subsequent career was closely interwoven with the broad economic and political fabric of Irish society. His thoughts were never far from the question of reform. To the end of his days his ambitions in the sphere of legal training marked him out as an original thinker. His personality gives life to this account of a significant epoch in the history of Irish professional education.

I have already mentioned my debt to Jimmy Heron and Daire Hogan, but there are others too who have helped this work to come to fruition. Simon Bailey, archivist at the University of London, searched his records for references to Kennedy's dealings with that institution. Theo Hoppen of the University of Hull generously transcribed relevant notes made during an inspection by him of the Bath papers at Longleat House. Tristram Kennedy's grandson, T. L. Stack, not only sent photographs and photocopies of papers and press-cuttings from his home in Somerset but also entered into a lengthy and useful correspondence. His involvement was fortuitous. I had written speculatively to another address in Somerset, at which Mr Stack's uncle had lived over fifty years earlier and whence his uncle had despatched certain papers to the National Library in Dublin. The present resident forwarded my letter to Mr Stack.

Yet another person who must be thanked is Professor W. N. Osborough, whose continuing enthusiasm and advice has been invaluable. Osborough's work as prime mover of the Irish Legal History Society has been responsible for elevating to a new plane the discipline of legal history in Ireland. I am also grateful to Dr Máirín Ní Dhonnchadha of the Dublin Institute for Advanced Studies for her permission to quote from her article, 'An address to a student of law', and to include at the beginning of this volume her translation of certain advice given to a law student who lived and worked in Ireland seven hundred years ago. I would also like to express my appreciation of the hospitality extended to me by Sister Bríd and her community during a visit to numbers 9 and

10 Henrietta Street, two fine Georgian houses which were formerly the location of Kennedy's Dublin Law Institute and Queen's Inns Chambers, and which today are maintained at considerable expense by the sisters. On 7 October 1994, the annual general meeting of the Irish Legal History Society was held in the parlour of no. 10.

Illustrations below are reproduced by kind permission of the following: Mr T. L. Stack (frontispiece and nos. 1, 19, 20); Mr Séamus Curran (no. 5); Mr Cathal Crimmins (nos. 29, 30); the benchers of the honorable society of King's Inns (nos. 8–11, 24); the treasurer and masters of the bench of the honourable society of Lincoln's Inn (no. 17); the masters of the bench of the honourable society of the Middle Temple (no. 23); Irish Architectural Archive (nos. 6–7); National Gallery of Ireland (nos. 3, 12, 14, 21); National Library of Ireland (nos. 2, 27); Smurfit Publications (nos. 15–16); Foyle and Londonderry College (no. 22). Letters in the appendix are published by permission of the Bodleian Library. Quotations from the Irish papers in the collection at Longleat House, Warminster, Wiltshire, are included by permission of the marquess of Bath.

The honorable society of King's Inns has granted me permission to publish extracts from the records of the society. The Royal Irish Academy has allowed me to reproduce my biographical article on Tristram Kennedy which was earlier published in the *Proceedings of the Royal Irish Academy*. It forms the basis for much of chapter 2 below. Some of chapter 10 has also appeared before, in an article written by me for the *Dublin Historical Record*. I wish to thank too certain librarians, keepers and archivists including those of Bray Public Library, County Wicklow; British Library, London; Cambridge University Library; Bodleian Library, Oxford; Dublin City University; Gilbert Library, Dublin Corporation; Gray's Inn; Inner Temple; Irish Architectural Archive; King's Inns; Lincoln's Inn; Longleat House; Middle Temple; National Archives, Dublin; National Gallery of Ireland; National Library, Dublin; National Portrait Gallery, London; Public Record Office, London; Public Record Office of Ireland; Public Record Office of Northern Ireland; Registry of Deeds, Dublin; Trinity College Dublin; University College Dublin; University of London.

Finally, permit me to thank my family, especially my wife Catherine Curran and my sons, Oisín, Conor and Samuel. Our sons' enthusiasm for life, their beauty and their joy fan the flame of creativity and demand some account of the world into which we have brought them. 'Gentle youths', the story begins. . . .

COLUM KENNY

Contents

	PREFACE	ix
	LIST OF ILLUSTRATIONS	xv
	ABBREVIATIONS	xvii
1	Tristram Kennedy and the revival of legal training	1
2	'Faithful and true to the poor': the life and times of 'honest Tristram Kennedy' (1805–1885)	17
3	'Gowned common people': patronage, professionalisation and the birth of the Dublin Law Institute	62
4	'A queer compound of individuals': the rise and fall of the Dublin Law Institute, 1839–42	83
5	'National institution': calendar of events relating to the Dublin Law Institute, 1839–42	93
6	'Wyse's committee': the Irish genesis of the select committee on legal education, 1846	132
7	'Low ebb': legal education in England and Ireland by 1846	147
8	'Creeping like snail unwillingly to school': innovation at the inns, 1846–76	161
9	'So many legs of mutton': Irishmen forced to the English inns, 1542–1885	186
10	'No memory of the past': King's Inns and Queen's Inns Chambers	218

EPILOGUE 236

APPENDIX: Kennedy Letters, Bodleian Library, Oxford 239

BIBLIOGRAPHY 245

INDEX 261

THE IRISH LEGAL HISTORY SOCIETY 270

List of illustrations

Illustrations appear between p. 142 and p. 143.

Frontispiece. Portrait of Tristram Kennedy. By Henry MacManus. Exhibited Dublin 1877 and now in the possession of Kennedy's grandson, Mr T.L. Stack of Taunton, Somerset.

1. Sarah Graham, who married Tristram Kennedy in 1862. Artist unknown but possibly Henry MacManus.
2. King's Inns and Registry of Deeds. By William Brocas, c.1818.
3. King's Inns and Royal Canal Harbour. By George Petrie, 1821. From Wright, *Historical guide to Dublin.*
4. No.10 Henrietta Street as it was in 1836 (then No.9), shortly before Kennedy acquired it for the Dublin Law Institute and for Queen's Inns Chambers. From the *Dublin Penny Journal,* 13 Feb. 1836.
5. No.10 Henrietta Street as it is today. By Séamus Curran.
6. Stairs and hall of no.10 Henrietta Street, 1980s.
7. Parlour of no.10 Henrietta Street in 1981.

8 & 9 Hand-bills advertising introductory lectures delivered for the Dublin Law Institute by Joseph Napier and James Whiteside.

10. Joseph Napier. By Thomas Bridgford. Exhibited Dublin 1844.
11. James Whiteside. By A. Scott.
12. Sir Thomas Wyse MP. By John Partridge, 1846.
13. J.A. Lawson. Artist unknown.
14. Sir Michael O'Loghlen, master of the rolls. By George Mulvany, 1843.
15. The old lecture room at King's Inns, 1958.
16. Benchers' council room, King's Inns, 1958.
17. Edward Burtenshaw Sugden, last English lord chancellor of Ireland. By his daughter, Charlotte Sugden.

18 William Conyngham Plunket, lord chancellor of Ireland. By Charles Grey. From *Dublin University Magazine*, xv (1840).

19 Salver accompanying a service of plate presented to Tristram Kennedy by the grateful electors of County Louth, 1857.

20 Tristram Kennedy, photographed in County Louth, 1865.

21 Philip Callan MP. By Sydney Prior Hall.

22 Photograph of Tristram Kennedy in old age.

23 Dining-hall, Middle Temple, mid-nineteenth century.

24 Dining-hall, King's Inns, mid-twentieth century.

25 Henrietta Street, from John Rocque's map of Dublin, 1756.

26 Elevation and design of the intended registry, record offices, &c. at the King's Inns, showing the intended line of buildings by the society of King's Inns, 1813. From *Rec. comm. Ire. reps.*

27 Henrietta Street, in an advertising handbill, *c.*1853.

28 Nos.3–10 Henrietta Street in 1910. All these houses once belonged to Kennedy. The photograph was taken for the *Georgian Society records of domestic architecture.*

29 Architectural ground-plan of the houses on Henrietta Street and King's Inns, 1987. By Cathal Crimmins, architect.

30 Aerial view of the King's Inns and Henrietta Street, 1980s.

Abbreviations

Ball, *Judges*	F.E. Ball, *The judges in Ireland, 1221–1921*
BL	British Library
Bodl	Bodleian Library, Oxford
Cal. S. P. Ire.	*Calendar of the state papers relating to Ireland*
Commons' jn.	*Journal of the house of commons*
DNB	*Dictionary of national biography*
Dub. Univ. comm.	*Royal commission on the University of Dublin, 1852–53*
Fry	*Royal commission on the University of Dublin, 1906–07*
G.I.P.B.	*The pension book of Gray's Inn, 1669–1800*
Hist Jn	*The Historical Journal*
IHS	*Irish Historical Studies*
ILT & SJ	*Irish Law Times and Solicitors' Journal*
Ir Arch Arch	Irish Architectural Archive
Ir Jur	*Irish Jurist*
King's Inns adm.	*King's Inns admission papers, 1607–1867*
L.I. adm. reg.	*The records of the honourable society of Lincoln's Inn: admission registers*
L.I.B.B.	*The records of the honourable society of Lincoln's Inn: 'Black Books'*
NGI	National Gallery of Ireland
NHI	*New History of Ireland*
NLI	National Library of Ireland
NUI	National University of Ireland
OED	*Oxford English Dictionary*

Ormrod Report	*Report of the committee on legal education [in England and Wales], 1971*
PRO	Public Record Office, London
PRONI	Public Record Office of Northern Ireland
Stack MS	Manuscript kept by Mr T. L. Stack, grandson of Tristram Kennedy
TCD	Trinity College Dublin
UCD	University College Dublin
RIA	Royal Irish Academy
RIA Proc.	*Proceedings of the Royal Irish Academy*
Robertson	*Royal commission on university education in Ireland, 1902–03*
Sel. comm. leg. ed.	*Select committee on legal education, 1846*
Stat. Ire.	*Statutes Ireland*
Waterloo directory	*Directory of Irish newspapers and periodicals 1800–1900*
Wyse committee	See *Sel. comm. leg. ed.* above

CHAPTER ONE

Tristram Kennedy and the revival of legal training

WHEN TRISTRAM KENNEDY opened the door of his Dublin law school in 1839, he welcomed students to classes in a discipline which had not been taught systematically in Ireland for centuries. It was an historic moment, marking not only a major educational development in legal training in the United Kingdom but also a growth in the confidence of the Irish middle classes nationally. This confidence was reflected both in the contemporary manifestation of professionalisation and in the movement for greater political independence for Ireland.

The English inns of court had provided more or less elaborate training exercises between the fourteenth and seventeenth centuries, declining rapidly thereafter. In Ireland, formal training appears never to have been a feature of life at the King's Inns from its foundation about 1541. So how then may one refer to legal training being 'revived' in Ireland in the nineteenth century?

For one thing, individual lawyers in that part of Ireland which was amenable to English law had in the past been known to instruct pupils. For another, there is a considerable and growing body of evidence which indicates that a range of law schools existed in Gaelic Ireland long before the inns of court in London assumed educational functions and that, as late as the end of the sixteenth century, these actively used law texts to instruct students in the brehon law and in aspects of civil, canon and, perhaps, common law. A thirteenth-century poetic exhortation, addressed by a prominent jurist to a student at one of these schools, has recently been translated and some verses from it are reproduced at the beginning of the present volume. It is a window on a vista which other scholars will hopefully continue to contemplate but which is merely glanced here.[1]

Turning firstly to the limited evidence which exists of earlier training in the common law within the areas of effective English

---

1. Kelly, *Early Irish law*, pp.242–63; Ní Dhonnchadha, 'An address to a student of law' in Ó Corráin et al., *Sages, saints and storytellers*, pp.164–70. I am most grateful to Ms Ní Dhonnchadha for permission to quote from her translation.

rule, it may be noted that this took place in a context where individuals had travelled from Ireland to England to learn law from at least the thirteenth century onwards. Some lawyers in Dublin appear to have been willing to prepare young men for such an excursion, grounding them in the texts and practices with which a student at one of the inns of chancery in London might have been familiar. In 1482–83 William Darcy and Thomas Kent were to be found with John Estrete 'at Divelyng', studying Littleton's *Tenures* and the standard law text known as *Natura brevium*. Estrete was then the king's serjeant in Ireland. On holy days Darcy and Kent joined their companions at the home of the chief justice 'to learn the harp and to dance', just as they might have done at Furnival's or Thavies Inn in London. This rounded off their preparatory education and readied them for the revels and banquets which they would encounter as formal manifestations of contemporary renaissance culture at the London inns of court.[2]

Our knowledge of the practice of pupillage in Dublin rests on just this one entry in the memoranda rolls referring to 1482–83. In 1541, in their petition for a grant of the site on which they had recently founded the King's Inns, the leading Pale lawyers mentioned 'othir to our charges committed', but it seems from the context that this 'othir' referred not to pupils but to certain types of causes besides those of the king. Nevertheless, the lawyers of King's Inns did at the time envisage using the premises somehow to facilitate 'the bringing up of gentlemen's sons within this realm in the English tongue, habit and manners', as required by law. They did not specify what this might involve and there is no evidence that legal or other training was ever provided subsequently at the King's Inns before 1850. The fact that the Irish parliament was pressed to pass the Statute of Jeofailles in 1542 suggests that a decision had been made by the king's officials that intending counsellors would be trained in English law by obliging them to reside at the inns of court in London.[3]

An informal system of pupillage also existed in Ireland in the early nineteenth century, something to which we shall return below when examining the state of legal education in the United Kingdom before 1850. Thus, about the time of his call to the bar, a young man might arrange to provide services to and receive guidance from an experienced barrister. This system served as an alternative to the standard service in chambers which was expected of the English law student but little is known of how it operated or

2. Kenny, *King's Inns and the kingdom of Ireland*, pp.14–22, esp. nn. 58, 63.
3. ibid., pp.35–39, 269–71.

of its origins and vintage. Was there an unbroken and unspoken tradition of such pupillage, going back centuries? Did every intending barrister have to have such a relationship? Was a fee ever involved? At what point in the nineteenth century was it settled that men in their first year at the bar 'devil' (serve an informal apprenticeship) with an experienced junior?[4]

What is clear is that systematic legal training was not conceived for the first time in the reign of Queen Victoria. Reading some modern British texts on the progress of professionalisation in the wake of the industrial revolution and, particularly, on the increasing public awareness of the value of formal instruction and examinations in the nineteenth century, one might be forgiven for thinking that there were no professions before then and no precedent for older lawyers training young men to follow in their footsteps. In fact, common lawyers had been enthusiastic educators centuries before the Victorian period and they long enjoyed a keen sense of their professional honour. What is needed is an author who will compare and contrast the earlier period studied by writers such as Baker, Prest and Ives with that later era which has preoccupied some sociologists. It is possible that there are certain threads which have run long and continuously through the fabric of legal training in the common law, with fundamental pedagogical patterns re-emerging over time. However, it must be admitted that for at least two centuries before their Victorian revival the English inns of court were undoubtedly in a bad way and the provisions which they had made for training were either entirely lapsed or else enforced in a derisory fashion. For its part, as remarked already, the King's Inns during the same period did not purport to train Irish lawyers.

Whatever the sparsity of information in relation to such forms of training in the common law as did exist in Ireland before the nineteenth century, it may be said that the history of legal education in these islands is not synonymous with that of the inns of court and is not confined by the ambit of common lawyers. The church, for example, had long provided instruction in the laws most relevant to the role of its clerics in society.

In Ireland cleric and lay needs were for centuries addressed under the same roof in various schools which studied what became known as 'brehon' law, 'breitheamh' being a Gaelic word for 'judge', 'lawgiver' or 'arbiter'. Gradually secular schools of law emerged, usually associated with particular families, and these lay centres

---

4. When it was said in the memoranda rolls that Darcy and Kent were with John Estrete 'at Divelyng', might it mean not 'at Dublin' but 'devilling'?

of brehon law had been training practitioners for centuries when leading common lawyers took over an old Dominican friary on the banks of the Liffey and founded the King's Inns. The Tudor military conquest of Gaelic Ireland would finally sound the death-knell of native law and learning, although some remnants of brehon practice may have survived into the seventeenth century. But before the Tudors resorted to brute force to tame the wild Irish they had been prepared not only to tolerate but also to recognise that the brehon lawyers were active participants in the administration of justice in Ireland.

I have suggested elsewhere that the Pale lawyers may have envisaged providing some type of education at King's Inns not only for their own children but also for young men from Gaelic parts of Ireland, perhaps in the hope of weaning the latter from older brehon schools which still existed. In making that suggestion I had not had an opportunity to read Patterson's recent study of brehon law in late medieval Ireland, which I believe makes my hypothesis more likely. Patterson argues forcefully that until the end of the sixteenth century the Irish jural or brehon tradition was continuous and functional, and that its persistence as a system with identifiable institutions depended upon the availability of the law tracts as an anchor for legal learning. Patterson points out that such legal learning 'took place either within the community setting of a monastery or the family setting of a law school, or by means of personal visits to friends at other establishments'. In this connection, it is perhaps merely coincidental that the King's Inns was established within an abandoned monastery and that the association of particular Gaelic families with the brehon legal profession was mirrored by a long association of certain Pale families with the practice of common law in Ireland. It would be wrong to jump to the conclusion that the visits by Kent and Darcy and their colleagues to the homes of prominent lawyers could be equated with the personal visits of brehons to friends at other establishments. Nor may too much be read into what appears to have been the attendance of some of the Gaelic Irish at the inns of court in London. But what is certain is that brehon law was still being taught and practised when the King's Inns was founded. Indeed, in 1548, seven years after the lawyers in Dublin had addressed the king on the merits of that new institution, some of those same lawyers as privy councillors allowed the O'Dorans, chief brehons of Leinster, to challenge the impending forfeiture of their estates before the privy council. However, in 1578 at Limerick, as the Gaelic tradition became increasingly unacceptable to government, a brehon who 'taught and practised' law was hanged.[5]

The address to the law student, cited above, was written about 1290, at a time when lay schools of law were first emerging in Ireland. According to the poem's modern translator, 'the role envisaged for the student is professional rather than academic':

> His education in the canonical law-tracts is to be put to use in a practical way in the deciding of legal cases. Whether he will act in the capacity of judge or advocate is not spelt out but as the ability to fulfil the higher role must have depended on both educational qualification and professional repute, the ambitious student will obviously aim for this. In exhorting the student to live up to his vocation, the poet gives us a glimpse of the temptations to malpractice to which any lawyer might be subject. Most obviously he must not be bribed to overlook the evidence against the guilty party. Other improprieties are of the kind which would only be spotted by fellow lawyers. While the poet defends the canonical texts as a basis for administering justice, they must be used properly. Memorised citations must be checked against the written text; citations must not be given from tracts of a spurious nature; the lawyer must not attempt to sway the court by quoting maxims of traditional law without demonstrating their appropriateness as precedents.[6]

The brehon schools took in students and taught them not only the old law-texts but also how these might be employed and developed to grapple with contemporary problems. As Patterson has indicated, 'the masters of the sixteenth-century law schools, far from being immobilised by tradition, actively manipulated the content of the law-tracts, selecting and editing materials as they saw fit'. Simms, too, indicates that brehon law continued to evolve to the end and she thinks that 'it hardly seems fair' to accuse the brehons of the later middle ages of having 'carried

---

5. Kenny, *King's Inns and the kingdom of Ireland*, pp.34, 38–39, 67 n.131; O'Rahilly, 'Irish poets, historians and judges in English documents, 1538–1615', 114–15; Cregan, 'Irish catholic admissions to the English inns of court 1558–1625', passim; Kelly, *Early Irish law*, pp.254–55; Patterson, 'Brehon law in late medieval Ireland: "antiquarian and obsolete" or "traditional and functional"', 46–51, 57–60. Dineen also gives 'brehon' and 'a judge of assize' for 'breitheamh'. A study of Irish manuscripts may provide some coherent insight into how brehon counsellors applied in practice the jurisprudence of their more academic colleagues, even if 'records in Irish of dispute resolutions are few in number, late in date' (Patterson, 'Brehon law', 44). For comparative purposes, unfortunately, there exists no yearbook or report of cases from the common law areas of Ireland prior to the seventeenth century (Osborough, 'Puzzles from Irish law reporting history', 89–94).
6. Ní Dhonnchadha, 'Address to a student of law', 161.

conservatism to unheard of lengths', as Binchy had suggested. Was the technique described by Patterson so terribly different from the common law use of precedents and the interpretation of statutes in classroom and court for the purposes of training? In recent years, the role of Gaelic lawyers in modifying tradition by intentional selection from, and emphasis on, particular old brehon texts and their application of this technique to contemporary circumstances right up to the late sixteenth century, has been studied by scholars in Ireland and abroad. The results of their research indicate that brehon law was neither frozen in some kind of time-warp nor rigidly applied.[7]

Researchers have also suggested that Gaelic practitioners saw themselves not only as experts in strictly legal matters but also as counsellors in a broader sense, advising on matters of public policy. This is worth bearing in mind when considering at what point 'barrister' became the term preferred by practitioners in Ireland and how 'counsellor' or 'lawyer' appears to have remained, well into the seventeenth century, a designation which was used not only by professionals themselves but by a government attempting to regulate the admission of catholics to practice. At a later stage, common usage dubbed Daniel O'Connell not 'the lawyer' or 'the barrister' but 'the counsellor', and this may have reflected a nostalgic folk memory. Indeed the role of catholic lawyers outside Dublin during periods of their exclusion from practice in the Four Courts is an important aspect of the history of the Irish legal profession between the decline of the brehon schools and the early nineteenth century. Those so excluded may have remained active as arbitrators. It is also the case that in Ireland, both for the government and for its opponents alike, lawyers played a role as political advisors to an extent which seems to have been exceptional by London standards. Perhaps they had once enjoyed an equivalent position in medieval English society and retained it later in Ireland or perhaps this was a legacy of the Gaelic past. A future researcher might fruitfully address the process of evolution of the concept of 'counsellor' in Ireland.[8]

---

7. Patterson, 'Gaelic law and the Tudor conquest of Ireland: the social background of the sixteenth-century recensions of the pseudo-historical Prologue to the *Senchas már*', 194; Simms, 'The brehons of later medieval Ireland' in Osborough and Hogan (ed.), *Brehons, serjeants and attorneys*, p.74; Binchy, 'Lawyers and chroniclers', 60.

8. Kenny, *King's Inns and the kingdom of Ireland*, pp.131, 140, 152; O'Connell, 'O'Connell: lawyer and landlord', 107; Kenny, 'The exclusion of catholics from the legal profession in Ireland', 342–56.

For students at the brehon schools there were what Kelly describes as 'ingenious academic exercises . . . to develop the forensic skill of aspiring lawyers'. There were also, as at the English inns of court when they developed, both oral instruction and readings. The extent to which the practice of 'reading' in each country shared some common European or general anthropological origin or, indeed, may even usefully be compared is far beyond the scope of this study. It is worth noting Ní Dhonnchadha's opinion that the act of *oirleighleann* (reading or reading aloud) in the brehon schools involved both understanding and interpreting legal texts. Similarly 'readings' at the London inns were lectures by senior members of an inn on the statutes of England, to which colleagues would respond by questioning and disputation. Patrick Barnewall took part in one such disputation at Gray's Inn, which he entered in 1527, but readings were never a feature of life at the King's Inns, despite one indication that Barnewall may have expected them to become so.[9]

The brehon students used texts especially written for the aspiring practitioner and 'mercifully free of the antique lumber that so clutters up the commentaries'. The vast majority of texts of all periods were written in Irish, although some Latin is also found. The early Irish law-texts are said to have been 'written in a context of cooperation and mutual influence between ecclesiastics and lay academics, which also included the involvement of practising members of the legal profession'. Irish jurisprudence appears to have accommodated the perspective of early church lawyers within the pre-Christian traditions of secular lawyers, an achievement celebrated by one poet who rejoiced that 'the learning that clerics speak of and our own truly wise art are two streams from one fountain-head'. From the twelfth century onwards there may have been an increasing European influence as Irishmen who wished to study civil and canon law to the highest level travelled abroad to obtain degrees as bachelors, masters or doctors at the various medieval universities.[10]

9. Kelly, *Early Irish law*, p.252; Binchy, 'Lawyers and chroniclers', 50; Ní Dhonnchadha, 'Address to a student of law', 168, 170; Kenny, *King's Inns and the kingdom of Ireland*, pp.9, 24. Dr J.H. Baker has told this author that it is unique to find evidence of Irish students participating in reading exercises at the London inns. Patterson, 'Brehon law', 56–57 quotes Dr Baker's work to draw comparisons between the two traditions, suggesting that 'medieval English and Irish [brehon] legal culture have much in common'. I had not read Patterson when I wrote the paragraph above.

10. Ní Dhonnchadha, 'Address to a student of law', 160; Breatnach, 'Lawyers in early Ireland', 3, 5; Simms, 'The brehons of later medieval Ireland', 55–56, 66. But the church gradually began to distance itself from the

The lay schools of brehon law which developed were usually associated with particular families but not necessarily confined to them. Students studied more than law. There was until late a common ground between jurists and poets or historians. Given a tradition that some students should be 'expert in every art', there is evidence that literary, poetic, historical and musical skills were imparted, and this 'liberal' rounding of a pupil's education, as a later age might describe it, was seen to have various practical benefits. For example, it might increase the likelihood of being highly regarded by one's colleagues ('a pure historian versed in genealogy is the due of every good company, having abundance of pleasing historical lore – it is he who is entitled to make a circuit') or facilitate an understanding of certain mythical judgments often cited in precedents. Against accounts of literary and musical training at Gaelic law schools may be set the instruction in dancing and harping which Darcy and Kent and their colleagues received in Dublin in the fifteenth century. Extravagant renaissance masques and revels may have been a part of life at the London inns but they were by no means the only source of immediate cultural inspiration for Irish law students during this period.[11]

There is a growing volume of research into the brehon law, its practitioners and their institutions. The picture of Irish legal training which emerges is that of a system which was multifarious and no less rich educationally than that which Fortescue described as being provided at the London inns of court in the fourteenth and fifteenth centuries. The old Irish schools and the newer English inns of court both expected men to aspire to become more than mere legal technicians and facilitated the acquisition of a broad education. Even in their understanding of law and of the role of lawyers, both traditions may have had more in common with one another than with later jural ideals of the centralising Tudor state. The significance of this in comparative terms and in the wider context of a European renaissance cries out for further study.[12]

    native legal tradition, the Gregorian reformers in particular frowning on what they saw as lax Irish ways and the church becoming more closely allied with anglo-normans (Simms, 'The brehons of later medieval Ireland', 56).

11. Simms, 'The brehons of later medieval Ireland', 63–65, Ní Dhonnchadha, 'Address to a student of law', 162 and 169 at verse 13. There was also, as Simms points out, a theoretical basis for this liberal education. The three grades of lawyers had each to achieve a different level of qualification, the highest 'advocate whom judgment encounters' being equated with the Old Irish *breithem tri mberla*, the judge of three speeches, law, poetry and Latin learning (Simms, op. cit., 65).

12. Fortescue, *De laudibus legum Angliae*; Patterson, 'Brehon law', 61–63. In this context the modern researcher must avoid unconsciously regarding so-

One thing is certainly clear. When in 1960 V.T.H. Delany reworked his earlier article on legal studies in Trinity College, his U.S. editor erred in publishing the later piece as 'The history of legal education in Ireland'. While Delany recognised that 'in the common-law courts the customary Irish law was frequently pleaded in causes, expert assessors being called by the courts to testify as to its nature', and that 'there must have been a considerable mingling of the two systems', he entirely ignored the Gaelic or 'brehon' law schools. This chapter hopefully goes someway towards rectifying that major oversight.[13]

Turning from the learned Gaelic tradition, one feels some sympathy for lawyers in Ireland of English descent. Having dutifully made their way in increasing numbers to the London inns to learn something of the common law, they attempted to come to terms with the Tudor reformation by founding the King's Inns in Dublin, only to be immediately constrained by the imposition of a statute which compelled law students to go to England. Deprived of an opportunity for formal training locally, they had abuse heaped upon them and were accused, by English officials in particular, of being venal, ignorant and incompetent. In turn, some of their class poured scorn on the brehons.

As religion became increasingly divisive in Ireland in the late sixteenth century, and as the English increasingly relied on new protestant settlers to administer the legal system, many of the old stock found themselves being squeezed out of the upper echelons of the profession and may have cast a longing backward glance at the brehon schools. Significantly, in the 1640s the Confederation of Kilkenny planned to found an alternative inn of court outside Dublin and even won permission from the king for that objective, shortly before the social fabric of Ireland was undermined by the Cromwellian wars and their aspirations were obliterated.

When, at the end of the eighteenth century, the protestants of Ireland in turn asserted their independence from England and catholics were at last readmitted to practice as junior barristers, some senior members of the King's Inns attempted to put in place a system of legal education. But they did so without consulting the profession as a whole, and the scheme which they envisaged was so bizarre in its reliance on the practices of the old English inns, as earlier described by Fortescue, that the bar feared it was being made to look ridiculous. Duhigg has suggested that the actual

    called 'customary law' as being necessarily less sophisticated or serviceable than the 'common law'.
13. Delany, 'Legal studies in Trinity College, Dublin, since the foundation'; Delany, 'The history of legal education in Ireland'.

objective of the graded system of qualification was to extend even further the opportunities for government to use patronage and place in Ireland as a means of controlling opposition. In the event, the whole plan was rejected and the question of legal education neglected for another four decades.[14]

In the early 1830s, the students of King's Inns considered debating 'what course of study is best adapted to a law student intending to practise at the Irish bar?' and 'would an examination of the student-at-law previously to being called to the bar tend to increase the respectability and promote the interests of the profession?' In the end, neither motion appears to have been discussed by the debating society. Perhaps, just as they had ruled out debates of a 'religious and party political tendency', the students baulked at the prospect of educational controversy.[15] However, current developments at the University of London and at the Law Society in London invited some response from Dublin and when in 1835, as will be seen, Thomas Wyse voiced criticism at Westminster of the deficiency of legal training in Ireland, he delivered the opening shot in a campaign which was to last half a century. Wyse was a member of an old catholic Norman family, like all catholics only eligible to sit in parliament since the passing of the Emancipation Act in 1829. He would be described later by Sir Robert Peel as 'the consistent promoter of education in all its gradations', and his championing of the cause of legal training in Ireland was no more or less remarkable than that two centuries earlier by the 'old English' catholic, Sir John Bath.[16] What gave Wyse's ambitions a considerable boost were the efforts of that 'indefatigable' and pragmatic Scots-Irish protestant, Tristram Kennedy. Descended from a family with impeccably loyal antecedents, Kennedy's foundation of the Dublin Law Institute in 1839 was timed perfectly to take advantage of the contemporary ecumenical spirit of political goodwill. Reformers, repeaters, liberals and even some tories united briefly to revive legal training in Ireland.

The campaign to reform legal education, upon which Tristram Kennedy and Thomas Wyse MP collaborated closely, was to have effects lasting into the late twentieth century. It stimulated the academic study of English law at universities in Britain and

---

14. Duhigg, *King's Inns*, pp.439–52; Littledale, *King's Inns*, pp.22–23; Kenny, *King's Inns and the kingdom of Ireland*, pp.247–53.
15. Law Students Debating Society, secretary's book, 1830–33 (King's Inns MS, at 24 Nov. 1831, 18 April 1832 and list of questions at back).
16. *DNB*, s.v. Wyse, Thomas; Kenny, *King's Inns and the kingdom of Ireland*, pp.95–98.

Ireland, hastened the introduction of qualifying examinations for both branches of the profession and pointed up the overwhelmingly ideological rationale for insisting that young men attend the English inns before being admitted to practice at the Irish bar. The report of the house of commons select committee on legal education of 1846, which the two men were almost wholly responsible for having appointed, has been described by a modern English authority as being of 'fundamental importance', in that 'the history of legal education in England over the past 120 years is largely an account of the struggle to implement the recommendations of the 1846 committee and the effects of that struggle'.[17] The history of legal education in Ireland has been no less influenced by the report.

Of course the responsibility for developments in legal training cannot simply be attributed to any single individual, or even to two men. Before Kennedy was called to the bar or Wyse had articulated his interest in legal education, the University of London had embarked on pioneering law courses and the Law Society was providing classes for its members in that same city. For decades past there had been those in England and Ireland who perceived a need for reform. However, innovations at Oxford and at Trinity College Dublin in the eighteenth century had not been sustained, and the indifference of benchers at the London and Dublin inns generally dampened any spark of professional enthusiasm for change.

Yet, gradually, change became irresistible, albeit circumscribed by considerations which were not entirely pedagogic. Perhaps the most compelling imperative was simply peer pressure. As other professions put their houses in order, by the standards of the nineteenth century, it became clear that the legal profession risked being regarded as unprofessional in its failure to introduce systematic teaching and examinations for law students. It also became necessary to find a socially acceptable way to limit the numbers in practice as both the English and Irish bars burgeoned. Insisting upon, and testing, the acquisition of information was one such means.

There were peculiar Irish circumstances which were conducive to reform. The Irish legal profession had been opposed to the Act of Union and continued to regard it as an imposition. Many barristers also resented the old law which required Irish men to attend English inns and which frustrated attempts to construct a

---

17. [Ormrod] *Report of the committee on legal education* [in England and Wales] . . . March 1971, pp.7–8.

systematic course of legal education in Ireland. Even the future leader of unionist opinion in Ireland, Edward Carson, is said to have described the provision as a 'badge of servitude'. With the support of professors of law at Trinity and at the Queen's colleges, the requirement was finally abolished in 1885. Until then, it had acted as a check on the efforts of Kennedy and other reformers to force the pace of change. The requirement was supported almost to the bitter end by the Irish benchers, most of whom were conservative protestants, who clung to it both as a symbol of political union and as a means of inculcating respect for what they regarded as a common, but ultimately English, jurisprudence.

For their part, the Irish attorneys and solicitors, eventually to be merged in one rank by the Judicature Act of 1877, grew heartily sick of the power of the benchers. Unlike their English counterparts, the former were forced to belong to the local inn of court, and this was dominated by a council which included not one of their rank. The benchers generally ignored or belittled their attempts to improve the training of practitioners. Eventually, the solicitors and attorneys escaped from under the yoke of the King's Inns and began to provide their own law classes and examinations.

As early as the 1830s, both branches of the profession had believed that change was in the air. This optimism reflected the new political environment in which for the first time since the union there was a liberal and reforming government in office. The fact that catholics had recently been emancipated was an augur not only of further political advances but also, with their admission to the ranks of king's counsel and to the senior law offices, of a shift in perspective on the bench. On the crest of a wave of reforming optimism Kennedy launched his Dublin Law Institute. The high degree of professional and intellectual enthusiasm with which his initiative was met may have misled its supporters into believing that its future was secure. But in almost every area of public life the Irish were to be disappointed by the liberal administration of 1835 to 1841, a disappointment compounded by the collapse of O'Connell's repeal campaign and brought to the verge of despair by the Great Famine. It would take many decades for the Irish to find again an effective way to stand on their own feet and to engage in concerted political action.

Nevertheless, in the decades between the success of O'Connell's campaign for catholic emancipation and the rise of the Home Rule movement, there were those who never entirely lost their faith in the possibility of rational reform in Ireland. Among them was Tristram Kennedy, called to the bar in 1834 just months before the Lichfield House compact between whigs, radicals and

O'Connellites stirred so many Irish expectations and as Thomas Wyse MP began to include legal training in his great plan for educational reform in Ireland. Although their hopes were soon to be brutally dashed, Kennedy and Wyse set in motion a train of events which largely defined the shape of legal education in England and Ireland until the contemporary period. Kennedy even lived to see the Statute of Jeofailles revoked in 1885. For three and a half centuries the statute had required Irish law students to attend the English inns and the repeal of this provision cleared the way for new developments in legal training in Ireland in the twentieth century.

Tristram Kennedy led a full life. Consideration of its course allows the foundation of the Dublin Law Institute and his other work to be placed in a broader context. The immediate political and professional environment in which the institute was born is also contemplated below, and it is discovered not to have been a freakish experiment so much as a collective gasp of exasperation. Yet the circumstances of its foundation always pointed to the possibility of its imminent demise. For the first time, the story of the Dublin Law Institute itself is told in detail. By including a calendar of relevant events between 1839 and 1842, it is possible to see how Kennedy grappled to sustain his support, and how, in the end, that effort defeated him. This was a very significant juncture in Irish political and legal history and, by employing the Dublin Law Institute as a case-study, one is afforded many fresh insights, not only into the attitudes and ambitions of Irish lawyers, but also into the contemporary power structures of Irish society.

Kennedy did not give up when, as seems to have been the case, Lord Chancellor Sugden pulled the rug from under his feet. Sugden was a tory and the last Englishman to hold office as chancellor of Ireland. Even before he was appointed to that position he withheld support from Kennedy's law school on the grounds that it was a waste of time to provide courses in a context where students were not obliged professionally to sit exams. Yet Sugden himself subsequently proposed the introduction of just such a system of courses without exams at the English inns, and his response to Kennedy's plan may have been influenced by political prejudice and professional jealousy. Lawyers such as Sugden or Brougham, or indeed Davies and Ley at an earlier period, enjoyed great reputations in England as far-sighted reformers but won less hearty encomiums in Ireland. Sugden's opposition did not deter Kennedy from continuing to seek reforms. The parliamentary petition which the latter persuaded Wyse to lay before the house of commons in 1843 led ultimately to the appointment of the important select committee on legal education in 1846.

The Irish genesis of, and contribution to, that committee has been ignored by English writers from Holdsworth to Manchester. But the Irish involvement was significant. It reflected a growing, if subdued, pressure for change in the relationship between centre and periphery in the United Kingdom, as well as increasing self-confidence on the part of the Irish professional middle classes. Such expressions of determination subverted one unspoken imperialist rationale for the provision which required Irish law students to reside in London, namely, that the Irish could not be trusted to formulate theories and to sustain practices equivalent by contemporary standards to those of the English. There was a long tradition of dismissing both Gaelic and common lawyers in Ireland as uncouth and pretentious. This attitude, as well as a fear that Irish lawyers might be only too willing and able to go their own way, underpinned support for the provision forcing law students to London.

As indicated above, it is not suggested by this author that the modern system of legal education in Britain and Ireland owes its origins solely to the efforts of Irishmen such as Kennedy and Wyse or indeed Joseph Napier, who was a leading lecturer at the Dublin Law Institute and who later was responsible for moving an enquiry into the English inns. There were already many in England, such as Andrew Amos or Henry Brougham, who had acknowledged the need for reform and had in practical ways encouraged the legal profession to adapt and change. But it does seem perverse to overlook the major contribution of Irishmen.

The Wyse report of 1846 underlined just how bad was the state of legal education throughout the United Kingdom at that time. In truth, the tide was already turning, but it had reached such a low ebb that it would be some time before the flow became particularly noticeable. During the decades which followed, benchers on both sides of the Irish Sea struggled to come to terms with changing attitudes and were roundly condemned in parliament for their lack of initiative. In their attitude towards education during this period, they evoke Shakespeare's schoolboy, 'creeping like snail, unwillingly to school'.

In particular, conservative Irish benchers clung like drowning men to the Statute of Jeofailles of 1542. This had introduced the requirement that intending counsellors must first attend English inns for a period of years before being allowed to practise in Ireland. The space of years had been left blank by parliament and what was actually demanded varied over the centuries from five years to four terms in the end, the last being the minimum which was felt capable of being reconciled with the plural usage of the statute. What also varied was how a term might be kept, with the improved communications of the nineteenth century allowing law students to do so if they wished by going over to London on a Monday night and returning to Dublin the following Friday.

Not everyone objected vehemently to the requirement for attendance in England, although there were those who found it insufferably offensive. There was a protestant tradition of defending it loyally. Moreover, many who agreed that it was educationally futile still enjoyed the break from home at their parents' expense, and savoured a taste of metropolitan if not cosmopolitan life. Nor did immersing people in the culture of London necessarily result in their docile acceptance of the English government's view of Ireland. The fact that politicians as diverse as Henry Grattan, Wolfe Tone and Daniel O'Connell were influenced in their thinking by their experiences in London while law students indicates that the effect of weaning young men from the breast of Mother Ireland might be more complex than some of its detractors suggested, although perhaps not beyond the fundamentally reformist paradigm of the Tudor framers of the statute. The latter, in their disdain for the Irish, would scarcely have been surprised to learn that the immediate parliamentary instrument of their improving statute's demise would be a spokesman for Irish inn-keepers. He was also a barrister, who had once acted as Tristram Kennedy's electoral agent and who had succeeded Kennedy as the parliamentary representative for Louth.

The story of Irishmen eating their legs of mutton in London is both infuriating and amusing. Also an interesting and hitherto untold tale is that concerning proposals to introduce a system of chambers in Dublin, along the lines of those in London. This is particularly relevant to any account of the development of legal training in Ireland. Gandon was asked to construct a range of chamber buildings at King's Inns but never got around to it. Later, in his seventieth year, Tristram Kennedy proposed that the society acquire all of the houses behind the King's Inns along Henrietta Street, erect a gateway at the foot of the street and turn the area into a warren of chambers. He published a pamphlet which indicated how the society might be enabled to fund such a development. He believed that the chamber system had certain educational advantages and had himself earlier turned three houses on Henrietta Street into what he styled 'Queen's Inns Chambers', the name indicating his admiration for Victoria. At the time of his imaginative proposal, Kennedy himself owned up to three-quarters of the houses in Henrietta Street, and he offered to sell these to King's Inns at their market value. But the benchers demurred and, following Kennedy's death, the quality of the street gradually declined to its present poor state.

The stories of the Irish being forced to attend the inns in London and of chambers that never came to be built in Dublin will be told in order to round off this account of how legal training came to be revived in Ireland between the reformist dawn of 1835 and the repeal of the Statute of Jeofailles in 1885. They are crucial for an understanding of the nature of changes in legal education in the nineteenth century, as is an appreciation of the sheer conservatism of the benchers in England and Ireland.

But it is necessary first to consider what kind of a person Tristram Kennedy himself was and what were the experiences and events which shaped the life of one who was so centrally involved in the development of professionalisation in Ireland.

CHAPTER TWO

'Faithful and true to the poor': the life and times of 'honest Tristram Kennedy' (1805–1885)

THROUGHOUT HIS LIFE, Tristram Kennedy stood for reconciliation and reform. By birth and upbringing a Derry protestant of settler origins, he was eventually promoted for the house of commons by catholic priests and nationalists. A landlord and land agent himself, he strove to ameliorate the lot of tenants, not least by establishing the renowned Carrickmacross lace industry. By profession first an attorney and subsequently a barrister, he established the Dublin Law Institute which was intended to reform radically the existing system of legal education. As a politician, he stayed loyal to his principles when surrounded by the more opportunistic and faint-hearted. During decades of frustration for Irish reformers, he was one of a small number of men who provided a parliamentary link between the movements of O'Connell and Parnell.

Kennedy's ancestors left their homes in Scotland to settle in Ulster during the early decades of the seventeenth century.[1] One of them, Horas Kennedy, was sheriff of Londonderry during the siege of 1688 and has been described as 'the chief promoter and main encourager of the memorable closing of its gates' in the face of an advancing army commanded by men loyal to the catholic King James. Tristram's father, John Pitt Kennedy, was a popular Church of Ireland clergyman who married Mary, the only daughter of Thomas Cary of Loughash in County Tyrone.[2]

The 'Carys of Innishowen' had been associated with Derry even longer than had been the Kennedys. Mary's great-great-great-grandfather, George Cary, was recorder of Londonderry in 1613. The Carys and Kennedys were close. Mary's two eldest sons by John Pitt married two of her first cousins, while their twelfth

1. Kennedy, *Family of Kennedy*, passim.
2. ibid., pp.22, 32, 36–38, 50–52; 'MacKenzie's narrative of the siege', in Hempton (ed.), *The siege and history of Londonderry*, p.161; *Londonderry Sentinel*, 3 July 1879.

child, Tristram, took his Christian name from a long line of Tristrams on her side of the family. It was possibly through his marriage to Mary that Tristram's father came to own land at Loughash, County Tyrone, as well as possessing two hundred and eighty acres on the Inishowen peninsula.[3]

Having been priested in 1782, Revd John Pitt Kennedy was instituted three years later to a 'living' at Carndonagh on Inishowen. The benefice was in the diocese of Derry but in the county of Donegal, and it was there at the glebe house that Tristram was born in 1805. Just six years later his father died, ending his days as rector of Balteagh, near Limavady in Co. Londonderry. He was survived by his wife and twelve children.[4]

The clergyman bequeathed his property at Loughash to his eldest son, William Pitt, but the rest he left on trust to be equally divided among all the surviving children, subject only to the condition that his widow enjoy the profits from it during her lifetime. Tristram was later to become a trustee of the land on Inishowen and of a small family property in the city of Londonderry.[5]

For the occupants of a remote rural glebe, John Pitt and Mary appear to have raised some remarkably active and extrovert sons. No fewer than five became members of the King's Inns, some as attorneys and some as barristers. Whether or not they were influenced in the choice of their profession by the fact that their father's sister had been married to Alexander Crookshank, lately a judge of the court of common pleas in Ireland, is not known. Two more sons went to sea, one becoming a commander in the Royal Navy, one a captain in the 'New India Service'. Yet another, who was to play an influential role in Tristram's life, had a distinguished military career overseas.[6]

The brother to whom Tristram was closest in age was Evory, who would later become a leading Dublin obstetrician. Evory was born just seventeen months after Tristram. On the same day in 1815 both were admitted to Foyle Diocesan College, formerly known as the Derry Free Grammar School. There they received a classical education in Greek and Latin before leaving in 1819.[7]

3. Lease, marquis of Donegall to T. Kennedy (PRONI MS); Kennedy, *Family of Kennedy*, contents p.ii, pp.96–100 and family chart no. 2.
4. ibid., pp.50–52, 66; Thom's *Dublin directory, 1866*, p. 449.
5. Registry of Deeds, nos.1846/4/47–8, 1882/35/124.
6. Kennedy, *Family of Kennedy*, pp.44, 50–74, 92. Admitted to King's Inns as attorneys were Thomas, Charles and Tristram. Called to the bar were William Pitt in 1812, Henry in 1821 and Tristram in 1834 (*King's Inns admission papers*, pp.263–64); Ball, *Judges*, ii, 221.
7. Kennedy, *Family of Kennedy*, pp.28–30, 70–72; Cameron, *Royal College of*

LAWYER

Tristram had already seen two of his brothers called to the bar when, aged sixteen, he himself embarked on a legal career. But his early inclination was to become an attorney, not a barrister, and in November 1821 he was taken on as an apprentice by his brother Thomas, then practising as an attorney in Londonderry. In 1824, the deaths of Thomas and of their eldest brother William, within months of one another, must have come as a great shock not only to Tristram but to the whole family. Both men were in their mid-thirties and both had young children. It was not long since Thomas had been appointed sheriff of the city. One immediate effect of his demise was that Tristram's indentures had to be assigned to a new master, Dominick Knox, under whom he completed his service as an apprentice.[8]

By the time that Tristram was admitted and sworn an attorney in the autumn of 1826, he was, by default, beginning to assume a position of responsibility within the family. Although the twelfth born among fourteen children, three of his older brothers had already died, one in infancy. Two more were at sea, while John Pitt, who had qualified as a civil engineer, was between 1819 and 1830 occupied on military service in the Greek islands under Sir Charles Napier.[9] Henry, called to the bar in 1821 and next eldest to Tristram, is said to have 'married twice, first a wealthy widow double his own age, but led a more or less wandering life and never practised his profession'.[10] In effect, therefore, Tristram was the most senior male to whom questions relating to domestic administrative and financial matters might be readily referred. It is unlikely, given the period in which they lived, that his two surviving elder sisters were allowed to take responsibility for such matters.

It was a sign of distinction for the family in general and for Tristram in particular that in 1828, at the young age of twenty-three, he was appointed sheriff of the city and county of

Surgeons in Ireland, pp.758–59; *Foyle College Times*, July 1941, pp.93–94; Pinkerton, 'Evory Kennedy', 77–81.

8. The memorial of Thomas Kennedy, gent., for liberty to take Tristram Kennedy as an apprentice, Michaelmas term 1821. The memorial of Dominick Knox, gent., to take an assignment of the indentures of Tristram Kennedy, Trinity term 1824 (King's Inns MSS, admission papers of Tristram Kennedy); Kennedy, *Family of Kennedy*, pp.50–52.

9. The memorial of Tristram Kennedy to be admitted a student, Michaelmas term 1829 (King's Inns MSS, admission papers of Tristram Kennedy); Kennedy, *Family of Kennedy*, pp.50–56; Ferriman, *Some English philhellenes*, pp.67–68; *DNB*, s.v. Kennedy, John Pitt.

10. Kennedy, *Family of Kennedy*, p.66.

Londonderry.[11] Not only his late brother Thomas but also a number of their ancestors had already held that position. But if, as noted earlier, one had been instrumental in closing the gates of the city against the forces of the catholic King James, it fell to Tristram to preside over an event which symbolically marked the emergence of a newly-found confidence among the catholics who lived in Derry. The manner in which he did so was to stand to his political benefit over twenty years later.

Between the years 1824 and 1828 proselytism by evangelical protestants was rife throughout Ireland. One of the tactics of those so vigorously promoting their Christian beliefs was to challenge local roman catholic priests to a debate about religious matters. But Irish prelates, in general, forbade their clergy to engage in such discussions, and in 1827 an attempt to stage in Londonderry a confrontation 'on the comparative merits of protestantism and popery' collapsed when the catholics failed to turn up.[12]

Some prominent Derry catholics were disappointed. According to one subsequent account by a catholic writer, 'the circumstances of the locality were peculiar and considerations all-powerful elsewhere were thought by many to be but secondary in Derry'. Given the history of Londonderry as a settlement town which had stood firm under siege from catholic forces, there was a particular resonance in the throwing down of a gauntlet by protestant clergy. With the repeal of the penal laws and the growing prosperity of the nineteenth-century bourgeoisie, catholics in Derry, as elsewhere, were kindling aspirations which had been unlikely to flare at an earlier date: 'Social ambition began to stir in their breast.... There was need of a triumph for them; there was need of a lesson to the ascendancy'.[13]

So when, in March 1828, a public meeting was called in Londonderry to set up a branch of the Reformation Society, catholics turned out in some force to oppose the proposition. There resulted 'a very tumultuous assembly' which had to be adjourned until the next day. No doubt fearing that matters might get out of hand, the sheriff, Tristram Kennedy, was asked to chair the resumed meeting. But, notwithstanding the charging of an

---

11. Memorial of Tristram Kennedy, 1829 (King's Inns MS, admission papers). He had been a sub-sheriff since 1824 (Londonderry council minutes, 6 May 1824 and 2 Nov. 1827; *The Times*, obituary, 25 Nov. 1885).
12. McGee, *Life of Maginn*, pp.12–13; *The Londonderry discussion, or a statement of an agreement between six R.C. priests and six Protestant clergymen to discuss the points at issue between both churches in which the former failed!; the speeches of the latter* (Dublin, 1827), passim.
13. McGee, *Life of Maginn*, pp.12–13.

entrance fee and the issuing of tickets, a still greater crowd turned up the next day and there was a 'very unpleasant conflict of opinion'. Eventually, the protestants decided to adjourn the meeting of the Reformation Society *sine die* when the catholics agreed to discuss the merits of the two churches in public. Six clergymen of the established church and six roman catholic priests were nominated to join battle. Among the latter was the future bishop of Derry, the 'militant' Edward Maginn. The debate lasted for twelve days, moving from court-house to cathedral. For the first four days Tristram Kennedy remained in the chair. Throughout, according to a report of the proceedings authorised by both sides, Kennedy 'continued most courteously and to the satisfaction of all to preside'. When, on the fifth day, Kennedy was replaced by another chairman whom he had nominated, it was a roman catholic who proposed the vote of thanks to the sheriff 'for his gentlemanly and impartial conduct in the chair'. If anyone had been expecting Kennedy to show bias towards the protestants because of his family background, then he clearly surprised them. His attitude at a sensitive moment in the city's history was to be recalled gratefully long after the event.[14]

Perhaps Kennedy's experience in the chair on that occasion whetted his own appetite for advocacy. For it was about this time that he decided to forsake the role of attorney and to become a barrister. In November 1829, at his own request, he was first struck off the roll of attorneys and then admitted by the benchers of King's Inns a student of the bar. Shortly afterwards, he entered Lincoln's Inn in London.[15]

Following his call to the bar in 1834, Tristram took up residence in Dublin, where most Irish legal business was conducted. His younger brother and class-mate at Foyle College, Evory, had already established himself in the city as a leading obstetrician, having been appointed master of the Rotunda Hospital in 1833 at the early age of twenty-seven and publishing a book on the foetus that same year.[16] In April 1835, Evory allowed Tristram the use

14. *Authenticated report of the discussion which took place at Londonderry between six Roman catholic priests and six clergymen of the established church in the diocese of Derry, March 1828* (Dublin, 1828), preface and fifth day; McGee, *Life of Maginn*, pp.15–16; Bowen, *The protestant crusade, 1800–1870*, p.190; *Londonderry Standard*, 7 Feb. 1874.
15. Memorial of Tristram Kennedy, 1829 (King's Inns MS, admission papers); *King's Inns adm.*, p.264, *L. I. adm. reg.*, ii, 135 (13 Nov. 1829).
16. Letter to author from M.R.N. Darling, master of the Rotunda Hospital (10 Dec. 1990); Cameron, *College of Surgeons*, p.758; Pinkerton, 'Evory Kennedy', 78–79; Evory Kennedy, *Observations on obstetric auscultation with*

of a house which the doctor owned on Cavendish Row.[17] Evory also appears to have provided at his own home in Rutland Square (now Parnell Square) accommodation for their older brother, John Pitt. In 1830, John Pitt returned to live in Ireland after more than a decade of service in Greece under Sir Charles Napier: in Caphalonia and elsewhere, they had overseen the creation of such infrastructural services as roads and market-places. John Pitt forged there a warm and lasting friendship with Napier, who was from Celbridge in Co. Kildare. Both felt strongly that extensive poverty in Ireland could be greatly eased by the adoption of pragmatic solutions. When a situation arose in which John Pitt might test his theories in practice, he decided to do so. Someone was needed to manage the estate at Loughash which had passed to the eldest Kennedy son and thence, following his early death in 1824, to his widow and two babies. John Pitt took on that responsibility. Subsequently, he became manager of a number of other estates also, including one in Donegal belonging to Sir Charles Style, whose daughter he married in 1838.[18]

That John Pitt, Tristram and Evory constituted a very distinctive trio is evident not only from subsequent events but also from references to them by both Thomas Carlyle and Charles Gavan Duffy.[19]

An incident in 1838 involving the family estate indicates that Tristram had a practical grasp of both legal and political procedures. He and John Pitt had become executors of their father's will, the two hundred and eighty acres at Inishowen and some property in Londonderry never having been sold. In 1838, a bill came before the house of commons in London for the purposes of draining and embanking certain lands along Lough Swilly and Lough Foyle, those stretches of water which define the peninsula of Inishowen. With rights upon the slob of Lough Swilly, the brothers saw an opportunity to seek compensation. They presented a

    an analysis of the evidences of pregnancy and an inquiry into the proofs of the life and death of the foetus in utero: with an appendix containing legal notes by John Smith esq., barrister-at-law (Dublin and London, 1833).

17. Registry of Deeds, 1844/1/236. Later in 1835 Tristram acted as trustee of Evory's marriage settlement with the Hamiltons of Donegal (Kennedy, *Family of Kennedy*, p.72; Registry of Deeds, no.1835/7/166–7).

18. Registry of Deeds, nos.1835/7/166–7, 1837/7/283; *DNB*, s.v. Kennedy, John Pitt; *Family of Kennedy*, pp.52, 58, 62, 102; Napier, *Life and opinions of General Sir Charles James Napier*, i, 438–42; John Pitt Kennedy, *Instruct; employ; don't hang them; or Ireland tranquilised without soldiers and enriched without English capital*, pp.44–48, 82–83, 159–61; *Fourth report from the select committee on the Poor Laws (Ireland)*, p.217.

19. Carlyle, *Reminiscences of my Irish journey in 1849*, pp.42–43; Gavan Duffy, *My life in two hemispheres*, i, 265.

petition to parliament against the bill, claiming that the work would injure their land. This led to a settlement under which the undertakers for executing the purposes of the act were obliged to agree to a scheme of compensation in return for the brothers withdrawing their opposition. Notwithstanding this successful encounter with parliament and the fact that he was already 'well and popularly known in Donegal' as an active member of the then Liberal Registry Association there, Tristram resisted any temptation to embark immediately upon a political career. It was to be another fourteen years before he made the trip to Westminster as a member of parliament and it would then be for Co. Louth.[20] In the meantime, educational concerns occupied his immediate attention, his Dublin Law Institute being opened in 1839.

It is difficult not to suspect that some degree of sibling rivalry was involved in Tristram's foray into education. Already his two brothers had established themselves in that field. As early as 1828 Evory had been appointed a lecturer in midwifery at the recently opened Richmond Hospital School, prior to his appointment as master of the Rotunda.[21]

John Pitt, for his part, became known throughout Ireland for his views on agricultural instruction. He had already built special national schools on the estates which he managed and had published regulations for promoting agricultural training when, in 1838, he was appointed the inspector-general of the nascent national schools system, 'on the understanding that practical instruction in agriculture was to become a prominent feature in national education'. It was he who in 1838, as inspector-general, acquired for educational purposes the site at Glasnevin in Dublin which afterwards became known as the Albert College. John Pitt intended to form there a central model farm and training establishment for teachers who would be taught to give instruction in agriculture in the national schools. He wished each national school to have a patch of land for practical instruction. So committed was John Pitt to educational improvement that he is said to have declined a governorship in Australia in order to continue promoting his plans. That he was offered such a position reflects his reputation as 'a practical man, not a visionary'.[22] Contemporaries strongly

20. *Londonderry Standard*, 28 & 31 Jan. 1874; lease, marquis of Donegall to T. Kennedy (PRONI MS); Registry of Deeds, nos.1845/17/158, 1846/4/48; Dun, *Landlords and tenants in Ireland*, pp.133-38 for a description of the area.
21. Cameron, *College of Surgeons*, p.758; Evory almost succeeded in being appointed professor of medicine at Edinburgh University (Pinkerton, 'Evory Kennedy', 78).
22. *DNB*, s.v. Kennedy, John Pitt; Napier, *An essay on the present state of Ireland*,

favoured education as a panacea for Irish problems. The ignorance of the Irish masses was seen to act 'not only as an impediment to practical schemes for the improvement of their condition but also prevented their developing habits of industry and systematic thinking, the lack of which left them an easy prey to the rhetoric of agitators'.[23]

Where his brothers had undertaken to provide medical and agricultural instruction, Tristram Kennedy turned his attention to the absence of legal training. As considered elsewhere in the course of the present book, between 1839 and 1846 Tristram was kept busy in campaigning to improve the standard of legal education in Ireland by establishing a special law institute in Dublin and by pressing parliament for reforms. During those years his contribution to the process of professionalisation was considerable, and the efforts of himself and of Thomas Wyse made a lasting mark on the history of legal training in both England and Ireland. At the time Kennedy himself travelled to Germany and to other European countries to learn about the well-established law schools there, as well as communicating with professors in St Petersburg and at Harvard about his objectives. These matters are merely touched upon here because they are treated in depth below. With the publication of the report of the Wyse committee on legal education, Kennedy appears to have decided that there was little more which he might do or try at that point in relation to legal training. The committee reported in 1846, the year when Ireland finally began to be overwhelmed by the full horrors of the great famine.

LAND AGENT

Widespread poverty and deprivation in Ireland during the 1840s did not leave Tristram Kennedy unaffected. His preoccupation with professional matters gave way to a determination to alleviate the misery of his fellow countrymen. In this he was influenced by the experiences of his older brother.

> *dedicated to the Irish absentee landed proprietors*, pp.31, 41; *Devon comm. digest*, p.48; Kennedy, 'Captain Pitt Kennedy's plan for Irish agriculture, 1835–45'; Edwards & Williams, *Great Famine*, p.120. The Albert College was for many years part of the Faculty of Agriculture of University College Dublin but is today the location of Dublin City University, formerly the National Institute for Higher Education, Dublin (Horgan, *Dublin City University*, pp.15–19).
> 23. Black, *Economic thought and the Irish question*, p.147; Ó Tuathaigh, *Ireland before the famine*, p.98.

John Pitt's reign as inspector-general of national schools had been even briefer and unhappier than that of Tristram as principal of the Dublin Law Institute. John Pitt's specific plans for a national education system had been thwarted. Even before his appointment, a second edition of his pamphlet on agricultural reform had expressed disapproval of the government's current proposals for a poor law, which were institutional in nature rather than structural.[24] John Pitt would later be described by Thomas Carlyle as 'headlong', and the dedicatory preface of his pamphlet appears to have aroused some abiding enmity by displaying too much relish for reform. An eloquent apologia published in London by his former and future commanding officer, Sir Charles Napier, failed to win him the additional powers or resources which he felt were needed if his plans for national education were to succeed. In 1839, John Pitt threw in the towel and resigned as inspector-general in order to return to estate management.[25]

However, before long the government again called upon his services. Although the full extent of the approaching disaster in Ireland was foreseen by few, there was a growing acknowledgment in official circles that problems caused by circumstances such as the absence of many landlords from their estates and the insecurity of title of tenants were creating a crisis. In November 1843 a commission was appointed under the chairmanship of the earl of Devon, a nobleman with extensive landholdings in Munster. Its purpose was to inquire into the state of the law and practice in respect to the occupation of land in Ireland. John Pitt Kennedy was invited to serve as its secretary, an appointment thought by some to strengthen its hand considerably. Members of the commission visited every Irish county and took an immense amount of oral evidence, including some from Charles Kennedy, the former secretary of the Dublin Law Institute who had succeeded his brother John Pitt as agent on the Style estate in Donegal. In February 1845, only some months before the beginning of the great famine, the Devon Commission issued its findings. These highlighted the sufferings of the impoverished tenantry.[26]

Clearly impressed by the secretary of the commission, whom he described as 'indefatigable', Devon asked him to become manager of his vast estates in Limerick. John Pitt was pressed for time

24. Kennedy, *Instruct; employ; don't hang them* (2nd ed.), dedications, introduction; Napier, *Essay*, passim; Ferriman, *Some English philhellenes*, pp.67–68.
25. Carlyle, *Reminiscences*, p.43; *DNB*, s.v. Kennedy, John Pitt; Napier, *Essay*.
26. *Devon comm. digest*, preface and p.1041; O'Brien, *The great famine in Ireland*, pp.34–36; Woodham-Smith, *The Great Hunger*, pp.20–21.

to complete for publication a digest of the commission's evidence, otherwise to be found only in bulky volumes. He turned, it is written, 'to a young relation, Mr Kennedy, of the Irish bar. To them belongs exclusively all the merits of the execution' of what was a highly-regarded abbreviation. The 'young relation' was perhaps Tristram, although it may also have been a nephew who had very recently been called.[27]

With Ireland being ravaged by famine both brothers found themselves being drawn into efforts to alleviate its effects. In 1845, the prime minister, Robert Peel, appointed John Pitt Kennedy secretary to the first Famine Relief Committee. The following year Tristram took a fateful decision when he became land agent for the Bath estate in the Ulster county of Monaghan. It is not known what finally pushed him into following in the footsteps of his two brothers, John Pitt and Charles, who had both managed other people's property. It may simply have been a philanthropic impulse. The measures which he took to relieve distress in Monaghan do not seem to have been particularly well calculated to enhance his employment prospects as a land agent. But they were to win him the lasting respect and affection of poor catholics in the area and to provide him with a platform upon which subsequently to stand for parliament. Indeed, even before he went to Monaghan, Tristram had already acquired a good reputation among catholics for his treatment of tenants in Donegal. There he acted as a trustee of the family property on Inishowen as well as himself leasing some additional land on the peninsula from the marquis of Donegal in 1830. The bishop of Derry, Edward Maginn, who had encountered Kennedy in the latter's role as chairman of the religious debate of 1828 in which Maginn participated as a priest, was so impressed by Kennedy that he went to some lengths to help him to settle in Monaghan. Maginn sought out the bishop of Clogher and assured him of 'the great blessings that must accrue to the tenantry of Farney' from Kennedy's appointment. Maginn wished 'to heaven' that 'all the estates in Ireland were under such management, and our country would not long be a bye word amongst the nations of the earth'. Writing to Kennedy in June 1846, Maginn assured the newly appointed land agent of 'a kind reception and co-operation in all the good works you may intend

---

27. *Devon comm. digest*, preface; *King's Inns adm.*, p.264; Kennedy, *Family of Kennedy*, p.66. Tristram was also described as 'indefatigable' about this time (*Legal Reporter*, ii, 87). John Pitt Kennedy, jnr., a son of the late Thomas, was called to the bar early in 1845. He later became a judge of the Indian high court in Calcutta (Foster, *Men-at-the-bar*, p.254).

to benefit the hitherto neglected tenantry of that locality'.[28] It was not to be the last time that a bishop gave his opinion on Kennedy's worthiness for a job.

Tristram's programme of action in Monaghan involved setting up national schools, encouraging local industry and taking steps to improve the quality of holdings occupied by tenants. In all of this, he could be seen to be representative of Irish reformers who had been arguing since the early 1830s for more imaginative responses to poverty than that represented by the Poor Law Act of 1838. That statute created the workhouse system, hated by tenants because of the humiliations which it entailed and disliked by landlords who saw the raising of rates to pay for the new institutions as a further burden on the occupiers of land.[29]

In determining what course to adopt in Monaghan, Tristram found a model to emulate in the estates in Tyrone and Donegal which John Pitt and Charles had managed. At Loughash John Pitt had arrived to find that in 1831 over three-quarters of the 1,150 acres were wasteland. On Sir Charles Style's estate in Donegal eleven thousand out of twelve thousand acres were waste in 1838. While reclamation of land was then being widely attempted or proposed (its utility as a remedy for over-population possibly being exaggerated), the particular efforts of John Pitt resulted in him being described by one modern writer as 'the most important advocate of waste-land reclamation in the years around the famine'. Allied to John Pitt's programmes of reclamation was his educational theory, which, as noted above, led to his establishing schools on both estates and to his receiving public recognition during a brief period in office as inspector-general of national schools. The teachers at Loughash doubled as overseers of improvements and were, in fact, the agricultural superintendents of their respective districts.[30]

On both estates women were encouraged to generate income from sources other than agriculture. In Donegal, where illicit distillation was said to have been 'the staple trade of the district', a female industrial school was set up with a boarding class attached to it, in which young women were trained to become teachers. There was also a small farm to demonstrate 'housethrift'. Even

28. Lease, marquis of Donegall to T. Kennedy (PRONI MS); Registry of Deeds, 1840/13/219; *Dundalk Democrat*, 13 and 27 June 1868; *Londonderry Standard*, 7 Feb. 1874; *DNB*, s.v. Kennedy, John Pitt.
29. Ó Tuathaigh, *Ireland before the famine*, pp.108–14.
30. Kennedy, *Instruct; employ; don't hang them*, pp.44–48, 82–83, 159–61; Napier, *Essay*, passim; *Devon comm. evidence*, i, 975–77 (evidence no. 278); Edwards & Williams, *Great Famine*, p.117.

more relevant to what Tristram would achieve in Monaghan was an experiment at Loughash. One of his sisters, Mary, had taken steps to revive a Tyrone costume, traditionally worn by women of the locality but by then almost entirely superseded by imported garments. The idea of reintroducing the costume was to encourage people to produce homemade articles 'in place of wasting their time in idleness'. Sir Charles Napier, whose continuing friendship with John Pitt was reflected in the latter naming his first-born son Charles Napier, visited Loughash and found the poor 'manufacturing in their cabins a strong, excellent cloth, made of woolen and flax'. The extent to which many landlords were sceptical of such undertakings is evident from Napier's feeling obliged to address the possibility that 'the establishment of a costume among the Irish labouring females, in place of the rags in which they are now clothed, may appear to be visionary, if not altogether ridiculous'.[31]

So Tristram Kennedy was neither without experience nor without example when, in the summer of the 'terrible' and 'disastrous' year of 1846, he arrived at Carrickmacross to take up employment as agent of the Bath estate in the barony of Farney in Monaghan, then the fourth most densely populated county in Ireland. 'Here he had a task to undertake which might well have appalled the stoutest heart'. The failure of the potato, upon which food the poor in many instances depended for survival, had intensified existing distress caused by the decline of the linen industries during the 1830s and 1840s. The miserable population on the Bath estate alone amounted to over 13,500 tenants, each one holding on average less than two acres:

The introduction of the new Poor Law . . . throwing upon landed proprietors a modicum of the Poor Rates, led in many quarters to an organised system of extinguishing the small-holders, lest they should become chargeable to rates, and 'extermination' upon a grand scale became the order of the day. The Bath estates, in common with the rest of the district, were greatly overpopulated, but Mr Kennedy sternly refused to adopt any of the cruel remedies applied in other quarters.[32]

---

31. *Devon comm. evidence*, i, 975–77; Napier, *Essays*, pp.65–67. Illicit distillation was already in decline everywhere. But domestic textiles were second only to agriculture as a major area of expanding employment (Connell, *Irish peasant society*, pp.1–50; Daly, *The famine in Ireland*, pp.11–13).
32. *Dundalk Democrat*, 1 Feb. 1851; Kennedy & Sullivan, *On the industrial training institutions of Belgium*, pp.53–54; Ó Mórdha, 'The great famine in Monaghan: a coroner's account', 32–41, 175–86; Kennedy and Ollerenshaw, *An economic history of Ulster 1820–1940*, pp.138, 143; *NHI*, v, 336–37; *Londonderry Standard*, 7 Feb. 1874 for quotation.

Kennedy's first task was to set people to work upon drainage schemes, reclaiming land as his brothers had done in Tyrone and Donegal. Labourers were paid remunerative wages out of a fund specially established by Tristram Kennedy in conjunction with local proprietors. He encouraged voluntary emigration and, it has been said by one writer,

> did, moreover, what scarcely any other Irish agent had ever before thought of, – he not only *permitted* tenant right sales, but he *enforced* the Ulster custom in all its unrestricted fullness, so that no tenant, however humble or poor, left the estate without the entire value of his tenant right interest in his pocket, as raised at a free, open, competitive sale.[33]

It is not clear what this writer meant be the 'fullness' of the Ulster custom. Unrestricted sales of tenant right were said by some landowners to encourage buyers to spend all of their capital in simply getting possession, leaving them without the means to work their farms. While it may be presumed that Kennedy himself did not actively encourage such rash transactions, he certainly supported fully the contemporary demands for tenant right. During the nineteenth century, the Ulster custom received much favourable notice from parliamentary reformers who wished to see it enshrined in legislation for the whole of Ireland. Those enjoying the benefit of Ulster custom, a form of tenant right largely peculiar to the northern counties, could continue in undisturbed possession of their farms so long as the rent was paid. Moreover, they were, in the case of ejectment, entitled to a payment from the incoming occupier for the enjoyment of the holding, in particular, for improvements which they had made and which continued to enhance the property. By comparison with tenants who did not, those who did benefit fully from the Ulster custom were fortunate.[34]

Kennedy appears to have won the affection of his tenants. Ten years later a deputation representing catholics and liberals from Louth would pay him a great tribute, recalling that

> we were so near the borders of the County Monaghan as to be familiarly aware of the extraordinary energy, charity and readiness of resources with which you grappled with the famine, and exterminated extermination – the words are no hyperbole – in one half of the barony of Farney.[35]

33. *Londonderry Standard*, 7 Feb. 1874; *Dundalk Democrat*, 26 June and 10 July 1852.
34. Hancock, *The tenant-right of Ulster considered economically*; [Steuart Trench], *On 'tenant-right'*, pp.16–21. For a modern critique of the limited advantages to tenants of the Ulster custom see Solow, *The land question and the Irish economy*, pp.24–45.
35. *Londonderry Standard*, 7 Feb. 1874.

Admirers claimed that it was Kennedy's agricultural improvements in Monaghan which finally persuaded the government to issue treasury advances for private works of abiding utility in cases where the owners allowed their estates to be charged with repayment of the advances made. These private loans represented a change in official policy and were announced in October 1846 by means of what became known as 'the Labouchère letter'.[36]

Like John Pitt, Tristram also appreciated the economic advantages of providing his tenantry with some useful form of education. But at first in Monaghan he had no opportunity of doing so for, between 1846 and 1848, 'my whole time was occupied in the attempt to procure employment and support for the population during the famine consequent on the potato failure'. Only afterwards could he consider the question of schooling the local people.[37] Upon his arrival in Monaghan, he had found 'a mass of population miserably ignorant and without any adequate educational provision'. Scarcely one in four of the population could read and write. So in 1848 Kennedy proceeded to set up within twelve months no less than seven national schools and one agricultural school, complete with its own model farm.[38]

Again, like John Pitt, Tristram sought ways in which to combine the usual so-called 'literary' curriculum of the standard national school with more vocational training. But where his brother had concentrated on providing agricultural skills, Tristram also drew inspiration from his sister Mary's efforts to revive local handiwork. A lace-making industry had been founded in Ulster in the 1820s, the idea having been imported from Italy. Some training was provided at a schoolhouse in Armagh but the experiment did not last. Kennedy now decided to incorporate in the curriculum of his Monaghan schools some instruction in lace-making, importing lace from Belgium to demonstrate a finely finished product. He went further by supplying materials on credit to, and acting as agent for, the nascent industry which his new system of education was creating. Carrickmacross lace became famous throughout Ireland and abroad, the industry which Kennedy established in

---

36. ibid.; *Dundalk Democrat*, 10 July 1852; O'Brien, *Great Famine*, pp.122–33; Black, *Economic thought and the Irish question*, p.116. Others too were given credit for the government's decision (de Vere, *Recollections*, pp.226, 250–51).
37. Kennedy & Sullivan, *Industrial training in Belgium*, p.53.
38. ibid.; 'Report by Tristram Kennedy esq. on the state and progress of education on the Bath estate, Carrickmacross, 17 May 1850' in *Nat. educ. crs. report, 1850*, pp.315–17. That rate of 75% was at the upper end of the incidence of illiteracy in central Ireland (*NHI*, v, 266).

1848 continuing to provide employment in the final decade of the twentieth century.[39] The commissioners for national education were impressed by Kennedy's approach. In their report for 1850, it was noted that

> the system thus carried out has already been attended with the best results. Through a wide portion of the barony of Farney the casual looker-on cannot fail to observe the neat appearance and gentle manner of the younger females, and in their looks an expression of self-reliance and content. To those who had known them ill-fed and ill-clad, careless of cleanliness and dejected, if not morose, the transition is at once extraordinary and most cheering.[40]

The reader of such an account might be forgiven for thinking that the chief objective of national education was a cosmetic one, intended to alleviate the sensibilities of the Victorian middle-classes. Indeed, the curriculum of national schools generally up to 1848 has been described as 'a turgid amalgam of social ethics and political docility'.[41] But there was certainly more to the Kennedy schools than charm. They were, in fact, a lifeline for some of the desperate tenantry. In 1851, with about 150 females being supplied with work by the Carrickmacross schools, an observer remarked that 'they have actually enabled many of the poor cottier families to struggle through all the calamities of the last two years by the earnings of the young girls and women'. Not everyone made lace. There was knitting, sewing and quilting too. Half of those employed were said to be aged between eighteen and forty, underlining the fact that the population as a whole, not only children, were in need of schooling. Kennedy was not exceptional in identifying this need for training in non-agricultural skills as well as agricultural ones. The popular, if short-lived, Manufacture Movement had attempted to have industrial training combined with national education in Ireland. That movement tried to unite all classes and religions in a campaign to persuade the Irish public to buy products made in Ireland.[42]

39. *Dundalk Democrat*, 10 July 1852; *Irish lace: a history of the industry with illustrations* (for Mansion House exhibition, 1883), pp.2–3; Boyle, *The Irish flowerers*, pp.32, 40–2; Livingstone, *The Monaghan story*, p.527. John Pitt and Mary are known to have visited Tristram together in Monaghan (Johnston family, Stranorlar diary (NLI MS, 3 and 8 Oct. 1847). I am obliged to Ms Mairead Dunlevy, National Museum, for drawing this reference to my attention).
40. *Nat. educ. crs. report, 1849*, pp.262–63; ibid. (*1850*), p.315.
41. Ó Tuathaigh, *Ireland before the famine*, p.106.
42. *The Nation*, 6 Sept. 1851; Kennedy & Sullivan, *Industrial training in*

Kennedy himself estimated that, in the five years following the foundation of the schools, the workers in Carrickmacross had earned between them a total of over £3,000. Kennedy relied largely on the existing state system to finance the national schools, observing that the Carrickmacross schools were erected 'without extraordinary individual exertion or local expenditure'. But his own efforts on behalf of the tenantry were widely recognised and remembered.[43]

Kennedy would later describe himself as having been 'always faithful and true to the poor people' and many indeed regarded him in his lifetime as 'the friend of the tenantry'. Yet his family background was such that there remained a social and cultural gap between himself and the residents on Bath's estate, and this did cause strains. While he boasted of the success of the lace industry, pointing to the total of over £3,000 which local women had earned from it in five years, his own income as land agent during this period was later said by one of his own supporters to have been £1,500 per annum.[44] And the divide between land agent and tenantry was not just a matter of money. He grew irritated by what he saw as certain distinguishing features of the poverty-stricken Irish, writing to his employer that

> from the characteristic ingenuity of the Irish peasant to evade truth, his statements can only be received with suspicion. He has I regret to say no sense of reciprocity in any engagement he enters into and if he evinced a tythe of the ingenuity, or devoted half of the time towards keeping his engagements, that he does towards eluding them, his country would rank amongst the most prosperous of agricultural nations. . . . This renders him very ruthless, cunning and exacting and in conveying all his views he looks upon the agent and his staff as his natural enemies and consequently every device that ingenuity or misrepresentation can afford is had recourse to as perfectly justifiable in his dealings with them.[45]

> *Belgium*, pp.48–54; James Murnane, 'The national school system in County Monaghan', 209–13; C.D.A. Leighton, *The Irish Manufacture Movement, 1840–43* (Maynooth, 1987), passim.

43. Kennedy & Sullivan, *Industrial training in Belgium*, pp.59, 117; *Nat. educ. crs. report, 1850*, p. 316.

44. *Freeman's Journal*, 4 May 1852; *Newry Examiner*, 15 Aug. 1857. By 1883 the marquis of Bath was enjoying an annual gross income of almost £20,000 from his Monaghan property (Bateman, *The great landowners of Great Britain and Ireland*, p.30).

45. Kennedy to Lady Bath, 2 Feb. 1849 (Longleat House, Wiltshire, Bath papers, Irish box). I am most grateful to Dr Theo Hoppen for having furnished me with a copy of his notes on correspondence between Kennedy and Bath. I have relied on his notes here and below when making reference to the Irish box.

That this was not simply an exceptional outburst of irritation is suggested by another letter in which he described how he received a tenant deputation asking for reductions in their rents. He sent them packing, pointing out that the Bath estate already afforded certain concessions which neighbouring estates did not, lecturing them on how they had contributed to their own problems through bad cultivation and subdivision and suggesting to them that they consider emigrating. His patronising tone in this respect was quite typical of landlords and land agents.[46] Yet there is no denying that he won the affection of tenant-league leaders and priests. This may have been due simply to the fact that he tried to manage the estate fairly and went to considerable lengths to make the best of things. Describing his efforts to Lady Bath in 1849, he wrote that he was concerned with

the infant state of our poor laws, the total want of unanimity amongst the gentry, the difficult crisis through which we have I trust passed, the recourse necessary to government aid through the Board of Works, Drainage Commissioners, and other public measures for relief, the establishment of schools in connection with the Education Board for industrial purposes and general education, the introduction of improved husbandry, the adjustment of the railroad question on behalf of both proprietor and tenant, the facilitating emigration, and the endeavour to establish manufacture.[47]

A benevolent Belfast quaker, named Lamb, visited Monaghan and reported of Kennedy that 'everyone, poor and rich, speaks well of him; the tenants adore him because in his dealings between them and his employers, he gives poor Paddy "honest justice and civil treatment"'. Sir Charles Gavan Duffy would later judge him to have performed his duties as agent for Bath both 'humanely and discreetly'. Lamb also remarked that Kennedy lived just two or three miles from where another land agent had been murdered but that Kennedy himself appeared to be in no danger: 'He spends most of his time going among the tenantry, accompanied by his practical agriculturalists, advising and instructing them in

46. Kennedy to Lady Bath, 27 Sept. 1848 (Bath papers, Irish box); Hoppen, *Elections, politics and society*, p.141.
47. Tristram Kennedy to Lady Bath, 2 Feb. 1849 (Bath papers, Irish box), cited at Hoppen, *Elections, politics and society*, p.141; Grant, 'The Great Famine and the poor law in Ulster: the rate-in-aid issue of 1849', 30–47. The railroad, like drainage, was seen as a way of stimulating economic growth. Between 1847 and 1851 the miles of railway track laid increased from 150 to 600 (Liam Kennedy, 'Regional specialisation, railway development, and Irish agriculture in the nineteenth century', pp.173–93).

approved modes of cultivations'. He even acted as one of the stewards at the Carrickmacross races of 1849. In contrast, William Steuart Trench, who for a period was land agent on the neighbouring Shirley estate, has written that when a previous land agent died there in 1843 'bonfires were lit by the tenants on every hill in the area in manifestation of joy at his decease'. Steuart Trench noted that when in 1850 the trial came up of those who allegedly murdered the land agent referred to above, 'the temper of a portion of the peasantry at this time around Carrickmacross was very bad indeed'.[48]

Trench may well have looked upon Kennedy's popularity with a baleful eye. When Tristram left the Bath estate in January 1851, it was Trench who took over from him there. The latter notes in his memoirs that Lord Bath was then a minor, travelling abroad with a tutor. It had fallen to the marchionness of Bath to play the role of absentee landlady. That may explain the gushing tone of Kennedy's letter to her in 1849, quoted above. Trench claimed subsequently that, on taking up his appointment in 1851, he discovered that 'on Lord Bath's estate the tenants had been allowed to fall into heavy arrears, so that not less than £30,000 were due upon the estate when I undertook its management. Many of the tenants had not paid any rent whatever for periods varying from two to six years'. If true, this may go some way towards explaining why Kennedy's views on the peasantry, if known to his tenants, were overlooked by them. Trench immediately undertook one of the most successful campaigns of assisted emigration, a modern local historian claiming that those who refused his offer to go were served with ejectment orders. Within a year, Trench was obliged to travel round the estate with his son, 'each with a brace of double-barrelled pistols in our breasts and large ones besides in holsters buckled before us'.[49]

The precise circumstances of Kennedy's departure as land agent are obscure. He appears to have believed that he was sacked, the Bath family that he had resigned voluntarily. There was clearly a disagreement, presumably over the arrears of rent which were due. But if his retirement was greeted with relief in

48. *Dundalk Democrat*, 10 July 1852; *Londonderry Standard*, 7 Feb. 1874; Gavan Duffy, *My life in two hemispheres*, p.265; Livingstone, *Monaghan*, p.525; Steurt Trench, *Realities of Irish life*, pp.52, 153. For a modern review of Trench's book, see *Clogher Record*, viii (1975), 300.

49. Trench, *Realities of Irish life*, p.140; Livingstone, *Monaghan*, p.227; *NHI*, v, 338, 591–98, 615; Trench to Lady Bath, 12 Feb. and 18 Dec. 1851 (Bath papers, Irish box), cited at Hoppen, 'Landlords, society and electoral politics in mid-nineteenth century Ireland', p.317.

Wiltshire, it was viewed with regret in Monaghan. The tenantry of the Bath estate and other admirers held a 'magnificent' public dinner at which they gave him 'the most superb piece of plate ever presented in the County Monaghan'. Tristram's brother Charles was there to witness the event. In language again evocative of that social gulf which the Kennedys crossed rather than closed, Charles was described by the foremost representative of the tenants as being 'a gentleman of the most kind and affable disposition, and easily approached by the most humble individual'. Those present expressed to Tristram 'their esteem for the manner in which he discharged his duties while agent on that property, more especially in the encouragement of industrial training amongst the female population, and the diffusion of education amongst the children of the tenantry'.[50]

Tristram Kennedy had arrived in Monaghan unknown locally. By the time he departed, his reputation had spread throughout the county and beyond. To his successes in chairing the fraught religious debate in Derry in 1828, and in bringing together a wide cross-section of lawyers to support the Dublin Law Institute in 1839, had now been added his popularity with the tenantry. A caring and practical protestant reformer, he had become politically attractive to catholic electors of the neighbouring county of Louth who were in search of a candidate to represent their interests.

LEGISLATOR

Where Tristram Kennedy was enticed into parliamentary politics after 1851, John Pitt had been tempted to take extra-parliamentary action in 1848. During that year of revolution across Europe, Dublin was awash with rumours of imminent insurrection. In the event an uprising by Young Ireland failed to win widespread support. But many protestant civilians, who were not allowed to arm themselves, feared a massacre. John Pitt bought 500 stand of arms at his own expense and secretly distributed them to protestants, maintaining that he had prevented an outbreak of disorder by his action. Gavan Duffy would later allege that John Pitt had become 'an agent to the Castle to furnish arms to the northern Orangemen to be used against the Nationalists'. Whatever the truth of the matter, he left Ireland shortly afterwards, taking advantage of an offer of employment from Napier, who had been appointed commander-in-chief in India. There John Pitt threw

---

50. Kennedy to Lady Bath, 8 May 1851 (Bath papers, Irish box); *Dundalk Democrat*, 1 Feb. 1851.

himself into the construction of railways and roads, one highway through Simla towards Tibet bearing his name into the twentieth century. For his part, brother Evory preferred poetry to politics, although later he would be tempted to join Tristram in a brief electoral adventure.[51] By then, Tristram would have been thrice returned to parliament.

The main thrust of Tristram Kennedy's political programme was to relate to the widely-perceived need for land reform. He was by no means the first or foremost to champion that cause, but he was persistent and consistent in his advocacy of it.

In 1847 a bill to improve the legal interest of tenants in their holdings by legalising the Ulster custom had been introduced at Westminster by Sharman Crawford, a reforming northern landlord, but it was defeated. In response, Crawford and others, with the widespread support of presbyterian ministers, founded the Ulster Tenant Right Association. Meanwhile, outside Ulster, 'tenant protection societies' began to spring up from 1847. Often these were under the guidance of local catholic clergy and included many tenants with substantial holdings. But it was not until three political journalists, John Gray, Gavan Duffy and Frederick Lucas, intervened that the various associations around the country were forged into a coherent movement articulating clear political demands. In August 1850 the three men played a central organisational role in convening a national conference of tenant farmers 'and their friends'. This body 'closed its labours by establishing the Tenant League at a public meeting at which catholic priests and presbyterian ministers succeeded each other in the tribune in support of each resolution'. As catholics and presbyterians combined to create a reform movement the government grew uneasy. Its action at this time in introducing an Ecclesiastical Titles Bill was seen by some of the tenant-right leaders as a deliberate ploy to break the back of the movement by creating sectarian division. The measure inhibited the freedom of the catholic church to structure, as it saw fit, the administration of the hierarchy in England. Whether intentionally or not, the bill opened old wounds and, for the first time since the granting of catholic emancipation two decades earlier, religious feelings in Ireland were widely and strongly aroused. Catholic clergy already active in the cause of tenant-right were now given another reason for political involvement.[52]

51. Woodham-Smith, *Great Hunger*, p.344; *DNB*, s.v. Kennedy, John Pitt; Gavan Duffy, *My life*, p.265; Kennedy, *Alliteration in poetry*.
52. Gavan Duffy, *The league of north and south*, pp.56, 112, 115; Whyte, 'The influence of the catholic clergy in elections in nineteenth century Ireland', 243; Lyons, *Ireland since the famine*, p.116.

Believing in 1852 that their electoral prospects would be enhanced by cooperation, tenant-right activists and outraged catholics came together in a political alliance which saw liberal and radical candidates seeking support on the same ticket as those members whose contributions to the outgoing parliament had earned for them the reputation of being 'the pope's brass band'. Forty members returned to parliament in the 1852 election, including Tristram Kennedy for Louth, would subsequently take a pledge to 'hold themselves perfectly independent of, and in opposition to, all governments which do not make it a part of their policy and a cabinet question to give to the tenantry of Ireland a measure embodying the principles of Mr Sharman Crawford's bill'. An equivalent formula was to be adopted on the religious question.[53]

The electors of the two-seat constituency of Louth were mainly catholic tenants of protestant landowners. The conservative and whig candidates relied on a substantial core of loyal supporters but the actual outcome of any election hung in the balance and depended upon a coalition between either the tories or whigs and those remaining electors who cast their votes in the catholic and nationalist interest: these usually found the whigs more palatable. For a generation after 1832, a whig-protestant, catholic-nationalist alliance generally shared the representation. Thus, prior to the election of 1852, Louth was represented by two liberals, R.M. Bellew and Chichester Fortescue, the former a catholic landlord, the latter a leading whig and later chief secretary of Ireland. Writing to Archbishop John MacHale in 1852, the editor of the *Freeman's Journal*, John Gray, expressed the political reality bluntly. Gray, who was also one of the founders of the Tenant League, noted that seats in Drogheda and Dundalk, as well as one of those in the county of Louth, were 'determined' by the archbishop of Armagh, who since 1849 had been Paul Cullen.[54]

In fact, Kennedy's reputation among catholics proved instrumental in his selection for the constituency in place of Bellew. Bellew failed to be reselected because he had retained office as one of Russell's lords of the treasury while the government was piloting the Ecclesiastical Titles Bill through parliament.[55] Central to the process of promoting Kennedy was an aged, catholic clergyman called Bannon. He appears to have been an astute politician

---

53. Beckett, *Mod. Ire.*, pp.354–56; *NHI*, v, 399–405.
54. Larkin, *The consolidation of the roman catholic church in Ireland 1860–1870*, p.318; O'Reilly, *John MacHale*, p.323.
55. Whyte, *The Independent Irish party*, pp.52, 169.

himself, recognising the damage that could be done to the interests of tenants by sectarian divisions.[56] In April 1852 Bannon chaired a meeting of the Louth tenant-right club, which had been recently established. Several catholic clergy participated, including a Revd Mr Campbell of Kilsaran who acted as secretary of the club. Campbell attacked the two sitting members of parliament, each a whig. He

condemned the political career of both members of the county, and declared that their places should be filled by gentlemen in whom the people could trust. He reprobated Mr Fortescue's opinion with regard to Mr Sharman Crawford's Bill, and stigmatised Mr Bellew as having taken a discreditable part with the late government, particularly in reference to the Ecclesiastical Titles Bill (cheers).[57]

Following this meeting a number of men were contacted in order to gauge their willingness to stand for Louth. They included Tristram Kennedy and John Sadlier MP, the latter shortly to engulf his parliamentary colleagues in damaging controversy by agreeing, rather too hastily, to a government appointment. But Bannon was in no doubt as to who should stand and, at a meeting early in May 1852, the old priest 'proceeded to eulogise the conduct of Mr Tristram Kennedy'. He was unlikely to have pronounced such an endorsement without at least the tacit approval of the primate in Armagh.[58] Central to Kennedy's attractiveness for Bannon and others was the protestant's reputation among catholics. His handling of the Derry debate in 1828 was mentioned regularly, the event's significance not diminishing with the passage of time. By 1857, it was to become 'one of the most momentous, controversial discussions that has ever taken place in Ireland'.[59] Moreover, in the past, Kennedy had also been willing to waive, or to mitigate, the unpopular tithe taxes which were intended to support the established church. Thus, he was now respected for

the just and equitable manner in which you dealt with the payment of tithes on your own property, when you arranged that the catholic tenant should be free from that impost, that the presbyterian should pay the half, and the protestant the entire tithes levied on his holding.[60]

56. Gavan Duffy, *League of north and south*, pp.115–16.
57. *Freeman's Journal*, 29 April 1852.
58. *Freeman's Journal*, 4 May 1852; *Dundalk Democrat*, 26 June and 3 July 1852; O'Reilly, *John MacHale*, p.323.
59. *Newry Examiner and Louth Advertiser*, 15 Aug. 1857.
60. *Dundalk Democrat*, 13 and 27 June 1868. For the tithe controversy, see Bowen, *The protestant crusade in Ireland, 1800–70*, pp.156–77.

It had been significant in the context of Kennedy's developing political ambitions that the farewell dinner given in his honour in Monaghan the previous year had been presided over by Thomas McEvoy Gartlan, 'the well-known tenant-leaguer'. At the selection meeting in Louth, Bannon now described Kennedy as 'the friend of the tenantry', noting that Kennedy had gone to great lengths to help those on Bath's estates in the neighbouring county and that, 'when he found himself so circumstanced as to be unable to carry out all his intentions towards them, he gave up the agency which was worth £1,500 a year (cheers)'. For his part, Kennedy promised Bannon and others that he would support a bill for the repeal of the Ecclesiastical Titles Act. Shortly before the election itself, Bishop Kelly and the catholic clergy of Derry publicly supported his candidature for Louth, describing him yet again as 'the friend of the tenant'.[61]

Kennedy made it clear that he was reluctant to stand should the tenant-right club select a second candidate. He feared that by challenging Fortescue as well as the tories the county 'might be embroiled' and that 'difficulties would arise between landlord and tenant which would be most calamitous in their results'. He got his way and, at first, the election campaign went smoothly, with a meeting in Louth being attended by 'about 2,000 people of the farming classes of the neighbourhood'. Once again the chair was taken by that 'patriotic parish priest', Bannon, who pointed out that, while Kennedy was the candidate of the local tenant-right club, he had the sanction of the national league. At this meeting the parish priest of Carrickmacross conveyed an address of support from Monaghan, 'signed by about 1,000 of the most respectable people, clergy and laity, in Farney . . . and indignantly repudiating the attacks upon his character'. One of the attacks being made identified Tristram with his brother John Pitt in the arming of Orangemen in 1848. To this, the candidate replied by way of a public statement: 'Never, never; the insinuation is a foul and wicked calumny; the question is a clumsy contrivance to impress the electors with a belief that Mr Kennedy was identified with an act which his whole public and private life disclaims and disapproves'.[62]

But if Kennedy thought that verbal insults were the worst form of abuse to which he might be subjected, he learnt the next day of greater dangers. A midday meeting of the tenant-right club was

61. *Dundalk Democrat*, 1 Feb. 1851, 10 July 1852, 27 June 1868; *Freeman's Journal*, 4 May 1852; Livingstone, *Monaghan*, p.227.
62. *Freeman's Journal*, 4 May and 6 July 1852; *Dundalk Democrat*, 3 and 10 July 1852, 13 and 27 June 1868.

arranged for the village of Dunleer, stronghold of the Bellew family, which was no longer being invited to represent Louth in parliament. The meeting had to be postponed when stones, sticks and other missiles were flung at Kennedy's carriage and when clergymen were threatened by a drunken crowd. One local priest was later knocked to the ground. The event made national news with readers of the *Freeman's Journal* learning that the meeting had been obstructed 'by a mixed mob of county desperadoes, armed with bludgeons and stones, instigated by the Hon. Edward Bellew, and led by Lord Bellew and his brother's menials'. Clearly Kennedy's earlier fears of Louth being embroiled in electoral disturbances were well-founded, albeit his appearance on the doorstep of the local magnate not being calculated to smooth ruffled feathers. He later claimed to have been 'obliged to retire from two towns in consequence of the intimidation exercised by paid bands of men in the adverse interest' during the election of 1852.[63]

Notwithstanding formidable clerical backing, Kennedy took the second seat in Louth only by defeating the conservative candidate, John McClintock, by less than one hundred votes. Top of the poll was Chichester Fortescue, 'a thorough-going whig', who had opposed the contemporary tenant-right campaign.[64] Kennedy's reluctance to split the independent vote by having a second tenant-right activist on the ticket had proven to be strategically correct. He appears to have won at relatively modest expense and his dependence on the support of priests was not held to invalidate the result. Some candidates in other constituencies were unseated when election petitions alleging 'spiritual intimidation' and 'undue clerical influence' were upheld, but an election petition against Kennedy is said to have been withdrawn. One modern electoral historian has highlighted the result in Louth in 1851 as being indicative of the extent to which tenants, 'galvanized by the specifically farmer issue of tenant-right', defied their landlords to a hitherto unprecedented degree.[65]

The result provided Kennedy with a wider audience for his ideas. In October 1852 he addressed a national tenant-league conference, describing the school system which he had established in Monaghan and 'explaining the method which had been

63. *Freeman's Journal*, 7 July 1852; *Hansard*, 3, cxxx, col. 443 (10 Feb. 1854); Beckett, *Mod. Ire.*, p.355.
64. Whyte, *Independent Irish party*, p.171; Walker, *Parliamentary election results in Ireland*, p.84.
65. Gavan Duffy, *League of north and south*, pp.210, 257; Whyte, 'Influence of catholic clergy', passim; Whyte, *Independent Irish party*, pp.63–82; Hoppen, *Elections, politics and society*, p.161.

adopted with a view to its extension'. A year later he spoke in favour of a model for industrial schools which was being advanced by Frederick Lucas, following the latter's visit to Belgium in 1853. Lucas, one of the leaders of the new independent parliamentary grouping, was highly impressed by the Belgian response to famine in that country. Shortly afterwards Kennedy himself, who earlier had obtained samples of lace from Belgium in order to set a standard for the women of Carrickmacross, travelled over to inspect its industrial training institutions. He was following not only Lucas but also his own brother, John Pitt, who twenty years earlier had inspected Belgian agricultural schools. Tristram's visit resulted in a booklet on training which he co-authored with William Sullivan, professor of chemistry at the Museum of Modern Industry in Dublin. Like many fellow lawyers, Tristram also joined the Dublin Statistical Society following its foundation in 1847 for the study and alleviation of social problems. Reflecting what appears to have been a contemporary eagerness among Irish intellectuals to look outwards, the new society was itself represented in Brussels in 1852 at the first International Statistical Congress.[66]

During his years in parliament, Tristram was from time to time to cite particular Belgian institutions as worth emulating. But his short maiden speech at Westminster related to a contemporary religious controversy rather than a question of agricultural or industrial reform. Some members were debating an incident which resulted in the government of the United Kingdom objecting to the persecution of protestants in Tuscany. Kennedy intervened to remark that the Grand Duke of Tuscany 'might have fairly retorted on the British government by pointing out the religious inequalities which unquestionably prevailed in these countries, and the adoption by the Imperial Parliament of such a measure as the Ecclesiastical Titles Bill'.[67] That first reported contribution in the commons was short and sharp. It reflected once again Kennedy's ability to be considerate of the catholic interest, although he explicitly described himself more than once as 'a protestant member'. Certainly, he depended politically upon the support of catholic voters and the organisational backing of catholic priests, but a speeech which he made at Westminster in

66. Gavan Duffy, *League of north and south*, pp.274–79; Edward Lucas, *Life of Frederick Lucas*, ii, 53–4; *DNB*, s.v. Kennedy, John Pitt; Kennedy, *Alliteration*, title page; Kennedy, *The patient, the physician and the fee*, title page shows that Tristram was a member of the Statistical and Social Inquiry Society; McEldowney and O'Higgins, 'Irish legal history and the nineteenth century', pp.204–07.
67. *Hansard*, 3, cxxiv, col. 239 (7 Feb. 1853).

1856 suggests a genuine respect for roman catholics and no mere playing to the gallery. He rose to defend the state grant to Maynooth College in the face of a motion opposing it. He brandished in his hand a list of converts to catholicism, including many titled men and women and others whom he described as 272 'gentry of distinction'. He said that he thought 'a greater degree of charity might be extended to a religion to which so many persons became associated in consequence of the investigation of truth'.[68]

Kennedy's parliamentary career was generally competent but unspectacular. During this first period in the commons his contributions were largely about landlord and tenant matters or about national and industrial education. He told the house that there was 'an ignorant population in Ireland but an industrious one'. However, he never let fall any of the unkinder observations on Irish peasants which he had shared with Lady Bath. He opposed the extension of the British income tax system to Ireland, noting in passing that 'the principle of England was always to divide Ireland when she wished to govern her'. On another occasion he 'objected to English and Scotch members deciding questions which had reference to Irish wants. Was Ireland to be legislated for by Scotch and English ignorance?' But apart from some such mild expressions of nationalist sentiment, he generally contented himself with making his points in a restrained and pithy fashion. He seldom strayed from areas of immediate concern to his constituents, although on one occasion he intervened to urge that the admiralty be provided with iron gun-boats to meet those of the Russians. The gunboats were for the use of Admiral Charles Napier and Kennedy was thereby advancing the interests of a first cousin of his brother's commanding officer.[69]

In January 1854 a banquet was held in Louth to honour Tristram Kennedy. It was preceded by a conference which considered 'the social and physical conditions' of the county and which was presided over by Fr Bannon. Guests at the dinner included Gavan Duffy, Frederick Lucas and John Gray. The former two were among those who made speeches which, according to one account, 'all breathed fervently the spirit of Irish nationalism'. One practical demonstration of that nationalism was Tristram Kennedy's own efforts to get agreement at Westminster on the establishment of separate select committees, 'by whom measures relating to Ireland and Scotland exclusively should be discussed

---

68. ibid., cxxxii, col.133 (30 March 1854); ibid., cxli, col.1076 (15 April 1856); ibid., clxxix, col.73 (17 May 1865).
69. ibid., cxxxiv, cols.1001–02 (30 June 1854); ibid., cxliii, col.533 (9 July 1856); ibid., cxxxiii, col.38 (9 May 1854); *DNB*, s.v. Napier, Charles.

and reported upon, before legislation had thereon in this house'. But despite his tabling a motion to that effect in the commons, and making clear through letters to the paper and by means of a pamphlet that his proposal was 'without regard to political interests of any kind or degree whatsoever', the initiative came to nothing.[70]

Even as he thus confirmed his reputation as a 'tried and well-approved representative', the political ground was slipping from under Kennedy's feet. While he himself would be accounted in the long run to have held firm to the principles of the Independent Party, as his parliamentary grouping soon became known, others were not so patient. The Independent Party lost its coherence within just three years of its electoral successes of 1852. Riven by recrimination, its numbers gradually dwindled away, and by 1856 the loyal rump was opposed by 'the government, the aristocracy, and the established church, and a decided majority of the catholic bishops; the middle class, if not hostile, were indifferent, and the peasantry were weary of a contest which had yielded such trifling results'. The northern section of the movement was particularly weak, having fared badly in the general election of 1852, and in 1856 not one presbyterian minister remained in the council of the league. By 1856 it had also lost its two principal leaders. Lucas was dead, having exhausted himself not least in a dispute with Archbishop Cullen, who wished to restrain the freedom of priests to participate in political causes as they so wished. Gavan Duffy had become disillusioned by events and emigrated to Australia. He stopped in London on the way to meet Tristram Kennedy. The two men are said to have gone together to visit Rotten Row.[71]

When the next general election came, in 1857, Kennedy stood again as an independent candidate in Louth, but the contest went against him. The whigs were particularly annoyed by the fact that the independents had challenged Fortescue in 1854 at a by-election which was brought about by Fortescue having to seek re-election upon his appointment as a commissioner of the treasury. Fortescue had survived only 'after a very hard fought contest in which the catholic clergy were deeply divided on the merits of the candidates'. Furthermore, the Bellew family had seen in the weakening of the independent movement an opportunity to reassert itself and sought to regain the support of disenchanted whigs. Richard Montesquieu Bellew's entry into the race in 1857 thus split the traditional whig-protestant, catholic-nationalist

70. *Anglo-Celt*, 12 Jan. 1854; *Londonderry Sentinel*, 8 Jan. 1857.
71. Whyte, *Independent Irish party*; *Anglo-Celt*, 12 Jan. 1854; Gavan Duffy, *League of north and south*, pp.322-23, 371; Gavan Duffy, *My life in two hemispheres*, ii, 119.

alliance, and ensured the return with Chichester Fortescue of the tory, John McClintock, who five years earlier had been pushed by Kennedy into third place. This time Tristram polled fewer than half the votes which were cast for his next nearest rival, Bellew. Yet Bellew and Kennedy together had more votes than the tory McClintock, this total underlining the fatal effect of splitting the vote.[72]

Kennedy was both angry and regretful. When some of his supporters, 'a deputation representing catholics and liberals of Louth', made him a presentation of plate in gratitude for his satisfactory services in parliament during the previous five years, Kennedy took the opportunity to criticise the successful candidates: 'Mr Fortescue and Mr McClintock represent each a certain social circle and cluster of estates rather than the people of Louth'. He observed that the fact that 'I had to exercise the serious trust of a seat in parliament at a time when popular rights were basely bartered for personal ends, and solemn public pledges shamefully broken, was a misfortune for me and for you'. He appeared personally wounded by his rejection, remarking that 'my great opponents in the county only assail me, I believe, as honest but impracticable'. He admitted that he was looked upon by some 'as a sadly speculative visionary today' and was disappointed that the church had not rallied to the independent cause in 1857 as it had five years earlier: 'When the priests and the people of Louth are united they are all powerful. Divide them and the landlords ride roughshod over you'. His supporters were even less restrained about local political machinations, claiming that he had been 'defeated by corruption, intimidation and the backsliding of some powerful friends', and castigating the 'base ingratitude and selfishness which was displayed by a section of the Popular Party at the election'.[73]

Tristram Kennedy, at the age of fifty-two, was hurt but not broken by this electoral set-back. Two years later, at the next general election, he left Louth to Fortescue and Bellew and journeyed to King's County (now Co. Offaly) to try his chances. There he was one of two partners in an independent liberal raid on two seats which had been thought to be secure by sitting whig occupants. The incumbents, however, were regarded by some influential constituents as having failed to display sufficient political independence and as being weak on the question of tenant-right. Most local catholics were said at the time to be disgusted with the whig party and in the ensuing contest one of the newcomers, John Pope Hennessy, topped the poll. However, Tristram Kennedy

72. Larkin, *Consolidation of the catholic church*, p.318; Walker, *Parliamentary election results*, pp.87, 91.
73. *Newry Examiner*, 15 Aug. 1857.

came last. A local newspaper suggested that he had only himself to blame for failing to capture the second seat and pointed out that Kennedy was

> not as prompt in addressing the constituency as was Mr Hennessy, for what reason we do not know, but the absence of any public avowal of his candidature for some days proved most injurious to his interests, and was strongly used by his antagonists to prejudice his chances.[74]

Given his defeat in 1857 as an independent oppositionist and in 1859 as an independent liberal, Kennedy may have felt at this point that his political career was over. Yet, he was to return to parliament in changed circumstances just six years later.

Meanwhile, in his fifty-seventh year, Tristram married Sarah Graham of Cossington, Somerset. The ceremony took place in London on 4 September 1862, and the people of Carrickmacross presented his bride with a lace shawl for her wedding day. If Tristram's many public activities had kept him long from a marriage bed, he found time with Sarah during the eighteen years following their wedding to father no fewer than seven children. The family lived mainly in England, between Somerset and the capital, their London home serving as an agency for the Carrickmacross lace industry.[75]

An opportunity for Kennedy to re-enter parliament arose in 1865 when Bellew resigned his Louth seat to accept a poor law commissionership. Influential constituents in Louth were eager to find a candidate who, in replacing Bellew, could be relied upon to represent the three major contemporary political objectives of Irish catholics; namely disestablishment of the Church of Ireland, tenant-right and educational reform acceptable to roman catholics. In order to further these catholic aims, Archbishop Cullen had lent his support to the creation of a new organisation, which provided a constitutional alternative to the growing Fenian conspiracy. Although styling itself the 'National Association', this grouping became closely associated in the public mind with Cullen himself and failed to prosper. But it had an impact on the election results

74. *King's County Chronicle*, 11 and 18 May 1859; Walker, *Parliamentary election results*, p.96.
75. Kennedy, *Family of Kennedy*, pp.68–70. In 1961 Tristram's daughter presented the veil or shawl to the National Museum, Dublin. It is described by the museum as 'a marvellous piece of Carrickmacross appliqué work' (Mairead Dunleavy to the author, 31 Dec. 1990); Livingstone, *Monaghan*, p.527; Kennedy was responsible for an order from Queen Victoria for the lace which was described as 'beau travail' at the Paris Exhibition in 1855 (Boyle, *The Irish flowerers*, pp.41–42).

of 1865, and was to provide a vehicle through which catholics could explore fresh forms of independent opposition which allowed the possibility of alliances with British politicians. The imminent emergence of the Liberal Party as, in R.V. Comerford's words, 'the first thoroughly popular parliamentary party in British history' provided the circumstances in which such a coalition might be both relevant and effective. In the past, a consensus on Ireland among English politicians and the absence of clear party lines had meant that the Irish had found it difficult to exploit their advantage when holding the balance of power at Westminster, and this had exposed independent opposition to the criticism that it was a sterile strategy. However, the political realignment which became apparent in England from the late 1860s onwards was to lead eventually to the birth of a distinct Irish Party in the house of commons. In the process of evolution towards that point 'Cullen's association' revived the prospect of distinctive national representation.[76]

That the catholic hierarchy in Ireland might agree with the broad objectives of the National Association while not entirely adopting its organisational strategy was reflected in Cullen's failure to prevent Tristram Kennedy from becoming a candidate in the Louth by-election of April 1865. As archbishop of Armagh, in 1852 Cullen had not stood in Kennedy's way when the latter was promoted for parliament by Bannon and other priests. But now, in 1865, he wrote to his successor at Armagh, the 'gentle' Joseph Dixon, to suggest that a better choice for the coming election would be Sir John Gray, protestant proprietor and editor of the *Freeman's Journal*. Dixon demurred, apparently letting himself be guided by the opinions of Dean Michael Kieran of Dundalk, who himself would shortly succeed Dixon as primate. E.R. Norman suggests that Kieran may have been planning an alternative strategy to that proposed by the National Association. He claims that Chichester Fortescue, the longstanding liberal representative for Louth, who would subsequently become chief secretary for Ireland under Gladstone, was party to just such a plan for a reconciliation of the Irish catholics with the English Liberal Party. In any event, Kieran convened a meeting of 'the clergy and liberal electors', where it emerged that a number of possible candidates had been approached but that the prospect of fighting Louth was too daunting for some. The meeting was told of Sir John Robinson's response: 'he would rather be at the head of an army (cheers and laughter)'. So it was down to Tristram Kennedy again, who appears

---

76. Walker, *Parliamentary election results*, p.101; Larkin, *Consolidation of the catholic church*, pp.290–308; *NHI*, v, 439.

to have been the only one of those considered suitable who was prepared to let his name go forward. The 'large and influential' attendance learnt that Kennedy 'felt somewhat sore relative to his defeat in this county; but in his principles he is still the same man', and that he was prepared to stand provided his expenses were met by the constituency. Whether he was party to any overall strategy possibly being concocted by Kieran and Fortescue is unknown, although his career indicates that he shared the objective of reconciling catholics and liberals. He was selected by the meeting as their candidate, Dixon informing Cullen that Gray would not be the best man in the circumstances. Shortly afterwards both Kieran and Dixon publicly endorsed Kennedy and the electors were exhorted as follows: 'Men of Louth, rally round Kennedy, your old and tried friend. Join your clergy in asserting the independence of your noble county'. At the time it appears to have been quite usual for clergy throughout the country to take such a prominent role at constituency level in the selection of candidates.[77]

Kennedy's candidature was welcomed on both sides of the Irish Sea, but for different reasons. Locally, people recalled his record on behalf of tenants. The *Dundalk Democrat* enthusiastically described the candidate's 'triumphant progress' through the constituency: 'men ran from the fields to the road and prayed God to bless Mr Kennedy, the people's candidate'. There was satisfaction in London too. *The Times* reported that 'the Roman Catholic leaders adroitly put aside the nominee of the National Association [Gray], while professing great deference for its authority'. But the paper noted that landlords were 'strenuously' pitted against clergy and that the outcome was still doubtful. Kennedy's selection was, 'at all events, an interesting fact as allowing that sectarian considerations are not likely to predominate'.[78]

In reality, Kennedy's nomination became an opportunity for catholics to exhibit their growing social and political confidence. When he went to the courthouse to hand in his nomination papers, the protestant candidate was flanked by Dean Kieran and followed by some fifty catholic priests. Also present was a twenty-eight year old catholic lawyer, Philip Callan, who represented the 'new and aggressive political factor' and who acted as Kennedy's barrister during the brief campaign. An electioneering photograph of

77. Larkin, *Consolidation of the catholic church*, pp.316–17; Norman, *The catholic church and Ireland in the age of rebellion 1859–73*, p.171; *Dundalk Democrat*, 3 and 10 July 1852, 1 and 8 April 1865; Thornley, *Isaac Butt and Home Rule*, p.29.
78. *Dundalk Democrat*, 8 April 1865; *The Times*, 8 April 1865.

Kennedy on the hustings at this time shows the candidate as a determined Victorian gentleman, firmly seated. On his left thigh is propped a book, the title of which, 'THE PEOPLE!', is clearly displayed on the binding. His right knee touches a copy of his address 'to the independent electors of Louth'. That election itself took place on a hot spring day and Kennedy won by less than ninety votes, a margin of just four per cent of those cast. A list was to be published shortly afterwards, showing precisely how each landlord and tenant voted in Louth in 1865. This list serves today as a striking reminder that the absence of secret balloting really did mean that everyone in the constituency knew where their neighbours stood politically, that tenants were thus caught between loyalty to their church and fear of offending their landlord, and that it was advisable, if not essential, for any candidate to enjoy the endorsement of one powerful group or the other. Kennedy was undoubtedly the catholic church's man and this clinched the contest for him. His supporters celebrated their victory, with 'immense crowds of young people' marching through the principal streets of Drogheda to the music of a temperance band.[79]

In London also there were those who were delighted at his win, if for reasons more complex than those of the youths of Drogheda. In Britain Kennedy's success was viewed as being of considerable significance to political developments there. In a report the tone of which tends to support Norman's suggestion of a political strategy being hatched in the Armagh diocese, as an alternative to that being supported by Cullen in Dublin, *The Times* wrote that 'the Louth election is a more satisfactory triumph for the Liberal Party than anything of the kind we have had in Ireland lately'. The writer accepted that Kennedy's return was due in great measure to the exertions of priests but noted that they had 'not, in this case, been moved by the bishops through the National Association'. Dixon's role was praised by *The Times* as being worthy of emulation by other bishops, the writer continuing that

we see from this example how cordially they would work with liberal protestantism, if Ultramontanism in high places, acting under foreign dictation, did not coerce them into a position of sectarian exclusiveness and political antagonism to the rest of the community.[80]

79. *Dundalk Democrat*, 15 April 1865; *The Times*, 15 and 17 April 1865; Kennedy, *Family of Kennedy*, pp.66–67; Larkin, *Consolidation of the catholic church*, p. 319; *An analysis of the parliamentary register of voters for the county of Louth with the names of the landlords and their tenants on the register of voters, shewing the candidate for whom they voted at the election in April 1865* (Dublin, 1865).
80. *The Times*, 17 April 1865.

The Fenians too were pleased, believing that Cullen, their opponent, had received a set-back in Louth. *The Irish People*, an organ closely associated with that movement, rejoiced that the 'unlucky' National Association had tried its hand in Louth, and 'another signal failure was the result. Mr Tristram Kennedy is not a member of the body'. The writer was satisfied that 'Dr Cullen was completely ignored in Louth'.[81]

With Kennedy's victory in the by-election of April 1865, his re-selection to contest the general election the following July came as no surprise. He and Fortescue were chosen as the liberal candidates for the two Louth seats. In a desperate response the tories placed an advertisement in the local paper in order to publicise a denial by catholic tenants that their landlord, the tory candidate, John McClintock, was a 'bigot'. If this was an attempt to sway catholic voters it failed miserably and both liberals were returned. It was also at this general election, down in Tipperary, that John Blake Dillon became a member of parliament for the first time. Dillon had been one of the Young Irelanders but had afterwards been converted to constitutional politics and had co-operated with Cullen and others in the establishment of the National Association.[82]

Kennedy now joined with Dillon to build a bridge between Irish catholics and independent liberals on the one hand and the English liberals on the other. If his disposition in this respect is not conclusively proven to have been the cause of his selection for Louth in 1865, it quickly became its consequence. It was soon clear that the National Association was not on its own a satisfactory parliamentary vehicle for Irish ambitions. Only about one in eight of the Irish representatives returned in 1865 had been elected on the whole programme of the association. But there were others with whom these might find common ground in alliance with a liberal government. If it was still too soon for the evolution of an Irish parliamentary party such as Parnell would later bequeath to the leadership of Dillon's son, there was no reason why the possibility of political cooperation might not at least be explored after 1865. Thus, Dillon and Kennedy came together in December 1865 as joint–secretaries of a special conference which was attended by twenty-two members of parliament who had been elected as catholics or liberals. In the event, this 'failed to articulate a programme for an Irish parliamentary party, not showing

81. *Irish People*, 29 April 1865.
82. *Dundalk Democrat*, 22 July 1865; Walker, *Parliamentary election results*, p.103; O'Cathaoir, *John Blake Dillon*, pp.150–66.

itself sufficiently prepared to vote against the government or to be separate from the whigs'.[83]

Nevertheless, the cooperation between the two men continued. In February 1866 they acted as joint-secretaries 'on behalf of a considerable number of the Irish representatives' at Westminster, in jointly arranging a 'personal interview' with Gladstone in order to explain their views on a bill for the amendment of the law relating to the tenure and improvement of land in Ireland. Gladstone at the time was Sir Robert Peel's chancellor of the exchequer.[84] Furthermore, while Kennedy's parliamentary colleague for Louth, Chichester Fortescue, was most prominently identified with the English liberal interest in Ireland, Kennedy himself was said to have acted informally on at least one occasion as an Irish political agent for the government. Indeed, Kennedy's election in 1865 had been specifically represented by *The Times* as 'a step to the formation of a new Liberal Party'. That new party became a reality following the election of Gladstone as liberal leader in 1867. But Dillon and Kennedy got no chance to forge with him a new Irish alliance or policy. For Dillon had contracted cholera and died a shockingly unexpected death 'at the height of his powers' in 1866 and Kennedy himself promptly departed the parliamentary stage shortly afterwards. Speculation about what might have been achieved had both been returned to Westminster in 1868 is beyond the scope of this study.[85]

Whatever about Kennedy's strengths as a reconciler and as a pragmatist, his contributions to parliamentary debates in the commons between 1865 and 1868 were no more sparkling than those between 1852 and 1857. He was solid if unexciting as an orator and even his supporters had to admit that he experienced some difficulty in catching the eye of the speaker so that he might be called upon to contribute. As in 1852, his first intervention in 1865 concerned a religious matter. But this time he was more pointed, addressing the question of disestablishment. It was an issue which Gladstone would shortly manipulate to win power as the head of a liberal government. Kennedy admitted that 'as a protestant he was ashamed to see the church to which he belonged maintained at the sacrifice of those good feelings and

---

83. Larkin, *Consolidation of the catholic church*, pp.364–70; O'Cathaoir, *John Blake Dillon*, pp.164–65.

84. Kennedy to Gladstone, 22 Feb. 1866 (BL Add. MS); Matthew, *The Gladstone diaries*, vi, p.421 (26 Feb. 1866) reads 'saw depn of Irish members on tenant right'; O'Cathaoir, *John Blake Dillon*, pp.167–72.

85. *Dundalk Democrat*, 27 June 1868; *The Times*, 17 April 1865; O'Cathaoir, *John Blake Dillon*, p.173.

kindly relations which ought to exist between inhabitants of the same country'. That Kennedy was a member of the Church of Ireland is clear from this intervention as well as from details of his birth, marriage and death. Yet his radicalism, particularly on tenant-right, misled some admirers into believing that he was a presbyterian. Indeed, in July 1867, he defended the continuation of the annual state grant to the presbyterian church as being acceptable for so long as the Church of England remained established. But this was of no more particular significance than his mischievous proclamation on the hustings in 1857 that 'I would be ashamed to come into the county, if I were not a better catholic than Richard Montesquieu Bellew'.[86]

On the need for a secret ballot at parliamentary elections, Kennedy pointed out to the house of commons that the voter in Ireland 'was a serf' and needed protection from reprisals for voting as he wished. According to Kennedy, the Irish elector was 'liable to be turned out at six month's notice after voting for the man of his choice, and liable to be distrained, as often happened, within a few weeks after he had recorded his vote'. On the insurrection in the Ionian islands, where not only his brother but also Gladstone himself had worked for the crown for a period, Tristram had a question for the foreign secretary.[87] But it was on the matter of tenant-right that once again he most regularly exercised himself. Even as his successor as land agent in Monaghan appeared before a committee of the house of lords in order to argue the opposite, Kennedy was continuing to urge the commons to extend the Ulster custom to the whole island: 'If a calculation were made of the improvements effected by the tenants since the confiscation of the land in Ireland, it would, he believed, be found that more than the value of the fee-simple had been paid for by the tenants'. His views were sometimes hotly rejected, as when he suggested that 'responsibility for the present state of Ireland devolved, from first to last, upon England (Question!)'. Later, to cries of 'No! No!' from across the house, he claimed that the constabulary was kept up by the state 'for sustaining class interests and landlord-made laws'. His very last act as a member of parliament was to plead with the prime minister in July 1868 for time to consider the

86. *Dundalk Democrat*, 27 June 1868; *Hansard*, 3, clxxix, col. 473 (17 May 1865); ibid., clxxxviii, col.1675 (18 July 1867); *Dundalk Democrat*, 27 June 1868; Kennedy, *Family of Kennedy*, pp.50–52, 68. Kennedy is buried at Cossington village Church of England church, Somerset. *The Times*, 17 April 1865, cites a report in *The Northern Whig* describing him as a presbyterian!
87. *Hansard*, 3, cxci, col.705 (2 April 1868); Steele, 'Gladstone and Ireland', pp.79–82.

Ejectments Suspension (Ireland) Bill. This proposed legislation had been introduced by Kennedy himself to limit the landlord's powers of ejectment but Disraeli rejected his request.[88]

Insofar as Kennedy spoke to the questions of disestablishment and tenant-right, albeit briefly during this period in parliament, he was true to two of the chief objectives of the National Association. But he was silent on education, a subject which he had not hesitated to address previously and upon which between 1865 and 1868 both the National Association and most of the bishops felt particularly strongly. It is unlikely that the views of Kennedy and the bishops coincided on the subject and his continuing enthusiasm for the national education system may have been one of the reasons why Cullen had suggested a different candidate for Louth in 1865. Cullen and most of the other bishops wished to see a system of denominational education introduced, having long dismissed efforts to establish non-denominational national schools and university colleges as being unacceptable. But where Kennedy believed that 'the root of all the evils in Ireland to be centred in the land question, and in the state of the Irish Church, which was an insult to the whole of the Roman Catholic population', there is no evidence that he shared fundamentally the bishops' position on education.[89]

Kennedy's restraint on the question helped to secure the Louth seat in 1865 but probably lost him the candidature in 1868. His vague electoral commitment to 'the furtherance of popular education, on terms of equality to all denominations' and his ambivalent promise to the 'independent electors of Louth' that his views on the subject were 'in harmony with those entertained by yourselves' were indeed enough to satisfy many of his constituents and have even led Emmet Larkin 'to include Kennedy in a list of those returned on the whole programme of the association'. But, as Larkin himself points out, when the National Association sought 'freedom and equality of education for the several denominations and classes in Ireland', their demand was actually for the setting up of a system of denominational education for catholics, and there is no evidence that Kennedy ever furthered that specific objective by word or deed. Between 1865 and 1868 the demand for a charter for a catholic university became the principal bone of contention between Irish bishops and English ministers, until Gladstone succeeded in diverting popular and clerical attention

---

88. *Hansard*, 3, clxxxvi, cols.1771–72 (29 April 1867); ibid., clxxxviii, col.584 (27 June 1867); ibid., cxciii, col.519 (2 July 1868); *Dundalk Democrat*, 6 and 13 June 1868 for the text of his bill; *Report from the select committee of the house of lords on the Tenure (Ireland) Bill . . . 1867*, 457.
89. *Hansard*, 3, clxxxv, col.748 (21 Feb.1867).

to disestablishment. But the former demand was not furthered by Kennedy in any of his reported speeches.[90]

Both *The Times* and *The Irish People* had spotted early on that Kennedy's interpretation of 'freedom and equality of education' might differ from that of the bishops. It could be argued that 'mixed' national schools and colleges fitted the formula of words to which he subscribed just as well as any system of denominational but equal institutions. Kennedy was unlikely to betray the memory and aspirations of the late Thomas Wyse, architect of non-denominational education in mid-nineteenth-century Ireland. As indicated elsewhere in this book, Wyse had been a good friend to Kennedy in the campaign to reform legal training and had backed the Dublin Law Institute. He was also closely associated with the national school system for which both John Pitt and Tristram had shown such enthusiasm over the years. It was Wyse's commitment to the 'godless' Queen's Colleges which had cost him his Waterford seat at the general election of 1847, following which contest he despaired of Irish politics and went to work in the diplomatic service as British minister at Athens.[91] Immediately upon Kennedy's victory in April 1865, *The Times* noted that Kennedy was 'attached to the national system of education, which the pope and the prelates have repeatedly condemned'. He reportedly expressed these views through Vere Foster, who proposed him. Foster himself had helped to fund the construction of many national schools. *The Irish People* reported that Foster had declared that the national schools were a blessing to Ireland and concluded, 'we may infer from this that Mr Kennedy does not go in for the three points' of the National Association.[92]

Given such circumstances and given his silence on educational matters, it is hardly surprising to learn that a challenger to Kennedy emerged in the months prior to the election of November 1868. By early June the attacks on Kennedy had begun. *The Ulster Examiner* denigrated his political performance and questioned where he stood on education. The writer doubted that Kennedy really supported a charter for the Catholic University. *The Dundalk Democrat*, ever enthusiastic for Kennedy, responded by claiming that their man was, in fact, a supporter of denominational education. But Kennedy himself appears to have kept silent. *The Dundalk*

90. Larkin, *Consolidation of the catholic church*, pp.300, 307, 348; *Dundalk Democrat*, 31 March and 15 July 1865.
91. *The Times*, 17 April, 1865; *Irish People*, 29 April 1865; *DNB*, s.v. Wyse, Thomas; Lyons, *Ireland since the famine*, p.94; Wyse, *Notes on education reform in Ireland*, pp.79, 102.
92. *The Times*, 17 April, 1865; *Irish People*, 29 April 1865.

Democrat noted significantly that Kennedy was now likely to be one of four candidates, with a third liberal entering the race. This was Matthew O'Reilly Dease, a catholic who had failed in 1857 to be returned for Cavan and who now in 1868 spent much money promoting himself under the slogan, 'Louth is entitled to at least one catholic member'. He thus introduced to the county what one correspondent in the local paper described as 'his golden and religious apple of discord'. Dease had a farm at Dunleer, stronghold of the Bellews, but there is no evidence that Kennedy's old opponents enticed him to run or that local catholic authorities encouraged him at an early stage. But Dease is said to have been urged on by the renowned Fr James Healy of Bray, County Wicklow, who reportedly acted as 'the puller of wires' to get the influential archdeacon of Drogheda to back him.[93]

At first, Kennedy's supporters tried to ignore Dease, suggesting that he posed a threat principally to Fortescue, if to either sitting candidate. *The Dundalk Democrat* dismissed as 'quite incorrect' rumours reported to have been circulated by 'some silly persons' that Kennedy might not stand. Readers were assured that 'Mr Denver, Mr Kennedy's conducting agent, has got the retaining fee in his pocket'. The editor regarded his re-selection 'as secure'. But it soon became apparent that Kennedy's religion was being made an issue. And to personal attacks was added attempted bribery when Dease offered Kennedy one thousand pounds to stand elsewhere. Although these efforts might have been ignored by Kennedy, he seems to have baulked at the prospect of an expensive and unpleasant contest. Protestants were continuing to be selected to represent catholics in other constituencies, notwithstanding the national growth of catholic triumphalism. But Kennedy may have suspected that, if forced to choose at the polls, the electors of Louth would revert to traditional religious loyalties. The author of a recent masterful monograph on the land legislation of 1870 has noted how at the heart of even the tenant-right question was a fundamental catholic grievance going back to confiscation. Kennedy himself acknowledged as much in the commons, and he may have decided that his record on behalf of the tenantry might not be enough to decide the contest in his favour, certainly without a sustained campaign. He had neither the money nor the stomach for one, and withdrew instead.[94]

93. *Dundalk Democrat*, 16 Oct. and 7 Nov. 1868, citing *The Ulster Examiner* (undated); *Dod's parliamentary companion, 1871*, s.v. Dease; Anon., *Father Healy of Little Bray*, pp.82–83. The anonymous author incorrectly suggests that Dease only entered the fray when Kennedy had decided upon retiring.

94. *Dundalk Democrat*, 30 May 1868; Thornley, *Isaac Butt*, p.39; Steele, *Irish land and British politics*, pp.19–22.

In a letter written in August, from Somerset, Kennedy let it be known that 'private and personal matters' had finally decided him against continuing in parliament. But he also took the opportunity to attack Dease for making the religion of candidates an issue, asserting that this should not be a test of fitness. To raise it at all was 'a blow to the faithful protestant representatives of catholic constituents', as well as 'an insult to your friends in England'. He urged electors to support Viscount St Lawrence, who had lately declared his interest in one of the liberal seats for Louth. But, as reported in the same issue of the local newspaper in which Kennedy's letter appeared, St Lawrence had already announced that he was withdrawing, having been persuaded that his candidature would be divisive. Dease responded to Kennedy's letter by rounding on him and accusing him of suffering from an 'irritation of disappointed ambition'. Dease claimed that he himself had become a candidate because Kennedy was not ready to defray the expenses of the election. It may well be true that one of the 'private and personal matters' which influenced Kennedy was financial. In 1862, in order to raise two thousand pounds, he had had to mortgage to his brothers some of the houses which, as we will see in chapter 10, he owned in Henrietta Street. This was, presumably, to pay certain bills associated with his wedding and settlement in England that year. In April 1865 he had insisted, before accepting a nomination, on the constituency paying his electoral expenses, their agreeing to do so being described as a 'special honour' by one observer. There had also been some disagreement over the same matter prior to his re-selection three months later but a compromise was agreed. So to come up in 1868 with at least another two thousand, a sum regarded as 'moderate' for electoral expenses, might have proven difficult. However, it would on its own scarcely have been decisive. The 'private and personal matters' may also have included the fact that he was now over sixty years old, was resident in England and had a young family of three surviving children, his second son having died in 1866 at the age of seventeen months. But it could also be the case that, like many politicians before and after him, Kennedy was simply consoling himself by taking refuge in personal matters when forced from public life by political considerations.[95]

Dease succeeded in winning the Louth seat, although he was given a fright by the tories who tried to beat him at his own game

---

95. *Dundalk Democrat*, 1 April 1865, 13 June, 1 and 29 August 1868; *The Times*, 8 April 1865 and 25 Nov. 1885; Registry of deeds, 1862/24/176–77; Hoppen, *Elections*, pp.83–85; Kennedy, *Family of Kennedy*, pp.68–70.

by producing as their candidate a member of the old catholic family of Gormanstown. It took a late intervention by Michael Kieran, who in 1866 had succeeded Dixon as archbishop of Armagh, to secure the seat for the liberals. It is not known if Kieran had earlier favoured the candidature of Dease or Kennedy, having in 1865 been instrumental in picking the latter against Cullen's wishes. But the bishops were determined to see a liberal government under Gladstone, committed as the new leader was to disestablishment, and Kieran explicitly endorsed Dease at the end of the day. Dease was first obliged to pay to the church a large arrear of dues on his land in the diocese.[96]

The election of 1868 proved to be the high-point of liberal fortunes in Ireland. The new government passed the land act of 1870, a milestone in Irish history which went some way towards meeting the recurrent demands of tenant-right advocates such as Tristram Kennedy, but which was also of great symbolical significance politically. Bitterly ironical for Kennedy must have been the fact that his former liberal colleague in Louth was instrumental in the drafting of specific provisions in the act of 1870. A landlord with a negligible personal record of tenant-right activism when compared to Kennedy's efforts of four decades, Chichester Fortescue as chief secretary was popularly regarded as Gladstone's Irish spokesman.[97]

LATE YEARS

Even while going to Monaghan as a land agent and seeking to represent Louth as a legislator, Kennedy had drawn strength from his ancestral city of Londonderry. As demonstrated above, he had received endorsements for his activities from the catholic bishops there. Indeed, his longest reported speech during the parliament of 1865–68 was not on the subject of tenant-right or the religious question but concerned the need to implement the recommendations of a report of 1854 which had advocated repealing the Londonderry charter of 1613 and appointing new trustees to administer the property of the Irish Society in Derry and Coleraine.[98] Now, as Tristram's seventieth birthday approached, he returned to the neighbouring county of Donegal, where he had been born and bred and where he had established his reputation

96. *Dundalk Democrat*, 7 and 14 Nov. 1868; Thornley, *Isaac Butt*, pp.41–22; *NHI*, v, 442–43; Anon., *Father Healy of Little Bray*, p.83.
97. *NHI*, v, 441–43; Thornley, *Isaac Butt*, pp.29, 37.
98. *Hansard*, 3, clxxxiii, cols.598–600 (8 May 1866).

as a fair landlord. He was approached by the tenant-right association of Castlefin and asked to stand on the liberal ticket at the general election of 1874. He accepted readily. Clearly, two decades in and out of the commons had given him a taste for Westminster. Evory Kennedy joined his brother in the contest, having earlier been selected but then stood down as the liberal candidate for Londonderry. Remarkably, the couple of septuagenarians were to come close to being returned for the two seats representing their county of birth.[99]

Evory had been continuing to play a prominent role in his profession, becoming president of the Royal College of Physicians of Ireland. His contributions to medical literature have been described as 'valuable', sometimes generating prolonged professional debate. He grew prosperous, acquiring Belgard Castle near Dublin. It was there that he had entertained Thomas Carlyle, apparently at the behest of Tristram who was then deeply involved in his work on the Bath estate in Monaghan. Carlyle repaid his host's hospitality in the characteristic style of his Irish reminiscences, by a patronising account of the evening and an unflattering description of Evory's wife and of the two older Kennedy sisters who were also present: 'pale, elderly, earnest-eyed lean couple of sisters, insipid-beautiful little wife'.[100]

But it was a big step from entertaining visitors whom his brother found interesting to sharing a platform with Tristram on the hustings. Nevertheless, the two men almost carried the day, coming within a total of 193 votes of both being returned. This was the first general election to be held since the introduction of secret balloting in 1872. However, 'contrary to general expectation', reported one Derry paper, 'the majority of the voters polled in favour of the former representatives', who were tories. According to Hurst, the secret ballot generally did not measure up to expectations in the degree to which it changed electoral preferences and patterns. Although the question of Home Rule dominated the 1874 election nationally, it does not appear to have been a major concern in Donegal. The Kennedys ran as 'liberal and tenant-right candidates', dedicated to amending land laws and abolishing income tax, and the proclamation by one of their opponents that he opposed Home Rule appears to have been a unique reference to the matter.[101]

99. *Londonderry Standard*, 28 Jan. 1874; Delany, *Christopher Palles*, p.66.
100. Cameron, *Royal College of Surgeons*, pp.758–59; Pinkerton, 'Evory Kennedy', 77–81; Carlyle, *Reminiscences of my Irish journey*, pp.42–3, 51, 60–61.
101. *Londonderry Standard*, 28 and 31 Jan., 4 and 14 Feb. 1874; Walker, *Parliamentary election results*, pp.110, 116; Hurst, 'Ireland and the Ballot Act of 1872', pp.326–52.

Meanwhile, in Tristram's former constituency of Louth, not only Dease but also Fortescue were being seen off by the Home Rule candidates, A.M. Sullivan and Philip Callan, the latter electoral barrister to both Fortescue and Kennedy in 1865. With the return of some sixty Home Rulers, the general election of 1874 effectively marked the destruction of the Liberal Party in Ireland. One unsuccessful Home Rule candidate was Charles Stewart Parnell, standing for the first time and one year later elected a member for Meath at a by-election. Where Tristram Kennedy's parliamentary career had now ended, Parnell's was just beginning. The latter thought that the independent opposition movement of the 1850s, of which Tristram had been such a stalwart, 'would be an ideal movement for the benefit of Ireland'.[102]

In retirement from politics, Kennedy turned his attention once more to issues which had long interested him. One was the assimilation of Irish with English law, the other the shortcomings of King's Inns. In both respects he shared to some extent the preoccupations of another liberal barrister, Bartholomew Duhigg, who seventy years earlier had published his opinions on these subjects. But where Duhigg allowed his whig emotions to undermine the accuracy of his various publications, including his book on the King's Inns, Kennedy was more restrained. His membership of the Dublin Social Inquiry and Statistical Society indicated a respect on his part for scientific methodology. Indeed, the long-standing secretary of that society himself published a short but useful history of King's Inns.[103]

In his pamphlet of 1878, Kennedy specifically examined how the benchers had earned and spent their income during the nineteenth century. He concluded that resources had been wasted which might have been better spent providing systematic legal education in Ireland. His own experiences with the Dublin Law Institute, which are considered in detail in later chapters, still rankled almost forty years after the benchers had thwarted his efforts. Yet, any residual bitterness which he may have felt did not prevent him from donating to the King's Inns judicial portraits of his uncle, Alexander Crookshank, who had been a judge of the common pleas from 1783 to 1800, and Joseph Napier, formerly a

---

102. Hanham, *Elections and party management: politics in the time of Disraeli and Gladstone*, p.185; Thornley, *Isaac Butt*, pp.180–81; *Special Comm. 1888 proc.*, ii, 694, cited at Foster, *Charles Stewart Parnell*, p.133. At elections a 'revising barrister' was appointed to revise the lists of persons qualified to vote for members of parliament (*O.E.D.*).
103. Kenny, 'Counsellor Duhigg, antiquarian and activist', 300–25; Littledale, *The society of King's Inns*.

leading lecturer at the Dublin Law Institute and chancellor of Ireland in 1858. These hang today in a vestibule of the library.[104] The other subject about which Tristram went into print in the 1870s was the codification of laws. Not only Duhigg and Kennedy but also many other Irish lawyers of the nineteenth century were convinced of the merit of codification – indeed codification is said to have been 'one of the major contributions made by the Irish diaspora in the United States and in Australia'. There were difficulties in establishing exactly where Irish law differed from that of the rest of the United Kingdom, a situation particularly anomalous in the aftermath of the act of union, and the fact that codification held out the prospect of clarification no doubt contributed greatly to its attractiveness. Kennedy himself was very conscious of the difficulties involved, having entertained the commons in 1855 by remarking that 'it seemed, however, to be a feature in all legislation for Ireland to assimilate the law of Ireland with that of England, where the circumstances were totally different, and to dissimilate it where the circumstances were exactly the same'. But he did not entirely confine his pamphlet of 1877 to the subject of codification. Even here he called for the reform of legal education.[105]

In 1877, a portrait of Tristram Kennedy by Henry MacManus was exhibited in the Royal Irish Academy (see frontispiece). A notice of it in the *Freeman's Journal* remarked that Kennedy was 'a handsomer man' than suggested by the artist. But the same critic confessed that the portrait 'boasts in especial an eye as like a real eye as ever a man painted'. Seen today, the painting suggests to this author a bull-like personality, attenuated by scepticism and even sadness. Tristram had struggled long and hard for justice and had witnessed much failure and misery, including between 1866 and 1874 the early deaths of three of his children.[106] His own death came in his eightieth year. On 20 November 1885, 'at his residence in Weston-Super-Mare, the earthly career of honest Tristram Kennedy came to a close'. The epithet 'honest', which had attached itself to Tristram when he represented Louth in parliament, now, in effect, became his epitaph.[107]

104. Tristram Kennedy, *The state and the benchers*, passim.
105. *Hansard, 3*, cxxxvii, col. 1544 (18 April 1855); ibid., cxliv, col. 1299 (25 Feb. 1857); Kennedy, *The patient, the physician and the fee*; McEldowney and O'Higgins, 'Irish legal history', p.218.
106. *Freeman's Journal*, 21 Feb. 1877; Kennedy, *Family of Kennedy*, p.70. The portrait today hangs in Taunton, Somerset – note 108 below.
107. *Londonderry Sentinel*, 3 July 1879; *Anglo-Celt*, 12 Jan. 1854; *Freeman's Journal*, 21 Feb. 1877; *The Times*, 25 Nov. 1885; *Dundalk Democrat*, 28 Nov. 1885.

Tristram was remembered fondly not only in Ireland but also in the south of France, where Charles Gavan Duffy was living in retirement. When word reached Gavan Duffy that his old parliamentary colleague was gone he penned a warm tribute to console the bereaved family, the youngest of whom was Caroline, aged just five and Tristram's only surviving daughter. Gavan Duffy addressed the letter to her second eldest brother:

My dear Pitt,

Your father died a death worthy of his life – which was placid and serene – in the bosom of his family and with every duty performed. I who must soon follow him feel how blessed he was in such an end, and that a man can desire nothing more, who has lived his life, than that he may be relieved from his post so tenderly.

It is scarcely a week since there was a paragraph in the newspapers announcing that I was at death's door – which was not so, but so many of the friends I esteemed are gone, that I am duly warned my time is coming. I would be well content to die as honest and gallant Tristram Kennedy died.

Pray say to your mother how sincerely I sympathise with her in the loss which can never be repaired. She bears the name of an honourable and upright man, and it will be her consolation to watch over the children in which he survives.

I hope to be in England next Summer – if life and health remain to me – and it would be a great pleasure to me to see you and if it be practicable I will visit Weston if you are still there.[108]

Tristram Kennedy was laid to rest in Cossington village in Somerset and was survived by his widow until 1916. His brother John Pitt had died six years before him. Less than six months after Tristram passed away, Evory died 'of gout', on Good Friday 1886.[109] Tristram had first come to public notice in Derry in

---

108. Kennedy, *Family of Kennedy*, pp.68–70; Gavan Duffy to Pitt Kennedy, 28 November 1885 (Stack family MSS). As stated earlier, Caroline's eldest son has been of considerable assistance to the author in the preparation of this book. Living in Taunton, Somerset, Mr T. Lindsay Stack has provided information on the Kennedy family, press cuttings, photographs of portraits of Tristram and his wife and letters. He believes that a box of papers belonging to Tristram Kennedy may be lost. Material relating to the Dublin Law Institute was deposited by Mr Stack's uncle in the King's Inns and the National Library in the 1930s, upon completion of the latter's *Family of Kennedy*.
109. Kennedy, *Family of Kennedy*, p.68; Letter from T.L. Stack to the author, 16 Dec. 1990; *DNB*, s.v. Kennedy, John Pitt; *Brit Med Jn*, i (1886), 911; Cameron, *Royal College of Surgeons*, p.759.

1828, just one year before the winning of catholic emancipation. He finally exited the political stage in 1874, just as Charles Stewart Parnell was walking on. In the week following Tristram's death in 1885, Parnell himself was electioneering in Louth, repudiating the candidacy of Philip Callan whom Parnell had come to regard as unreliable and self-serving. A local newspaper at the time commented favourably on Tristram's contribution to Irish political life and Parnell himself may have been struck by some of the similarities between his own biography and that of the former representative for the county which he was visiting. Both were members of the Church of Ireland; both born into the middle of large families; both having an older brother John, whose experience of managing bad farmland in Ulster influenced their thinking on reform; both had been high sheriff of their home county; both stood for election in a Leinster county to which they were strangers; both landlords advocating tenant-right; both bachelors until late in life; both backed actively by catholic clergy. Both were finally undone politically by that 'golden and religious apple of discord' to which one of Tristram's constituents had ascribed his parliamentary fall. However, it is certainly not claimed that Kennedy enjoys an historical importance equal to that of Parnell. What may be said is that, over and beyond any fortuitous personal similarities, the Irish Parliamentary Party which Parnell led was the inheritor of that independent opposition to which Kennedy was so deeply committed and for which Parnell had a high regard.[110]

Kennedy flourished during a period of difficulty which saw the repeal movement flounder, which witnessed the efforts of Irish members to unite in common cause at Westminster confounded and which was, above all, marked by the holocaust of the great famine and the misery of many Irish tenants. Throughout, his response was positive and determined, transcending traditional religious boundaries and justifying his own description of himself as having been 'always faithful and true to the poor people'.[111]

Tristram Kennedy's achievements were modest but they were also pragmatic and significant, as we shall begin to understand in more detail as we turn to survey his important contribution to the revival of Irish legal education.

---

110. *The Times*, 30 Nov. 1885; Foster, *Parnell*, passim; *Dundalk Democrat*, 19 Sept. 1868, 28 Nov. and 5 Dec. 1885; *Freeman's Journal*, 30 Nov. 1885.
111. *Newry Examiner*, 15 August 1857; Gavan Duffy, *League of north and south*, pp. 210, 371.

CHAPTER THREE

'Gowned common people': patronage, professionalisation and the birth of the Dublin Law Institute

THE ESTABLISHMENT OF the Dublin Law Institute was a significant event in the development of the legal profession in the United Kingdom. It signalled on the part of many lawyers not only a desire for decentralisation from London but also a consciousness that the bar's standards of training and practice stood in need of improvement. Although the institute itself did not survive for long, its supporters were to have an important influence on the future of legal education in both Britain and Ireland.[1]

The second quarter of the nineteenth century was marked by a surge in professionalism throughout the United Kingdom.[2] Irish barristers were infected by the mood of the times, being conscious of their own standing in relation both to their colleagues in England and to their brethren, the attorneys and solicitors of Ireland. In London the English profession witnessed the birth of competent courses in legal education at a number of new colleges. In Dublin attorneys were straining at the bit of King's Inns, an institution unlike the London inns of court in that attorneys and solicitors were obliged to join it. Since its foundation three centuries earlier, King's Inns had provided no legal education. Neither branch of the profession could avail of formal training in Ireland, a deficiency which the attorneys attempted to remedy in the 1830s. For their part, those wishing to practise at the Irish bar were bound by law to spend time at the English inns. Doing so was thought generally by the Irish to be a waste of both

---

1. Below, chapter 6. Neither Holdsworth, *History of English law*, passim, nor Manchester, *Modern legal history of England and Wales 1750–1950* nor Manchester, *Sources of English legal history: law, history and society in England and Wales 1750–1950* indicates the major role played by Irishmen in this context.
2. Duman, 'Pathway to professionalism: The English bar in the eighteenth and nineteenth centuries', 616.

time and money. But the fact that the inns in London had to be attended was a deterrent to the provision of training in Ireland.[3]

In these circumstances, it was not surprising that in 1839 many Irish barristers enthusiastically supported the opening in Dublin of a special law school, which had been devised by their young and industrious middle-class colleague, that protestant from Derry, Tristram Kennedy.[4]

In 1835, the year following Tristram's call to the bar, there was a major change in the political landscape of Ireland. For the first time since the Act of Union had been passed, the tory interest ceased to be dominant. This created opportunities for innovation and Tristram was inspired to found a law school to serve the needs of his profession. Few contemporaries would have argued with the opening line of his prospectus, published in the autumn of 1839, that 'the want of any preparatory course of legal education in Ireland has been sensibly experienced'. By examining here the professional context in which the Dublin Law Institute was formed, rather than by concentrating upon the details of the institution's day-to-day existence from 1839 to 1842 and again from 1845 to 1846, it is intended to demonstrate in this chapter that the fate of Kennedy's experiment depended to a great extent not upon the quality of its courses but upon political and professional goodwill. Unfortunately, such goodwill was a commodity in diminishing supply from 1840 onwards.

PATRONAGE AND THE LEGAL PROFESSION

Both before and after the passing of the Act of Union in 1800 successive governments used patronage on a wide scale in Ireland to advance their interests and to reward their supporters. It was a factor of great relevance to the professional aspirations of Irish barristers, amongst others, and its deployment as an instrument of policy in the years leading up to the foundation of the Dublin Law Institute exacerbated the sentiments of conservative lawyers. This rendered more tenuous the chances of sustaining professional reforms.

3. Kenny, *King's Inns and the kingdom of Ireland*, passim.
4. Forty practitioners, either serjeants-at-law or queen's counsel, signed one resolution supporting the institute. 'If any man in Ireland could have induced the within forty subscribers to agree upon any one other question in which the common interest of both countries were concerned', wrote an observer, 'he would have been worthy of the post of lord lieutenant and governor-general of Ireland!' (below, ch.5, June 1840 – see pp.112–13).

In 1835, the tory government, having been defeated in the house of commons by a small majority, retired from office and was succeeded in power by the whigs. The British members were then almost equally divided between whigs and tories. But a whig majority was obtained and a whig government established 'by the support of Irish popular members'.[5] At the election of 1835 Irish 'anti-tories' – whigs, liberals, radicals and repealers – had made common cause. The most prominent of these was Daniel O'Connell, successful champion of catholic emancipation.[6] As it subsequently transpired, the alliance between Irish reformers and whigs was ultimately to prove a disappointment. It resulted in very limited gains for the Irish before the Melbourne administration finally fell in 1841. But at least in the application of patronage to legal offices there was an important development. As recently as 1831 Daniel O'Connell had written that

> the administration of Earl Grey is doing all it can to drive the people to despair . . . first, they appointed the leading Orangeman of the bench, Mr Joy, Chief Baron; second, they appointed a fifth or sixth rate barrister, Mr Doherty, Chief Justice of the Common Pleas; third, they appointed a dogged, pertinacious Orangeman, Mr Blackburne, Attorney General. . . .[7]

The change after 1835 was one of practice rather than principle. Future appointees would be found, as Ó Tuathaigh puts it, 'among friends of the people'. Thus, McDowell has noted that

> all the six judges placed on the bench between 1835 and 1841 were liberals (four had been liberal MPs) and three were catholics. During the same period the attorney- or solicitor-general was always a catholic, and his colleague a liberal protestant, and religio-political considerations played a part in a wide variety of appointments, including stipendiary magistrates, legal officials and police inspectors.[8]

To that list of positions MacDonagh has added the assistant barristers, an office described by one writer in 1851 as being 'the first appointment to which the lawyer can aspire'.[9]

5. Anon., *Memoranda of Irish matters by obscure men, of good intention. Part 1: the rules of Irish promotion*, p.50.
6. MacDonagh, *The emancipist*, p.159.
7. *Correspondence of Daniel O'Connell*, iv, 375.
8. Ó Tuathaigh, *Thomas Drummond and the government of Ireland, 1835–41*, p.9; McDowell, *Irish public opinion*, p.179.
9. *NHI*, v, 179; Anon., 'The present condition and future prospects of the Irish bar', 74; Kenny, 'Counsellor Duhigg', 310–11.

The central administrator responsible for implementing the new patronage was Thomas Drummond, under-secretary for Ireland from 1835 to 1840. He enraged the most reactionary elements in society by his support for reform and by his fairness in government. When the magistrates of Tipperary wrote to him following the murder of a local landlord, Drummond lectured them in reply on the responsibilities of members of their class to the tenantry. Even today the full text of his letter, in which appears the celebrated dictum that 'property has its duties as well as its rights', is breathtaking in its disregard for their sensitivities. The government had little time for the old magistracy and had decided that new blood was needed. Indeed, according to MacDonagh, 'the greatest single gain, in O'Connell's eyes, from the continuance of the liberals in office was the widespread changes wrought by the Morpeth administration in the Irish magistracy in the spring of 1838'.[10]

Daniel O'Connell himself was not only a prominent politician and a leading barrister but also became the first catholic to be admitted to the senior ranks of king's counsel following the passage of the Roman Catholic Relief Act of 1829. In 1838 he declined a government offer to make him master of the rolls and the position went instead to Michael O'Loghlen, a friend of his and the first catholic to be appointed to judicial office since the reign of King James II (1685–88). Notwithstanding the fact that this appointment followed almost a full decade after the granting of catholic emancipation, the patronage of catholics was deeply resented by some tories. They purported to see in it an unholy alliance between the pope, O'Connell and Drummond. To one such suggestion by the representative for Dublin University, O'Connell replied dismissively in March 1839:

It was said that the government had distinguished none but agitators, had given to none but agitators the emoluments of place; nay it was said that they had abused the seat of justice, and placed none but agitators on the bench. Was Sergeant Ball an agitator? Was Mr Woulfe an agitator? Was Sir Michael O'Loghlen an agitator? These were the last appointments made by the government.[11]

But, notwithstanding general agreement among government supporters concerning patronage and the legal profession in

10. Ó Tuathaigh, *Drummond*, pp.7–18; O'Hegarty, *A history of Ireland under the Union*, pp.85–87; MacDonagh, *The emancipist*, pp.173–74.
11. Kenny, 'The exclusion of catholics from the legal profession in Ireland, 1537–1829', 356–57; O'Brien, *Thomas Drummond*, p.326; Ó Tuathaigh, *Drummond*, p.9.

Ireland, English and Irish reformers disagreed about other matters and thus left the way open for the return of a tory administration. Indeed, within just months of the political alliance being formed in 1835 the first major blow had been dealt to Irish expectations by the whigs. They decided, for reasons of political expediency, to extend the English poor law system to Ireland. Tristram Kennedy's brother was prominent amongst many critics of this extension, which was seen by most Irish liberals as being very inappropriate in Irish circumstances. In making its decision, the government had ignored the relevant recommendations of a government-appointed commission, chaired by Archbishop Richard Whately of Dublin. The new poor law was disliked by tenants, who saw it as demeaning, and by landlords, who saw it as financially oppressive. Its adoption was the first of many disappointments for Irish supporters of the administration. Insofar as the reformers in Ireland made gains under the whig administration, their final consolation would be the limited municipal reform act of August 1840. That year also saw the death of the sympathetic under-secretary, Thomas Drummond. Within eighteen months the tories would return to power.[12]

It was in 1839, in this increasingly charged political atmosphere, that Tristram Kennedy founded the Dublin Law Institute. Whatever its intrinsic merits, the institute could not escape the bleary eye of those who regarded contemporary changes as lamentable and who waited patiently for a return of the old order. This was despite the fact that a number of tories individually backed the liberal-minded Kennedy. Where between 1836 and 1841 the Royal Dublin Society was suffering materially because its council had offended the sensibilities of whigs, the Dublin Law Institute would experience from 1841 the practical consequences of having become too closely associated with the reform movement.[13]

There was, as shall be seen later, one particular tory whom Kennedy ultimately would blame for the closure of his institution in 1842. This was Edward Sugden, the last English lord chancellor of Ireland. As I have written elsewhere, Sugden established himself early in his professional career as a highly-regarded lawyer. He had also the reputation of being one of the best-paid barristers in the first half of the nineteenth century. It was reported that before his appointment to the Irish judiciary he was earning 'upwards of

12. Kenny, 'Tristram Kennedy', 8–9; Ó Tuathaigh, *Ireland before the Famine*, pp.108–14; Beckett, *Mod. Ire.*, pp.319–21; *NHI*, v, 216–17.
13. Berry, *A history of the Royal Dublin Society*, ch.xvi, esp. pp.258–68, 273–77; White, *The story of the Royal Dublin Society*, pp.92–103, 107–13.

£17,000 per annum' at the English bar. Later to become chancellor in England, Sugden first became chancellor in Ireland for a few months in 1835, replacing William Conyngham Plunket. But when the whigs took power later that year, Sugden went back to England. Plunket then resumed the great seal and continued to hold it until forced to retire in 1841. He was then again succeeded by Sugden, following a brief interlude when Campbell held the office as a sinecure.[14] The polarity between Plunket and Sugden was not confined to politics and place. In legal argument, too, they had a reputation for holding opposite opinions, although Plunket's grandson has suggested that the extent of their disagreement has been exaggerated. But the biographer may have done so because his grandfather was considered by some to be inferior to Sugden as a lawyer.[15]

Because the lord chancellor of Ireland traditionally presided over the council of King's Inns the fate of the Dublin Law Institute was caught up with the personalities and inclinations of these two contrasting figures. It had been during Plunket's tenure as chancellor that the benchers agreed provisionally to support the institution, but during Sugden's that the crucial decision whether or not to continue that support fell to be made. Sugden had declined from the outset to endorse the Dublin Law Institute, ostensibly on pedagogic grounds. Kennedy courted his support in April 1840 but eventually, over three months later, received an unfavourable reply. Marking the letter 'private', Sugden wrote that he was 'adverse to lectures, as [well as?] a law school, unless accompanied by a compulsory examination'. Sugden, as will be seen below in chapter 8, later recommended the introduction of a system of legal education for England which was in principle similar to that which he ruled out for Ireland.[16]

Having been unsupportive in 1840, Sugden was even more unlikely to respond warmly to the ambitions of local reforming

---

14. Duman, *The judicial bench in England 1727–1875: the reshaping of a professional elite*, p.109; Kenny, 'Irish ambition and English preference in chancery appointments, 1827–41: the fate of William Conyngham Plunket' in Osborough (ed.), *Explorations in law and history*, p.152. In the latter article I state, clearly by mistake, that in the sketch by Grey – again reproduced below – Plunket holds his spectacles in clasped hands. Other images reproduced in that article show him with spectacles in hand.
15. Ball, *Judges*, ii, see reference to Plunket and Sugden; Plunket, *Life, letters and speeches of Lord Plunket*, ii, 327; O'Flanagan, *Lives of the lord chancellors of Ireland*, ii, 584–85; Burke, *History of the lord chancellors*, pp.246–62; Kenny, 'Irish ambition', 166–74.
16. Letter from Edward B. Sugden to Tristram Kennedy, 16 July 1840 (Stack MS).

barristers when he returned to Ireland as chancellor in 1841. For the Irish bar had made little secret of the fact that it resented the continuing appointment of Englishmen to Irish judicial office, particularly since opposition among English lawyers to the earlier appointment of Plunket as English master of the rolls had led to the government revoking their decision in that instance. O'Connell had described Sugden's appointment as Irish chancellor in 1835 as 'an insult and gross injustice to the Irish bar', and there was considerable agitation surrounding the latter's return in 1841. Sugden knew this but reportedly felt secure in his reputation to lord it over the legal profession. One writer would later claim that in 1841

His [Sugden's] profound learning, and great quickness of comprehension, were expended in snarling at the decisions of Lord Plunket; his chief energy appeared directed to drilling the solicitors; and his great pleasure seemed to consist in insulting those of the bar who did not resent it; and in snubbing those who were too manly to endure tamely his insolence.

Where patronage and professional advancement in the legal profession were clearly related to one's opinions, it is not surprising to read of 'coyish, nervous hesitation in public conduct' on the part of many ambitious barristers during these years. In the period 1830–45 generally, the intellectual and social aspirations of lawyers were often entangled with individual political loyalties.[17]

Among his other activities, Sugden specifically set about weeding the magistracy of the repealers 'and he accordingly superseded about twenty . . . while several others, of their own accord, resigned the commission of the peace'. His actions then, sustained in parliament in July, gave great offence in Ireland. But this did not deter him from signing the infamous proclamation banning the 'monster' meeting which O'Connell had called for Clontarf on 8 October 1843 as part of the popular campaign for repeal of the Act of Union.[18]

PROFESSIONAL STATUS

Prior to the second quarter of the nineteenth century, the social significance of the Dublin professional classes, especially lawyers

17. Anon., 'The Irish bar', 74, 76–77; *NHI*, v, 193; Burke, *Chancellors*, p.241; Holdsworth, *History of English law*, xvi, 42–43 admits that Sugden was 'very surpercilious in his manner towards opponents' but claims that 'the Irish appreciated his qualities'.
18. *DNB*, s.v. St Leonards [Sugden, Edward]; Burke, *Chancellors*, p.253.

and doctors, had been rising steadily for some time. Such mobility may have reflected patterns of social change internationally but it had also distinctively Irish features. Thus the passage of the Act of Union was felt to have had a stultifying effect on Irish commercial activities and, it was noticed, 'as trade glided from our shores, and manufactures passed to the more enterprising and happy sister island, that the Four Courts became the rallying point for all the aspiring talent in the country'.[19]

Throughout the United Kingdom at this time lawyers, doctors, churchmen and civil servants were being professionalised.[20] It was a process in which parliament took an interest and in 1834 the appointment of a select committee of the house of commons to investigate the state of medical education was a precedent which would later be followed in relation to legal education. The committee of 1834 'was not friendly to the physicians (nor to their sister institution, the Royal College of Surgeons) and it did its best to build up a case against them'. One of its members was Daniel O'Connell, later appointed also to the select committee on legal education. It seems likely that Kennedy was well aware of developments in the medical profession for, as we saw earlier, he had a very close affinity with his brother Evory, who was a reforming obstetrician and lecturer.[21]

The burgeoning professions dreamt that the future belonged to them, that talent and training would supersede patronage. In 1840 this middle-class optimism found expression in an anonymous article published by the Dublin *Legal Reporter*, a journal supportive of the Dublin Law Institute:[22]

> There never was a time in which more exertion was necessary to obtain any position in society than the present. We live in days when every man is obliged to present his credentials, ere he can obtain admission at any door. The strictest, the most zealous searching scrutiny is adopted on the frontiers, if we may use the expression, of every occupation. . . . Success is become the test. . . . A fair field is opened; an equal contest is taking place; rewards are before every man. Patronage and favour are of little account, and will be less.

19. Anon., 'The Irish bar', 75; *NHI*, v, 193.
20. Manchester, *Modern legal history*, pp.50–51. For a review of some recent studies of professionalism see Burrage and Torstendahl, *Professions in sociology and history: rethinking the study of the professions*, passim.
21. Reader, *Professional men: the rise of the professional classes in nineteenth-century England*, pp.16–17; *The Citizen*, i, no. 1 (Nov. 1839); Pinkerton, 'Evory Kennedy', 77–81.
22. *Legal Reporter*, i (7 Nov. 1840), pp.1–2.

Practitioners at any time we can have in scores, ready and ingenious, and quick-witted enough, but of lawyers, men who when the high-roads are broken up can find a way, – who when oppression stalks abroad can meet it powerfully, and drive it back, – who can invoke the spirit of our laws in the hour of danger, – THEIR number must depend upon the direction given at the outset to their pursuit of legal knowledge.

That same year, Kennedy signalled his approval of such rhetoric by picking a line from Juvenal's *Satires* to adorn the first published proceedings of his institution. The line was 'Qui juris nodos et legum aenigmata solvat'. The full verse from which it is taken, in the eighth satire, reads, 'Veniet de plebe togata, qui juris nodos et legum aenigmata solvat'. This is, in translation: 'Someone will come from the common people [toga'd plebs] who can solve the knotty points of jurisprudence, and the riddles of the law'. By a generation weaned on the classics, such an allusion was unlikely to be misunderstood. Kennedy's contemporaries may have noted that the entire eighth satire was devoted to advancing the proposition that nobility does not consist in statues and pedigrees, but in honourable and good actions. Such action 'displays the worth of persons meanly born', according to Juvenal. The Roman author's sentiments suited ambitious Victorian professionals.[23]

Advancement on the basis of merit might be facilitated by the provision of training, particularly where courses or examinations were compulsory. But there were other reasons, too, for the erection of entry barriers. These, as Richard Abel has pointed out, 'perform two tasks essential to the construction of any profession: they limit the number who can offer the service, thereby lessening competition, and they simultaneously shape the demographic characteristics of practitioners by making entry easier for some than for others'.[24] Limiting the number of persons newly admitted to practice must have been an attractive proposition for the ever-growing legal profession in Ireland. Even in the eighteenth century there had been complaints that Ireland had too many lawyers. But in the mid-nineteenth century, especially, the total in

23. Juvenal, *Sat.* viii, 1, 50. For a contemporary translation see Hickie, *The satires of Juvenal* (Dublin, 1820); *Proceedings of the Dublin Law School comprising the four introductory lectures of the several professors and a prospectus of the plans of instruction to be adopted in the several departments of the institution*. A copy of this, presented to TCD in 1975 by the Law Library, the University of Seattle, may be inspected at OLS 178 n. 12, no. 5. There is another copy at RIA Haliday pamphlets, vol.1777, no.4.
24. Abel, *The legal profession in England and Wales*, p.37 and generally ch. 3, 'The age of reform: the professions 1825–75'; Duman, 'Pathways to professionalism', 615–18.

practice increased rapidly. During the decade preceding the foundation of the Dublin Law Institute, the number of students admitted to King's Inns was greater than in any other decade of the century. The average number of new apprentices was also at its height at this time. Both branches of the profession were becoming very competitive.[25]

Throughout western Europe generally at this time there appears to have been an excess of supply over demand in the professions. One modern author who has studied the problem has concluded that in England 'the problem was most marked in the legal profession',[26] and that may also have been the case in Ireland. With the King's Inns slow to respond to what many saw as a very clear problem, attorneys and barristers began to take matters into their own hands.

THE SOCIETY OF KING'S INNS

Founded by local lawyers during the mid-sixteenth century, in a flush of enthusiasm for the Tudor reform of government in Ireland, the society of King's Inns had never been allowed to attain the status of an English inn of court. As noted elsewhere in this volume, no sooner had the King's Inns opened its doors than a statute was passed at the behest of the crown obliging those who wished to practise as counsellors in Ireland to reside for a number of terms at one of the inns of court in London. The society in Dublin was never permitted to call to the bar and it lived permanently in the shadow of the English inns. It also differed from them in that the judges and senior law officers continued to be members of the Dublin inn even after their elevation to office, and these rather than the barristers long dominated its government. Furthermore, attorneys and solicitors, who were made unwelcome at the English inns, were actually obliged to subscribe to the King's Inns.

The founders of King's Inns may have had educational aspirations for their institution but these came to nothing. The provision of legal training in Ireland was not one of the society's functions during its first three centuries in existence. An attempt to introduce an elaborate set of reforms at the close of the

---

25. Howard, *A compendious treatise of the rules and practice of the pleas side of the Exchequer in Ireland*, i, preface; Hogan, *Legal profession*, pp.39, 95, 158–62 for appendix on 'numbers and social background of lawyers'; Joy, *Letters on the present state of legal education in England and Ireland*, pp.84–85.
26 O'Boyle, 'The problem of an excess of educated men in Western Europe, 1800–1850', 478.

eighteenth century had included plans for training. That attempt was unsuccessful. By the beginning of the second quarter of the nineteenth century there was still no institution in Ireland providing professionally relevant courses for someone aspiring to practise law. The position in London was little, if at all, better. The English inns had long since descended from their once splendid pedagogic past to a position where such training as they purported to provide was a mere formality. But then, from 1826, the new University of London began to experiment with practical courses in law. Other English colleges and the Law Society in London responded to this development by experimenting with courses of their own, as will shortly be seen in more detail. Yet still the benchers in London and Dublin were slow to recognise the need for reform. Notwithstanding the fact that the King's Inns enjoyed a substantial annual income from the many barristers and attorneys who were obliged to subscribe to it, the Irish benchers showed no inclination to meddle in matters educational. The judges were all protestants and the conservative protestant interest in Ireland had, for ideological reasons, long approved of the statutory requirement that Irishmen attend the London inns. In the polarised aftermath of the Act of Union, that interest was unlikely to be enthusiastic about the development of a national law school in Ireland.[27]

Comparing the numbers in practice in London and Dublin in 1839, the Irish barrister James Hardey pointed out that in London there were about 1,500 barristers, 100 conveyancers and pleaders and about 3,000 solicitors and attorneys, who all 'had the advantage of three regular incorporated law schools in active operation'. Hardey estimated that at the same time there were in Dublin no less than 700 barristers and 1,800 solicitors and attorneys, none of whom had a law school to attend. In his petition to the house of commons in 1843, Tristram Kennedy pointed out that the society of King's Inns then consisted of about 3,000 members, of whom 1,700 were attorneys, 900 were barristers and 400 were law students. He also explained that the society was governed by benchers who were self-elected or self-perpetuating and unrepresentative, being

in number about forty-two, consisting of all the judges, several high legal officials, the law officers of the crown, a few members of the inner bar, with but one member of the outer bar, and not even one individual from the profession of attorney and solicitor.

27. Kenny, *King's Inns and the kingdom of Ireland*, passim; *Return of the amount of all moneys received by the Hon. Society of King's Inns, Dublin, in each year since 30 June 1839 to the present time . . . with a statement of the expenditure of the same . . . 1856.*

There was no one to whom an appeal could be lodged against a decision of the society; the judges being themselves benchers could not constitute a plausible board of visitors. Kennedy was to continue for over thirty years more to argue against this system of governing King's Inns.[28] In 1834, a parliamentary commission on the superior courts in England inquired into the regulations and practice of the London inns of court. This was an indication of public disquiet about the function and organisation of those institutions. The King's Inns escaped scrutiny at the same time, the scope of the inquiry not being extended to Ireland.[29]

RESENTFUL ATTORNEYS, 1837–39

The figures on membership of the King's Inns which Kennedy presented to the house of commons in 1843, in connection with his efforts to revive legal education in Ireland, were a salutary reminder that attorneys were not only permitted but were obliged to be members of the inns in Dublin. This was contrary to past practice for at least two centuries in England. That attorneys indeed constituted a majority of its members was nowhere reflected in the constitution of King's Inns: as indicated already, the society's governing benchers included in their number not a single attorney or solicitor, and the law students who were allowed to join the society were only those intended for the bar and not apprentices. But the society benefited financially from the membership of attorneys. Not surprisingly, there were tensions between, on the one side, the lower branch of the profession and, on the other side, the society to which its members were obliged to belong but by which they felt poorly served. Recently, W.N. Osborough has traced the regulation of the admission of attorneys and solicitors in Ireland between 1600 and 1866. In the context of the rise of the 'lower branch' of the legal profession, both he and Hogan have stressed the importance of the founding of the Law Society in Dublin in 1830, just five years after its sister society had been constituted in London.[30]

28. *Saunders's News-letter, 2 Dec. 1839; Petition of Tristram Kennedy presented in the House of Commons, 22 May 1843*; Kennedy, *The state and the benchers*, passim. In the years leading up to the Great Famine far more people lived in Ireland than have done so ever since. Thus, in 1841 the population of Ireland was just over eight millions or about half that of England and Wales at the time.
29. *Report of the commissioners appointed to inquire into the practice and proceedings of the superior courts in England . . . 1834.*
30. Osborough, 'Admission of attorneys', 101–53; Hogan, *Legal profession*, pp.91–143.

An increasingly ambitious and self-confident group, the attorneys and solicitors resented being governed by the society of King's Inns and saw in the independence of their English brethren a model for their future organisation in Ireland. The fact that many attorneys were catholic, while the benchers and the bar were overwhelmingly protestant, would have given the tension between the groups a certain resonance. Relations between the benchers and attorneys appear to have been especially bad from 1836 to 1840, a factor relevant to Kennedy's ambitions for the Dublin Law Institute. One particular area of concern to the lower branch in Ireland was that relating to training. Dissatisfied with the existing system, under which there took place only a cursory scrutiny of young men by so-called 'moral examiners', the society pressed the benchers for reforms in legal education. It was to be 1860 before the benchers were induced to introduce written examinations, although these had been approved by English judges for their attorneys a quarter of a century earlier.[31]

In the autumn of 1837, Villiers Fowler, secretary to a committee of the Irish attorneys and solicitors, wrote twice to the benchers and enclosed a draft bill for the better regulation of his side of the profession. He sought a meeting to discuss the proposals but the benchers rejected his request out of hand.[32] In the following year, a Dublin solicitor, Theophilus Digges La Touche, 'caused a bill to be brought into parliament' by Daniel O'Connell. Digges La Touche had been practising since 1828 and was a member of the Irish Law Society. His bill, too, was 'for the better regulation of the profession of attorney and solicitor in Ireland'. Its terms proposed that attorneys and solicitors would no longer be members of the King's Inns, but that they would constitute instead an incorporated society, which would have power to make rules governing the whole body and admission to it, 'subject to approbation of the judges'. The bill was to get no further than a first reading.[33]

A deputation of attorneys and solicitors was eventually allowed to meet the benchers in order to discuss the former's proposals to reform the profession. Among other points made by the deputation was that they wished 'to ensure a proper system of education for young gentlemen intended for apprenticeship to the profession'. But the bill did not make specific provision for instruction

31. Osborough, 'Admission of attorneys', 150–51.
32. Benchers' minute book, 1835–44 (Kings Inns MS, p.51 (11 Jan. 1837), p.70 (2 Nov. 1837)).
33. Bills for the better regulation of the profession, prepared by Mr O'Connell, 1838–39 (King's Inns MSS); *Commons' jn.*, xciii, 381, 409, 461, 526, 543, 570, 602, 624; *Sel. comm. leg. ed.*, p.liv and q. 2579.

'within the halls of the [Law] Society itself', and in this respect, as the select committee on legal education of 1846 was to find, it differed from the act which had incorporated the English Law Society. That act specifically made the establishment and maintenance of courses of lectures an objective of that society. The foundation of a library had been its primary object. The English Law Society had begun to offer its own lectures from 1833.[34]

While the benchers of King's Inns expressed 'approbation of the views of the attorneys so far as related to education and qualification for admission to the profession', they objected generally to the proposals being put forward. The reforms were opposed by the King's Inns as a denial of the authority of the benchers to make regulations for the attorneys and 'also a denial of the legality of the society'. The records of King's Inns show that the benchers were particularly concerned about a potential loss of revenue. In 1840 the King's Inns received from the fees levied on apprentices and attorneys and from the stamp duty on attorneys' indentures a total of £3,428. That was just £96 less than the society's total annual income from barristers. The council of King's Inns decided to use the influence of such benchers as were members of parliament to help to kill the attorneys' bill.[35]

With relationships deteriorating, a bill to incorporate the King's Inns itself was originated by Villiers Fowler. In January 1839 he sent the benchers twenty-one propositions relating to his proposal for incorporation. Proposition 19 envisaged 'a course of education and examination for those intended for apprentices' and 'a course of examinations for persons seeking to be admitted attorneys or solicitors'.[36] That same year, the house of commons ordered the King's Inns to make a return of its income and expenditure. The benchers delayed responding because they guessed that the attorneys and solicitors were behind the move and did not wish to facilitate them. However, a communication from under-secretary Drummond persuaded them to cooperate.

34. *Sel. comm. leg. ed.*, pp. xv, liv and app. ix, i, 388–89 ('Case on behalf of the attorneys and solicitors of Ireland in reference to the Society of King's Inns') and q.2762.
35. ibid., qq.2353, 2763–65; Benchers' minute book, 1835–44 (King's Inns MS, pp.94–95: 5 May 1838); Hogan, *Legal profession*, pp.99–100; Osborough, 'Admission of attorneys', 148–50; *Return of moneys received by King's Inns . . . 1856*.
36. *Sel. comm. leg. ed.*, 392–94 ('Letters and propositions'); *Commons' jn.*, xciv, 71; Benchers' minute book, 1835–44 (King's Inns MS, p.4: 2 Feb. 1830, p.119: 15 April 1839); Letterbook, 1836–69 (King's Inns MS, p.29: 4 April 1839); Bill for the incorporation of King's Inns, prepared by Mr O'Connell, 1839 (King's Inns MS).

The returns which they then made showed that the society had an annual income of £8,000. But it had recorded losses for the period 1832–39. These losses were said to have arisen from the cost of construction both at King's Inns, where the new library and dining-hall had been completed, and at the back of the Four Courts, where rooms were being built and fitted out for the use of barristers and solicitors. The benchers were peeved that the attorneys and solicitors, being advantaged by the construction of buildings for them at the courts, were so ungrateful as to press for professional reforms. In the event, attempts by the attorneys to change the law in 1839 were no more successful than they had been the previous year. Digges La Touche would claim in 1846 that the bills 'fell to the ground' because introduced against the opinion of the benchers.[37]

Another source of friction was the fact that apprentices to solicitors and attorneys were not eligible to become members of King's Inns, although students for the bar were admitted. This reflected the relative status of the two branches of the profession. On 11 January 1837, a solicitor's apprentice who had tried to break with tradition was refused his request to be admitted a student of the King's Inns. The fact that apprentices paid duties, out of which the government made grants to the King's Inns, was particularly galling to both apprentices and their masters. In 1838, the latter sought an opinion of counsel about this. Counsel suggested that apprentices were, of right, entitled to have their indentures enrolled without any payment to the King's Inns, and that they were similarly entitled to be sworn once they had complied with certain statutory requirements. But he noted realistically that he could see no way of enforcing such rights without legislative interference. In December 1839, a complaint was lodged with the benchers concerning their refusal to allow apprentices to use the new library.[38]

Yet, in spite of such frustrations, apprentices were still considered by some observers to be better prepared for professional life than were those intending to practise at the bar as counsel. In 1846, J.A. Lawson, the professor of political economy at Trinity

37. Benchers' minute book, 1835–44 (King's Inns MS, pp. 94–95: 5 May 1838, p.127: 10 June 1839); *Sel. comm. leg. ed.*, qq. 2353, 2780–81; ibid., app.iv (ix), 348–49 for 'Returns made to parliament by the benchers of King's Inns for 1832–39'; Letterbook, 1836–69 (King's Inns MS, pp. 27ff. – for letters to members of parliament).
38. Benchers' minute book, 1835–44 (King's Inns MS, p.51: 11 Jan. 1837); Letterbook, 1836–69 (King's Inns MS, p.35: Dec. 1839, p. 82: June 1843, p.83: 3 Nov. 1843, p.96: 25 June 1845); *Sel. comm. leg. ed.*, p.xv and qq. 2801–2; ibid., app. ix, pp.389–90 ('Opinion of Richard B. Warren, 6 June 1838').

College Dublin and a qualified barrister, pointed out to the select committee on legal education that, in contrast to students for the bar, apprentices were at least 'obliged to attend the courts, and to go through all the established forms of law; it is impossible for any person to be admitted as a solicitor without having some knowledge of his business'.[39]

THE BAR IN THE 1830S

If during the 1830s 'the lower branch' of the profession was quite agitated, the 'upper branch' generally appears to have been relatively subdued. Individually, barristers might belong to one of the circuit bars and they were obliged to join King's Inns. But, collectively, the bar had not yet a mouthpiece of its own, the King's Inns having been ever dominated by the judiciary. Although barristers had earlier clubbed together to create the Law Library at the Four Courts, not until the very end of the nineteenth century did there emerge a constant organised expression of their professional opinion, namely the General Council of the Bar. Before then, when they shared a concern, barristers appear simply to have circulated petitions or to have called meetings on an *ad hoc* basis under the chairmanship of the 'father' or most senior practising member of the bar. Thus, for example, they petitioned the benchers in 1818, and again in 1822, to make available a larger space at the Four Courts for the Law Library. Those petitions were unsuccessful, but in the 1830s, as indicated above, the benchers agreed to fund from the resources of King's Inns new accommodation at the Four Courts for barristers as well as solicitors.[40]

During the second quarter of the nineteenth century, established practitioners may have felt increasingly threatened as the number of barristers-at-law rose steadily and as catholics began slowly to be admitted to the inner bar and to be appointed to the bench. In such a context the dominant protestant elite was unlikely to be enthusiastic about any initiative which might diminish their power of patronage by determining access to the bar on the basis of academic qualifications. But the professional order was changing, a fact reflected in the gradual appearance of reliable reports of Irish judgments from 1830, and there were some lawyers who felt concerned about the professional status of the Irish bar, both in terms of its provincial subordination to the inns of court in London and in terms of its failure to take account of developments

39. *Sel. comm. leg. ed.*, q.1856.
40. Kenny, *King's Inns and the kingdom of Ireland*, pp.196–217; Hogan, *Legal profession*, pp.42–43, 55–75.

in English legal education. While the requirement for attendance at an English inn would not be rescinded until 1885,[41] a development which will be considered in chapter 9 below, there was now an attempt to provide in Ireland training fit for the modern counsellor. When, in 1839, Tristram Kennedy founded the Dublin Law Institute, such was the sense of relief amongst barristers that Kennedy won for his initiative the broad support of barristers of many shades of opinion. Indeed, from the start, the Dublin Law Institute was intended primarily to serve the needs of students for the bar, and belated attempts by Tristram Kennedy to involve attorneys and solicitors cannot conceal the fact that in its government, personnel and preoccupations the institute was principally a manifestation of the professional concerns of the Irish barrister in the second quarter of the nineteenth century, concerns to which we have already drawn attention. For a full understanding of its significance, it is necessary to consider what was perceived to be the role of education in the contemporary process of professionalisation.

PROFESSIONAL EDUCATION

Even such basic educational provisions as those sought by Irish attorneys and solicitors between 1837 and 1839 had, as noted already, at least two professional advantages. Firstly, they helped to improve the standards and status of practitioners. Secondly, they might be used as a relatively equitable mechanism for restricting entry, especially if examinations were compulsory.

During the eighteenth and early nineteenth centuries, educational requirements for the professions generally in England and Ireland were either minimal or non-existent, and were particularly deficient in the case of lawyers. The inns of court in London had long ceased to provide effective training, and the universities were only very slowly beginning to provide satisfactory courses in the common law. Eighteenth-century initiatives by William Blackstone at Oxford and by Francis Stoughton Sullivan at Trinity College Dublin had subsequently collapsed, with most of their successors treating their chairs as sinecures. But by the 1830s pioneering courses had been established in London at two new institutions, University College and King's College, and at the East India Company's College at Haileybury. Tristram Kennedy was to seek support from these colleges for his new

---

41. Barristers' Admission (Ireland) Act 1885 (48 & 49 Vict, c.20).

institution in Dublin.[42] The London inns were slow to respond to this development of legal education elsewhere in the city. In 1833, two lectureships were set up at the Inner Temple, but by 1835 they had failed, due to a lack of support, and not for more than a decade was the experiment to be repeated. However, it was also in 1833 that the English Law Society, which had been founded eight years earlier for attorneys and solicitors, began its lectures. Attendance was voluntary but, in Trinity term 1836, 'under the judges' authority and with help from the Law Society, which was represented on the examining board, the first serious qualifying exams for any branch of the legal profession were held'.[43]

As the nineteenth century progressed there were, throughout the United Kingdom, growing demands that intending civil servants, doctors and lawyers follow certain courses and sit examinations. Walker has gone so far as to say that 'the triumph of the examination system is a major historical landmark. It marks the end of a whole set of social assumptions'. But in the first half of the nineteenth century there was not yet widespread acceptance of the advantages of examinations, and such examinations as were set were often optional. These were vulnerable to attack as being of limited value, with conservatives scorning them as ineffective while radicals dismissed them as inefficient.[44]

In contrast to the legal profession, the medical establishment adopted educational reforms early, and critics were not slow to point at the lawyers and to draw what Abel describes as 'unflattering comparisons with physicians'. One such critic was the great educational reformer and member of parliament for Waterford, Thomas Wyse. In July 1835, a select committee was enquiring into schools of public foundation in Ireland. The committee had been set up on foot of a successful petition from Wyse two years earlier and it had decided that its terms 'embraced the whole question of education in Ireland, with the exception of that given in Dublin University'.[45] One of the witnesses was John D'Alton, who appeared before the committee to give evidence on an exhaustive tabular

42. Hanbury, *The Vinerian chair and legal education*, ch.5; Abel-Smith and Stevens, *Lawyers and the courts: a sociological study of the English legal system 1750–1965*, p.26; Duman, *The judicial bench*, pp.28–38, 173–74.
43. Holdsworth, *History of English law*, xiv, 231; Reader, *Professional men*, p.54; Abel-Smith, *Lawyers and the courts*, pp.25–27.
44. Reader, *Professional men*, p.116; Perkin, *Origins of modern English society*, pp.256–61.
45. Abel, *Legal profession*, p.41; Atkinson, *Irish education: a history of educational institutions*, p.109; *Report from the select committee on foundation schools and education in Ireland . . . 1838*.

digest of charitable funds for education in Ireland. But D'Alton was a barrister of twenty-five years standing, and Wyse digressed to ask him,[46]

Has it struck you as an anomaly, that whilst we require previous education for the profession of medicine, no such course is required either for entrance at the bar, or for any of the various civil situations held under government?

D'Alton agreed that it was anomalous and was then asked by Wyse whether it would not 'raise considerably the general character of the bar, and at the same time be a great advantage to the public at large, that a previous course of education should be required by the professional body before any gentleman is admitted to practice?' At this point D'Alton became hesitant, suspecting, perhaps, that his testimony might be used by the committee as the basis for some proposal which could displease his colleagues at the bar or their judicial superiors. He replied cautiously that,

When I look at the profession of the bar as it exists, I should be unwilling to think that there was such a necessity, for I know that very few men can maintain rank or character at the bar without great exertions in the study and practice of their business, although no course has been prescribed to qualify for being called.

But Wyse was unwilling to let go. He retorted that his question had in view 'a number of individuals of inferior knowledge, who by being at the bar have an opportunity frequently of misleading people'. He then pressed D'Alton by again contrasting the position in respect of doctors with that of lawyers. But he was losing the tussle when D'Alton retreated even further:

Medicine is pursued, if I may so express it, in loneliness; one individual goes forth. . . . but the profession of the bar is carried on in a perpetual communication of its members one with the other, meeting altogether at the courts; from the habits of their profession, conversing upon law subjects, mooting knotty points, consulting each other on difficulties that may have met them, or on the consequences and changes of frequent legislative provisions, and in that way I think that more serviceable knowledge is often acquired by barristers, after they are called, than by years of unpractised and often ill-directed reading in their chambers.

---

46. *Report on foundation schools and education*, p.78, qq. 872–76.

Wyse, of course, had been contemplating formal education, not 'ill-directed reading' in apprenticeship. However, he recognised a conservative argument against educational reform and let the matter drop for the moment. But he could not resist a parting reference to the 'great advantage' to be derived from including legal studies as a considerable portion of any college education in Ireland.

Wyse's committee reported in December 1837, the report being published the following August. The committee proposed four provincial colleges for higher education in Ireland. This recommendation was the germ of the future Queen's Colleges. Among the committee's many recommendations was one referring specifically to legal education, now argued to be a necessary part of the proper training of middle class professionals:[47]

> To a well-educated middle order, the state must mainly be indebted for its intellectual and moral progress. Such a class is especially desirable at the present time in Ireland. Your committee are of opinion that a liberal, judicious, and appropriate system of education for the middle class is the only means by which they may be enabled to acquire and maintain that proper position in society to which they are entitled, and by the maintenance of which the community can be fully protected from the chances of internal disorder. They are further of opinion that such system is not likely to be provided as rapidly and extensively as may be required, by voluntary efforts; and that it thus becomes the duty of the legislature to intervene.
>
> The present deficiency of institutions for the regular study of law is generally admitted. It is submitted that the establishment and maintenance of law schools, either in connection with or separate from the [proposed provincial] colleges, under the joint administration of the Board [proposed new Board of National Education] and the legal profession, like other professional schools, might be found desirable.

The inclusion of this recommendation on legal education had been personally suggested by Thomas Wyse, the only evidence directly relevant to it being that of D'Alton. But Wyse would later explain to Tristram that the recommendation was made because 'there appeared to me no reason why the legal profession should be subjected to an exclusion from that systematic course of special teaching deemed so essential by every other'.[48]

---

47. ibid., pp.64, 78.
48. Anon, 'The Dublin Law Institute', *Citizen*, ii (June, 1840), p.431. Printed copies of letter, Wyse to Kennedy, at NLI pamphlets, ref. 'Ir 308 p.11', and *Saunders's News-letter*, 28 April 1840.

FOUNDATION OF THE DUBLIN LAW INSTITUTE

Kennedy came to rely on the report of 1838, particularly on its reference to a 'deficiency of institutions for the regular study of law', when explaining what had 'dictated' the founding of the Dublin Law Institute by himself and those whom he described as 'divers distinguished members of the Irish bar and others'. The institute was launched in the autumn of 1839, when a series of special public inaugural addresses was delivered at Leinster House, headquarters of the Royal Dublin Society. The lecture-hall of Leinster House did not then resemble in any way the chambers of parliament which are today located in the same building. For most of the nineteenth century, in fact, the lecture-hall consisted of an outbuilding, sometimes known as the kitchen, which was appropriated as a laboratory and theatre. In 1836, it was noted that 'there is a small range of furnaces and sandbaths in the theatre for the purposes of exhibiting some chemical processes', and that the place was 'singularly deficient' as regards heating and ventilation. Only the introductory lectures, which were open to the public, took place at this venue. The courses proper, which were given by busy practitioners, began in January 1840 in Henrietta Street in premises which Tristram Kennedy himself had acquired and which immediately adjoined the rear of King's Inns, standing directly opposite the society's new library.[49]

---

49. [Kennedy], *First report on the progress of legal education in Ireland, 22 October 1840*. Reprinted without final page at *Sel. comm. leg. ed.*, app. iv, pp. 332–35; *Petition of Kennedy* (cf. note 28 above); Berry, *A history of the RDS*, pp. 325–26; *Proceedings of the Dublin Law School comprising the four introductory lectures and a prospectus*.

CHAPTER FOUR

'A queer compound of individuals': the rise and fall of the Dublin Law Institute, 1839–42

BY NOVEMBER 1839 Tristram Kennedy was ready to open his law school in Dublin. All of the necessary arrangements were made by a small provisional council which consisted of himself and the four persons who had consented to act as part-time teachers or 'professors'. Their inaugural lectures, delivered at the theatre of the Royal Dublin Society in Leinster House, were very well attended. Thereafter, as has just been indicated, they gave their classes at the Dublin Law Institute's own premises in Henrietta Street.[1]

Having circulated amongst senior law officers and barristers an invitation to become members of the law school's council, Kennedy was gratified to receive many enthusiastic and favourable replies. The press, too, praised his venture. There was no member of the bench of the four courts on the new council, although the admiralty judge, the chief remembrancer, the attorney general and the solicitor general were included. The five chief judges for the time being were subsequently invited to join, but they kept their distance. At this time no solicitor or attorney was asked to become a member.

In December 1839, Kennedy and the professors explored with the Irish chief secretary, Lord Morpeth, the possibility of government support for the Dublin Law Institute. The following month, Kennedy invited members of the Irish Law Society to make suggestions concerning the future of the institute. In February, he celebrated the launch of his venture by inviting a large number of guests to a party in honour of the marriage between Queen Victoria and the future prince consort, Albert.

With strong public support for his institution continuing, Kennedy set up another meeting with Lord Morpeth. This time he brought with him a delegation of members of parliament, led by Thomas Wyse. They pressed the Irish secretary to perpetuate by charter the law school and to give it a leading role in the train-

1. As this account is based largely on events listed and referenced in the calendar in chapter 5 below, I have almost entirely dispensed with footnotes.

ing of barristers, attorneys and solicitors. Morpeth seemed to be in favour of the proposal, but refused to commit himself to any course of action before consulting the lord chancellor of Ireland.

During this period, Kennedy also sought discreetly to have the Dublin Law Institute associated with the University of London, so that his students might sit examinations and receive degrees there. Just such an arrangement, relating to candidates for medical degrees, had recently been concluded between Mercer's Hospital in Dublin and the University of London. Kennedy's proposal had serious ramifications for both Trinity College and King's Inns. While the University of London appeared to be well-disposed towards his suggestion, the home secretary, the Marquis of Normanby, embroiled it in bureaucratic complications, and in the end it came to nothing.

By April 1840, it was clear that the law school would not be incorporated quickly. Kennedy was in communication with Wyse about the matter, but political circumstances were changing for the worse, and the solicitors and attorneys were also showing signs of concern about the proposed terms of any charter. The Law Society took offence at Kennedy's attempt to bring the education of apprentices under the control of a council composed largely of barristers, notwithstanding his proposal to include a minority of solicitors, and disclaimed any interest in the charter being sought by him. He responded by adjusting the terms of his proposal in order to leave open the possibility of the attorneys and solicitors having their own school: but it was too late to divert them from passing a resolution opposing a charter for the Dublin Law Institute.

Kennedy had misjudged the mood of the attorneys and solicitors and mismanaged his relationship with the Law Society. If he had been afraid of alienating the bar and bench by courting too early the involvement of attorneys and solicitors in the council of his law school, it was now the case that the institute's future relied entirely on the support of barristers. This he continued to command in large measure, a resolution recommending the incorporation of his school being signed in June 1840 by forty serjeants at law and queen's counsel, men who were not often persuaded to find common cause.

In January 1841, at a banquet held in the Dublin Law Institute to acknowledge the services of Thomas Wyse to education, the master of the rolls, Michael O'Loghlen, pledged himself 'to do anything in his power to advance the interests of this praiseworthy and important institution'. Such an endorsement from a member of the bench no doubt encouraged Kennedy, but the fact that O'Loghlen was the first catholic to sit as a judge in Ireland since the reign of King James II may have diminished his persuasiveness in certain quarters. He was to die in 1842.

There were undoubtedly some senior lawyers in Ireland and Britain who were not enthusiastic about Kennedy's activities. Amid the clamour of very many expressions of professional and editorial goodwill directed towards the Dublin Law Institute there was a note of caution struck by Joseph Napier, one of its professors and a future attorney general and lord chancellor. At his inaugural address, Napier referred obliquely to the fact that 'the project to be submitted to your judgment is encountered by the powerful resistance which its novelty creates'. Three months later, in February 1840, Napier mentioned again that opposition had been got up 'by some parties' against the institution. On neither occasion did he identify the opponents, but it is safe to assume that they were not all solicitors or attorneys. A number of the benchers cannot have been pleased at the prospect of the Dublin Law Institute effectively wresting control of the qualifying process from the society of King's Inns. Ardent unionists were likely to be suspicious of proposals which would result in Ireland going its own way educationally, thereby weakening the rationale for requiring Irish law students to travel to London. Napier defended the school against allegations that it had been founded on principles which were calculated to create a division between the profession in England and Ireland. But he and others also described it as a 'national institution', potentially evocative if not provocative terminology to those who supported union precisely because it suggested the abolition of national differences. Amongst those who failed or refused to endorse the law school was, as we have seen, Edward Sugden, a leading English practitioner and both former (1834–35) and future (1841–46) lord chancellor of Ireland. From correspondence in the Bodleian Library in Oxford, it is clear that Kennedy was frustrated by the attitudes of some members of the bar and of the bench. But having alienated the solicitors and attorneys, he had to be careful not to antagonise any of his remaining supporters. He wrote that he was obliged to work with 'some strange and mighty peculiar members in the society', explaining that 'we are seeking both endowment and charter for the institute and in our own body we have a queer compound of individuals whose taste we must endeavour to consult'. He pledged himself to avoid making enemies of any party or of the government, and to that end vetted the proposed text of at least one guest's lecture.

However, Kennedy's ambitions received a setback when the Irish chief secretary, Morpeth, indicated that a charter would not be issued for the Dublin Law Institute until such time as Kennedy could ensure the stability and permanence of his institution. This was generally understood to mean that Kennedy needed to win for his law school the full support of the benchers before the government would even consider making a decision on issuing a charter. Accordingly, in January 1841, a memorial from the Dublin Law Institute was sent next door seeking 'a proper endowment' from the society of King's Inns. The meeting at which it fell to be considered happened to take place on the same day that Daniel O'Connell launched a national campaign of agitation for repeal of the union. The benchers proved to be in no humour to rush into what might fairly be regarded as a commitment to the radical reorganisation of legal education. Four months were to pass before the society finally made up its mind.

The fact that by June 1841 Kennedy still had supporters not only at the bar but even on the bench was reflected in the terms of the society's eventual decision. The benchers agreed to make a modest contribution of £400 to the running costs of the Dublin Law Institute. This, they added somewhat grudgingly, was to be for one year 'and no longer'. The amount of their grant was relatively insignificant in the context of their other expenditure but the principle had been established, at least tentatively, that the society should spend money on the provision of legal training in Ireland. Yet Kennedy had to pay a big price for even this level of support. He had originally sought the endowment from King's Inns in order to strengthen his institute's case for a charter of incorporation. To win the benchers' financial backing, he had to agree to change the constitution of the Dublin Law Institute and he dropped the demand for a charter. In fact, he had little option but to do so. He could at least hope that the grant might yet be renewed and increased annually and that his initiative would be permanently sustained in some way, notwithstanding the terms of the benchers' decision. But a change of government and the return of Sugden as chancellor saw his hopes dashed.

Thus, when the benchers came to consider renewing the grant in 1842 they declined to do so, referring cryptically to 'events' of the past year which had influenced their decision. It is possible that they would have declined anyhow to continue supporting the Dublin Law Institute, but they felt most comfortable sheltering behind what they considered to be self-evidently vitiating circumstances. It is not difficult to see what they had in mind.

From early in 1841 the political climate had become increasingly stormy as Daniel O'Connell stepped up his campaign for repeal of the union. By the end of the year he would be elected the first catholic lord mayor of Dublin since 1688. He and his nephew had always supported the reform of legal education, and this fact possibly heightened hostility towards Kennedy's plans. Moreover, from May 1841, Irish law students launched into a sustained campaign for the abolition of that provision which required them to attend the inns of court in London. Kennedy was suspected by some people of encouraging the campaign. His supporters denied that he was involved, and he himself sought and obtained modest financial support from the London inns for his law school. But it was scarcely an atmosphere in which the unionist benchers of King's Inns would eagerly support his institution, the very existence of which was a reproach to the inns on both sides of the Irish Sea and an argument against the necessity of sending young men to London.

During the month of June 1841 tensions rose even higher when junior barristers in Dublin called a meeeting of the bar to protest at the forced retirement of Lord Plunket and, more particularly, at his replacement as chancellor by John Campbell, a Scottish lawyer practising at the English bar. One of the large number of barristers responsible for convening this meeting was Tristram Kennedy. It was a divisive action, which led to other juniors disassociating themselves from the proceedings and seniors staying away on the grounds of 'the disastrous consequences of patriotism in Ireland'. In August, matters took a turn for the worse, from the perspective of Kennedy and other reformers, when the whigs were forced from office and the tories returned to power for the first time in seven years. The new government appointed Edward Sugden chancellor of Ireland once more. There was no love lost between him and the junior bar. His politics were radically different from those of Kennedy and, as we saw earlier, he had rebuffed Kennedy's earlier invitation to support the Dublin Law Institute. He would have been aware that Kennedy was one of those who had actively opposed the appointment as lord chancellor of anyone who was not Irish. Given that the lord chancellor wielded great power, Sugden's appointment was not propitious for the future of the Dublin Law Institute or of its principal.

In such circumstances, Kennedy was tempting fate when, in January 1842, he told his students that the Dublin Law Institute had 'survived the pestilential attacks of ignorance, folly, prejudice and malevolence'. His claim that the reform of legal education united 'protestant, dissenter, roman catholics, whig, tory, conservative and radical' could only be sustained in terms of the most general principles. If in 1839 Napier had grounds to worry about opposition to the Dublin Law Institute, by early 1842 Kennedy certainly had good reason not to be complacent.

It was in May 1842 that the benchers received Kennedy's formal request for a second grant to his law school. Referring the matter to the same committee which had responded positively one year earlier, the benchers attached a double qualification to their terms of reference. The committee was 'to enquire into the proceedings of the past year and into the expediency of making any further grant to the institute, having regard to the consideration of the expediency of maintaining a law school in Ireland'. The latter qualification was later said by one bencher to have been added at the behest of Lord Chancellor Sugden, who expressed a doubt as to whether such law schools were of value or not. This was entirely consistent with Sugden's earlier refusal to give his personal backing to the venture, on grounds which we saw above, namely that a law school without compulsory examinations was ineffective. As has already been remarked, Sugden later proved inconsistent by agreeing to recommend the introduction of just such a system at the English inns.

The benchers' committee set about considering the question of whether or not to give Kennedy a second grant. It was to take them six months to report back their findings. In the interim, Sugden appears to have discovered that James Hardey, one of the professors of the Dublin Law Institute, had forged some legal documents in order to conceal his professional negligence in hastily drawing a particular deed of re-settlement. The scandal, although unconnected with the affairs of the Law Institute itself, may be assumed to have damaged any remaining chance that the chancellor and his fellow benchers might yet be persuaded to continue supporting Kennedy's plans. In any event, a number of members of the committee, who had once enthusiastically backed Kennedy's attempts to establish a law school, had in the interval found themselves embarrassed by his support for those who opposed the appointment of an English chancellor. Even Michael O'Loghlen felt that he had to sign the report of the committee declining to recommend any further grant to the institute.

In November 1842, the benchers accepted the report of their committee, recording their decision in vague and general terms. The Law Institute was now doomed, as the government would not grant it a charter when it had the support of neither the benchers nor the attorneys and solicitors. Kennedy regarded Sugden as the chief culprit in his misfortunes. Taking a narrow view of developments, he now publicly rounded on the chancellor and blamed him personally for the decision of the benchers. In this atmosphere, the professors of the institute felt obliged to withdraw from it, and classes ceased. The refusal of the King's Inns to continue supporting the law school immediately sealed its fate. But this disappointment did not end Kennedy's efforts to reform legal education and, with the help of his friend Wyse, he would later succeed in focusing the attention of parliament on the issue in a way which was seen to force the pace of change. He even revived the institute briefly at a later stage.

While it lasted, the Dublin Law School appears to have been popular with students. Its curriculum drew to some extent on the new courses being taught by the London colleges and by the Law Society in England. Kennedy actively sought and received moral support for his venture from some of the lecturers at these institutions. He also decided to hold examinations in Dublin but felt unable or unwilling to insist that his students sit these. The tentative and experimental nature of the whole examination process at the time may be deduced from a statement which in November 1839 was made on this subject by Echlin Molyneux in his introductory lecture on equity and which is given in the next chapter. In a situation where examinations would be seen as a radical innovation, Kennedy might have alienated many supporters by insisting that his students sit them. Yet, rather than measure the advances which Kennedy was making in legal education, Sugden had chosen to carp at the absence of examinations.

The first four courses of the Dublin Law Institute, introduced before Christmas 1839, were in Common Law (Joseph Napier), Equity (Echlin Molyneux), Real Property and Conveyancing (James J. Hardey) and Medical Jurisprudence (Thomas Brady M.D.). Early in 1840 came introductory lectures in Criminal Law (Joseph Napier) and Nisi Prius (James Whiteside). There were, in addition, occasional lectures on subjects such as Master and Servant or Procedure. At one stage, some attempt was made to cover aspects of international and constitutional law, and a course in civil law was contemplated. There were occasional guest talks from prominent persons such as Archbishop Whately. One guest lecture was also given by Mountifort Longfield, professor of feudal and English law at Trinity College Dublin, who thus demonstrated his goodwill towards the institute. The latter appears to have regarded the teaching of criminal law at the institute as superfluous to the needs of the profession, informing the select committee on legal education in 1846 that he personally never lectured in it and that the only principle involved in it was that 'men must not commit certain crimes, and if they do, there are certain punishments'. Napier himself admitted in his opening lecture that the study of criminal law was so little regarded among practising lawyers that a total ignorance of it was considered quite acceptable professionally.[2]

Those who had rallied around Kennedy and agreed to deliver the courses included some of the brightest young barristers of the day. They became part-time professors at his new institute, making their way to Henrietta Street when their work at the bar ended at 4.00 p.m. Molyneux was later to be one of the first professors of law in the Queen's Colleges, delivering lectures in Belfast, while Napier and Whiteside were both ultimately to be elevated to the bench, Napier in 1858 becoming lord chancellor of Ireland and Whiteside in 1866 being appointed chief justice in queen's bench. That this pair were also to be elected conservative members of parliament, both in turn representing the University of Dublin, underlined the breadth of support which Kennedy was able to muster at the bar. For his part, Hardey in 1839 had a considerable conveyancing practice, albeit doomed because of what Sugden found out. The course in medical jurisprudence was taught not by a lawyer but by a doctor, Thomas Brady, who was also a professor in the College of Physicians.

The principal readings for students on these courses were from Blackstone's *Commentaries*. Other works listed were Stephen on *Pleading*, 'with the references', selections from Smith's *Leading Cases*, Cooper's *Treatise on Pleading in Equity*, Watkin's *Conveyancing* and Sheppard's *Touchstone*. In this connection, Joseph Napier 'strongly recommended to the students to confine their attention, during the first year, to the class books'. But,

in addition to lecture and class instruction, it was not unusual for the pupils to attend the courts, and the professors were in the habit of taking advantage of this circumstance, and placing before their classes, in the common law department, the pleadings of cases pending at the time; a practice which had the effect of exciting the attention of the student, who, in many instances, watched with a lively interest the progress and issue of such proceedings.[3]

As regards the actual numbers attending the courses of the Dublin Law Institute, it has to be said that these were somewhat disappointing for those who hoped that such a voluntary venture might meet with a wholehearted response from all intending lawyers. There were in 1843, for example, some four hundred law students on the books of King's Inns.

2. *Sel. comm. leg. ed.*, q. 2835; *Freeman's Journal*, 10 Feb. 1840.
3. *Sel. comm. leg. ed.*, p. xlii, qq. 1199, 1202, 2993.

Although the inaugural lectures of the Institute had been greeted with enthusiasm and had attracted large numbers, the select committee of 1846 would note that the attendance at ordinary lectures 'does not appear to have been at any time very general'. This impression is borne out by an examination of Kennedy's own figures. He gilded the lily by adding together those registered for individual courses in order to arrive at the total number attending his institution. On this basis fourteen students registered for the equity course and another twenty-four for the real property and conveyancing course could be counted as thirty-eight. In fact, only about one in six of his students appears to have taken and paid for the entire range of courses on offer. However, by calculating it his way, Kennedy was able to inform the benchers of Kings Inns that the number of students attending lectures in 1840 was 121, declining to 106 in 1840. Lest this drop be misconstrued, Kennedy pointed out that

this falling off of attendance is not, however, to be ascribed to remission of zeal. A greater number entered the first year, as might be expected: the list comprised the students not only of the last but of three or four years previous, and who had hitherto no opportunity of attending any similar institution in the country.

Attendance at the Dublin Law Institute was voluntary, and many students opted not to avail of the opportunity to improve their legal knowledge. But Kennedy did point out that, on a proportional basis, the number of subscribers to the institute, as compared to the number of students admitted to King's Inns, was rising when the benchers withdrew their support.

The income generated by students was never sufficient to support Kennedy's ambitions for his institute, and he not only put his own property at its disposal but also relied on the goodwill of fellow barristers who provided lectures for modest remuneration. Without official backing from both the benchers and the government, Kennedy's Dublin Law Institute was set to wither on the vine.[4]

Nevertheless, it is clear that the number of students who paid for courses at the Dublin Law Institute was considerably greater than the number annually sitting law examinations at the University of London or usually attending lectures at Trinity

---

4. Benchers' minute book, 1835–44 (King's Inns MS, p.156: 22 May 1841); *Sel. comm. leg. ed.*, pp.xli–ii, app. iv, no. 21. In making some of his calculations, Kennedy appears to have been assisted by the professor of mathematics at Trinity College Dublin (*Saunders's News-letter*, 24 June 1842).

College, notwithstanding the fact that the latter were open to intending practitioners. In the 1840s, there were, on average, four or five candidates for the degree of bachelor of laws in London, while the average number of students at a class given by the respected professor of feudal and English law in Trinity was just seven. When the Dublin Law Institute was revived briefly in 1845, the number of students who registered for the course in common law was said to be 115, and for the equity course, thirty.[5]

Kennedy attracted enough students to allow him to construct a working model of professional legal training and to draw the attention of the public to deficiencies in the existing system of professional education in Britain and Ireland. How he did so is demonstrated in the following two chapters.

---

5. *Hansard, 3*, lxxxv, col.677 (7 April 1846); *Sel. comm. leg. ed.*, qq. 682–85, 2833, 3777.

CHAPTER FIVE

'National institution': calendar of events relating to the Dublin Law Institute, 1839–42

BETWEEN 1839 AND 1842 the fate of the Dublin Law Institute was spun at a fast rate. As the momentum built up during these years of political and social excitement, Kennedy tried hard to stitch together the various strands of his support long enough to convince the government of the advantages of making his school a permanent national institution. But from the start he encountered some opposition, and little by little his designs began to fail. He was as much overwhelmed by external circumstances as undermined both by his own mistakes and by the too enthusiastic backing of certain supporters.

In the preceding chapter, the rise and fall of the institute has been discussed in broad terms. But to understand better how precisely Kennedy's plans for the Dublin Law Institute were undone, it is necessary to look closer at the daily struggle in which he was engaged. With the help of an annotated calendar it is possible to gain some insight into Kennedy's perspective on developments. Ultimately, it was the day-to-day 'events of the last year' which were taken into account by the benchers when deciding not to continue supporting the institute.

The circumstances in which in 1845 the institute was briefly revived will be considered in context in chapter 6 below.

1839

5 October 1839 Kennedy's plans for a Dublin Law School are published in the *Dublin Evening Post* and are welcomed by that paper's editor. Although a member of the Church of England, the proprietor of the *Post* was said to 'advocate all the national interests' in Ireland. By this time, too, there was circulating a prospectus or statement of intent relating to the Dublin Law School, or 'institute' as it would soon be dubbed in the new year. This pointed out that 'the great purpose of the course proposed is to elevate the standard of professional knowledge, to cultivate diligence and provide for regular and permanent benefits by a system more intended for utility than display'. The statement added that 'the plans and details of the several law schools in London have been accurately ascertained and examined, and a system formed upon the experience thus acquired, in which all that appears most useful and practical has been combined'.[1]

31 October 1839   The *Ulster Times* enthusiastically greets the foundation of the Dublin Law School. Although conservative and protestant, this paper was said to be committed to 'every reasonable and necessary reform'.[2]

7 November 1839   Kennedy applies for and receives permission for Joseph Napier to deliver a lecture in the theatre of the Royal Dublin Society at Leinster House in Kildare Street. This will be his new institution's inaugural lecture. The theatre was used by the R.D.S. not only for lectures in science, agriculture and the fine arts but also for occasional special addresses, such as that delivered this same year by William Betham on the advantages to be derived from the study of antiquities.[3]

9 November 1839   Joseph Napier delivers his introductory lecture on the common law, at the R.D.S. The lecture took place at 4 o'clock on Saturday afternoon. Long before the appointed hour, every seat in the theatre was filled. Napier was said to have been 'most enthusiastically greeted by an overflowing audience', which reportedly included some members of the inner bar and a large number of practising barristers and solicitors. Also reported as present were several of the judges, including Philip Crampton, who had been professor of feudal and English law at Trinity College Dublin until elected to parliament in 1829. In the audience, too, was the senior remembrancer, Acheson Lyle. So many people wished to attend that a large number could not be accommodated and went home disappointed. In the course of his discourse, which was a 'very beautiful and pleasing composition' and 'of extreme rhetorical beauty', Napier was reportedly interrupted with animated applause.

1. Dublin Law Institute, *Proceedings*, passim; *Waterloo directory*, p.166.
2. *Waterloo directory*, p.483.
3. Scrapbook (King's Inns MS, unpaginated); Berry, *Royal Dublin Society*, p.269. For a description of the lecture theatre see above, p.82.

Rather cryptically, Napier announced that 'the project to be submitted to your indulgent judgment is encountered by the powerful resistance which its novelty creates . . . ', but failed to elaborate. He said that the institute was being founded 'in imitation' of the several law schools which had been established in London. He described the rise of the inns of court 'and the many defects in the present mode of study in them'. It is clear from comments which he made on this occasion that he intended his students to sit examinations as an intrinsic part of his course. However, when his introductory lecture was subsequently published, it was explained that examinations in his subject would be voluntary. Napier decided to apologise for the standard of his lecture: 'I feel it due to myself to request, that it should be indulgently criticised, as it was entirely composed during the few hurried instances I could snatch from business, in the first week of the present term'. Nevertheless, he concluded amid general and sustained applause.[4]

11 November 1839   In a report on Napier's lecture, the *Freeman's Journal* writes that 'the English system of teaching law appears to consist, in fact, more in pleasing the palate than in refining or improving the understanding'. It is not clear from the context if this is an exact report of something which Napier himself said or an observation by the newspaper upon his comments. John Mitchell, the nationalist leader and solicitor from County Down, regarded the *Freeman's Journal* as 'the recognised organ' of the liberal Irish party.[5] This same day the neutral *Saunders's News-letter* extends best wishes to the institute, 'as we look upon it with some degree of national pride'. Apparently, unlike Napier, the writer was unaware of any resistance to the institution: 'we have not heard of any difference of opinion as to the value and importance of it to the candidates for both professions'.

12 November 1839   In a report on Napier's lecture, the *Evening Packet* expresses the view that, 'although we are not usually inclined "to meddle with those who are given to change", yet we must admit that a more enlarged and intellectual course of training should be added to the masticatory process which our present

4. Dublin Law Institute, *Proceedings*, at 'Prospectus', p.ix, at 'N. B.'; *Saunders's News-letter*, 11 Nov. 1839; *Morning Register*, 11 Nov. 1839; *Freeman's Journal*, 11 Nov. 1839; *Dub. Ev. Post*, 12 Nov. 1839; *Dublin Monitor*, 12 Nov. 1839; *Londonderry Journal*, 19 Nov. 1839; Napier, *Introductory lecture on the study of the common law*; McDowell and Webb, *Trinity College*, p.139.
5. Cited at *Waterloo directory*, p.418.

law students are doomed to undergo'. The *Packet*, which was tory in sentiment and sometimes anti-catholic, welcomes the institute's plans.[6]

16 November 1839 An introductory lecture to the course of medical jurisprudence is delivered at Leinster House by Dr Thomas Brady, professor in the College of Physicians. Two nights earlier Brady had given a lecture on the same subject at the College of Physicians. He began on this later occasion by saying that the object of his lectures was 'to communicate such a knowledge of medicine, and its collateral sciences, as is absolutely required in the practice of the profession of the law'. It was reported that 'a most numerous' and 'highly respectable' audience had gathered for the occasion, but the *Morning Register* felt obliged 'to express our regret that the number of professional persons was rather scant'. The *Freeman's Journal* did not agree. It referred to 'a most numerous assembly of members of the legal profession'![7]

Brady remarked that

it may be said men have risen to eminence at the bar without the aid of lectures, or the laborious study we now propose. No doubt; but the bar was not then, as now, 'filled to overflowing'. In the course of his talk, he noted that 'in a very large portion of the cases in which members of the bar are engaged – such as infanticide, abortion, murder, poisoning, lunacy and insurances – the evidence of medical witnesses forms the principal portion of the investigation; and the success of counsel engaged on either side must depend, in a great measure, on the ability which he shows in examining and cross-examining medical gentlemen on subjects immediately connected with their profession'.

Brady was reported to have concluded his address

amidst repeated demonstrations of applause, by some excellent observations on the necessity of unceasing application and study to all barristers who wish to rise in their profession. It was not by fawning on governments, or those in power, as is too frequently the case, that they were to expect to arrive at eminence or rank.[8]

23 November 1839 An introductory lecture on equity is delivered at Leinster House by Echlin Molyneux, esq. According to the

6. *Waterloo directory*, p. 204.
7. *Ev. Packet*, 14 and 19 Nov. 1839; *Saunders's News-letter*, 18 Nov. 1839; *Morning Register*, 18 Nov. 1839; *Freeman's Journal*, 18 Nov. 1839.
8. *Freeman's Journal*, 18 Nov. 1839; *Dub. Ev. Post*, 19 Nov. 1839; *Dublin Monitor*, 19 Nov. 1839.

Freeman's Journal, 'the audience was fully as numerous as at the two preceding lectures and expressed their pleasure during the deliverance of the discourse, which was possessed of great rhetorical merit, by repeated marks of approbation'. Before addressing the subject of equity, Molyneux made some general observations on legal education:

> the learned lecturer commenced by referring to the want, which has been strongly felt by all who have made the study of the law their profession, of some guide in the commencement of their labours to direct them in the practical part of the science, and in the profitable mode of employing their time.

Molyneux, whose contribution to legal education was to be sustained, continued by pointing out that

> a library, containing even the initiatory works which are recommended to the young barrister, would alone fill a large room; and, in the absence of a master, the student finds himself in a labyrinth of doubts and difficulties, from which many years of close application are scarcely sufficient to extricate him. The new law school is intended to remove these obstructions, and while the profession will give practical oral instruction in the several branches of the science, they will also direct the student what books or passages he is to read in the interim between the lectures.

He announced that he intended 'to distribute written questions through the class, which may be answered or not, at the option of the student, the answers to be in writing, under signatures either fictitious, or if real, to be deemed confidential by the lecturer'. At the conclusion of his lecture, Molyneux made some observations on the subject of law reform. In a report on his lecture, the tory *Evening Packet* remarked that, 'as these delightful reunions progress, their interest increases'.[9]

26–29 November 1839 A circular was sent by Kennedy from 'Queen's Inn Chambers', Henrietta Street, inviting certain law officers and barristers to become members of the council of the 'Dublin Law School'. Until then the provisional council appears to have consisted solely of himself and his four part-time profes-

---

9. Molyneux, *Introductory lecture on equity*, p.26; Dublin Law Institute, *Proceedings*, passim; *Freeman's Journal*, 25 Nov. 1839; *Ev. Packet*, 26 Nov. 1839. Molyneux later became professor of law at Queen's College, Belfast (Mark O'Shaughnessy, 'On legal education in Ireland', 125. O'Shaughnessy himself was a barrister-at-law and professor of English law at Queen's College Cork).

sors. He enclosed a prospectus and a copy of Napier's introductory lecture. Kennedy wrote to those whom he was inviting to become council members that 'it is to be hoped that the general purpose of the undertaking will commend itself to those members of the profession whose names are identified with the reputation of the Irish Bar'. During the following weeks, he received warm replies from many of those whom he had invited, including the attorney general and the solicitor general. Extracts from these replies were printed and circulated.[10]

30 November 1839 The ill-fated James J. Hardey delivers his introductory lecture on property and conveyancing in the theatre of the R.D.S. at Leinster House. Once more there was 'a very numerous attendance' and applause. Hardey spoke for about three-quarters of an hour. Praising the Dublin Law Institute, Hardey struck a cautionary note:

When first the formation of this – I might almost say national – establishment was mentioned to me, and my assistance solicited in its behalf, I felt assured that it would receive support from a great proportion of the legal profession in Ireland – yet there are so many in all professions, and in all countries, who are, as it were, *constitutionally* opposed to every improvement (which they brand with the reproachful name of novelty), that I was prepared to meet with some opposition, or at least disapprobation.

However, he felt able to reassure his listeners that he had been 'delighted to find, from the press and various other sources, that all the shades of difference which divide public opinion in Ireland had been merged in one general sentiment of approval of the Dublin Law School'.

Hardey concentrated on demonstrating that the institute was neither novel nor experimental – 'after the great success which has for the last eight years attended the establishment of similar institutions in the sister metropolis'. He continued by pointing out that 'in America the advantages of such establishments have long become so well known that there legal education is considered incomplete unless the student has attended for some time at one of the law schools established in that country'. Hardey expressed his hope that, before long,

both in England and Ireland, it will be a condition imposed upon the candidates for admission into both branches of the legal profession that

10. Scrapbook (King's Inns MS).

they shall previously have attended some regular practical course of legal education. Such has long been the rule with respect to the medical profession.

Then, having read some extracts from the introductory lecture of the late Professor Park, delivered in 1831 upon the occasion of the establishment of the first law professorship in the King's College, London, Hardey stated that the Dublin institute had received advice and assistance from several law professors in England and from many of the English legal profession. One particular law teacher in England was said to be so delighted with what he called 'our admirable combination of all that was most beneficial in the several law schools existing in London' that he was convinced students would shortly cross from England to study law in Ireland. Hardey concluded his lecture 'amid loud cheers'.[11]

3 December 1839 The sympathetic yet conservative *Evening Packet* notes that the introductory lectures, concluded by Hardey, were 'all that could be open to the public'. Future lectures were intended solely for students of the institute. The writer says of the institute itself that 'parents and guardians who design their sons and wards for the practice of the law, and also those who design themselves for . . . taking part in either of the legislative assemblies, should avail themselves of the opportunity thus afforded'. The *Packet* reminds its readers that

from the outset we hailed the law school in Dublin with feelings of gladness and national pride, and we are now convinced of its perfect success, almost in an instant. In this opinion, it is highly gratifying to know we are joined by some of the most eminent practitioners at the Irish Bar, and we do not know of a single dissentient from that opinion among the learned body.

9 December 1839 Kennedy had an interview with the attorney general and reported that the latter 'said he would have pleasure in being on council either ex officio or otherwise'.[12]

16 December 1839 At a meeting of the 'provisional council' of the Dublin Law School, held in Kennedy's house in Henrietta Street, at which were present Kennedy, Molyneux, Hardey, Napier and Brady, it was resolved that the council be restricted to the

---

11. Dublin Law Institute, *Proceedings*, passim; *Freeman's Journal*, 2 Dec.; *Evening Packet*, 3 Dec. 1839.
12. Scrapbook (King's Inns MS, note by Kennedy on list of members invited).

twenty-six law officers and barristers who had consented to act with the principal and the professors, 'with power however for the five chief judges . . . for the time being to sit on council'. Most of these barristers were queen's counsel. The council included the attorney general, the solicitor general, three serjeants, the second remembrancer and the judge of the admiralty.[13]

17 December 1839   Kennedy writes to the five chief judges (Lord Chancellor Plunket, Lord Chief Justice Bushe, Master of the Rolls O'Loghlen, Chief Justice of the Common Pleas Doherty and Lord Chief Baron Woulfe), informing them of the decision of the previous day and enclosing a list of the council members together with a copy of Napier's lecture and a prospectus. In each case, he wrote, it was 'most anxiously hoped' that his lordship would become a member of the council for the time being.[14]

(n.d.) December 1839   Under the heading 'legal intelligence', one anonymous writer in the monthly *Citizen*, a liberal periodical, praises the Dublin Law School and notes that

the want of such a school is not yet sufficiently understood by the uninitiated. The public is aware that eating a certain number of appointed dinners is the only preparation, actually insisted upon, as a qualification to be called to the bar, and the process is sufficiently the subject of ridicule and contempt among the people; but there is no adequate estimate in the public mind of the trying, depressing and discouraging nature of the pursuit upon which the student, who really aspires to practise the law in Ireland, enters.[15]

13. Scrapbook (King's Inns MS). Shortly afterwards, the names of the council members were published in the *Ev. Packet*, 26 Dec. 1839. They were the attorney general (Maziere Brady, who in 1840 would become chief baron and in 1846 chancellor), the solicitor general (David Pigot), Serjeant Greene, Sergeant Jackson, Sergeant Curry, the judge of the admiralty, the second remembrancer (Acheson Lyle), Robert Holmes, George Bennett QC, Francis Blackburne QC, Thomas Stapler QC, Richard B.Warren QC, John Gilmore QC, Richard Moore QC, James Bessonet QC, Edward Litton QC, T.B.C.Smith QC, Robert Haire QC, Richard Keatinge QC, William Brooke QC, James Major QC, George B.Hickson QC, John Brooke QC, James H. Blake QC, James Clancy and William E. Hudson. The principal and professors of the institute would be ex-officio members of the council.
14. Scrapbook (King's Inns MS).
15. *The Citizen*, i, no. 2, p.140. This journal later became the *Dublin Monthly Magazine* and then simply the *Dublin Magazine*. Mitchell said that its proprietor 'took a deep and lively interest in assisting with his pen and purse every effort calculated to raise the character of his country and race' (cited, *Waterloo directory*, p.112).

The anonymous contributor to the improving and reforming *Citizen* reflected upon the complexity and range of legal writings, and noted that this was not all with which a student intent on the bar must contend. It was also necessary to acquire a knowledge of the business and practice of the Four Courts, a requirement which could leave a young man nonplussed:

He is utterly at a loss; and for this reason, the majority of students abandon every hope of acquiring any knowledge of practice, until they are actually in the profession. What would the public think of a proposal to teach anatomy by the dissection of living subjects?

The writer did not confine the *Citizen*'s 'legal intelligence' column to educational matters but raised also the controversial question of the chancellorship. Reports were circulating that Sir John Campbell, a Scot in practice at the English bar, was to supersede Lord Plunket as chancellor of Ireland and many members of the bar were opposed to this possibility. Putting to one side 'professional and personal and political objections' to Campbell, the *Citizen* contended that 'the great and lofty ground of hindrance is that the chancellorship is the highest legal office in Ireland and that it belongs indefeasibly to the Irish people'. The reports about Campbell's appointment were somewhat premature but would prove ultimately to have been well-founded. Campbell would replace Plunket in 1841.

21 December 1839 The tory *Evening Packet* reports that Kennedy

and the professors had an interview with Lord Morpeth . . . relative to the claims of the institution to public patronage, which it is unquestionably well entitled to. The noble Lord received them with his usual courtesy, and listened to their application with apparent satisfaction.[16]

26 December 1839 The *Evening Packet* reports that the founders of 'the Irish Law School, . . . this excellent national establishment', have succeeded in completing their arrangements for courses in common law, equity, property law and conveyancing and medical jurisprudence. A different lecture was planned to take place each weekday evening, Monday to Thursday, beginning in January 1840 and 'thence till the July following, and so on through each year with but one alteration, – namely that in future the session will commence in Michaelmas Term (Autumn) instead of Hilary. Students might attend all or part of any course, with charges

16. *Evening Packet*, 26 Dec. 1839.

adjusted accordingly'. The *Packet* publishes a full list of the council members of the institution and its 'consulting correspondents' in England.

1840

January 1840 During this month the Dublin Law School begins to style itself the Dublin Law Institute.

13 January 1840 Kennedy writes at last to the secretary of the Irish Law Society, enclosing some 'papers connected with the proceedings in the Dublin Law School or Institute', and asking that these be left in the reading room of the society. He points out that any suggestions about the institute would be welcomed,

> the Dublin Law Institute having been established with a view to elevate the standard of knowledge in all branches of the legal profession, to cultivate diligence, to encourage the study of law as a science and to enable the junior members of the profession to participate in the guidance of the experienced.[17]

Next day he is thanked on behalf of the society, which had agreed to place the papers in its reading room.

14 January 1840 Class instruction for the 1840 session begins at the Dublin Law Institute. Lectures take place in the evenings from Monday to Thursday. These, as noted earlier, are on equity, property and conveyancing, common law and medical jurisprudence. From 8 February lectures will commence on Fridays and Saturdays on *nisi prius* and criminal law.

5 February 1840 Referring to a lecture on tenures which James Hardey had delivered at the institute the previous evening, *Saunders's News-letter* says that the institute was 'rapidly progressing'.

8 February 1840 In the afternoon at the R.D.S. Napier delivers his introductory lecture on the criminal law. In the evening at the institute in Henrietta Street it is the turn of Whiteside to lecture on the law of *nisi prius* (see the accompanying handbill reproduced below). Napier's earlier introductory talk, delivered on 9 Nov. 1839, had been on the common law. On this occasion 'the

---

17. Scrapbook (King's Inns MS).

audience, which was extremely numerous, consisted exclusively of professional gentlemen'. He was interrupted by loud and frequent bursts of applause. According to the *Freeman's Journal*, Napier began 'by briefly referring to the opposition which had been got up by some parties against their institution'. He believed that there was little to dread from such opposition and stated that 'the opening labours of the professors had been well received by the public'. The school itself, which he claimed was regarded already as a national institution, 'was encouraged by the highest authoritites at the Irish bar'. Napier asserted that

the principles on which the school were founded were not, as was alleged, calculated to create any division between the profession in England and Ireland. They were, on the contrary, intended to have precisely the opposite effect, as the professors appeared each to be anxious that his motto, as far as the union between the two countries were concerned, should be *connubia jungam stabili.*

Turning to the subject of his lecture, Napier remarked that, 'however extraordinary it may appear, it is an undoubted fact that the study of criminal law is so little regarded among the profession at present, that a total ignorance of it is not considered incompatible with a high professional character'. Six years later the attitude which Napier here categorised was to be reflected in Longfield's admission to the select committee on legal education that criminal law was not taught by him at Trinity because he did not consider it worth calling the attention of students to, there being 'no fixed principles in it, except that men must not commit certain crimes, and if they do, there are certain punishments'.

The prevalence of this same attitude may explain why 'the want of sufficient funds prevented the publication' of Napier's introductory lecture on criminal law. Funds were found to publish the talk on *nisi prius* which James Whiteside delivered that same day. Whiteside was said to have been 'eloquent and highly interesting'.[18]

11 February 1840 The *Evening Packet* reports that Kennedy had thrown open his chambers in Henrietta Street 'for the reception of members of the council and the professors, in celebration of the queen's nuptials', Victoria having married Albert:

18. Whiteside, *Introductory lecture on the law of nisi prius*; *Freeman's Journal*, 10 Feb. 1840; *Sel. comm. leg. ed.*, q.2835; *Morning register*, 12 March 1840; [Kennedy], *First report on the progress of legal education* (Dublin, 1840), p.12; *Ev. Packet*, 27 Feb.; *Saunders's News-letter*, 31 Jan. 1840. The Latin maxim appears to mean that 'marriage is stabilised by union'.

the building was tastefully illuminated, and the several transparencies with which it was decorated were much admired for their elegance. The large centre figure of the Queen, surrounded by the allegorical emblems of the arts and sciences, was beautiful in the extreme, and the judicious application of the gas-light tended much to heighten the effect.

Gaslight had come to Henrietta Street in 1825. Among the company, who enjoyed dancing and refreshments that evening in 1840, were not only leading lawyers but also Kennedy's brothers and sisters. Queen Victoria was greatly admired by liberals and remained respected by Kennedy for many years. Having called his own premises in Henrietta Street 'Queen's Inns Chambers', he would in 1875 suggest

a more appropriate name for the so-called King's Inns, that of Victoria Inn; thus affording both a land-mark to the country and a time-mark of the age in which originated the systematic study of law as a science now established in Ireland, followed by examination tests of fitness for call to the bar.[19]

15 February 1840   The *Evening Packet* reports that a 'considerable' number of students have been enrolled by the Dublin Law Institute and that 'the lectures . . . are confined to the students and to the members of the press, to whom the principal (Mr Kennedy) has afforded the privilege of admission at all times'.

25 February 1840   The *Evening Packet* reports that most of the lecturers connected with the institute are 'compelled to attend to their professional avocations on circuit' and that the school has 'necessarily' closed for over a month. It is intended to resume lectures on 27 March.

7 March 1840   The *Evening Packet* reproduces a favourable notice of the Dublin Law Institute from the London *Legal Observer*.

12 March 1840   The *Morning Register*, soon to be identified with the repeal movement, refers approvingly to the circulation amongst the profession in England of the text of the institute's introductory lectures, believing that this 'must tend to produce a juster appreciation of the claims and character of the Irish bar, with our

19. *Ev.Packet*, 11 Feb. 1840; *Saunders's News-letter*, 12 Feb. 1840; Minutes of benchers, 1819–30 (King's Inns MS, pp.146, 158, 171, 174); Kennedy, *The state and the benchers*, p.15. One of Tristram's brothers, Charles Horatio, acted during these years as secretary and registrar of the institute. He is not to be confused with Charles R. Kennedy.

English brethren, and a spirit of emulation and generous unanimity in its members at home'. The writer adds that 'the Dublin Law Institute has within itself all the elements of success; and the time has now come when it must rank amongst our national institutions'.

17 March 1840   It is St Patrick's Day and Kennedy writes to Lord Morpeth's secretary seeking a meeting between Morpeth and a delegation of members of parliament 'with the view to them bringing under his lordship's consideration the claims for perpetuating by charter a system of legal education in Ireland'. Morpeth was chief secretary from 1835 to 1841 and has been depicted by McDowell as a strong and good-natured liberal.[20]

20 March 1840   Lord Morpeth meets the deputation of members of parliament at the Irish Office in London. Tristram Kennedy is also present. The members of parliament are Thomas Wyse, chairman of the late select committee on education in Ireland, Serjeant William Curry (Armagh City/Liberal), A.H. Lynch (master in chancery/Galway City/Liberal-Repeal), J.E. Tennent (Belfast/Conservative), Fitzstephen French (Roscommon Co./Liberal), N.A. Vigors (Carlow Co./Liberal-Repeal), J.A. Yates (Carlow Co./Liberal), John O'Connell (Athlone/Liberal-Repeal), George Dunbar (Belfast/Conservative), W.V. Stewart (Waterford Co./Liberal). These members are, according to Kennedy, 'identified with the advancement of legal education in Ireland'. Robert Hutton MP subsequently wrote to Kennedy to say that he had intended to attend but that he had been prevented from so doing by the illness of one of his children. Hutton was not only the Liberal representative for Dublin City but was a member of the council of University College, London. It appears that twenty members of parliament were invited, of whom ten attended the meeting:

The object of the deputation being to obtain a charter of incorporation for the institution, Mr Wyse brought under his lordship's consideration the want as sensibly experienced in Ireland of the system in legal education, and directed attention to the very different courses pursued in that department of study throughout the rest of Europe.

The attention of his lordship was also called to that portion of the report made in 1838, by the select committee of the house, which had reference to professional education in Ireland, and to the recommendation of the committee submitted for the establishment and maintenance of a law school in Ireland.

20. Scrapbook (King's Inns MS); McDowell, *Public opinion and government policy in Ireland 1801–46*, p.177 ('The Whigs and Ireland 1835–41').

Explanation was given of the plans and proceedings in the Dublin Law Institute, established to meet the recommendation of the select committee and supply to students the want of a system of legal education in Ireland, as also the success which had attended the undertaking since its foundation.

Claims were submitted for a charter and 'Lord Morpeth was pleased to express his opinion favourable to the object, deeming it right however, before pledging himself to any course, to submit the matter to the consideration of the chancellor in Ireland'.

Daniel O'Connell was absent from the delegation which met Morpeth but was effectively represented in the person of his son, John, who was both a barrister and the member for Athlone. At this period Daniel O'Connell himself was 'the complete ministerialist, largely taken up with British issues and the local manoeuvrings at Westminster'.[21]

30 March 1840 *Saunders's News-letter* announces the resumption of classes at the institute and reports that 'the professors will continue their lectures till the Summer circuit'.

That same day, in a scathing attack, the catholic *Pilot* describes the existing mode of preparation for the bar as 'an idle mockery', leading to 'various little make-shifts of conscious incapacity'. Supporting a charter for the Dublin Law Institute, the writer says simply that the necessity and value of the institute 'appears to be universally felt and acknowledged with respect to the barrister'. The writer expands on the opportunity which the institute also presents to attorneys. Then a note of caution is struck. The institute is

> calculated to produce advantages truly national; but, in this impoverished and struggling country, its progress must be slow, its success doubtful, and its beneficial influence long confined to a narrow circle, unless in its early struggles it be sustained and invigorated by the favour of the government.

Also on this date Kennedy writes from his London address in Molton Street to the University of London to request that its senate consider 'the expediency of extending the benefits of the Dublin Law Institute by connecting that establishment with the University of London'. A fortnight earlier the senate of that uni-

21. Scrapbook (King's Inns MS, for Kennedy to Morpeth, 17 Mar. 1840, Kennedy to Arthur French, 8 Mar. 1840 – two copies with note on one re invitees, Hutton to Kennedy, 21 Mar. 1840; *Morning chronicle*, 21 Mar. 1840; Walker, *Parliamentary elections*, passim; MacDonagh, *The emancipist*, pp.184, 354.

versity had decided to admit to their medical degrees candidates from Mercer's Hospital in Dublin. The University of London held examinations and awarded degrees only, having neither professorships nor lectures itself. Its charter, dated 1836, did indeed make provision for institutions other than the original constituent colleges of King's College, London, and University College, London, to submit candidates for examinations. But the first degree had been conferred only in 1839 and seven years later the only institution affiliated with 'any considerable facilities' for legal education would still be University College.[22]

2 April 1840 Kennedy writes from his London address to the former and future lord chancellor of Ireland, Edward Sugden, who was also a leading English barrister:

The advantages derived by the legal profession both in England and in Ireland from your labours and experience tend alike to elevate the tone of thinking and raise the standard of legal knowledge and, at the same time, encourage a hope that the object for which the Dublin Law Institute has been founded will commend it to one who cannot but have the interest of the legal profession in both countries sincerely at heart and whose approbation, no doubt, would evince the success to which it is suggested this undertaking is entitled.[23]

Kennedy receives a reply from the University of London to his request that its senate consider 'connecting' his establishment with the university (above, 30 March). He is told that the senate, 'as it possesses no power in the matter, has referred the communication in question to the secretary of state for the home department'. The home secretary was the marquis of Normanby. From 1835 to 1839 Normanby, a strong liberal, had been a popular viceroy in Ireland, whence he moved to the home office. On receipt of the letter Kennedy immediately writes to Normanby's department seeking to have the Dublin Law Institute 'placed in connection with the University of London agreeable to the provisions of the charter of the university'. Kennedy encloses various papers, including copies of the opinions of 'the several law professors in London who have investigated the system of instruction adopted'. The application is for the attention of a Mr Phillipps at

22. *Morning Register*, 31 Mar. 1840; *Sel. comm. leg. ed.*, pp.ix, 94–109; Bellot, *The University of London*, pp.4–7; Thomas, *Universities*, p.20; Sanderson, *The universities in the nineteenth century*, pp.58–60; Mr Simon Bailey, archivist, University of London, to the author (1 Oct. 1985).
23. Scrapbook (King's Inns MS).

the home office. Kennedy informs Phillipps that William Empson, professor of law and jurisprudence at the University of London, 'has expressed his entire approbation of the proposed connection and has allowed me to state that he will be happy at any time to confer with you upon the subject'.[24]

4 April 1840   It is reported that Mr Tudor is giving lectures on real property and conveyancing, in place of Hardey.[25]

7 April 1840   The anti-tory *Dublin Monitor* reports on the meeting between the Dublin Law Institute's deputation and Lord Morpeth, 'to solicit a charter of incorporation for that valuable society' (above, 20 March). The reporter writes that Morpeth 'expressed himself favorably to the delegation and promised to submit the matter to the consideration of the chancellor'. The writer notes that the institute 'has commenced under the most favourable auspices', but cautions that it cannot succeed 'unless a charter be obtained to secure to it the permanency and the advantages enjoyed by incorporated bodies'. The paper argues that students cannot learn professional principles 'by idling away their time in pleaders', or conveyancers' offices in London' and points out that throughout the rest of Europe many courses in law exist.

10 April 1840   Kennedy sends to the Law Society in Dublin some more papers relating to the Dublin Law Institute and promises further information on the proposed charter.

Kennedy also writes to William Empson, the professor of law and jurisprudence at the University of London, to inform him that he had just returned from a meeting with Phillipps (above, 2 April 1840), who had given him to understand that it was necessary for the senate of the university formally to make a recommendation if the possibility of a connection between it and the Dublin Law Institute was to be entertained by the home secretary. Kennedy suggests that the professor might call attention to this difficulty at the next meeting of the senate, 'and perhaps they may be induced to remove it by passing a resolution upon the subject'. Empson will reply on 14 April.[26]

13 April 1840   Kennedy writes to the benchers of Lincoln's Inn, enclosing the introductory lectures and other papers relating to

24. Scrapbook (King's Inns MS); Kennedy to Normanby, 2 April 1840 (PRO, London, MS); McDowell, *Ir. public opinion*, p. 177.
25. Scrapbook (King's Inns MS, source not given).
26. Scrapbook (King's Inns MS).

the institute and inviting suggestions 'that emanate with a tendency to promote the advantageous working of the plans'.[27]

14 April 1840 Kennedy writes to Wyse that the number of students at the institute is increasing and that 'the Irish journals have been advocating our plans since our last application and I have heard of some of the bench speaking of the institution in the warmest terms'. From the letter it appears that he awaits anxiously some suggestions from Wyse before forwarding 'our claims' for a charter to the Irish chief secretary, Morpeth.

William Empson of the University of London expresses surprise at the 'supposed difficulty' of connecting his institution with the Dublin Law Institute (above, 10 April 1840). Empson writes that he is not aware that the senate had ever in any case made such a recommendation as was now being proposed. He regards it as probable that the senate will do as requested.

Kennedy writes to Phillipps at the Home Office, enclosing a copy of the charter of the University of London and pointing out why, in his opinion, its senate was not required to make a particular recommendation in the matter of a connection.[28]

15 April 1840 Thomas Drummond, under-secretary for Ireland since 1835 and 'generally adjudged the greatest Irish public servant of the nineteenth century', dies. His death, rather than the actual demise of the whig administration, has been seen by historians as effectively the extinction of the liberal and reforming spirit in that age. Significantly, this is also the day Daniel O'Connell constitutes the National Association, which on 16 July will be renamed the Loyal National Repeal Association.[29]

16 April 1840 The secretary of the Irish Law Society calls at Kennedy's house in Dublin to convey the society's views on the proposed charter. Finding that Kennedy is in London and no date fixed for his return, the secretary sends him a letter requesting further information on the proposed charter for consideration at a meeting of the society scheduled for 22 April.[30]

21 April 1840 Continuing to wax eloquent about the merits of the Dublin Law Institute, the tory *Evening Packet* supports the

27. ibid.
28. ibid.
29. Beckett, *Mod. Ire.*, pp.322–23; MacDonagh, *The emancipist*, p.127.
30. Scrapbook (King's Inns MS).

granting of a charter of incorporation to the institution: 'The precedent has already been established in reference to several establishments in Great Britain, and cannot be departed from, in this instance, without the most palpable injustice to the Irish people'.

The same day Wyse writes to Kennedy, identifying a charter of incorporation as being 'almost a necessity'. He believed that few would be inclined to endow an institution 'which may be here to-day and gone to-morrow. A charter gives a legal air and imposes a public character upon all your proceedings'. Wyse stated that he had learnt, with real pleasure, of

the increasing success of your efforts to establish a law college or institute in Ireland. So early as 1832, when occupied with the question of national education, the subject engaged my attention. In 1838, I suggested the recommendation which appears in the report of the committee on Irish education.

Praising the 'long and laborious' courses for law students in other European countries, Wyse remarked sarcastically that 'they have not discovered the magic of certain dinners, under certain roofs'. Pointing out that 'the second great faculty, in every foreign university, is that of jurisprudence', he argued that the purpose of legal education was to 'form not merely lawyers but men, not tradesmen or mechanists in their profession, but thinkers'.

Wyse complained that

the common phrase that 'a good lawyer must be nothing else' has led to this, that from too often being nothing else but a lawyer, the good lawyer is not near so good as he might otherwise have been; and the very best, when thus exclusively educated, are nothing better than mere lawyers after all.

He expressed concern about possible limitations on the freedom of the Dublin Law Institute to govern its own affairs, in that 'how far you can, in the peculiar relation it bears the bar, adopt the regulations for its internal management usual in other institutions, is a fair subject of discussion'. He suspected that modifications must be made 'to harmonise the activity and energy of the younger with the judgement and discretion of the elder members of the profession'.

Wyse urged the involvement of both branches of the profession, for 'there is no reason why we should have well educated lawyers and ignorant solicitors', and recommended the inclusion in the curriculum of courses in administration, diplomacy or 'even the elementary branches of constitutional or international law'.[31]

28 April 1840 Wyse's letter to Kennedy of 21 April is made public through the pages of *Saunders's News-letter*. Kennedy adds, in response to Wyse's recommendations on the curriculum, that it had always been intended, 'in the general arrangement of the institution', to include instruction in constitutional and international law.

In a letter to the professor of civil law at Oxford, Joseph Phillimore, Kennedy seeks his support for the institute and writes that it is intended to have a professor of civil law at the Dublin Law Institute.[32]

29 April 1840 At a meeting of the united committees of the profession of attorney and solicitor in Ireland, held for the purpose of considering the draft of a charter proposed to be obtained by 'certain barristers' to establish a law institute in Ireland, it was resolved unanimously that:

Any course of education for the instruction of attorneys or solicitors in Ireland should be regulated by that profession with the sanction and under the control of the judges only, and not placed under the control or direction of members of the bar. And as the profession are now unanimously seeking to promote measures for the education and better regulation of their own body, they disclaim any participation in the charter now sought for by Mr Kennedy on behalf of the Dublin Law Institute.

Kennedy will respond by dropping the proposal to include twelve attorneys on the council of his institute (below, 9 May 1840).[33]

8 May 1840 Kennedy writes to the Irish chief secretary, Lord Morpeth, submitting the proposed form of charter. He encloses a copy of 'the expressed opinions of the highest authorities in London on legal education, as also the opinions of those distinguished individuals whose character is identified with the reputation of the Irish bar and who at present are members on the council of the institution'. He adds that 'the present institution is not intended to interfere with the rights of any existing body' and notes that attendance at courses is voluntary.[34]

31. Wyse to Kennedy (21 Apr.) in *Saunders's News-letter*, 28 Apr. 1840.
32. Scrapbook (King's Inns MS). For Phillimore, see *Sel. comm. leg. ed.*, pp.14–24.
33. Scrapbook (King's Inns MS, for William Goddard – chairman and future president of the Law Society – to Kennedy).
34. ibid., for Kennedy to Morpeth.

112   *Tristram Kennedy and the revival of legal training*

9 May 1840   Kennedy points out that two changes have been made by the Dublin Law Institute to its proposed charter. Firstly,

in not inserting that a fourth of the council must be attorneys and solicitors. We leave that perfectly open to the world, the committee of the body of attorneys having declined to participate in our plans as they speak of having a separate school established for themselves unconnected with the bar. Our leaving it open will enable them to join either as fellows, council men or otherwise, if they change their minds (above, 29 April 1840).

The second change is that allowing the professors to be ex-officio members of the council, 'such being the general wish of all parties here'.[35]

12 May 1840   Morpeth writes to Kennedy from the Irish Office, acknowledging receipt of the proposed charter and promising to 'bring the subject under the immediate consideration of the government'.[36]

31 May 1840   Apparently ignorant of the fact that Kennedy has already decided to alter the terms of the proposed charter for his institution, the united committees of the attorneys and solicitors resolve 'that a caveat be lodged against granting a charter to a body styling themselves the Law Institute for the reasons set forth in a resolution dated 29 April 1840, transmitted to Lord Morpeth, the attorney and solicitor general and Mr T. Kennedy'. This resolution itself is agreed to be transmitted to the same people.[37]

(n.d.) June 1840   A resolution, signed by forty serjeants at law and queen's counsel in Ireland, recommends that the Dublin Law Institute be incorporated and approves 'the establishment of a school in Dublin for facilitating the acquisition of legal knowledge'. Among the signatories are Daniel O'Connell, Thomas Lefroy, Richard Moore, George Bennett and Robert Holmes. Scrawled on the original copy of the resolution, now in the National Library, is the following anonymous observation:

if any man in Ireland could have induced the within forty subscribers to agree upon any one other question in which the common interest of both countries were concerned, he would have been worthy of the post

35. ibid., for Kennedy to Wilde.
36. ibid., for Morpeth to Kennedy.
37. ibid., for Josias Dunne – president of the Law Society – to Kennedy.

of lord-lieutenant and governor-general of Ireland!!! and the British Government would have been safe in a pledge to comply with *any* request emanating from the forty subscribers within.[38]

24 June 1840 At the general quarterly meeting of the Law Society, the committee of the society presented its annual general report. In a reference to the activities of Kennedy and other supporters of the Dublin Law Institute the report contained some swingeing comments:

> Your committee cannot help expressing how much they were surprised to find that a few members of the bar had not only conceived a project for obtaining a charter of incorporation, but had actually prepared a draft of a charter, including therein our profession as parties, without ever having made a communication of their intention (so far as your committee have been able to ascertain) to any member of the profession. Your committee have, however, to state that subsequently a copy of the proposed charter was submitted for their consideration, and that having maturely and dispassionately considered the same, they were of opinion that it was not in any way calculated to advance the interests of their profession and, accordingly, communicated such their sentiments to the particular members of the bar interested in the project through the promoter of it, as well as to members of the government, and law officers of the crown; and at the same time published for the general information of their own profession a resolution entered into, expressive of their feeling on the subject.[39]

16 July 1840 In a letter marked 'private', addressed from his English home at Boyle Farm, Sugden replies to Kennedy's letter of 2 April and declines to support his objectives. He tells Kennedy:

> Sir,
> I should long since have answered your letter of the 2nd. April (for which and the papers sent with it I beg you to accept my best thanks) could I have written an answer which was likely to be agreeable to you.
> Your plans can hardly fail to be useful but my opinion has always been adverse to lectures, as a law school, unless accompanied by a compulsory examination.
> I however heartily wish you success in your undertaking.
> I have the honour to be etc.[40]

10 August 1840 The Municipal Reform Act is passed. While this act would provide O'Connell with an opportunity to become

38. Dublin Law Institute papers (NLI MS); *Sel. comm. leg. ed.*, pp.355–56.
39. *Saunders's News-letter*, 30 June 1840.
40. Sugden to Kennedy, 16 July 1840 (Stack MS).

mayor of Dublin, its terms were a disappointment to liberals and reformers and its passage had been so grudging that it marked the demise of any effective alliance between the Irish and the whigs. The government's end was in sight.

28 October 1840   Kennedy presents his 'first report on the progress of legal education in Ireland'. In it Kennedy writes that it is 'desirable that the instruction should be given by barristers of experience, derived from extensive practice'. He places on record the fact that he has regularly been in communication with Thomas Wyse, and remarks that 'I cannot sufficiently express the obligation due to him for his important co-operation in support of our institute'. Kennedy reports that he himself has visited the law schools of the universities of Heidelberg and Bonn to learn from their experiences. Wyse is known to have held up 'the Prussian system' at Bonn as a good example of college education. In doing so, he attracted a rebuke on religious grounds from Archbishop McHale. In his report Kennedy also raised the question of how 'the several claims of the institution for support should be brought before parliament'. The report was subsequently published.[41]

29 October 1840   Kennedy receives from Dublin Castle a qualified response to his request for incorporation of the institute. He is informed that,

although the lords justices approve highly of the objects sought for by the Institution, and have every reason to believe that as far as the plan has yet been tried, it has been found to operate most beneficially, they still feel themselves constrained for the present to withhold the grant of a charter simply upon the ground of there being nothing attached to the Institute which might fairly be supposed to give assurance of its stability and permanence.

Should, however, any legal body think proper to confer an endowment upon the Institute, and thereby recognize it as a permanent and beneficial aid to legal study, one of the main objections to the grant of a charter would be removed.

This answer to Kennedy's petition had been prompted finally by a specific request for a charter signed by four members of the institute's council, including Kennedy and the then second remembrancer and bencher, Acheson Lyle.[42]

---

41. Kennedy, *First report on the progress of legal education in Ireland*; Wyse, *Notes on education reform in Ireland*, pp.39, 47, 60; *Sel. comm. leg. ed.*, pp.332–36.
42. *Sel. comm. leg. ed.*, p.358; [Kennedy], *Legal education in Ireland* (London,

(n.d.) November 1840 In an article in the *Citizen* an anonymous author praises the institute. Citing the reference by the 1838 commons committee on education in Ireland to the deficiency of institutions for the regular study of law, the author explodes: 'Deficiency! – non-existence would have been the word in truth descriptive of the fact'. The author disagrees with the suggestion, which the *Citizen* attributes to William Empson of the University of London but which actually originated with Kennedy himself, that the new institute be connected with London University, and demands for the Irish bar 'education at home'. As regards the institute itself, the author talks of the 'valuable assistance that it is likely to afford in procuring the abolition of the gross injustice inflicted upon our law students by compelling them to serve terms in London'. The latter practice is described by *The Citizen* as being 'utterly ruinous and absurd'.

Significantly, the writer suggests that the Dublin Law Institute apply to the benchers for financial assistance. The benchers are described as 'a body which has hitherto done much to impede . . . legal education in Ireland'. This, thinks the writer, is all the more reason why they ought now to be asked for money: 'The experiment should therefore be made, and the utility of the honorable society of the King's Inns, as a means of legal education, properly tested'.[43]

9 December 1840 At a general meeting, subscribers to the Law Library at the Four Courts pass a motion thanking the benchers 'for their kindness in providing the new apartments for their accommodation, and for the liberal grant for the fitting up and furnishing same'.[44]

1841

7 January 1841 A memorial is despatched from the Dublin Law Institute addressed to the benchers of King's Inns. It recites that 'your memorialists have been most successful in their efforts to found an institution for the advancement of legal education in Ireland'. Accompanying it was a copy of the reply from the lords justices to the request for a charter (above, 29 October 1840).

> 1843). This contains Kennedy's petition to parliament of that year and various supporting documents, including at no.3 the request from Kennedy and Lyle.

43. *Citizen*, ii, no. 13 (Nov. 1840), pp.431–34.
44. Minutes of benchers, 1835–44 (King's Inns MS, p.147).

The memorialists inform the benchers that 'to secure the advantages conferred by the institute, a proper endowment is essential, and your memorialists feel happy in being enabled to state that they have satisfactory reason to expect a parliamentary grant for double the amount of private endowment'.[45]

11 January 1841 The 'Address of the Repeal Association to the people of Ireland', signed by Daniel O'Connell, is published. The association declares that it is 'commencing the first year of the agitation for the repeal, – for what we have hitherto done we consider as nothing . . . '. McDowell has written that 'the most striking feature of the new agitation was the number of intelligent young professional men, who, convinced of the supreme value of national independence, joined the association'.[46]

This same day the memorial from the Dublin Law Institute, despatched on 7 January, falls to be considered at King's Inns. The benchers decide only that the under-treasurer is to retain the memorial. It was to be over three months before they appointed a committee to consider it further and another two months before they made a decision in the matter.[47]

21 January 1841 A banquet for Thomas Wyse is held in the hall of the Dublin Law Institute, Henrietta Street, 'in acknowledgment of the services he had rendered to the cause of education'. Among the speakers is Sir Michael O'Loghlen, who remarks that

the difficulties he had himself experienced in the direction of his own course of study, on entering the legal profession, were too deeply impressed on his mind to be easily forgotten. The ordinary obstacles to which all men were exposed who made the law their study induced him to hail with extreme satisfaction the foundation of this institution in Ireland. He had watched with anxious care the proceedings and progress of the Law Institute from its earliest foundation up to this truly interesting and important era of its existence; and the result of his judgment was, that to secure the success of so valuable an undertaking, its direction and guidance could not have been placed in safer or abler hands. He would only add, on his own behalf, that in whatever position he might at any time be placed, he would be found ever ready to do anything in his power to advance the interests of this praiseworthy and important institution.

45. ibid., p.147 (11 Jan. 1841); *Sel. comm. leg. ed.*, p.337.
46. *Saunders's News-letter*, 11 Jan. 1841; McDowell, *Ir. public opinion*, p.231.
47. Minutes of benchers, 1835–44 (King's Inns MS, p.157: 15 April 1841, p.169: 14 June 1841).

The Church of Ireland archbishop of Dublin, Richard Whately, and several judges are among the large attendance at the banquet. Whately had earlier lined up with Kennedy's brother and other opponents of the government on the poor law issue. He had also founded and endowed the chair of political economy at Trinity College Dublin. During 1841 this came to be occupied by James Lawson, a young barrister who had attended the courses in criminal law and *nisi prius* at the Dublin Law Institute and who had found them 'very profitable indeed'.[48]

29 March 1841 Kennedy writes to General Sir William Napier in England:

Whenever you can dedicate a few hours to the Dublin Law Institute do not forget to throw together your ideas on any subject connected with International Law likely to interest our society in Dublin. The general who is to give me a paper on military law suggested that I should call your attention to a subject you have already given your consideration, –'American slavery and the power given thereby to our country over theirs in case of war'. This would be a matter of interest.

William Napier's brother, Charles, was both the commanding officer and an old friend of Tristram's brother, John Pitt. Referring to the possibility that one of the Napier children might become a conveyancer in Dublin, Kennedy told William that 'I could obtain considerable advantages for John through the professors in our institute if he were disposed to attempt the undertaking'. Kennedy pointed out that it was intended to extend considerably in April his own premises in Henrietta Street.[49]

15 April 1841 The benchers agree a motion from Judge Torrens that a committee be appointed at last to consider the memorial from the Dublin Law Institute (above, 7 and 11 January 1840). At the head of the committee of thirteen benchers was Sir Michael O'Loghlen, master of the rolls, treasurer of the King's Inns since November 1840 and a supporter of the Dublin Law Institute. Also on it was Judge Crampton, who was a former professor of law at Trinity College Dublin and who had attended the institute's inaugural introductory lecture on 9 November 1839.

48. *Sel. comm. leg. ed.*, qq. 1771–75, 1892–98; ibid., pp.358–59 for 'Views of Sir M. O'Loghlen, late master of the rolls in Ireland, on the working of the Dublin Law Institute'; Kennedy, *The state and the benchers*, p.20.
49. Letters from Tristram Kennedy to Sir William Napier (Bodl. MS, f.97 and appendix below).

The committee's other members were either judges or senior barristers and included five council members of the institute.

At this same meeting in King's Inns, O'Loghlen gave notice that he intended to propose on the first day of next Trinity term that 'the number of benchers be enlarged by the addition of ten solicitors and that at all times at least ten solicitors shall be benchers'. O'Loghlen's proposal proved to be unacceptable to his colleagues.[50]

17 April 1841   Kennedy writes to William Napier, acknowledging receipt of the former's essay on the poor law, which it is intended will be read to the students of the Dublin Law Institute. He is having a copy made and will send this to Napier, 'marking any portion which might not suit the taste of *some strange and mighty particular members of the society I have to work with*' (underlined by Kennedy).[51]

8 May 1841   As he promised he would (17 April 1841), Kennedy returns to Napier the paper on the poor law and writes that,

I send a copy of the essay with a few red ink marks in the margin at those parts where the alteration of a word or two might make the subject more palatable to some who may hear or read it. It is desirable our society should at this moment avoid making enemies of any party, of the government, as we are seeking both endowment and charter for the institute and in our own body we have a queer compound of individuals whose taste we must endeavour to consult.[52]

22 May 1841   The committee, which on 15 April last had been appointed by the benchers 'to enquire and report whether any and what sum of money should be given out . . . and if so upon what terms', so reported. The report was signed by seven benchers, headed by O'Loghlen. The other six were Crampton, Torrens, Holmes, Curry, Blackburne and Bennett. This group of seven sympathetic lawyers, most of whom were on the council of the institute and others of whom had attended its gatherings, recommended merely that the modest sum of £400 be granted to the

50. Minutes of benchers, 1835–44 (King's Inns MS, p.152). The committee consisted of O'Loghlen, Crampton, Perrin, Torrens, Ball (all judges), Foster and Richards (both barons), Thomas Goold, William Curry, Richard Moore, Francis Blackburne, George Bennett and Robert Holmes. The last five of these were members of the council of the Dublin Law Institute (*Ev.Packet*, 26 Dec. 1839); *Sel. comm. leg. ed.*, q.2453.
51. As note 49 above.
52. ibid., f.100.

Dublin Law Institute for the current year. This grant may be viewed in a context where the benchers annually were then receiving large amounts in fees from law students, barristers and solicitors and spending £625 alone on the wages of tipstaffs for the judges.

The committee set down certain terms, on the basis of propositions which had been laid before it by the principal and council of the Law Institute. Under these terms, which were to be adopted into the rules of the Dublin Law Institute, ultimate control of the institute was yielded to the benchers.

Kennedy and his council had proposed, firstly, that the benchers should have either the nomination of all future professors or the veto in every such appointment. The benchers' committee now proposed in reply that the appointment of the several professors by the council should be subject to the approbation of the benchers, 'which shall be deemed to be essential to their appointment'.

The second proposal was that the benchers should have the power of requiring such additional lectures as might be desired by them and this was accepted 'with minor modification to some details'. It was envisaged that these lectures might even be delivered 'in the hall or chambers of the King's Inns'.

The third proposition was similarly acceptable, namely that the benchers, 'in addition to the control they will have as benchers, shall also be ex-officio fellows of the institute, and that a portion of their members shall at all times be members of the council'.

However, there was some difference in respect of the fourth proposition. The institute had stated blankly that 'a course of lectures peculiarly adapted for the apprentices of solicitors and attorneys shall be delivered'. But the benchers referred this back to the council of the institute, 'reserving to the society of the benchers the power of directing and controlling such lectures, in such manner as they shall think expedient'.

The committee's recommendations were to be adopted by the benchers as a body the following month.[53]

24 May 1841 Irish law students, meeting in London, passed a number of resolutions condemning as 'derogatory' the requirement that they attend an English inn of court and regretting that

---

53. Minutes of benchers, 1835–44 (King's Inns MS, pp.94–95, 155–57); Dublin Law Institute, rules and bye-laws 1841 (King's Inns MS); Original rules, 1841 – in Dublin Law Institute papers (NLI MS); *Sel. comm. leg. ed.*, q. 2296 (Lyle), p.329 for 'rules of the society of the Dublin Law Institute'; ibid., p.348 for 'returns made by the benchers of King's Inns to parliament'; ibid., p.356 for 'views of the benchers'.

this 'should continue to be considered by the benchers of the King's Inns, Dublin, an essential qualification for admission to practice'. The debate became 'somewhat warm and protracted when some people turned up at the meeting who were of opinion that the existing system was unexceptional'. But the main body of students went on to appoint a committee and this in turn agreed to send copies of the proceedings to each of the benchers of King's Inns and to publish an account of the proceedings in the press.[54]

25 May 1841 Thomas J. Beasley, solicitor, author of the standard work on *Precedents for the masters' office*, is invited by the institute to deliver lectures aimed at the needs of solicitors and attorneys (see 8 and 19 June, below). On or shortly before this day, a resolution was passed at a meeting of the institute, 'signed by several of the fellows, intimating that it was their desire to establish a course of lectures for the profession of attorney and solicitor'.[55]

28 May 1841 The three rooms called the Solicitors' Rooms, in the new building behind the Four Courts, completed the previous October, were delivered to the solicitors and attorneys by the benchers. The benchers also paid for furnishing the rooms.[56]

29 May 1841 Kennedy acknowledges the return from William Napier of the poor law essay, as altered by the latter. He writes to Napier that 'whatever you dictate me I will do, publish it now or keep it until November for our society'. He says that he can get the essay published in the next number of the *Citizen*, which he will later identify as 'the only liberal periodical we have in Dublin of any stamp'. He encloses a review from the *Citizen* of William Napier's *Peninsular war*.[57]

8 June 1841 Beasley delivers the first of two lectures, as invited on 25 May. These were open to both branches of the profession and took place at the institute. During his first lecture, on the origin and duties to their clients of attorneys and solicitors and on the benefit of a liberal education, Beasley expressed regret that

54. *Saunders's News-letter*, 11 Jun. 1841; *Sel. comm. leg. ed.*, pp.339–48. The committee chairman was F.L. Smyth and H. Cooke was secretary.
55. Beasley, *Lectures* (copy at RIA Haliday pamphlets, vol. 1805, p.1).
56. Benchers' minute book, 1835–44 (King's Inns MS, pp.144, 162–65).
57. Letters, Kennedy to Napier (Bodl. MS, ff. 102–03v, 106); *The Citizen*, iii, no.20 (June 1841), pp.340–46. Kennedy wrote to Napier that the author of the review 'is a great admirer of yourself and your works and will be delighted to correct any mistakes he may have made in fact or opinion . . .

the two branches of the profession are not joined together in one *common* cause, for the general education of the practitioners of the law, and the diffusion of useful and necessary knowledge. But yet, I do hope the time is not far distant, when such may be the case, when petty jealousies will be thrown overboard . . . [58]

14 June 1841 The benchers adopt the recommendations of their committee in relation to the Dublin Law Institute (22 May 1841), 'it being expressly understood that the grant of £400 therein mentioned is made for the current year and no longer'. Bearing in mind that the lords justices had held out no prospect of a charter being granted to the Dublin Law Institute without some 'assurance of its stability and permanence', the qualification which the benchers placed upon their grant was unhelpful. Not surprisingly, thereafter, the attempt to gain a charter was dropped. Kennedy put the best face on this subsequently when he told the select committee of 1846 that, 'on the benchers becoming connected with the institute, it was deemed that the connection was equivalent to any advantage which a charter could confer, and the intention of obtaining a charter was abandoned'.[59]

N.B: On 23 May 1842, when considering whether or not to renew this grant to the Dublin Law Institute, the benchers would refer to '*the proceedings of the past year*'. While the reference to a year ought not to be taken too literally, clearly from this point whatever reservations the benchers had in relation to the institute were to be exacerbated by the course of events.

17 June 1841 The inaugural meeting of the Society of Attorneys and Solicitors of Ireland, formerly the Law Society, takes place. Rules are adopted which show that the society intends 'providing means for the instruction of apprentices'. The committee of twenty-one, which had been 'selected by the profession at large to prepare rules', reported that it had been 'strongly impressed with the opinion, that the education of apprentices should be retained in the hands of the profession, under the control of the judges, and under no circumstances should that control be permitted to fall into other hands'.[60]

    and in future reviews . . . his attention will be directed to any portion or subject you may like the public mind brought to bear upon'.
58. *Legal Reporter*, i (1840-41), pp.356, 259-61; Beasley, *Lectures*.
59. Benchers' minute book, 1835-44 (King's Inns MS, p.169); *Sel. comm. leg. ed.*, q.1172, p.356.
60. *First report of the Society of Attorneys and Solicitors of Ireland, with appendix* (Dublin, 1841).

18 June 1841 A letter from one John Beresford Alcock appears in *Saunders's News-letter* begging the attorneys and solicitors of Ireland not to adopt the report of their committee (see 17 June). The author, who appears to have come from England especially to avail of courses at the Dublin Law Institute, describes the committee's report as a 'jealous or narrow-minded policy'.

19 June 1841 In his second lecture, on the practical duties of attorneys and solicitors and on legal education, Beasley points out that 'until lately, we had no law school; now that one is formed, the two branches of the profession appear to disagree about it, – a sort of puerile jealousy seems to exist'. He hopes that 'jealousies, either public or private, will yield to the general prosperity, and the legislation for the education of the profession will be solid and useful'. The two lectures by Beasley, on 8 and 19 June, were presumably the introductory lectures by a solicitor in Dublin which would be referred to by Kennedy in 1846 as a 'first step' towards an intended special course of education for solicitors.[61]

22 June 1841 Agitated by the continuing advancement of British lawyers to high judicial office in Ireland, and against the backdrop of a general election campaign brought on by the collapse of Melbourne's whig ministry, members of the bar meet to consider the forced retirement of Lord Plunket and his replacement as chancellor by John Campbell, a Scot. The meeting had been requisitioned by eighty-five members of the outer bar. One of these junior counsel was Tristram Kennedy. While two hundred barristers turned up for the meeting, 'the seniors of the profession, instructed by experience, and aware of the disastrous consequences of patriotism in Ireland, had prudently absented themselves'. The meeting resolved that all judicial appointments in Ireland ought to be made from the Irish bar and appointed a committee to convey to the queen an address expressing their views. That address was afterwards delivered to the home secretary and reportedly misplaced by him.

Later, 144 barristers were to declare that they had been absent from the meeting of 22 June and that they disagreed with 'the principle of its proceedings'. The fact that they signed their declaration meant that the government could see where they stood and it was alleged three years later that they were subsequently 'showered' with honours and advancement by the tories, who

---

61. *Saunders's News-letter*, 22 June 1841; Beasley, *Lectures*, p.82; *Sel. comm. leg. ed.*, q.1205.

won the general election of July 1841. O'Flanagan has stated that the disunity of the bar during this period was exploited politically.[62]

July 1841 In a piece published in the *Citizen*, William Napier attacks the poor law in Ireland, writing that 'a direct poor law has been at last forced upon her rulers'. This piece, presumably, is basically the same paper as that which he had prepared for the Dublin Law Institute (above, 29 May).[63]

19 September 1841 Lord Campbell having departed with the whig ministry, the committee of the bar which had opposed his appointment now approach the home secretary appointed by the tory Sir Robert Peel, and once again press the case for an Irishman to be made lord chancellor of Ireland. In his letter on the subject, the chairman of the committee digressed to note that 'the Irish student is forced to spend two years at the English Inns of Court, by an unequal and insulting law, which brands an Irish legal education as insufficient or worthless'. But this protest was just as ineffectual as that against the appointment of Campbell had been, and Edward Sugden became the next lord chancellor of Ireland, a position which he had held also in 1834–35. He was to be the last Englishman to hold the office.[64]

(n.d.) October 1841 Kennedy applies to the London inns for aid, noting that those societies have 'the power and the means . . . of rendering more enduring the existing connection which unites the legal profession of both countries'. These were ambiguous words which did not necessarily signal his approval of the form which that connection then took.[65]

16 October 1841 Beasley publishes his two lectures to the Dublin Law Institute, 'with additions'. Kennedy promises William Napier that he will send to the editor of the *Citizen* a copy of the latter's address to the government on the corn laws.[66]

62. *The Citizen*, iv, no. 23 (Aug. 1841), pp.92–104; Anon., *Memoranda of Irish matters by obscure men of good intention*, pp.1–2, 27–28, 55–73, 80; O'Flanagan, *Lives of the lord chancellors of Ireland*, p.593; Hogan, *Legal profession*, pp.58–59; Plunket, *Life, letters and speeches of Lord Plunket*, ii, 329–46; Kenny, 'Irish ambition', pp. 160–65.
63. *The Citizen*, iv, no.21 (July 1841), pp.73–80.
64. Anon., *Memoranda by obscure men*, p.75.
65. [Kennedy], *Legal education in Ireland*, document no. 6.
66. Letters, Kennedy to Napier (Bodl. MS, f.106); Bruce (ed.), *Life of General Sir William Napier*, ii, 77–8, 568–71; Beasley, *Lectures*.

1 November 1841 Daniel O'Connell becomes lord mayor of Dublin, the first catholic to hold that office. He sees his role as 'offering a first trial in self-government'.[67]

11 November 1841 At a meeting in Radley's Commercial Rooms, Dame Street, Dublin, 'numerously attended', law students adopt a memorial to the benchers of King's Inns. The memorial attacks the current statutory obligation to resort for a period to one of the London inns of court in order to be eligible to be called to the Irish bar. The students suggest that, 'even if the system were acted on, as originally designed, . . . such system would be inadequate . . . [because] the numerous and important differences in the law and practice of the English and Irish courts render it essentially necessary that a system should be established which would have, for its actual as well as declared object, the study of those differences'. The students ask the benchers to procure the abolition of the present system and its substitution by a better one. It was agreed to publish minutes and to send copies to the bar and benchers. Press reports of the meeting include much colourful language from the students, including this:

Shall we say, as we were taunted at the meeting of 24 May last in London, that the Irish bar has not within itself the means of legal education, but that to English offices alone we must look for this advantage? What! When such works are issuing from our press as The Equity and Law Reports, and the Legal Reporter, the works of Messrs. Ferguson, Barry and Keogh, Yeo and Billing, Smythe, Kelly, Longfield and others, the first fruits of awakened activity in the Irish bar.

The students were also complimentary about the Dublin Law Institute. But, with repeal sentiment running high, there were those whose support of the school as a national institution might not enhance its chances of continuing support by the benchers.[68]

1842

7 January 1842 Moving to quash certain rumours in anticipation of the benchers considering the students' memorial of 11 November last, the committee of the law students agitating for an end to the requirement that they attend the London inns issues a statement that they

---

67. MacDonagh, *The emancipist*, p.202.
68. *Legal Reporter*, ii, 22; *Sel. comm. leg. ed.*, pp.339, 341–7; *Saunders's News-letter*, 16 Nov. 1841.

feel it their duty to take notice of a report in circulation derogatory to the character of a body of such respectability as the Dublin Law Institute, that they (the Law Institute) are 'at the bottom' of the proceedings of the Irish law students, thereby insinuating a charge of a support being given by them clandestinely to the committee. The committee, therefore, take this opportunity of contradicting the rumour since neither directly nor indirectly has there been a communication between any of the members of the Law Institute and the committee of the Irish law students.

The committee goes on to proclaim that 'to treat the question of the present system of legal education, divested of reference to nationality, had been our anxious desire', and pointed out that the committee itself had been appointed without regard to religious belief or political creed, 'consisting alike of Protestant and Roman Catholic, Liberal and Conservative'.[69]

11 January 1842 Benchers read the memorial of law students agreed on 11 November last. They record 'no rule' in the matter.[70]

31 January 1842 Both Tristram Kennedy and the archbishop of Dublin, Richard Whately, address members of the institute. The theme of the archbishop's address is 'the intellectual and moral influences of the professions'. Kennedy, in his talk, purports to be confident for the future. He says that the institute 'had its early struggles and difficulties, but these were of shorter duration than might have been reasonably anticipated'. He adds that 'it has survived the pestilential attacks of ignorance, folly, prejudice and malevolence' and claims that, on legal education at present, 'Protestant, Dissenter, Roman Catholic, Whig, Tory, Conservative and Radical stand all united'. Kennedy announces that the societies of Lincoln's Inn and Gray's Inn have each contributed a sum of £100 to support the Dublin Law Institute.

Whately's address steered clear of current controversy. He himself has been said by McDowell to have, 'from the outset of his episcopal career assumed an attitude of contentious detachment from all Irish parties', but John Pitt Kennedy and he shared a very negative view of the Irish poor law.[71]

69. *Saunders's News-letter*, 7 Jan. 1842; *Sel. comm. leg. ed.*, pp.345–46.
70. Benchers' minute book, 1835–44 (King's Inns MS, p.177); Letterbook, 1836–69 (King's Inns MS, for Jan. 1842).
71. Kennedy. *Opening address by the principal of the society, 31 January 1842*; Whately, *Address by his grace the archbishop of Dublin, 31 January 1842*. Copies of full address at RIA Haliday pamphlets, vol.1834. Also see Dublin Law Institute, *Papers*; McDowell, *Ir. public opinion*, p.198.

5 April 1842   Sir Valentine Blake introduces a bill to abolish the requirement for persons wishing to be barristers in Ireland to spend terms in London. But he would have students wait longer for a call in Ireland. His bill also proposes to allow English barristers to practise in Ireland and sets out the circumstances in which Irish barristers might practise in England. Lord Eliot, for the government, reserved his position 'as he had not any representations made to him from Ireland on the subject'.[72]

15 April 1842   Supporting Blake's bill insofar as it proposed to abolish the requirement for residency in London, law students despatch a petition to the benchers of King's Inns asking that their memorial of January last on the subject be reconsidered. But, as before, the benchers record 'no rule'. The benchers appointed a committee to consider Blake's bill and to watch its progress in parliament.[73]

16 April 1842   At a general meeting of the law students of Ireland held at the Commercial Buildings to take into consideration Blake's bill it is unanimously resolved that the secretary of the student group be directed to communicate to Blake the 'surprise and regret of this meeting that any Irish member could be induced to introduce a bill so utterly subversive of the interests and rights of the law students of Ireland'. It was further resolved that the Irish members of parliament be written to soliciting their opposition to the bill, principally on the following and somewhat alarmist grounds:

1st. Because of the bill English barristers as such are permitted to practise at the bar of Ireland.
2nd. Because Irish barristers, after a double term of preparatory study, are by it merely admitted to the degree of special pleader, equity draftsman and conveyancer in England . . . but they are not admissible to the English bar.
3rd. Because of the greatly increased length of previous preparation imposed by it on students before admission to the Irish bar, a monopoly is created in favour of the wealthy and those who have early in life determined to pursue this profession and a manifold additional difficulty is placed in the way of all persons desirous of engaging in it.

72. Hansard, 3, lxi, cols. 1294–5 (5 April 1842); below, pp.197–98.
73. Benchers' minute book, 1835–44 (King's Inns MS, pp.182–83). The benchers' committee consisted of the master of the rolls (Michael O'Loghlen), Judge Crampton, Judge Foster, Baron Lefroy, David Pigot QC, 'Mr Holmes', 'Mr Attorney-General' (Francis Blackburne), 'Mr Blake'.

4th. because by its operation the King's Inns Society of Ireland will be virtually annihilated, inasmuch as it would be competent to practise at the Irish bar by being merely called to the English, the latter course offering inducements of less expense and less time to the Irish student.

Later that evening there was held the first of what were intended to be weekly meetings of the Dublin Law Institute debating society. On this occasion the students debated a matter relating to liens. It was envisaged that debates would involve principles of law or equitable jurisdiction: 'These questions are litigated by them and decided upon by one of the professors, who takes the chair on the occasion, in the same manner as they may have been already, or might be argued in court'. Hardey took the chair on this occasion. Students at the University of London had founded a similar debating society in earlier days under the guidance of Andrew Amos. Both Napier and Whiteside had belonged to it. The debating society at King's Inns in the 1830s was less strictly devoted to legal questions.[74]

18 April 1842   In compliance with the resolution of 16 April, the honorary secretaries of the law students, James Coffey and John Pigot, write to William Smith O'Brien MP asking him to oppose Blake's bill, and adding that 'we believe we express the sentiments of the Irish law students generally when we state to you, that the present system faulty and objectionable as it appears to us is highly preferable to the one proposed to be enacted by Sir Valentine Blake'. John Pigot was a son of David Pigot QC, who had supported the establishment of the Dublin Law Institute and who had been appointed one of the benchers to monitor Blake's bill.[75]

20 April 1842   Blake moves the second reading of his Barristers (Ireland) Bill, saying that 'the student had such a means of obtaining a knowledge of his profession in Dublin, that it was unnecessary for him to come to London'. Mr Serjeant Jackson opposes, stating that he had received a letter from Pigot, as secretary to the Irish law students, expressing 'on the part of nearly the whole body, their opposition to the bill'. John O'Connell and Mr Hardy spoke briefly. Mr Murphy presented a petition from law students. The house decided to put off the bill.[76]

74. William Smith O'Brien papers (NLI MS); *Saunders's News-letter*, 20 Apr. 1842; *Sel. comm. leg. ed.*, q.1269; Law Students Debating Society secretary's book, 1830–33 (King's Inns MS, passim).
75. William Smith O'Brien papers (NLI MS).
76. *Hansard, 3*, lxii, col. 894 (20 April 1842); Copy of letter, Pigot to Jackson,

30 April 1842 James A. Lawson, newly appointed professor of political economy at Trinity College Dublin, delivers a lecture at the institute on 'law as it relates to the economic condition of a people'. Recently called to the bar, Lawson himself had earlier attended some of the institute's courses as a student.[77]

7 May 1842 Thomas Wright BL delivers a lecture to the institute on 'the duties and licence of counsel'.[78]

10 May 1842 The Society of the Attorneys and Solicitors of Ireland, formerly the Law Society, issues its first report. This shows that one of the principal objects of the society is 'the instruction of apprentices'. The report refers to the difficulty which the society has encountered in obtaining possession of all of that building behind the Four Courts

which was avowedly erected for the use of the profession, and more especially the large room on the ground-floor, which it was hoped they would have had it in their power to appropriate as a lecture-room, but which, instead of being available for so desirable a purpose, has been allotted to be accommodation of a coffee-room-keeper, thus throwing, at least for the present, a serious obstacle in the way of one of the most important objects of the society.

The report adds: 'it will be the duty of the society to provide proper accommodation for the delivery of lectures, and otherwise improving the practical education of their apprentices'.[79]

23 May 1842 The benchers consider Kennedy's memorial for a renewal of the first grant to the Dublin Law Institute, 'or such further grant as the benchers shall think proper'. They refer the matter to the same committee which had considered the application of 1841 and instructed its members, '*to enquire into the proceedings of the past year*, and into the expediency of making any further grant to the Institute, having regard to the consideration of the expediency of maintaining a law school in Ireland'. That portion of the terms of reference which has been italicised here was to be omitted by Bencher Lyle in evidence to the 1846 select

18 April 1842, at William Smith O'Brien papers (NLI MS); *Saunders's News-letter*, 23 April 1842.
77. Dublin Law Institute, *Papers*, p.21; *Sel. comm. leg. ed.*, qq.1771–79, 1892.
78. Dublin Law Institute, *Papers*, p.29. Also copy at ref. 'NLI Thom, p.29'.
79. *Report of the Committee of the Society of the Attorneys and Solicitors of Ireland, 10 May 1842* (Dublin, 1842).

committee on legal education. Lyle would also express his belief that the last phrase in the resolution, 'having regard to . . . the expediency of maintaining a law school', was added 'upon the expression of a doubt by one of the benchers, as to whether such law schools were of value or not. . . . and my recollection is that it was the late lord chancellor, Sir Edward Sugden, who was in the chair, and who desired that these words should be included in the reference'.[80]

4 June 1842 Michael Barry delivers a lecture in the criminal law course on 'legal calculation and the division of time'. He would later appear before the select committee on legal education.[81]

24 June 1842 At the R.D.S. Joseph Napier delivers a lecture closing the current session of the Dublin Law Institute. His theme is 'Master and Servant'. At the end of the lecture he refers to the benchers' decision of 23 May last, and says that 'the professors of the Law Institute have suddenly and unexpectedly discovered that they may soon stand discharged'. He remarks that he and his colleagues have consented 'to the almost gratuitous toil of taking charge of the professorships. The extent of our sacrifices I will merely say was not inconsiderable'. Napier says that it had been expected that 'attendance on a course of lectures would soon be required as a systematic accompaniment to, if not a substitute for, a course of dinners'. So he purports to be puzzled by the apparent about-face of the benchers and notes that

in the course of the present session some unexpected movement has taken place, and the propriety of continuing the annual grant has recently been referred to a committee of the benchers, who are prepared to recommend the discontinuance of this paltry grant to the Law School of the Institute.[82]

28 June 1842 Thomas Beasley, solicitor, delivers a special lecture 'on the records of Ireland'.[83]

September 1842 Andrew Palles, father of the future chief baron, is committed to prison for debt and struck off the roll of solicitors

80. Benchers' minute book, 1835–44 (King's Inns MS, p.186: 23 May 1842, p.189: 2 Nov. 1842); *Sel. comm. leg. ed.*, q.2358.
81. Dublin Law Institute, *Papers*, p. 37. Also copy at ref. 'NLI Thom, p.37'; *Sel. comm. leg. ed.*, pp.119–33.
82. *Saunders's News-letter*, 24 June 1842.
83. Dublin Law Institute, *Papers*, p.45. Also copy at ref. 'NLI Thom, p.45'.

by Chancellor Sugden. He would later be restored. Related proceedings reveal that James Joseph Hardey, occasional professor at the Dublin Law Institute, has forged some papers in order to conceal professional neglect on his part. Sugden orders that Hardey's behaviour be investigated by the King's Inns.[84]

October 1842   *The Nation* newspaper is founded by Duffy, an experienced catholic journalist, Dillon, a catholic barrister, and Davis, a protestant barrister and pamphleteer.[85]

2 November 1842   The committee of the benchers, appointed in May, finally reports on the matter of a renewal of the grant to the Dublin Law Institute. Its report confirms Napier's suspicions of 23 June 1842 as the committee has decided that 'we are not prepared to recommend any further grant to be made to the Institute out of the funds of the honorable society'. Notwithstanding that many of the council of the Institute were also benchers, the King's Inns immediately accepted the advice of its committee. Kennedy noted later that, 'the application not having received their favourable consideration, the professors of the institute decided upon discontinuing their course of instruction for the future'.

The benchers who signed the report, effectively a death warrant for the institute, were Michael O'Loghlen, Francis Blackburne, George Bennett, Richard Moore, Robert Holmes and Thomas Lefroy. The first four had personally and warmly endorsed the institute when it was first mooted and Blackburne, Bennett, Moore and Holmes had allowed themselves to be made members of its council. It has been seen how O'Loghlen waxed eloquent on legal education at a dinner in the Dublin Law Institute in January 1841 and even Lefroy, although not directly associated with the institute, was a person one might have expected to be well disposed towards any experiment in legal education, given his own experiences in his youth. But it was also the case that Blackburne, Bennett and Holmes had been among those who signed a public protest against the action of their colleagues in deciding in June 1841 to address the government on the appointment of English

---

84. Delany, *Christopher Palles*, pp.16–18. Delany says that of Hardey's fate 'history is silent' but the records of King's Inns certainly are not. They show that, eventually, in 1845 he was struck off for his unprofessional conduct in connection with the preparation, alteration, cancellation and execution of the deeds. An appeal, in which Hardey was represented by his fellow professor, Joseph Napier, was to no avail. (Benchers' minute book, 1844–49: King's Inns MS, pp.33–38, 101–02.)

85. McDowell, *Ir. public opinion*, p.231.

lawyers as chancellors in Ireland. Moore and Lefroy had held aloof from signing either the address or the protest (above, 22 June 1841).[86]

18 November 1842 Saunders's News-letter reports allegations by Kennedy that Sugden had been responsible for the decision of the benchers not to continue funding his institution. In 1846, the evidence of two witnesses, one a bencher and the other a professor of law at Trinity College, would lend weight to Kennedy's opinion.[87]

26 November 1842 The *Legal Reporter* carries statements by professors of the institute who disassociate themselves from Kennedy's remarks of the previous week and withdraw from the institute. Ambitious lawyers were unlikely to risk a direct confrontation with the chancellor.[88]

---

86. Benchers' minute book, 1835–44 (King's Inns MS, pp.189–92: Nov. 1842); Scrapbook (King's Inns MS); *Sel. comm. leg. ed.*, p.lxii; Lefroy, *Memoir of Chief Justice Lefroy*, pp.11, 20.
87. *Sel. comm. leg. ed.*, qq. 2358 (Lyle), 3111–12 (Longfield).
88. *Legal Reporter*, iii, 29–30.

CHAPTER SIX

'Wyse's committee': the Irish genesis of the select committee on legal education, 1846

IF KENNEDY WAS BITTERLY disappointed by the collapse of his Dublin Law Institute, he did not give in to despair. His ambition was to improve the standard of legal education in Ireland and this objective might be achieved in other ways. He had a powerful ally in parliament in the shape of Thomas Wyse, who was very active in highlighting Irish grievances during the conservative administration of Sir Robert Peel, from 1841 to 1845. On 22 May 1843, Kennedy had Wyse lay on the table of the house of commons a petition 'for better regulating the legal profession in Ireland'. This was intended to be the basis on which to ground a motion for the appointment of a parliamentary committee to enquire into the subject. It must be said that this was just one of many different petitions presented on that day alone, hundreds of others relating to a variety of matters from the Factories Bill to the pawnbrokers of Tipperary. Kennedy's petition was simply 'presented and read and ordered to lie upon the table', but it would later prove to have been a slow-burning fuse which eventually ignited parliament's impatience with the legal profession in Ireland and England.[1]

The petition recited a brief history of the Dublin Law Institute, and noted that 'Ireland is probably the only civilized country in the world in which facilities are not afforded for the study of jurisprudence'. It took a sideswipe at the constitution of the King's Inns, noting that there was no solicitor and only one junior counsel a bencher and that the judges themselves now constituted 'little more than one fourth' of the council, most of the benchers being queen's counsel. There was a hint here of tension between the outer and inner bar, similar to that reflected in the absence of queen's counsel from the meeting of 1841 which had been called to press for the appointment of an Irish chancellor. Kennedy's petition concluded by asking parliament, firstly,

1. *DNB*, s.v. Wyse, Thomas; [Kennedy], *Legal education in Ireland*; Kennedy, *The state and the benchers*, p.21.

to facilitate the acquisition of legal knowledge in Ireland, whether through the instrumentality of the Dublin Law Institute, or in any other manner that may be thought more advisable. Second, in order to [sic] a revision of the laws which regulate the admission to, and government of, the legal profession in Ireland, upon a basis which may at least afford to this country the advantages enjoyed by the respective branches of the profession in England. Thirdly, with a view to [sic] securing that the future expenditure of the funds of the society of King's Inns shall be in unison with the wishes of the body at large, conformable to the act hereinbefore referred to, and in furtherance of those important objects for which the benchers have declared themselves responsible.

On the morning following the presentation of this petition, George J. Bell, law professor in the University of Edinburgh, despatched to Kennedy a solicited letter supportive of the Dublin Law Institute. The principal of the institute was slowly gathering ammunition to use against the benchers, and in November that same year won from Professor Simon Greenleaf of Harvard University a letter conveying the supportive opinion of the judges of the U.S. Supreme Court on the general question of reforming legal education.[2] But the time was not yet ripe to move for further parliamentary action, and again in 1844 and 1845, under the advice of Wyse, a motion for the appointment of a committee of the house of commons was deferred. But in the latter year Wyse undertook to move for an enquiry in 1846.[3]

In the interim, Kennedy continued to muster support for the provision of legal education, although some who backed him may have alienated as many potential supporters as they won over. Thus, during 1844, an anonymous pamphlet was published protesting against the appointment to office in Ireland of Englishmen and of those Irish who were 'hearty supporters of the English Interest'. The author recalled that,[4]

during the relaxation of the maintenance of the English Interest, under the ministry of Melbourne, some members of the legal profession in Ireland, supported by an Irish chancellor, made an effort to form a legal college, under the name of the 'Irish Law Institute'. It was expected that this college would have afforded the means of acquiring and giving evidence of intellectual eminence, of Irish growth, and of Irish education; and its opening was attended with great success. But immediately after the restoration of the English Interest, in the year 1841, this college was closed and the attempt altogether crushed – a consummation which was

2. *Law Times*, vi, 245, 281; *Sel. comm. leg. ed.*, app. iv, no.11, pp.349–50.
3. Kennedy, *The state and the benchers*, p.21.
4. Anon., *Memoranda by obscure men*, pp.27–28.

effected, according to the published charge of the principal of the Law Institute, by the active interference of the English Chancellor in Ireland.

The author did not advance Kennedy's cause by recalling his indelicate outburst of 1842. Moreover, the writer also attacked the requirement that Irish students attend the English inns, thereby associating Kennedy by implication with a campaign which had interfered with his immediate ambitions in the past. Not that the principal of the Dublin Law Institute himself avoided bruising conservative sensibilities. Thus, in February 1844, he wrote to the King's Inns asking how he could gain access to the accounts of that society. He was informed that the only way in which he might achieve this was by an order of the house of commons. Later that month the benchers may have been taken aback when, on a motion from Hayter, they were actually instructed to make financial returns to parliament.[5]

In May 1844, Kennedy received a reply from Judge Joseph Story of the U.S. supreme court, who extended his support to the institute's efforts. According to one authority, it was Story's appointment as a professor at Harvard in 1829 that, more than any other factor, popularised the law faculties in the American universities: 'While the majority of students still read law in offices, the best went to Harvard to study under Story and his successors'.[6] But if Kennedy was primarily focused on legal training, his friend Wyse was not. The latter was deeply involved in the general university question, making a major speech to parliament in July 1844, and easing the way for the bill which would soon establish Queen's Colleges in Belfast, Cork and Galway. Yet Wyse always bore in mind the need for professional legal education. In August 1844, in the course of a long letter to the Provincial Colleges Committee of Cork, which was largely devoted to the contemporary debate about the nature of university education, Wyse noted incidentally that 'the Provincial Colleges offer great facilities for preparatory or elementary general legal instruction . . . but a special institution might with great advantage be established in Dublin'. He praised the Dublin Law Institute and, passing over the awkward matter of its demise, wrote that

---

5. Letterbook, 1836–69 (King's Inns MS, p.91: 5 Feb. 1844); *Sel. comm. leg. ed.*, app. iv, no.10, p.349.

6. Abel-Smith and Stevens, *Lawyers and the courts: a sociological study of the English legal system 1750–1965*, p.26, n.3. In 1811 Story, aged 32, had been appointed to the U.S. supreme court. He continued to hold the judgeship when appointed at Harvard.

it is not here necessary to refer to the circumstances which checked its progress, but a hope may be entertained that it may yet be resumed under still more favourable auspices. I took the first steps to obtain at least a parliamentary inquiry into the practicability of such measure, and yet trust such inquiry will be granted.[7]

From the terms of this letter, it seems that Wyse and Kennedy had jointly worked out a strategy, whereby the benchers would ultimately have to respond constructively to parliamentary pressure for reform, or face the likelihood of the Dublin Law Institute finally receiving statutory recognition. But the progress of the Queen's Colleges bill and the furious sectarian debate which erupted around it early in 1845 kept Wyse occupied and provided unfavourable circumstances for parliament calmly to consider the matter of legal training. In May 1845, with controversy raging over various educational issues, some law students presented a memorial to the benchers of King's Inns requesting the publication of lectures in Common Law which had been given by Whiteside and Napier. The students wishfully described the Dublin Law Institute as 'the law school of your honourable society'. It was to take the benchers six months to decide against the students' request. They did so just as the Dublin Law Institute reopened its doors for the first time in four years and recommenced lectures with a course in Common Law, delivered again by Joseph Napier, who by now was a queen's counsel. To this course there was free admission and the average attendance was 115 daily. There followed another course in Equity, with 30 students attending. Also in November 1845 the English inns of court began a series of lectures by three readers. These ran until March 1846.[8]

The need for further instruction in legal matters was underlined in 1845 by the publication that year of a second edition of Samuel Warren's *Popular and practical introduction to law studies*. It was essentially a new work, running to around 1,000 pages and including chapters on the law in force in Ireland and on the requirements for entry to, and call at, the English inns of court. In his preface, the author referred to 'the fearful extent to which our profession is over-stocked'.

7. *Hansard*, 3, lxxvi, cols.1121 f. Atkinson, *Irish education*, pp.125–26; Wyse, *Notes on education reform in Ireland*, pp.93–94.
8. Benchers' minute book, 1844–49 (King's Inns MS, p.43: 3 Nov. 1845); *Hansard*, 3, lxxv, col. 677 (7 April 1846); *Sel. comm. leg. ed.*, app. iv, no. 6, p.338; Kennedy, *The state and the benchers*, p.21; Holdsworth, *History of English law*, xiv, 231; *Ormrod Report*, p.9. Only a few of the inaugural lectures and some guest talks had been published in 1839–42.

As the year drew to a close, the Dublin Law Institute attracted further attention in London with the *Law Times* noting that the institute had just published certain 'interesting papers on legal education'. These were various letters of support and other documents which set Kennedy's experiment in an international context. Printed and circulated in small numbers they included, 'Imperial Law School of St. Petersburg', 'Views of the judges of the Supreme Court of the United States in reference to legal education, as communicated in a letter from Professor Greenleaf of Harvard University to the principal of the Dublin Law Institute', 'Letter from the late honorable Joseph Story of the United States Supreme Court to the principal of the Dublin Law Institute' and 'Letter from the late George J. Bell, law professor in the University of Edinburgh, to the principal of the Dublin Law Institute'.[9]

In the spring of 1846, with both winter and the Queen's Colleges act behind him, Wyse turned his attention once more to legal education. He had never forgotten Kennedy's petition of 1843, each year considering a way of advancing its objectives at an appropriate moment. Finally, on 24 March 1846, he gave notice of his intention to move in April for the appointment of a select committee to enquire into the state of legal education in Ireland, and the means for its further improvement and extension. At this stage the motion did not encompass England. An anonymous author in the *Law Times* of London rejoiced at Wyse's action, recognising it as 'in fact being a renewal of the proceedings commenced by that honourable member in the house, the session of 1842–3'. This author also referred to the recent revival of the Dublin Law Institute, claiming that

Whatever success attended that undertaking has been the result of almost individual exertion; the talented professors, during this session, are giving gratuitous courses of instruction to the law students, who eagerly avail themselves of the only aid Ireland now affords towards the study of the law. But, we would ask, should this important branch of national education be left thus unprovided for in the sister kingdom? What higher test of its importance could be desired than the fact that men of unrivalled talent, such as Messrs Whiteside and Napier, come forward during the pressure of term, and contribute their valuable time towards the guidance of the hitherto neglected student.

The *Law Times* further reported that Kennedy was finding new ways to stimulate interest in his revived institute. A book prize

---

9. *Law Times*, vi, 245, 281. For a copy of these papers see NLI ref. 'Thom, NL, 1846, pt 2'. This includes a copy of the argument of Joseph Napier, QC, in the house of lords in *Dungannon* v. *Smith* (44 pp.).

had been offered by him 'for the most approved original essay to be delivered to the secretary of the institute before 25 May 1846, on "The necessity and advantages of an enlightened system of legal education as affecting the social improvement of the country"'. It was also announced that there would be voluntary exams held by the institute in Trinity term 1846 and that certificates would be awarded on the basis of these.[10]

As he had promised in March, Wyse rose in the house of commons on 7 April and moved for the appointment of a select committee to enquire into the state of legal education in Ireland and the means for its further improvement and extension. In the course of doing so, he gave the commons background information relating to the experiences of the Dublin Law Institute. He recalled the address which, in January 1841, Michael O'Loghlen had delivered at a dinner in the institute in Wyse's honour. This, as we saw above, illustrated the difficulties faced by law students. He also acknowledged the fact that the English inns had under consideration the establishment of a teaching institution to comprise representatives of the four London inns. His motion was passed, the terms of reference of the committee at this stage still confined to legal education in Ireland.[11]

Three days later, again in the *Law Times* of London, an anonymous author returned to the subject of Irish legal education. This time the King's Inns came under attack:

There are advantages in fixing the Irish student in London, which would make it undesirable to dispense with that portion of his apprenticeship. It must tend greatly to the removal of prejudices of nation, sect, and party, enlarge the sympathies, widen the experience, and assist mightily in preparing him for the duties of an advocate, so infinitely varied in their demands.

But something should be done to teach him a little *law*, either at home, or here, or at both. Ireland may fairly claim a professor or two for her law students, and if King's Inn [sic] be too poor to provide them, they should be furnished by the state. But surely the admission fees of the Dublin students would amply provide for their instruction, if properly applied. Before the hand is put into the public purse, it should be ascertained that the corporation entrusted with the nursing of the embryo lawyers is too poor to provide teachers for them. Should it prove to be, then let the state help them. But the revenues of King's Inn and their applications, must first be investigated, and we trust that an inquiry will be instituted without delay.[12]

10. *Law Times*, vi, 530–31.
11. *Hansard*, 3, lxxv, col.677 (7 April 1846); *Sel. comm. leg. ed.*, preface. O'Loghlen had died at Brighton in 1842.
12. *Law Times*, vii, 37.

On the last day of April, the members of the select committee were nominated and appointed by the commons. Seven were Irish and nine British. Most were lawyers themselves. Their politics were a balance of conservative and liberal. The bulk of the British represented constituencies far from the capital, a fact which may have inclined them to view the London inns with some scepticism.

It was scarcely surprising that seven members were Irish when the committee was still mandated only to consider the position in relation to legal education in Ireland. The seven were *Thomas Wyse* himself, who became chairman, *Sir William Somerville*, a liberal from Drogheda, *William Watson*, a liberal from Kinsale, *Sir Edmund Hayes*, a tory from Donegal, *Alexander McCarthy*, recently elected on the repeal ticket in Cork city, *George Hamilton*, a tory for Dublin University and *Daniel O'Connell*. The endorsement of O'Connell may have been considered important by the chairman but 'the counsellor' never attended any sessions of the committee. O'Connell, Watson, McCarthy and Hamilton had all been called to the bar in Ireland. A number of the British members were also barristers. Thus, *Sir Howard Elphinstone* was a magistrate and deputy-lieutenant for the county of Sussex. A barrister, he had formerly practised as an advocate at Doctors' Commons. He was regarded as a radical reformer and represented the constituency of Lewes. *William Christie*, representing Weymouth, was a barrister on the western circuit in England. A liberal, he had been private secretary to the earl of Minto when the latter was first lord of the admiralty. *William Ewart* (who was added to the committee on 24 July) was a barrister and a member of the council of University College, London. Although representing the Scottish constituency of Dumfries, he had sat for a decade for Liverpool and Wigan, and was the son of a merchant and broker at Liverpool. He was a radical reformer, approving of triennial parliaments and the ballot amongst other progressive measures. For his part, *Andrew Rutherford* of Leith was a leading advocate at the Scottish bar. He tended to hold conservative sympathies. *Spencer Horatio Walpole*, elected for Midhurst earlier in 1846, had been called to the bar in 1831, while *Richard Godson* of Kidderminster was a queen's counsel and author of *A practical treatise on the law of patents for inventions, and on that of copyright*. Appointed counsel for the admiralty in February 1845, Godson was a conservative who voted against the admission of dissenters to the universities. But he favoured the emancipation of jews and negroes. *Sir Thomas Wilde* of Worcester, afterwards became Lord Chancellor Truro. The other British members were *Richard Milnes* of Pontefract, who had published an account of his tour in Greece, and *Henry*

Bingham Baring of Marlborough, an East India proprietor and tory. The East India Company's college provided its students with some instruction in law.[13]

If in theory there were so many weighty members that the committee ran the risk of being unwieldy, in practice only a few of them participated actively in its proceedings. Indeed, four of the members never attended any of the eighteen sessions at which witnesses appeared or the final session at which the report was agreed. These were O'Connell, Wilde, Rutherford and Godson. Moreover, Hayes and McCarthy attended only the very first session, while Baring, Walpole, Watson and Elphinstone were present on only four or five occasions. So who then was most active? For his part, the chairman, Thomas Wyse, never missed a session. This was notwithstanding the fact that half-way through the committee's hearings he was appointed secretary to the board of control for India, the liberal Lord John Russell having replaced the conservative Robert Peel as prime minister. Most attentive after Wyse was William Christie, the barrister from the western circuit in England, who missed only one meeting of the committee. George Hamilton of Dublin University, who may have held an informal watching brief for the Irish benchers, was present at sixteen of the nineteen sessions, while Richard Milnes, the gentleman from Pontefract, attended twelve. William Somerville's attendance improved markedly following his appointment in July 1846 as under-secretary of state for the colonies. Having missed nine of the first eleven meetings, he managed to make it to seven of the last eight. William Ewart attended three of the five meetings which took place after he joined the committee on 24 July. As might be expected, most of the questioning of witnesses was conducted by the chairman himself. But a number of other members also intervened from time to time.[14]

On 5 May 1846, just ten days before the committee heard its first witness, the house of commons extended its terms of inquiry to include the state of legal education in England. Before the end of August twenty-seven witnesses would appear before the committee. The benchers of King's Inns took a relaxed attitude towards the whole investigation. On 22 May, when two sessions had already passed, the benchers in Dublin appointed a special committee to take such steps as they should think fit on the subject of the enquiry. But the special committee does not appear to have met

13. *Dod's parliamentary companion 1851*, passim; *King's Inns adm.*, passim; *Sel. comm. leg. ed.*, pp.46–56. The committee's report gives only 'Mr O'Connell' but O'Shaughnessy, 'Legal education', 126, identifies this member as Daniel.
14. *Sel. comm. leg. ed.*, passim; *DNB*, s.v. Wyse, Thomas.

until 22 June. At this meeting, the benchers were read a letter from 'the recorder', presumably of Dublin, who pointed out that his 'colleague', George Hamilton, who was on the select committee and who represented Dublin University in parliament, could be counted on to 'give every assistance in his power'. The recorder added that he had seen Wyse and that 'Wyse professes great anxiety to do nothing hostile to the feelings of the benchers and the authorities of the profession'. The committee of benchers decided merely to write to Hamilton to be kept informed. There is no explanation as to how one of the benchers, Acheson Lyle, came a fortnight later to give evidence to the select committee in London. He had been present in 1839 at the first introductory lecture of the Dublin Law Institute and appears always to have supported it, being a member of its council. His evidence was not particularly flattering of the King's Inns and Hamilton's interventions during it seem intended, if anything, to point up deficiencies. There is no other information in the records of King's Inns to indicate that the benchers gave the select committee or its deliberations further attention. They seem to have been much more concerned at this time with matters relating to the accommodation of records and taxing officers at the Four Courts.[15]

On 14 August 1846, the committee heard from the last two witnesses to give evidence before it. In three months it had met eighteen times and examined twenty-seven witnesses. Seven of these had travelled over from Ireland (Kennedy, Barry, Lawson, Lyle, Mahony, La Touche and Longfield), while two more were Irish barristers working abroad (Moriarty, Norton), and the testimony of these nine Irishmen (33% of the witnesses) accounts for 115 (38%) of the 302 printed pages of evidence. In the appendix to the report, papers delivered to the committee by Irish witnesses take up 51 (57%) of the 89 pages devoted to documents which were submitted. The vast bulk of these Irish papers were provided by Tristram Kennedy and related to the Dublin Law Institute.

The witnesses fell into two main categories, those from the universities and those from the professions. The former, of which there were twelve, were *Thomas Starkie* QC, professor of civil law at Cambridge and a former pupil of Chitty; *Edward Shepherd Creasy*, professor of ancient and modern history at University College, London, Rev. *Joseph William Blakesley*, formerly a tutor at Trinity College, Cambridge; *William Empson*, law professor in

---

15. Benchers' minute book, 1844–49 (King's Inns MS, p.84: 22 May 1846); Standing and education committees, 1846–73 (King's Inns MS, p.3: 22 June 1846).

the East India college at Haileybury; *John Thomas Graves*, examiner in laws and jurisprudence in the University of London; *Andrew Amos*, previously the innovative lecturer in law at University College, London; *John Robert Kenyon*, a successor of Blackstone's as Vinerian professor of common law at Oxford; *James Anthony Lawson*, professor of political economy at Trinity College Dublin; *Mountifort Longfield*, by now professor of feudal and English law in Trinity College Dublin; *Philip Bliss*, registrar of the University of Oxford; *Edward Moriarty*, an Irishman abroad, who was a specialist in continental law and who had taught at the Royal Academy of Trade in Berlin. Last of the witnesses was *Allan Maconochie*, professor of law in the University of Glasgow and an advocate. Some of these men, like Maconochie, Starkie, Creasy and Amos, had considerable personal experience of legal practice, but they appeared principally in connection with their academic roles. Most of these witnesses did not think that the prime object of law courses in the universities was to train professionals, an education in legal principles being held to be equally desirable for that general class of people from whom magistrates were appointed or for those likely to occupy various administrative or official positions in church and state. Creasy, for example, wished to avoid examinations which were 'too frequent, too stringent and too emulative', fearing that they would discourage the sort of people who become magistrates, but who would not wish to practise law: 'you might drive away all but mere lawyers from the inns of court', he warned the committee.[16]

But from the testimony of these witnesses it became clear that some college professors gave little or no instruction of any kind in law, while those who did so found few students in attendance. As noted earlier, the numbers who flocked to the Dublin Law Institute, albeit something of a novelty, might be compared favourably with the seven students on average who attended Longfield's lectures in Trinity or the four or five candidates who presented themselves annually for the degree of bachelor of laws at University College, London.[17]

The fifteen other witnesses, called principally because of their professional experience, were *Joseph Phillimore*, a civil lawyer and 'advocate exercent in Doctors' Commons'; *Richard Bethell*, bencher in the Middle Temple; *Thomas Taylor*, a solicitor of long standing who provided a description of the origins and functions of the Manchester Law Association; *Tristram Kennedy* of the Dublin

---

16. *Sel. comm. leg. ed.*, q. 426.
17. ibid., pp.iv–v, qq. 682–85, qq. 2833, 3777.

Law Institute; *Michael Barry*, an Irish barrister in his thirteenth year of practice; *Sir George Stephen*, thirty years a solicitor in London and author of *The adventures of an attorney in search of practice* [!]; *Robert Maugham*, secretary and solicitor to the Incorporated Law Society, London; *Acheson Lyle*, by now chief remembrancer of Ireland; *Pierce Mahony*, an Irish solicitor of thirty-two years standing; *Edward Turner Payne*, articled clerk to an English solicitor; *Theophilus Digges La Touche*, Dublin solicitor since 1828; *Thomas Norton*, an Irish barrister who had acted as first puisne judge of British Guiana before becoming chief justice of Newfoundland; *James Stewart*, twenty years at the English bar; *Lord Brougham and Vaux*, the former chancellor of England who had recently chaired meetings of the twelve benchers deputed by the four inns of court in London to consider the future of legal education; *Lord Campbell*.

It is clear from the questioning of the witnesses that the committee believed legal education to be completely inadequate, both in relation to the needs of the public generally and the profession specifically. The chairman felt strongly that some education in law ought to be part of the general education of any person intent on holding an administrative position in public life. The universities were seen by the committee as the places to provide such basic training, and it was thought desirable that substantial law faculties should be established to give a range of new law courses, leading together to the award of law degrees or constituting individually portion of the requirement for certain other degrees such as the bachelor in arts. Future barristers and solicitors ought then to attend the university courses, but they would also need special professional training, which could be provided at some new institution run by the profession itself. Committee members found themselves contending with the view, which nobody appeared before it to represent but which clearly found expression over drinks in the clubs, that many brilliant and very many adequate lawyers had risen in the profession without any elaborate scheme of legal education and that there was no need for great and possibly burthensome reforms, 'or, in other words, there is nothing to be hoped for which we do not now possess, from an improved system of legal education'. Questions were regularly aimed at eliciting rebuttals of this viewpoint. The chairman of the committee also angled for witnesses to support examinations, and some did so willingly. Amos believed that the inns should test students and, he added, 'I would let the comparative proficiency of every individual be made public'. Brougham purported to share this view, claiming that without exams 'lecturing is of no real use'.

1 Sarah Graham, who married Tristram Kennedy.
  Artist unknown but possibly Henry MacManus.

2 The King's Inns and Registry of Deeds, by William Brocas, *c.*1818.
   The ground in front of the buildings was not yet laid out.

3 King's Inns and Royal Canal Harbour, by George Petrie, 1821. The spur of the Royal Canal which led by the Foster aqueduct to the Royal Canal Harbour at Broadstone was long ago filled in. See *D.H.R.* xiii (1952), p.63.

4 No. 10 Henrietta Street as it was when Kennedy acquired it (then no. 9), from *Dublin Penny Journal*, 13 Feb. 1836.

5 No. 10 Henrietta Street, as it is today, by Séamus Curran.

6 Stairs and hall of no. 10 Henrietta Street, 1980s.

7 Parlour of no. 10 Henrietta Street, 1980s.

A LECTURE,
"Relating to Master and Servant,"
WILL BE DELIVERED
IN THE THEATRE
OF
THE ROYAL DUBLIN SOCIETY,
On FRIDAY, JUNE the 24th
AT FOUR O'CLOCK,
By PROFESSOR NAPIER, Esq.

8–9 Hand-bills advertising introductory lectures for the Dublin Law Institute by Joseph Napier and James Whiteside.

DUBLIN LAW INSTITUTE.
An Introductory Lecture
On the Study of the Criminal Law,
Will be delivered in the Theatre of the Royal Dublin Society,
On Saturday, 8th February, at half-past 4 o'Clock, p. m.
By JOSEPH NAPIER, Esq.
Professor of Common Law in the Institute.

FREE ADMISSION TO THE ABOVE LECTURE.

The Separate Course of Class Lectures
IN THE COMMON LAW DEPARTMENT,
Will be delivered in the Lecture-Room of the Dublin Law Institute, previous to the Spring Circuit, according to the following arrangement:

JAMES WHITESIDE, Esq.
On the Law of NISI PRIUS,
On Saturday, the 8th February, at half-past 7 o'Clock, p. m. and each succeeding Wednesday and Saturday, at the same hour

JOSEPH NAPIER, Esq.
On CRIMINAL LAW and CIVIL BILL PROCEEDING,
Each Tuesday, (commencing 11th February), at half-past 4 o'Clock, and each Friday, at half-past 7 o'Clock.

TICKETS TO THE ENTIRE - 2 GUINEAS.

Printed at John Hoare's General Printing-Office, 14, Hawkins'-Street.

10 Joseph Napier by Thomas Bridgford, exhibited Dublin 1844.
11 James Whiteside, by A. Scott.

12 Sir Thomas Wyse MP, by John Partridge, 1846.

13 J. A. Lawson. Artist unknown.

14 Sir Michael O'Loghlen, master of the rolls, by George Mulvany, 1843.

15 The old lecture room at King's Inns, 1958.
16 Benchers' council room, King's Inns, 1958.

17 Edward Burtenshaw Sugden, last English chancellor of Ireland, by his daughter, Charlotte Sugden.

18 William Conyngham Plunket, lord chancellor of Ireland, by Charles Grey, 1840.

19 Salver accompanying a service of plate presented to Tristram Kennedy.

The inscription reads: 'Presented to Tristram Kennedy by the electors of the county of Louth and others his admirers as a memorial of their sincere respect for the incorruptible integrity and inflexible consistency of his public conduct and steadfast fidelity to the liberties of the people during the period in which he represented that county in the commons house of parliament, 1852–7'.

For further details see *Newry Examiner*, 15 Aug. 1857.

20 Tristram Kennedy, photographed on the hustings in Louth, 1865.

21 Philip Callan MP by Sydney Prior Hall.

Although scrawled on this sketch are the words, 'Phil Callan (?) suggested forger of the letters', the question mark appears to refer to the matter of forgery and not to the identity of the person sketched. That this is Callan may be seen by comparing the sketch with the group and key at *The Illustrated London News*, 9 March 1889, reproduced in Kissane, *Parnell*, pp. 74–75.

22 Photograph of Tristram Kennedy in old age.

23 Dining hall, Middle Temple, mid-nineteenth century.

Mrs J. E. Edgell, librarian and keeper of the records at the Middle Temple, writes of this unsigned drawing:

> The print itself is undated; and the board on which it has, at some unknown date, been mounted bears only a pencilled annotation: 'Middle Temple Hall 1840. "Taking Commons"'. Whether the print was produced as a strictly contemporary illustration of the 'status quo' in 1840 or was an historical depiction in some later publication we cannot say; and the annotator may have added '1840' either from exact knowledge or from a position of surmise. The internal evidence however does narrow the field from the nineteenth century to the years 1830–64: for it was in 1830 that the central hearth (of which there is no sign in the print) was removed; and the busts of the Caesars (which had been 'in situ' since at least the late-eighteenth century and are very much in evidence in the print) were taken down in 1864. The absence of the gas flambeaux which subsequently projected from the walls is another indication that the print cannot be late-nineteenth century.

24 Dining-hall at King's Inns, mid-twentieth century.

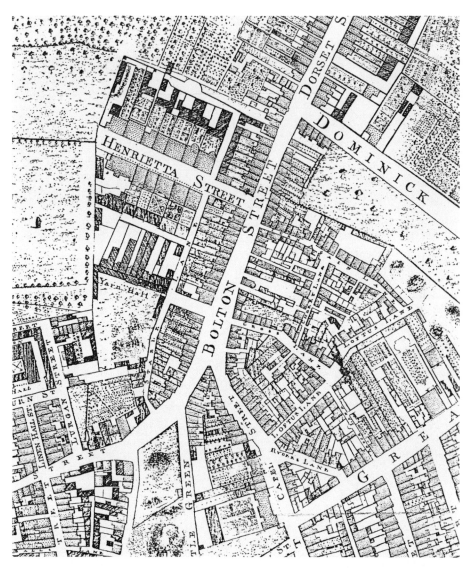

25 A section of John Rocque's map of Dublin, 1756, showing Henrietta Street leading to lands which were later acquired as the site for the present buildings of King's Inns.

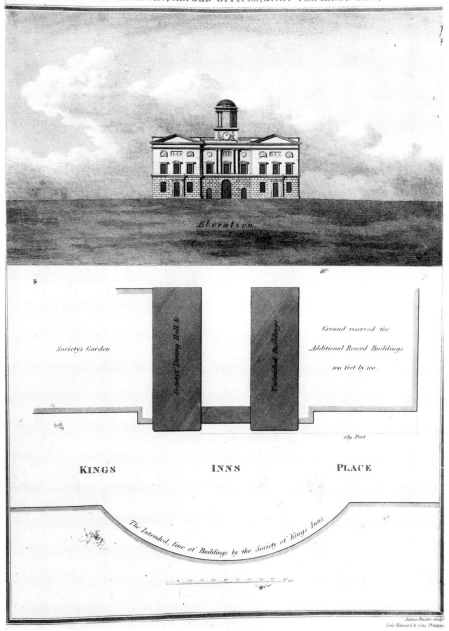

26 Elevation and design of the intended registry, record offices, &c. at the King's Inns, showing the intended line of buildings by the society of King's Inns, 1813.

27 Henrietta Street in an advertising handbill, *c*.1853.

28 Nos. 3–10 Henrietta Street in 1910. All these houses had belonged to Tristram Kennedy.

29 Architectural ground-plan of the houses on Henrietta Street and King's Inns, 1987, by Cathal Crimmins, architect.

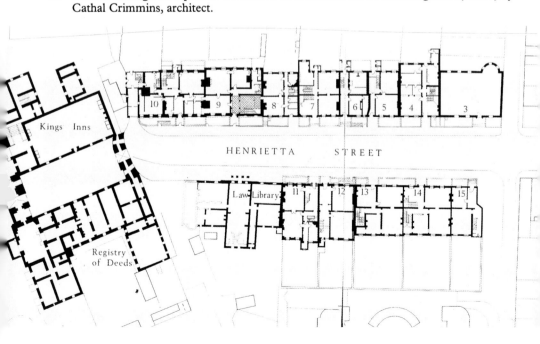

30 Aerial view of the King's Inns and Henrietta Street from the west, 1980s. This photograph was taken before the present car-park was laid out on the southern side of the inns.

But he also argued that the inns had no right in law to insist upon examinations. Lord Campbell disagreed.[18]

The fate of the Dublin Law Institute was also touched upon, but the decision of the King's Inns not to continue funding it was not investigated in any depth. Given the recorder's comment to the benchers on the disposition of Hamilton and Wyse, there may have been a deliberate decision taken not to antagonise the benchers by investigating too minutely their past deliberations. But some light was thrown on their earlier decision in the course of cross-examination. Asked by the chairman was there not 'some demur formerly on the part of the benchers to the Law Institute', Mountifort Longfield, the professor of feudal and English law at Trinity College, Dublin, confirmed that there had been, and said that he believed that this was so because 'some thought that there was a feeling of hostility to connection with England, and they felt that it did not arise from the proper source'. Another witness confirmed that

it was found difficult to command public support, in consequence of an apprehension that it might not continue, or become a mere private speculation, uncontrolled by the general interests or authority of the bar . . . although the professors were exceedingly well qualified men, yet as they were self-elected, of course there could not be the same feeling with regard to them, nor the same influence possessed by them, as if they had been appointed by such persons as the benchers . . . and however eminently qualified the actual professors might be, yet no sufficient guarantee could be given to the public that their successors might be equally so . . . .

Kennedy himself reminded the committee that 'there was a good deal of jealousy evinced by the solicitors' society' towards his institute. But if anyone expected him to throw further light on its earlier demise, they would have been disappointed. If there was a strategy on the part of his friend Wyse not to get the benchers' backs up, he may have agreed with it, not least because he had been making some attempts to revive the institute in 1845–46. A number of witnesses indicated that there was widespread goodwill in the profession at large towards the establishment of a special institution for legal training.[19]

On 25 August 1846, the Wyse committee read and agreed its report and evidence. This, as it happened, was also the month during which blight struck the Irish potato crop for the second

---

18. ibid., pp.xxx, 1, 274–95; qq. 1378, 3777.
19. ibid., p.lii, qq. 1206, 1219–20, 1761–67, 1931–36, 2358–60, 2994, 3111–12.

year running. Ireland was being overwhelmed by the Great Famine, and its public figures may have found little time to reflect on Wyse's considerable achievement.

Within what Ormrod would later describe as 'the amazingly short period of three months', the Wyse committee had completed its work and produced a document which ran to over 450 pages in print. Its fundamental finding was that 'the present state of legal education in England and Ireland ... is extremely unsatisfactory and incomplete'.[20]

In a flourish of idealism, the committee in its report discussed at some length the effects of what it saw as a lack of systematic education in the law, especially in its 'scientific' or 'philosophic' aspects, and concluded that it had led to 'a hypercritical attention to the technicalities', and reduced the arguments before the courts to the 'citation of what are more or less apt instances of adjudication of similar points found in the reports', and to the absence of 'the enunciation and application of legal principles'. They dealt head-on with the view that

as the English and Irish Bar have already produced men of high eminence in all departments, notwithstanding all these educational deficiencies and defects, it is difficult to expect better results from any changes in the present system, or, in other words, there is nothing to be hoped for which we do not now possess, from an improved system of legal education.

The committee's response was to point out, firstly, that whatever the high eminence to which some distinguished men had risen, they might rise higher 'under still more favourable circumstances'. Secondly, the committee noted that it was a fallacy to assume that 'the superiority of the few is conclusive as to the abilities, acquirements and character of the many'. A system of education might enable the public to assure itself, 'with as near an approach to truth as may be, of how far the many as well as the few are qualified to perform satisfactorily their respective duties'.[21]

The committee recommended that the universities should play a leading part in providing an education in law, not only for future practitioners but also for future legislators, administrators and magistrates. They recognised that this would not be sufficient for the future practitioner because the universities in England and Ireland were not designed for, and were unwilling to play the role of, their continental counterparts in providing professional training. The members thought it necessary that some institution

20. *Ormrod Report*, p.5.
21. *Sel. comm. leg. ed.*, pp.xxx–xxxi.

more special and characteristic should be provided; in other words a 'College of Law'. They conceived of this proposed institution as being along the lines of the existing Colleges of Physicians and Surgeons, and believed that it ought to be provided within the framework of existing institutions, rather than by 'the erection of new ones . . . no violent or inappropriate innovation is attempted to be forced upon them'. There might be one such college in Ireland, connected with King's Inns to which both barristers and attorneys belonged, and two in England, one connected with the four inns of court and one with the Incorporated Law Society. The committee gave due credit to the Dublin Law Institute for its achievements, recounting its history and noting that 'the first exertions to meet the demands of the profession, especially of the barrister, are to be met with in Ireland'. But it believed that Kennedy's school 'laboured from its birth under the defect incidental to such associations, arising from precariousness, uncertainty and want of efficient authority and control'. It added that the Law Institute 'is not only a purely voluntary association, but one which, after the recent transactions, is regarded as scarcely sanctioned by the bench or higher bar'.[22]

The King's Inns itself was recommended for incorporation and it, together with the inns in London, were advised to substitute attendance at term lectures for term dinners. Furthermore, the committee believed that a much stricter system of qualifying examinations was essential in order to induce the students to undergo that education which members thought to be desirable. Members favoured holding compulsory examinations to test the knowledge of those wishing to become law students and further compulsory examinations prior to admission to practice. In addition to such ordinary tests, there might be other optional exams for those seeking honours: 'Eligibility for admission to certain higher situations at the bar should be the prize for passing through the extraordinary courses', in the same way that some positions already required the holder to have spent a certain number of years at the bar. But it was pointed out that none of the four London inns were contemplating such public examinations and the powerful Lord Brougham and Vaux was against compulsion in such matters. This served as a reminder to the reader that the committee was ultimately in the position of a plaintiff appearing before the bench. The chances of parliament forcing the legal profession to adopt changes was remote and never openly advanced or seriously entertained at the time. Reflecting considerable concern that their findings would be ignored, the committee raised the possibility of a royal

22. ibid., pp.xli–ii, xlvii–iii.

or parliamentary commission to implement change and to oversee progress. On it would sit the most eminent members of the professional and academic bodies, 'with one or two officers of the crown, in order to ensure parliamentary responsibility'. But having suggested this, the committee immediately acknowledged that the idea was, 'with few exceptions' opposed by many, including those who were 'known to be zealous for this change'. The report noted that 'any imposition of laws upon such bodies except by themselves, would be resisted if not resented'. As an alternative, it suggested that the inns, universities and solicitors' societies of both Britain and Ireland ought to meet in common to co-ordinate change. They were not in fact to do so.[23]

The committee had completed its work, and its report stood not only as a major record of deficiencies in the system but a blueprint for future generations. Over a century later, legal education had still not been organised in the comprehensive way recommended by the committee of 1846 and recognised as desirable by many in public life. When, in 1971, the Ormrod committee on legal education in England and Wales reported, it acknowledged that Wyse's committee had provided 'a remarkable and far-sighted study of the whole problem of education for the legal profession'. Ormrod believed that the findings of 1846 had been 'of fundamental importance to legal education in this country' and that 'the history of legal education in England over the past 120 years is largely an account of the struggle to implement the recommendations of the 1846 committtee and the effects of that struggle'.[24] But even Ormrod did not acknowledge the Irish context out of which Wyse's committee had been born, and Manchester later ignored it in his account of the committee. The fact remains that the earlier report was owed largely to the efforts of Tristram Kennedy and Thomas Wyse to reform legal education in Ireland by, in the first instance, founding a special institute for legal studies and, subsequently, campaigning in the commons and elsewhere for reform. The considerable contribution of Irishmen to the deliberations of the committee of 1846 must not be overlooked, especially the central and dominant role played by Wyse himself. If being forced to London to eat dinners made the Irish more sensitive to deficiencies in the system, the lack of institutions at home made them even more eager for change. But the changes which eventually came, welcome though they were, bore out the fear of Wyse's committee that little would happen quickly without the effective authority of co-ordinated supervision.

23. ibid., pp.xliii, l, lv–lxi.
24. *Ormrod Report*, pp.5–8.

CHAPTER SEVEN

'Low ebb': legal education in England and Ireland by 1846

IT TAKES LITTLE SPACE to give an account of formal legal education in England and Ireland in the eighteenth and early nineteenth centuries, because there was virtually none. Whatever may be said about the inns of court or the brehon schools as educational establishments in earlier periods, by the end of the seventeenth century the former had ceased to provide valuable instruction for law students and the latter had ceased to exist. 'Since then', as Lord Campbell pointed out in 1846,

> all that has been required has been that the candidate to be called to the bar should be of fair character; that he should have been a certain number of years upon the books of the society; that he should have kept a certain number of terms, by eating a certain number of dinners in the hall each term, and have gone through the form of performing what are still called exercises, but which consist of a mere farce of a case being stated, and a debate on each side; but the parties being stopped by the time they have read three words of the case, or the argument on either side, the case and argument being furnished to them by an officer of the society.[1]

For a moment, in 1796, it had looked as though the benchers of Lincoln's Inn might be encouraged to be innovative. They then agreed to a request from Michael Nolan, a Dubliner practising at the English bar, that he be permitted to read in their hall a course of lectures on municipal law and law and equity. On the basis of this precedent, two further courses would later be permitted to be delivered, one by James Mackintosh and the other by Joseph Chitty. However, the benchers ignored Nolan's proposal that they create the office of law lecturer, and the opportunity which he had afforded them of providing systematic legal training was not taken. In 1846, another Irish practitioner considered it 'very remarkable that the bar is the only profession for which no education at all is required; a person may become a member of the bar who can only sign his name; education is not at all required, nor

1. *Sel. comm. leg. ed.*, q. 3819; Holdsworth, *History of English law*, xii, 78–101.

any other qualification whatever'.² Of course, this was a slight exaggeration for, as the above comments by Lord Campbell indicate, it was necessary to eat a number of dinners. The benchers might point out defensively that the number of dinners required was less for those people holding a university degree than for those who did not. Without a university education of some kind the barrister was obliged to keep seventeen terms, whereas with a university education he was obliged only to keep twelve. This could be said to encourage intending barristers to go to college and to pursue a course of studies there, although it might also be seen as favouring those who were privileged enough to attend university. The same could be said of that privilege which reduced for graduates the period required for registration at an inn prior to one's call.³ But, either way, the requirement for dining scarcely increased the level of legal knowledge significantly. To qualify for the exemption it was unnecessary for the student to have chosen even one legal course as part of his degree programme and, where he did, such courses were either nominal or minimal. In the case of those wishing to be attorneys, there was also an advantage for university graduates in that their period of apprenticeship was shortened from five to three years. In the case of apprentices it was also recognised that certain practical skills might be picked up in their masters' offices, although the pupil ran the risk of simply becoming preoccupied with minor details of his master's business.⁴

Overall, apart from certain modest exceptions in the case of both Oxford and Dublin, training in the common law had been utterly neglected by the universities and the inns of court. The position in relation to civil, canon and Roman law was scarcely any better. The founding of law courses at the new University of London in the late 1820s had raised expectations that the tide was turning, and that the position in relation to legal training might improve quickly and dramatically. But, as had been the case at Oxford with Blackstone and at Trinity College with Stoughton Sullivan, the new courses in London were closely associated with one individual, Andrew Amos, and when he passed on to other things, his initiative was not so enthusiastically sustained or, as Lord Brougham put it, the university 'fell off very much'.⁵ In the absence of official backing from the government or support from the inns, it was difficult for

2. ibid., q.1825 (Lawson).
3. *Sel. comm. leg. ed.*, q.1919 (Lawson); *L.I.B.B.*, iv, 66, 76–77, 121; *L.I. adm. reg.*, i, 511.
4. Osborough, 'Admission of attorneys and solicitors', pp.134–36; *Sel. comm. leg. ed.*, p. lii, qq. 1825, 1857–58, 1875–78.
5. *Sel. comm. leg. ed.*, q. 3777; Holdsworth, *History of English law*, xii, 77–101.

Legal education in England and Ireland by 1846   149

the universities to reform the system of legal education, since those destined for professional practice were not obliged to take courses or to sit examinations. This absence of effective endorsement, as has been demonstrated, also undermined the radical efforts of Tristram Kennedy and the Dublin Law Institute to bring about lasting changes in the Irish system.

Commenting on the whole situation in 1846, Lord Brougham, who shortly beforehand had chaired a joint committee of the inns appointed to consider designing a new system of education, remarked that 'anything more entirely nugatory, and more of a mockery, as a test of legal acquirements, cannot possibly be imagined'. He was sorry to say that the state of legal education was 'at as low an ebb as it is possible for education to be in any country'.[6]

BARRISTERS

There were certainly ways in which a student might learn something about law and legal practice, but these were highly individualistic, and were unsupervised by any professional or public institution. As Brougham told the select committee on legal education, 'A person is called, as is well known, to the bar, merely because his name has been five years upon the books, or three if he has a degree of master of arts, and because he has what is called kept twelve terms'.[7] Young men were always free to read books, as the humour took them, or to glean what they might from proceedings in the law courts. English law students also paid fees to attend the chambers of practising lawyers. As Lord Campbell explained in 1846,

During the whole of the eighteenth century it was left entirely to the student themselves to acquire a knowledge of their profession. In the early part of the century they went into attorneys' offices, and towards the middle of the century, and afterwards, there was a system established of going into the chambers of special pleaders and equity draftsmen and conveyancers, paying them a fee of one hundred guineas a year, and assisting them in carrying on their business, and seeing how their business was to be transacted; and that, down to the present time, has been the only teaching, for any of the branches of the profession of a barrister.[8]

---

6. *Sel. comm. leg. ed.*, qq. 3771–74; *L.I.B.B.*, iv, 229 (8 July 1845); *L.I.B.B.*, v, liv, 5 (12 Jan. 1846), 11–12 (22 July 1846).
7. *Sel. comm. leg. ed.*, q. 3774.
8. ibid., qq. 1265, 3823. The role of the special pleader in the system was singled out by Dicey in 1899, by which time a rapid growth in the number of those studying for the bar and changes in the legal system had exposed weaknesses in the English system: 'The conjecture may be hazarded that

It was considered necessary by English students to stay at least one year in chambers but many remained for two. Yet Brougham observed that,

in attending his master, the pupil is not taught by interposition of the pleader or draftsman; generally speaking he is left entirely to himself; he has the precedents; he may copy them or not as he chooses; he sees cases brought to be answered by the pleader, or draftsman, or conveyancer; he sees the answers, and he may obtain information by speaking to his master and discussing the subject; but, generally speaking, he is left very much to himself.[9]

There were some exceptional masters and those pupils whom Professor Amos personally took on, when wearing his wig as a practising barrister, no doubt considered themselves lucky. Overall, it was not an attractive system and to the Irish it was burdensome. Attending the inns in London cost a great deal, and many Irish felt that entering chambers was simply too expensive and did not do so. Moreover, there were differences between the law and practice in England and the law and practice in Ireland, and students might learn ways of drafting and pleading which could prove fatal in their early days at the Irish bar. In any event, many Irish students did not stay long enough in London to pass the two years which most English students regarded as the minimum period necessary to benefit from attending chambers.[10]

One of the minority of Irish law students who did enter chambers in London was Michael Barry. He told the 1846 select committee on legal education that this was 'an exception, it is not usual', and that those who did so stayed usually for a very short period, 'sometimes but for six months':

If a candidate for admission to the Irish bar enter the chambers of a conveyancer in England, for which there is a fee of one hundred guineas required for one year, with respect to which my experience has been, that in one year he really learns nothing, and he is about to leave the chambers just as his eyes, as it were, are about to open upon the subject

---

reading in a lawyer's office, which resembles the office of a solicitor, is not the intellectual equivalent to reading in the chambers of a leading barrister or (what is now to the great loss of students impossible) to reading in the chambers of a special pleader' (Dicey, 'The teaching of English law at Harvard', 748, note).

9. *Sel. comm. leg. ed.*, p.xii, qq. 66–69.
10. ibid., pp.viii, xii, qq. 1669 (Wyse), 3025–28 (Hamilton and Wyse); 'The Irish law students' in *Saunders's News-letter*, 16 Nov. 1841.

Legal education in England and Ireland by 1846 151

of real property and conveyancing; and if he hopes to repay the time lost, he must stay a second year, that is 200 guineas'.[11]

In Ireland, as we will see in chapter 10, barristers generally had their domestic studies or libraries, but they usually kept no chambers, at least not in the sense that the term was used in England to designate private offices in the vicinity of the courts. Most barristers preferred instead simply to resort daily to the law library and to the hall of the Four Courts. Their library at the courts was a sort of legal exchange, whence they sallied forth to huddle with clients or to appear before the bench. On a winter's morning in Dublin in the early nineteenth century you might have glimpsed through the shutters of Daniel O'Connell's house in Merrion Square

> a tall able-bodied man standing at a desk, and immersed in solitary occupation. Upon the wall in front of him hangs a crucifix. . . . no sooner can the eye take in the other furniture of the apartment, the bookcases clogged with tomes in plain calf-skin bindings, the blue-covered octavos that lie on the table and the floor, the reams of manuscript in oblong folds and begirt with crimson tape, than it becomes evident that the party meditating amidst such objects must be thinking far more of the law than the prophets. He is unquestionably a barrister, but, apparently, of that homely, chamber-keeping, plodding cast, who labour hard to make up by assiduity what they want in wit. . . . Should you happen in the course of the same day to stroll down to the hall of the Four Courts, you will not be a little surprised to find the object of your pity miraculously transformed from the severe recluse of the morning into one of the most bustling, important and joyous personages in that busy scene.[12]

In an era of industrialisation, the difference between the work practices of English barristers, who shared chambers, and Irish barristers, who did not, was ascribed by some to the existence in England of a greater volume of work, the belief being that this necessarily encouraged specialisation and that specialisation in turn somehow bred the peculiarly English system of chambers. But other observers saw no intrinsic reason why Irish barristers might not specialise or might not have chambers like their English brethren, and appeared to attribute the existing modes of operation simply to custom and tradition. The fact that the Americans,

11. *Sel. comm. leg. ed.*, qq. 1647, 1651.
12. Curran, *Sketches of the Irish bar*, cited at Pakenham, *Dublin*, p.11. For a thumbnail history of the bar's law library to 1846, see *Sel. comm. leg. ed.*, q.2247 (Lyle). For a description of it later, see Marjoribanks, *Life of Lord Carson*, i, 18–20. Hogan, *Legal profession*, p.117, has a photograph of the library at the turn of the century.

like the Irish, did not ape the English system lent weight to the latter argument.[13]

The lack of specialisation in itself did not preclude the possibility of barristers taking chambers in the city of Dublin. Indeed, as will be seen below, the King's Inns had decided in the late eighteenth century to develop chambers for Irish barristers, although their plans came to nothing. And later, in the nineteenth century, Tristram Kennedy used the establishment of the Dublin Law Institute to encourage his colleagues to establish chambers and to take pupils but, while a number adopted the former course, only a very few of these appear to have had an arrangement with pupils comparable to that which was common in England.[14] However, Irish law students might and did read over the briefs of Dublin practitioners and assisted them in various ways. They would go to a barrister with whom they were acquainted and make themselves as useful as possible. The most diligent students were trusted not only to peruse the briefs but to mark them and were expected to turn up relevant cases, of which a growing number were reported. According to Acheson Lyle in 1846, 'very many' students attended barristers in this way, either at the Four Courts or at their homes.[15]

In 1846, J.A. Lawson, the latest in a succession of brilliant young lawyers to occupy the new chair of political economy at Trinity College Dublin, was examined about this Dublin custom by members of the select committee on legal education. Lawson, a former student of the Dublin Law Institute and a practising barrister, was questioned by George Hamilton, the member for Dublin University:

HAMILTON: Is it not the habit in Ireland, as it respects chambers, on the part of barristers, that they have not chambers separate, but that they are in their own houses?
LAWSON: They have not; they do their business in their own houses.
WYSE: Does any inconvenience arise from that?
LAWSON: No.
WYSE: Not in the present state of legal education; but if a great number of pupils were taken would it not be inconvenient?

13. *Sel. comm. leg. ed.*, qq. 1070–75 (Kennedy), 2519 (Mahony); Dicey, 'The teaching of English law at Harvard', 748. The way in which Irish lawyers each practised in a number of different areas is said to have hindered the development of law reporting (Osborough, 'Puzzles from Irish law reporting history', pp.95–96).
14. *Sel. comm. leg. ed.*, qq. 1652, 1880, 2397. According to Brougham, it was also uncommon for students to attend chambers in Scotland (*Sel. comm. leg. ed.*, p.xxi, q.3774).
15. *Sel. comm. leg. ed.*, qq. 1880, 2403–06.

LAWSON: Certainly it would be an inconvenience if that were the case.
WYSE: Would it not be advisable that there should be chambers, like those of Lincoln's Inn and the Temple, for instance?
LAWSON: Yes.
HAMILTON: Practically, as long as the barristers' offices are at their own houses, would it not operate as an impediment in the way of a proper system extending itself?
LAWSON: It would.

Lawson claimed that 'almost all the students who have a friend at the bar, who will take the trouble with them, and who are anxious to proceed and avail themselves of that mode, do so; it is almost the only mode they can take'. But he admitted that 'the course of the law student is beset with difficulty, and if he does not have a friend at the bar who will guide him and take a great deal of trouble with him, I think his attempts to arrive at any adequate knowledge of his profession are attended with very great difficulty indeed'.[16] One alternative, to which John Adye Curran resorted and to which he refers in his memoirs, was made possible

by the indulgence of an old friend of my father's in the solicitors' profession, Mr Thomas Geoghegan, who enjoyed a very considerable practice, and who allowed me to frequent his office for six months before my call. There I learnt much of the practical work of the profession.[17]

Another person unable to avail of the services of a 'friend at the bar' before he was called was Michael O'Loghlen, who subsequently floundered in practice until he came to the paternal attention of Daniel O'Connell. Thus the picture of O'Connell at home in his study, which was sketched above, may be enhanced

16. Akenson, *Whately*, p.105; *Sel. comm. leg. ed.*, qq.1881–88, 1892, 1899. Lawson later became president of the Statistical and Social Inquiry Society, of which many lawyers were prominent members (Black, *Statistical and Social Inquiry Society*, pp.61–62).

17. Curran, *Reminiscences*, p.9. In 1846, Lawson had told the select committee on legal education (q.1880) that, 'of course there is no remuneration, and therefore with respect to a barrister, except he is a friend of yours, there is very little inducement to him to take the trouble of instructing you, which he must do for some time, before you are of any use to him'. But John Adye Curran, who was called in 1860, gave as the reason for his attendance on a solicitor the fact that his father could not afford the fee for him to read with a barrister. Three decades later, Edward Carson paid 50 guineas to 'devil' for a year with an experienced junior, this becoming by the twentieth century the common sort of arrangement for those who had just been called to the bar (Marjoribanks, *Carson*, i, 23). It appears that formerly the system of pupillage straddled one's call and only gradually came to involve payment in some instances.

by imagining at his side the young barrister and future master of the rolls, whom he tutored and loved 'as my son'.[18]

But such chance arrangements and makeshifts were a poor substitute for formal legal education, and no one appeared before the select committee of 1846 to defend the existing system of leaving law students to teach themselves whatever law they felt inclined to learn. There was no difficulty in finding agreement to the proposition that the present system was inadequate. But agreement in principle that changes were needed did not in itself ensure that these would be introduced in a coherent fashion. As the select committee of 1846 foresaw, the absence of a fully co-ordinated approach to reform was to result in courses being introduced by the inns and the universities in an unsatisfactory manner. Efforts to reform the system were also to be hampered by the requirement that Irish bar students go to London to eat dinner.

ATTORNEYS AND SOLICITORS

If barristers were unhappy at the state of legal education for the higher branch of the profession, members of 'the lower branch' were equally dissatisfied. The position in which Irish attorneys and solicitors found themselves in the first half of the nineteenth century was quite different from that of their English colleagues. The latter were free to organise their own affairs through the Law Society, incorporated for educational and other purposes in 1831, whereas the Irish were obliged to belong to the King's Inns and depended on the benchers for reforms. In London, from 1833, the Incorporated Law Society had provided some lectures. In 1836, a rule of court was made by the English judges under which articled clerks were required, for the first time, to pass an examination in law before admission to the roll of practice. In 1843, this became a statutory requirement. In Ireland the only test was one for general fitness to practise as an attorney which, under a statute of 1773, was administered by 'moral examiners'. But this soon came to be regarded as a mere formality by those who had kept out of trouble for the period of their apprenticeship. A minor improvement in the provisions governing admission to practice as an

---

18. 'Recollections of the late Sir Michael O'Loghlen', 93–98; Beckett, *Mod. Ire.*, pp.308–09, 316. O'Connell abandoned regular practice at the bar about 1830, although he continued to appear in court from time to time. He subsequently rejected invitations to become the first catholic attorney general or master of the rolls since the reign of James II, recommending O'Loghlen instead for that honour (MacDonagh, *The emancipist*, pp.14, 42–43, 56–57, 73, 122–23, 175).

attorney was that from 1843 the benchers insisted that the petitions and affidavits of prospective apprentices should be lodged at the King's Inns.[19] The Dublin benchers were exclusively men who had been called to the bar and in 1841, as we have already seen, they rejected a proposal from Sir Michael O'Loghlen to add some attorneys to their ranks. For his part, as we have also observed, Tristram Kennedy failed to win the broad support of the lower branch of the profession for his Dublin Law Institute, not least because he did not welcome them to its council until late in the day.[20]

Asked in 1846 to describe the system of education for articled clerks in the offices of Dublin attorneys, the Irish barrister and professor, J.A. Lawson, replied:

> There is no system of education, except doing their master's business that arises in the office . . . to copy the different papers there, and prepare them; to go down to the courts, and attend the different proceedings, the different motions, and the arguments there.
>
> HAMILTON: Is that practically such a system as is calculated to give a tolerably good legal education to the clerk?
>
> LAWSON: It gives him an acquaintance with the practical forms of law; I should say nothing more than that; there is no provision made for his receiving any instruction in the principles of conveyancing.
>
> HAMILTON: Can you state whether there be any attorneys, men of standing and eminence in their profession, who, on receiving articled clerks into their offices, take any pains to instruct them in the principles or practice of law?
>
> LAWSON: I never heard of any.[21]

There was an unincorporated Law Society in Dublin, with which the benchers at times were willing to deal in relation to some professional matters. But by the time Wyse and his fellow members began their deliberations in 1846, the Irish solicitors and attorneys were still organisationally weak, and they failed to defend their interests in the face of some very harsh criticism at Westminster. The committee condemned the practice of allowing Irish solicitors to prepare the first draft of deeds, which were then sent to counsel for revising:

19. Holdsworth, *History of English law*, xiv, 231–41; *Ormrod Report*, p.5; *Stat. Ire.*, 13 & 14 Geo III (1773), c.23; Littledale, *King's Inns*, p.19; *Sel. comm. leg. ed.*, qq. 1857–58 (Lawson); Hogan, *Legal profession*, pp.16, 96–97, 115; Osborough, 'Admission of attorneys and solicitors', pp.114–115, 120–23.
20. Benchers' minute book, 1835–44 (King's Inns MS, p.152: 15 April 1841); *Sel. comm. leg. ed.*, q. 2453 (Mahony).
21. *Sel. comm. leg. ed.*, qq.1875–78.

this of itself is only another evidence of the gross neglect allowed to prevail. Questions of great nicety, reposing upon important principles, and those principles requiring great judgment and knowledge, and therefore great study and thought for their application, which in England are reserved, on this conviction, to the higher branch of the profession, who especially devote themselves to such studies, are devolved without concern to the ordinary solicitor throughout Ireland, whose means and zeal for the acquisition of legal knowledge are, as we have seen, confessedly inferior to those possessed by the solicitor in England.[22]

The committee of 1846, being dominated by barristers, was scarcely inclined to approve of 'the lower branch' in Ireland doing legal work which was reserved to the higher branch in England. The committee proceeded to take a side-swipe at the attorneys' society in Dublin. Notwithstanding the fact that they had been told that as early as 1821 some professional men in Ireland 'did all that they possibly could' to have a system of tests established, tests previous to being admitted as an articled clerk and tests previous to being admitted as an attorney or solicitor, and recognising that in 1838–39 the Irish attorneys had attempted to have the benchers introduce examinations at King's Inns, the select committee, nevertheless, took its lead from one of two Irish attorneys to appear before it, the 'incorrigible' Pierce Mahony, who said that in Ireland 'the chief part of litigation is the fruit of incompetency on the part of the attorneys'. The budding Irish Law Society was hastily dismissed by the committee as being simply a body for the purpose of forming a library and for holding meetings, a body 'which in no wise contemplates the education of its members'. This was quite untrue as the objectives of the Law Society, since its foundation in 1830 and specifically under new rules adopted in 1841, had ranked above the establishment of a library the need 'to give lectures and to provide better education in the laws and practice of the courts'.[23]

Having thus dealt with the Law Society, the select committee concentrated its attention on one particular aspect of Irish legal practice to which it took exception, namely that the Irish solicitor had entrusted to him the management of cases of an intricate and serious nature,

for the professional conduct of which he may, and in most cases must be, from his want of previous studies, altogether incompetent. The

22. ibid., p.xvii.
23. ibid., pp.xvii, liii, qq. 2440, 2454–64, 2513; *Report from the select committee on admission of attornies and solicitors . . . 5 March 1821*; Hogan, *Legal profession*, pp.92–4, 101–02. The select committee of 1846 did not distinguish between the Law Society and the Law Club.

Legal education in England and Ireland by 1846   157

result of such a demand of qualifications, for which no adequate means of supply exists, is obvious; discussions *ex parte* and at random, fatal errors, and ruinous or expensive appeals. These functions, too, happen to fall into the hands of that class of the profession which is not looked on as the most creditable.[24]

The report cites the evidence of Irish solicitor Pierce Mahony against the professional standards of his own colleagues who are

persons who have been mere copying clerks, scriveners to attorneys, and by their diligence been able to scrape as much money together as would pay the stamp duty; their masters have taken them without any fee, and they ultimately become attorneys, and are thrown for their subsistence upon the lower classes; they are the persons who conduct that class of litigation, which is a very great evil in Ireland.[25]

The committee decided that

the greater proportion of the minor litigation in that country [Ireland] arises out of instruments prepared by this class of persons; that is to say, leases, settlements, and wills; and these documents afterwards become the question of debate in the very courts where these solicitors are now allowed to practice.[26]

Reviewing the evidence which had been placed before it concerning Irish attorneys and solicitors, the committee of 1846 recommended the establishment of a series of lectures, class instruction and examinations. It left open the question of whether the King's Inns should 'conjoin' students for both branches of the profession in the one institution or allow the solicitors to be incorporated into a separate body for the purpose of educating apprentices. The benchers implicitly chose the second option for, as will be seen below, the system of education which they introduced in 1851 was intended for those wishing to become barristers. For its part, the Society of the Attorneys and Solicitors of Ireland finally secured a royal charter, becoming incorporated on 5 April 1852. This charter recognised the society's determination to facilitate the acquisition of legal knowledge, a determination which would soon see the benchers yield to its demands for reform. Meanwhile, however, neither in Ireland nor in England had a majority of attorneys yet been persuaded to join the respective law societies and this weakened the lower branch in its dealings with the benchers.[27]

24. *Sel. comm. leg. ed.*, p.xxxvi.
25. ibid., qq. 2444-49.
26. ibid., p.xxxvi.
27. *Sel. comm. leg. ed.*, pp. liii-iv; Hogan, *Legal profession*, p.113; *Ormrod Report*, p.9.

THE UNIVERSITY OF DUBLIN AND THE QUEEN'S COLLEGES

There had long been nominal provision for instruction in civil, canon and common law at the University of Dublin. As Nial Osborough observes, 'from the time of Trinity's foundation to the middle of the nineteenth century, formal legal education in Ireland, in so far as it meant anything at all, was synonymous with formal legal education in Trinity'. Osborough thinks it 'probable' that at some point regular instruction in the civil law was available. But Arthur Browne may have been exceptional in treating the chair of civil law as other than a sinecure and, certainly by the nineteenth century, the degrees of bachelor of laws and doctor of laws were conferred upon graduates simply on payment of a fee and the performance of merely formal exercises. The degree of bachelor of laws formed part of the qualifications for some important offices in the ecclesiastical courts, while the degree of doctor of laws was the qualification for advocates in the ecclesiastical and admiralty courts. Yet, both degrees might be obtained 'without the slightest study or knowledge of the law'. As regards the common law there was a brief period at the beginning of the 1830s when an energetic deputy replaced the then part-time professor, Philip Crampton, and seemed set to bring to the chair of feudal and English law a vitality which it had lacked since the days when it was first occupied by Stoughton Sullivan. The enthusiast was Mountifort Longfield, a young barrister from Cork who was apprised of recent developments in the field of legal education in London. But shortly afterwards Longfield became Ireland's first professor of political economy, being appointed to the new chair which Archbishop Whately had founded at Trinity. He was the first in a line of lawyers to fill it. A condition of Whately's endowment was that no individual should hold the position for longer than five years, but by the time Longfield returned to the law school he was in the process of developing professional commitments which dampened his ardour for exhaustive teaching.[28]

28. Osborough, 'Review of McDowell and Webb', 187–88; O'Higgins, 'Arthur Browne (1756–1805): an Irish civilian', 255; *Dub. Univ. Comm . . . 1851–3*, p.32; Anon., 'Law School of the Dublin University', 93–97; Black, 'Mountifort Longfield: his economic thought and writings reviewed in relation to the theories of his time and of the present day'; Akenson, *Whately*, p.105; Moss, *Mountifort Longfield: Ireland's first professor of political economy*, pp.14–15, 225. There does not appear to exist any sketch or photograph of Longfield. He was one of fourteen children and he spent part of his youth at his grandfather's big house, near Mallow (Longfield, 'Visits to Longueville c.1805–1815').

In 1846, the select committee on legal education found that the position in relation to legal education at the University of Dublin was then a little better than that at Oxford or Cambridge but that the degrees in law at Dublin were still 'mere formal honours; no examination, no previous attendance on lectures are required'. There were just two professors, both part-time, and two courses, one in civil law and one in what was known as 'feudal and English law', which was interpreted for practical purposes as real property and the common law. That in civil law was described by the committee as 'a perfect sinecure' and the holder expressed his readiness to cede it to another. He gave no lectures. The lectures in English common law which Mountifort Longfield delivered were regarded affectionately by those who attended them, including a few young barristers. Law lectures at the university were open to undergraduates to select as part of their preparation for a general arts degree. But no class of student was obliged to attend them and there was no particular incentive for future professionals to go along. Longfield, in the chair of English law, lectured about thirty times a year, endeavouring in a two-year course to go through the body of the law, with the exception of the criminal law which, in words we have already quoted, he dismissed as unworthy of attention. The average number who attended the lectures which he did give was seven, perhaps because the lectures were given at nine o'clock in the morning. In Longfield's opinion, the one or two young barristers who sometimes attended would not come if a fee was charged, and he also found that they were unwilling to have questions put to them in the presence of younger people. Overall, the report of 1846 was dismissive of the arrangement at Trinity College, finding that 'the university provides little legal education for the professional or unprofessional classes'.[29]

The older universities of Dublin, Oxford and Cambridge were in danger of being passed by. The report of 1846 was enthusiastic about the law degree programme of University College, London and saw in the creation of the Queen's Colleges at Belfast, Galway and Cork in 1845 an opportunity for innovation in Ireland:

The charter of the new Irish provincial [queen's] colleges empowers them to found 'chairs of law'. It may be thought that taking into view the position in which they are likely sometime to be placed, there is little chance of much demand for such instruction. But it must be remembered that these colleges are at a later period to be aggregated into a university. They offer in a remarkable manner the opportunity sought for in the existing universities, of introducing a popular course of elementary

---

29. *Sel. comm. leg. ed.*, pp.iii–vii; qq. 2830–05, 2956–59.

law or jurisprudence for all classes.... it would form a good preparation for those higher studies to which the student would have to proceed, in institutions intended for the more special education of the barrister or solicitor.[30]

The new Queen's Colleges opened to students in 1849 and were 'aggregated into a university' the following year. Each employed two part-time law professors. The circumstances enticed authorities at Trinity College and the benchers to co-operate with each other, as envisaged a number of times in the course of evidence before the select committee of 1846, rather than see a system develop which they might not dominate or control. At the time, Trinity better suited the social and religious sensibilities of many benchers than did the new provincial, middle-class and non-denominational Queen's Colleges. At Trinity College scholarships and fellowships remained closed to all but members of the established church, and nearly all of the professors were clergymen in the Church of Ireland. In 1846, only the two law professors and a physician were laymen. While catholics could and did attend the college, there was understandable concern in the ranks of their church about such a state of affairs. Unfortunately, in the course of the nineteenth century, the organisation of Irish education generally became an increasingly contentious political issue, with the catholic bishops demanding that the state support the establishment of denominational institutions. The bitterness of the debate, which extended from primary to tertiary level, contributed to the departure from public life of Thomas Wyse, whose support for the reform of legal education in general and for the Dublin Law Institute in particular has been considered above. Wyse's commitment to educational reform extended far beyond the field of law, and he was regarded as 'the apostle' of non-denominational education. Wyse himself was a member of an old catholic landed family and a graduate of Trinity College. But he and other supporters of the Queen's Colleges saw the institutions denounced by critics such as O'Connell as 'godless', and in 1847 Wyse lost his seat in parliament as a result of the bishop of Waterford mobilising the electorate against him. 'Turning away from his unkind countrymen', Wyse accepted a post as ambassador to Greece and never again sat in parliament.[31]

30. ibid., p.xlvi.
31. ibid., q. 3085; Wyse, *Notes on education reform in Ireland*, pp.39, 47, 60; *DNB*, s.v. Wyse, Thomas, which blames his defeat partly on his refusal to join Young Ireland; Atkinson, *Irish education*, pp.122–28; Dowling, *History of Irish education*, pp.164–66. Despite their titles these last two works ignore legal education in general and the King's Inns in particular; Andrew Burke, 'Trinity College and the religious problem in Irish education', 98–100.

CHAPTER EIGHT

'Creeping like snail unwillingly to school': innovation at the inns, 1846-76

THE SELECT COMMITTEE of 1846 recommended that the reform of legal education be carried out by common consent and co-operation between the English and Irish inns, the solicitors' societies and the universities. But the recommendation was ignored. Delegates from the professional bodies did not take up the suggestion, although the four inns of court in London continued to co-operate among themselves. As forecast by Wyse, the absence of a royal commission to oversee reform resulted in 'detached efforts, a reform here, and an improvement there'.[1]

Even before Wyse's committee had published its report, the English inns, on an experimental basis, appointed three readers to give lectures to law students, thereby recognising that some change was inevitable. In 1847 they attempted to establish a system of education which might be permanent, but their efforts at the time were unsuccessful. Not until 1852 did a new joint Council of Legal Education, representing all four inns, finally issue generally accepted rules with respect to legal training. This was two years after the King's Inns had published its response to the demands for reform, and the system established in London, as will be seen, varied considerably from that earlier adopted in Dublin and discussed below. Both had their own strengths and weaknesses. Where the Irish benchers provided only lectures, the English also introduced a system of voluntary qualifying exams. The students were induced to sit the optional exams by the award of prizes and by being ranked in seniority above other students called on the same day. If they chose to sit the exams, they need not attend any lectures. If they did choose the lectures, and provided they spent at least the usual minimum period of one year in chambers, just one year's attendance at classes was made compulsory. In Ireland lectures could not be avoided and were spread over two years. In both countries one could still get to the bar without any examination of

1. *Sel. comm. leg. ed.*, pp.lv, lxi.

proficiency. As one of the editors of the 'Black Books' of Lincoln's Inn has caustically remarked, 'mere attendance at lectures, without any obligation to pay attention while present, was indeed a singular method of instruction'. Irish students going to London were not obliged to attend any of the new courses there as a condition of keeping their terms in accordance with the Statute of Jeofailles. But, if they wished, they were permitted to attend classes on payment of the same fees as were required from their English colleages. Before long some of the more eager Irish students, such as James Wylie, did so. He was one of a string of graduates of the Queen's Colleges to win examination prizes at the English inns.[2]

THE KING'S INNS AND TRINITY COLLEGE DUBLIN

That the benchers of King's Inns had never provided any legal education before 1850 has been noted above. In 1792 a bizarre plan to introduce an elaborate, anachronistic and decorative system of training had been advanced. It must be regarded as an aberration and was roundly condemned by barristers at the time, one styling it 'the vacation exercises of busy, meddling men'. Little remained of the original ornate proposal in the end, but from that time 'students' were at least obliged to register with the society a number of years before their presentation for admission as barristers and also to 'keep terms' in the new dining hall.[3] If the benchers felt any shame about the absence of legal education at King's Inns, they managed to conceal it very well. Their tentative and short-term support for the Dublin Law Institute did not impress the select committee on legal education of 1846, and the only Irish bencher to give evidence before that committee, Acheson Lyle, the chief remembrancer, does not appear to have done so on behalf of his colleagues. But they could not entirely ignore the report of 1846, even if it had been spawned by the efforts of Kennedy and Wyse and, like the Dublin Law Institute, 'did not come exactly from the proper quarter'.[4]

An ideological framework within which the benchers could rationalise reform, without being seen to bow to radicals like

---

2. *L.I.B.B.*, v, liv–vi, 18, 36; Reader, *Professional men*, p.56; *Dub. Univ. comm.*, pp.60, 361; *Ormrod Report*, p.9 and p.12, where it is said that, while some who subsequently sat exams did rely on the council's courses, 'most preferred to go to law tutors or to read privately for the examinations'; O'Shaughnessy, 'On legal education in Ireland', 145.
3. Duhigg, *History of King's Inns*, pp.437–50; King's Inns, *General rules . . . 1794*, nos. ix–xvii; Kenny, *King's Inns and the kingdom of Ireland*, pp.240–55.
4. *Sel comm. leg. ed.*, q. 2994 (Longfield).

Wyse and Kennedy, was provided by Henry H. Joy, barrister and tory and one of those who had publicly disassociated themselves from the action of their professional colleagues who called a meeting in 1842 to protest at the appointment of English lawyers as Irish chancellors. In 1847 Joy published his *Letters on legal education*. These were said by him to have been inspired by conversations with George Hamilton, the member for Dublin University who had sat on the committee of 1846 and who, like other members for that university in the nineteenth century, appeared to represent the interests of the benchers at Westminster. In his *Letters* Joy ignored the experiences of Tristram Kennedy and the Dublin Law Institute. Although in the course of 151 pages he relied extensively on evidence given to the committee on legal education, he did so with minimal acknowledgment of this fact, and it seems likely that his pamphlet was intended to make more palatable the argument for what had become, in effect, inevitable educational reforms, while allowing conservatives to avoid admitting the achievements of Kennedy and Wyse. Joy writes in relation to legal education that 'public attention is at length aroused, and the judges, the benchers and the bar appear equally alive to its importance'.[5]

The committee of 1846 had raised the possibility that King's Inns and the University of Dublin might establish jointly a scheme of legal education. There already existed an arrangement between Trinity and Sir Patrick Dun's hospital in the case of medical studies. Joy took up this theme and urged the provision of legal education by the benchers, with some reliance upon lectures being given at Trinity College Dublin. Whether he made this suggestion at the behest of some of the benchers is unknown but a writer at the college responded positively. Welcoming the publication of Joy's *Letters*, an anonymous author wrote in the *Dublin University Magazine* that

> we are glad to see that this subject has at last attracted, in this country, the attention of sensible and competent men. Previous attempts had been made, not, however, calculated, in our opinion, to effect the desired object; such systems must carry with them the impress of the authority of men of eminence and consideration in their profession, in order to possess the confidence of the public.

There were still differences in the legal and academic perspectives. Where Joy notes in an ingratiating fashion that 'in respect of the Irish bar, nothing is more striking than the advance in legal knowledge within the present century', the college author claims

5. Joy, *Letters on the present state of legal education*, pp.1, 6.

that 'the Irish bar, whether as regards the qualification, the talent, or the education of its practitioners, has greatly deteriorated within the last fifty years'. Where Joy believes that 'a compulsory public examination is to be deprecated, as an essential preliminary to admission to the bar', the university writer asks 'is this profession alone to be excluded from the benefit of a test, of which every other possesses the advantage?'[6]

In a postscript, added as his article went to print, the university author of 1847 noted that Joy's letters had already 'had the effect which we would naturally have expected. At a meeting of the benchers it has been resolved that some prompt measures shall be taken, and the introduction of a system similar to that proposed by Mr Joy has been recommended'. This was a reference to the fact that at a meeeting on 15 April 1847 the benchers had adopted a resolution that the special committee, appointed on 22 May 1846 to consider what Wyse and others at Westminster were doing, be transformed into a committee on legal education and

that it be referred to such committee to enquire and report whether it would be expedient for the society to establish a School of Legal Education to be in connection with and under their own superintendence, and if the committee shall be of opinion that such a School of Legal Education should be established then to report what scheme or system of such education it would be advisable to adopt.

It appears from the deliberations of this special committee that the society had not in its possession by May 1847 a full copy of the select committee report of 1846! A sub-committee wrote to the London inns to discover what was being done there by way of response to the pressure for reform.[7]

By December 1848, the Committee on Legal Education at King's Inns was recommending that the benchers appoint no less than four professors, one each in real property, common law, equity and civil law, and general jurisprudence. But Judge Jackson had undertaken to communicate with Mountifort Longfield at Trinity College 'on the feasibility of combining his professorship of Feudal and English Law in the university with our professorships here'. The proposal for a system of joint lecturing was subsequently

---

6. *Sel. comm. leg. ed.*, qq. 3029, 3039–44; *NHI*, v, 479; Joy, *Letters on legal education*, p.6; Anon., 'Legal education' (July, 1847), 57, 59–61. For a sustained attack on the standards of the bar at this time see [Madden?], *The reign of mediocrity*.
7. Anon., 'Legal education' (July 1847), 65; Benchers' minute book, 1844–49 (King's Inns MS, pp.139, 173–79).

agreed in principle by the society and the college, although the actual scheme which came into operation in 1850, as will be seen, had just two professors at King's Inns instead of four and relied upon two courses at the college rather than just one.[8]

The King's Inns decided to proceed with the introduction of courses and of new educational requirements, although the benchers in London were hesitating. In December 1849 the council of King's Inns had heard a report that the English inns of court in England had 'either wholly or in part abandoned the propositions respecting legal education'. Two months later the Irish benchers agreed that these circumstances in England 'constitute no just ground for altering but rather tend to confirm the recommendations already made' by a sub-committee of benchers in Dublin to establish compulsory courses for law students. So it was that in 1850 the benchers established under their supervision at King's Inns a School of Legal Education and agreed 'that the system of compulsory attendance on lectures shall be recognised as part of the system to be adopted by the society'. However, this trumpeted recognition of 'the principle of compulsory attendance on lectures' was compromised in practice by a decision to insist only that non-graduates attend all four courses at Trinity College and King's Inns. Graduates in law or arts need only attend on any two of the four courses. The possibility of having compulsory oral examinations was also raised at this time, but was rejected by a slim majority. Rules to give full effect to the benchers' decision were published on 3 November 1851.[9]

This was an historic juncture, for not only was the society in Dublin about to commence legal training for the first time, but it was to do so independently of the London societies. Moreover, the system was quite different from that which the English inns would adopt two years later, especially insofar as there was a formal connection with a university. The lectures required to be

8. Benchers' minute book, 1844–49 (King's Inns MS, p.229: 2 Dec. 1848, p.238: 11 Jan. 1849); Benchers' minute book, 1849–56 (King's Inns MS, pp. 1–6: 23 April 1849, p.27: 1 Dec. 1849, p.34: 9 Feb. 1850); Building, Standing, Education and Library Committees, 1844–52 (King's Inns MS, p.99); Standing and Education Committees, 1846–73 (King's Inns MS, p.14 for identical entry except that the date is corrected to 1848); Board registers (TCD MSS, mun. v/5/8, p.318 and mun. v/5/9, pp.223, 235, 237); *Dub. Univ. Comm.*, p.36.

9. Benchers' minute book, 1849–56 (King's Inns MS, p. 27: 1 Dec. 1849, p.33: 9 Feb. 1850, pp.36–38: 15 April 1850); 'Dr Longfield on Law School, 30 June 1849' (TCD MS, mun. p/1/1799); *Dub. Univ. Comm.*, pp.46–47, 358–59; *Law Times*, xvi, 185. The minority who voted against establishing a law school at King's Inns were Thomas Staples, Judge Ball, Baron Richards, Judge Torrens and the master of the rolls, Smith.

attended by English students for the bar were all delivered by the five professors of the inns. Students in Dublin had from the start access to the courses of two professors at Trinity and two at King's Inns, the total rising to five from the 1870s, so that, quantitatively, they were not in a significantly inferior position to their London counterparts and, qualitatively, they were possibly better off. Moreover, the Dublin courses lasted two years, whereas in London students were obliged to attend lectures for just one year – if, as usual, they were attending chambers. Indeed, London students could avoid going to any lectures simply by volunteering to sit a final examination, this option not being available in Dublin until later. It is ironic that Edward Sugden was the third signatory of the report which recommended to the English benchers the system then adopted in London. For, it will be recalled, Sugden had earlier refused to endorse Kennedy's Dublin Law Institute on the basis that 'my opinion has always been adverse to lectures, as a law school, unless accompanied by a compulsory examination'.[10]

Under the new regulations of King's Inns two professorships were established by the benchers in Dublin, one of the law of personal property, pleading, practice and precedent; the other of constitutional, criminal and other crown law. In selecting these subjects, the benchers pointed out that they had taken into account the subjects to be taught at Trinity College Dublin, by the professor of feudal and English law and by the professor of civil and canon law. The benchers announced that John Hastings Otway had been appointed to teach the first course, Edmund Hayes the second. The appointments were made for just three years and subsequent appointments were to be similarly limited. The benchers' intention was to avoid men holding the positions indefinitely and to ensure that a succession of practitioners would refresh the syllabi. Each professor was expected to give at least thirty-eight lectures during the year, each lecture together with an opportunity for questions lasting from 4.00 p.m. to 6.00 p.m. The lectures, on Mondays, Wednesdays, Thursdays and Saturdays, were to be open to the public at large, but the public were obliged to withdraw at the end of the formal written lecture and the benchers reserved the right to suspend even this privilege 'if any abuse should arise'.[11]

10. *Dub.Univ.Comm.*, p.362; Sugden to Kennedy, at p.113 above.
11. 'Rules of the King's Inns with respect to legal education, 3 Nov. 1851' at *Dub.Univ.Comm.*, pp. 358–59; 'Rules of the four inns of court, England, 1852, rule 3' at *Dub.Univ.Comm.*, pp.360–62, shows that the English inns also favoured appointing readers for just three years. Again in 1853 Otway presented himself as a candidate for appointment at King's Inns but was

As part of the arrangements for connecting the law school at the University of Dublin with King's Inns, the board of Trinity College had in 1850 reorganised its courses and raised the salary of its professor of civil and canon law, formerly a mere sinecure, and adopted a rule of not electing to the professorship anyone who was not a doctor of laws and a barrister of six years standing. John Anster was appointed to the post shortly afterwards. For his part, the professor of feudal and English law was already required to be a barrister of two years standing, and Mountifort Longfield long continued to hold the position which he had already occupied for over a decade, notwithstanding growing professional commitments. The college also issued a decree at this time requiring the taking of an annual law examination by certain undergraduates who wished to accrue credits by attending the law courses instead of, for example, Hebrew. The new arrangements gave rise to a somewhat anomalous situation in that the two professors at Trinity issued a certificate to students who attended their courses and who sat their exams, but the King's Inns did not ask students to pass the exams, only to attend the courses. Thus, further certificates had to be issued to students who only attended individual courses.[12]

Moreover, the rules of King's Inns allowed graduates of a chartered university to complete their two required law courses in two years, but insisted that non-graduates spend three years taking their four law courses at Trinity and King's Inns. There was no intrinsic reason for this, as it was physically possible to attend any and all four courses each week, and the fact that graduates need

---

    rejected in favour of Richard Bolton McCausland. William Drury then replaced Hayes, the benchers deciding against Denis Caulfield Heron – see List of candidates (King's Inns MS, dated 1853). In 1843 the catholic Heron had won a scholarship at Trinity, only to have it denied him on purely religious grounds. By 1853 he was professor of civil law and jurisprudence at Queen's College, Galway, and a selection of his examination papers had been published in London in 1852, the editor noting that 'the uses of law lectures are now gradually becoming understood in both countries' (Walsh, *The Irish university question: the catholic case*, p.29; *Law Review*, xvi (1852), 100–14; Dowling, *Irish education*, p.164; O'Shaughnessy, 'Legal education', 132–33).

12. *Dub.Univ.Comm.*, pp.29, 32–33, 38. Anster may be better remembered today as the translator of Goethe's *Faust*. Longfield, one of the first three commissioners appointed to the encumbered estates court in 1849 and later first judge of the landed estates court in 1858, was 'our most famous conveyancer' – in Delany's opinion. In 1859 Longfield was elected a bencher of King's Inns. In 1867 he left the landed estates court for a seat on the privy council. He was vice-president of the Statistical Society from its foundation in 1847 and was its president, 1863–67 (Longfield, 'Address by the president', 128; Delany, 'A note on the history of legal education in Ireland', 218; Moss, *Mountifort Longfield*, pp.170–74, 225–26).

only attend for two years meant that a professor could not devote more than that to covering a cycle of topics. The privilege enjoyed by such graduates was additional to that which allowed them to keep but six terms in the dining hall of King's Inns and six at a London inn, whereas non-graduates were obliged to keep nine and eight terms respectively at this time. The rules were, in effect, a modest incentive to attend university, although they did not at the time distinguish between arts and law degrees and they did not apply to graduates of the Catholic University in Dublin.[13]

SOLICITORS AND ATTORNEYS

By an act of 1851 solicitors' apprentices were encouraged by parliament to concentrate their attention on legal studies. Those who attended the lectures and passed the examinations of the professors of law either in Dublin or in the new Queen's Colleges during two years had their period of apprenticeship shortened. But the Dublin University Commission reported in 1853 that the purpose of this act was frustrated in many cases because of the heavy stamp duty of £120 imposed on articles of apprenticeship, for 'the great expense which this stamp duty imposes on young men, or on their parents, must often exhaust the funds that would be much more advantageously applied in securing a liberal education'. This duty and the expense incurred by students for the bar by having to go to London were described by the commission as

> heavy taxes on the entrance to the legal profession [which] counteract in a great measure the benefits of exhibitions and scholarships as means of assisting young men to enter such professions; for what the successful student gains by the public endowment in the form of an encouragement to the diligent cultivation of his talents, is shortly afterwards taken from him in the form of a tax on his admission to the professions in which he can best make his talents and acquirements serviceable to the community.[14]

The new regulations which the benchers introduced in 1850 had ignored solicitors' apprentices. These might attend the law classes at King's Inns as members of the public but, as we have seen, such 'members of the public' had to withdraw from the class at the end of the formal written lecture and prior to the commencement of any discussion. This was a humiliating requirement for

13. *Dub.Univ.Comm.*, pp.356, 358; ibid., p.34, q.18, where Anster says that at that time most law students attended all of the Trinity lectures.
14. ibid., pp.32, 73; 14 & 15 Vict, c. 88.

apprentices, but it appears that some who applied to remain for the full two hours were refused their request. In any event, the timing of the lectures was very inconvenient for apprentices, delivered in term, and at 4 o'clock, when the courts were still busy. It was not long before the Law Society was seeking an improvement in their situation. It was strengthened in its campaign by the fact of its incorporation in 1852.[15]

In 1855 the newly incorporated Law Society presented a memorial to the benchers asking that examinations be introduced as a test of suitability both for intended apprentices and for admission as a practitioner. A committee of the benchers bluntly refused the first request, referring as follows to the education of persons previous to their admission as apprentices:

however insufficient the present system may be, and however inadequate to carry into effect the spirit and object of the old printed rules of the society [of 1793], we are not prepared to recommend any course of preparatory study so advanced and extreme as to be scarcely attainable in practice, more especially in remote parts of Ireland, and by young men of humble means, but endowed with those moral and intellectual qualities calculated and likely to render them most eminent and honorable members of the profession.

The committee complained that 'so advanced a course of preparatory study as that suggested is not required for the admission of students of law [bar students]'. Why, the very notion of solicitors being better educated than barristers! As regards the education of those admitted as apprentices, the benchers argued weakly that the society did not possess the funds to establish a separate course of lectures for apprentices, and suggested that the latter attend part of the classes given by the society's professors for the benefit of bar students. They rejected a proposal in the memorial that apprentices be allowed to use the King's Inns library on the same basis as bar students, unconvinced that the former would 'devote their limited leisure to legal study, in preference to lighter and more agreeable reading'. The benchers clearly did not share parliament's level of confidence in the educational ability of apprentices who, as noted above, were now empowered to shorten their period of apprenticeship upon successful completion of the law courses and examinations at the universities.[16]

15. *Dub. Univ. comm.*, pp.356, 358; Littledale, *King's Inns*, pp.32, 39; Charter and rules of the Incorporated Society of the Attorneys and Solicitors of Ireland, 1852 (King's Inns MSS); Hogan, *Legal profession*, p.113.
16. Benchers' minute book, 1849–56 (King's Inns MS, pp.207–08: 26 Apr. 1856); Littledale, *King's Inns*, p.38.

But the benchers' committee of 1856 could not hold out against all change and in one important respect it bowed to pressure from the Law Society by recommending the institution by King's Inns of a test of fitness for admission as an attorney. It still took another four years of mounting pressure for the benchers to give effect to this recommendation. Meanwhile, the recent statutory provision whereby apprentices were encouraged to reduce their period of apprenticeship by taking law courses and examinations at Trinity or at the Queen's Colleges proved impractical and inadequate as a means of having them trained. In 1858, commissioners enquiring into the Queen's Colleges found that only one apprentice had availed of the privilege and recommended a greater degree of compulsion. In 1859, the benchers' response to the general demands of solicitors and attorneys for improved training came under heavy attack when William Littledale, barrister and secretary of the Statistical and Social Inquiry Society, published his brief account of the history of King's Inns. At last in 1860, with parliament also taking an interest in the matter, the society of King's Inns finally relented. 'It appears to us', the benchers ruminated,

> that the present system of a young man swearing to his literary qualifications should be altered and that in lieu thereof there should be a bona fide examination on a prescribed course of learning before he should be permitted to become an apprentice to an attorney. There should also be a bona fide examination to test his professional attainments before his admission as an attorney.

The benchers appointed William Hickson professor for the legal education of apprentices.[17]

The benchers had completely alienated the solicitors and attorneys and responsibility for the affairs of the lower branch was about to be taken away from King's Inns. In 1866 the Incorporated Law Society successfully promoted a bill in parliament to put its members on the same footing as members of the Incorporated Law Society in England. Under the new act solicitors were no longer required to belong to the King's Inns and responsibility for the education of apprentices was transferred to the Law Society in the first instance. The Law Society thereupon obliged apprentices to attend during two years its new courses of lectures in Dublin.

17. Benchers' minute book, 1856–69 (King's Inns MS, p.80: 19 Jan. 1860, p.105: 22 May 1860); *Report of commissioners on the Queen's Colleges, 1857–58*, pp. 228–90 (Heron), 345–47 (Littledale); Littledale, *King's Inns*, pp.36–40; O'Shaughnessy, 'Legal education', 153–54; Hogan, *Legal profession*, pp.110–11; *NHI*, v, 479–80.

Until 1898, the society still required the consent of the benchers in relation to educational provisions.[18]

In 1872 Mark O'Shaughnessy, the professor of English law at the Queen's College in Cork, complained that any young man who wished to avail of the earlier statutory provision, whereby he might shorten his period of apprenticeship by attending the courses and passing the exams in law at Trinity or at the Queen's Colleges, could not have such performance taken into account when it came to the general requirement that all apprentices spend two years on the Law Society's own new courses. Although such a person could reduce his apprenticeship from five to four years, the courses at Queen's extended over three years, so that having to spend a further two years at courses of the Law Society in Dublin meant that it still took an apprentice at least five years to get into practice.[19]

BARRISTERS

The solicitors were not the only ones who were unhappy with the response of the inns of court to the contemporary demands for reform. In 1853 the report of the Dublin University Commission reflected dissatisfaction on the part of the academics at Trinity with the new arrangement for training barristers which had just been agreed with King's Inns, although criticism was muted because the connection was still so recent. In England the new regulations of the inns of court there left some observers distinctly unimpressed, and in 1854 there was general support when Joseph Napier QC rose in the commons to move for the appointment of a royal commission to investigate the affairs of the London inns. The former student of the University of London and professor of the Dublin Law Institute was motivated largely by a concern for the fate of Irish students in London. Napier recalled the state of education when he himself had entered Gray's Inn twenty-six years earlier:

He remembered well having to ask experienced friends what course of reading they recommended a student to follow, for when he came to London for the purpose of eating a certain number of dinners, the mere dining was all that was required, and the opportunity thus afforded of learning anything was over a bottle of wine. Having an experienced

18. 29 & 30 Vict, c. 84; Hogan, *Legal profession*, pp.122–23; O'Shaughnessy, 'Legal education', 154–55 for details of the Law Society's new courses; Plunkett, 'Attorneys and solicitors in Ireland', p.61. The Law Society was freed from its last link with the benchers by 61 & 62 Vict, c. 17.
19. O'Shaughnessy, 'Legal education', 156.

friend, however, who had once practised at the Irish bar, he asked him in his simplicity, what course of study he would recommend him to take up. The answer was, 'If you are going to the Irish bar the best thing you can study is *Joe Miller*'.

If Napier's Irish pride had been wounded by the suggestion that all he need do to qualify for practice in Ireland was engage in light reading, then he now had a chance to stand up for his countrymen's honour in the matter of educational standards. The Dublin Law Institute was paid a tribute by him, the select committee of 1846 was described pointedly as 'Wyse's' and the King's Inns was given due credit for its reforms, such as they were. Napier suggested that the Irish society would like to go further: 'the Dublin benchers proposed to introduce substantial improvements, but they were hindered by the arrangements in England'. He raised the statutory provision requiring Irish students to go to London and suggested that the English inns of court had an obligation to put their houses in order for those Irish who were obliged to attend. Speaker after speaker supported his motion, although almost exclusively with reference to indigenous English needs. The English attorney general displayed his impatience at being lectured by an Irishman when he expressed a hope that Napier would be as quick to support reforms at the University of Dublin. But the attorney general appeared to be ignorant of the fact that a royal commission had recently investigated Trinity and Napier pointed this out. He added that 'no other university in the kingdom had gone so far in the way of making voluntary reform as the University of Dublin'. At the close of the debate his motion was carried, and he found himself subsequently the only Irishman included in the commission. He and his colleagues investigated the arrangements of the English inns of court for promoting the study of law, the revenues properly applicable and the means most likely to secure a systematic and sound education for students. Conservative thinking at the inns was exposed in the course of evidence given by their treasurers. The commissioners, who included several leading lawyers, held twenty-nine meetings in London and presented their report on 10 August 1855. They recommended that the inns establish a legal university, with powers to grant degrees in law on the basis of performance in examinations. They pointed out that the clergyman, the doctor, the solicitor [in England] and officers in the navy and army were required to pass examinations before being admitted to practice or to hold a commission. The inns, however, were unmoved and took no further steps at the time in the matter of legal training. For its part, the King's Inns itself was not included in the deliberations of the commission of 1855, an omission which later caused Tristram Kennedy to marvel. Littledale believed that 'the labours of the commission were at first intended to extend to Ireland', but was unable to explain why this did not happen. However, it seems clear from reading Napier's speech in the commons that the enquiry was from the start directed exclusively at flaws in the London inns, and certainly most of those who addressed Napier's motion or who sat on the commission had no particular interest in Ireland.[20]

Napier's personal interest in the matter of education was evident again in 1859, during his brief tenure of office as lord chancellor of Ireland. In his ex officio capacity as chairman of the benchers, he was instrumental in having the society's legal education committee consider ways of improving legal training, 'with the view to adapting it better to the wants of those for whom it is intended, having regard to the question of an examination on law preparatory to admission to the bar'.[21] After due consideration by this committee, and some prevarication, the benchers decided in 1864 that they would indeed introduce a final voluntary examination. However, they gave into the temptation of aligning their rules with those of the English inns, insofar as they agreed that such students as chose to sit the exams voluntarily would no longer be obliged to attend lectures. That this was a mistake was recognised within a few years, and in 1872 compulsory lectures were reintroduced for all students at King's Inns. These students were also now obliged to spend three years instead of two preparing for their call and to sit the final examination. In 1876, the benchers admitted that 'during the interval between 1864 and 1872, when the lectures were optional, the attendance upon them was sparse and irregular; students preferred the chance of passing an examination on hasty preparation to the slow and laborious process of attending lectures'.[22]

20. *Hansard*, 3, cxxxi, cols. 147–69 (1 March 1854); *Report of the royal commission on the arrangements in the inns of court and inns of chancery for promoting the study of the law and jurisprudence . . . 1855*; Littledale, *King's Inns*, p.33; Kennedy, *The state and the benchers*, p.22; *Ormrod Report*, p.9; Reader, *Professional men*, pp.55–56. Napier, who had earlier revived the 'Hist.' at Trinity, was said by Amos to have been 'a distinguished member' of the debating society at the University of London (*Sel. comm. leg. ed.*, q.1269 – Amos).
21. Benchers' minute book, 1856–69 (King's Inns MS, p. 66: 26 May 1859). A portrait of Napier painted during the years of his association with the Dublin Law Institute was later donated to the benchers by Tristram Kennedy. It hangs today in the entrance hall at King's Inns library (Ryan-Smolin, *King's Inns portraits*, p. 51).
22. Benchers' minute book, 1856–69 (King's Inns MS, pp.70–71: 23 June 1859, p.121: 15 Apr. 1862, pp.174–75: 15 April 1864, with interleaved

Examinations at the English and Irish inns now became compulsory more than a quarter of a century after Wyse's committee had made its recommendations in the matter. Bowing at last to pressure, the four inns of court in England had resolved that any student admitted from January 1872 could only be called to the bar following success in a final examination. Soon afterwards the benchers of King's Inns introduced their rule that all students admitted from January 1873 would be obliged to pass the general examination if they wished to be called. In England the rule that those who sat exams could avoid lectures remained unchanged. Thus, Ormrod notes that while some of those who sat exams in London did rely on courses at the inns, 'most preferred to go to law tutors or to read privately for the examinations'. Ormrod indicates that the lectures of the English inns 'never played a leading part in education for the practising bar in England'. Pupillage, although not yet obligatory, continued to be the method by which most, if not all, young English barristers learned the techniques of their profession. The form of such pupillage in London was, as has been mentioned, admission to chambers. For their part, as noted above, the Irish benchers between 1850 and 1864 had observed the benefits of compulsory lectures and regretted having made them voluntary as in England. It was for this reason that, as part of the reform of 1872 which also made examinations compulsory for the first time, they reintroduced compulsory lectures for all students. Four years later they noted that once again 'the professors have well-filled classes, the character of the lecturers stands high, and . . . the system works satisfactorily'. The benchers in Dublin were deliberately going their own way and, asked to review the Irish system in 1876, the society's education committee stood firm:

When we recommended the compulsory system we were aware that we were making a step in advance in the line of legal education, which would be much criticised, and would be disliked by those who preferred an examination, for which students might be prepared in a few months, to lectures extending over years. We were, by doing so, in advance of the inns of court in England, where lectures have not as yet been made compulsory, but we felt that the establishment and payment of professors was practically useless, unless the student were obliged to avail himself of their teaching.[23]

    printed rules). *Report of the education committee, King's Inns* (Dublin, 1876), p.6 (copy bound with Benchers' minute book, 1870–85).
23. *Report of the education committee, King's Inns* (1876), p.6; *Ormrod Report*, p.12; Kennedy, *The state and the benchers*, p.23.

Not everyone shared the benchers' sense of self-satisfaction. In June 1872 Mark O'Shaughnessy, who was not only the professor of English law at Queen's College in Cork but also a barrister, had read a detailed critique of the system of legal education in Ireland to the influential Statistical and Social Inquiry Society, of which many lawyers were members and of which both Lawson and Longfield had been president. He described the system as being 'faulty particularly as unmethodical, unsuitable and incomplete', and observed that 'the meagre extent of such instruction' could not fail to strike anyone who glanced, for example, at the range of legal subjects taught at Harvard. Nor could he support a system of professional education which failed to require those who wished to practise as barristers to sit *regular* examinations. He advocated both preliminary and periodical compulsory examinations and suggested that combining these with a final one might achieve 'the exclusion from the profession of the incompetent and indolent'. But the benchers obviously did not share his view on the advantages of such an extensive scheme of examinations. The final ones were quite enough for them.[24]

One person clearly worried that the introduction of final examinations had undermined the campaign for a more systematic reform of legal education was Tristram Kennedy. Kennedy had been remarkably and inexplicably silent on all professional matters during his terms in parliament between 1852 and 1857 and again between 1865 and 1868. But now in his seventieth year, in 1875, he published *The state and the benchers – being an account of undischarged obligations on the part of both the state and the benchers to the law student and the society of King's Inns*. In this he argued in vain for the creation of a formal chambers system, with special training in pleading, drafting and conveyancing. Notwithstanding their very different political opinions, he may have been acting in concert with Chief Justice Whiteside, one of the former professors at his Dublin Law Institute. For, shortly beforehand, Whiteside had been instrumental in establishing a committee of Irish benchers 'to consider and suggest such plans as might be judiciously adopted for promoting the establishment or extension of chambers, to meet the requirements of those entering upon, or engaged in, legal study, in both branches of the profession'. This, as will be seen in chapter 10 below, was just the latest in a long line of such proposals which came to nothing. For the young Irish barrister in such circumstances, the system of 'devilling' with an older man in the

24. ibid., pp.9–11; O'Shaughnessy, 'Legal education', 126, 133–36, 143, 160–61; Anon., 'Legal education in Ireland' (July, 1872), 364.

year after one's call proved indispensable. Much of Kennedy's pamphlet, like Littledale's in 1859, was devoted to contemplating the society's actual and potential income.[25]

The changes on both sides of the Irish Sea during the early 1870s were the minimum to be expected in an age when, as Ormrod would put it, 'great faith was beginning to be placed in examinations as a means of protecting the public from unqualified or incompetent professional men, and the age which saw the professions emerging into their present form, which has depended to a considerable extent on the principle of qualifying examinations'. But Ormrod also made an observation about developments subsequent to the introduction of examinations in England which applies equally well to the history of Irish legal training after 1873, namely that

Thereafter, the educational arrangements for the bar remained substantially the same, with minor changes from time to time, until after the 1939–45 war.[26]

The benchers in England did not yield to continuing pressure for the establishment of some kind of legal university, while those in Ireland did not feel compelled to take any further action, having superimposed a simple final examination upon the structure introduced in 1850. Indeed, standards may even have declined again during the last quarter of the nineteenth century. Thus, in 1889 the benchers in England reported that their system had gradually undergone 'alteration for the worse' from 1873. In 1896, one Irish observer complained that there were not enough lectures for the law student in Ireland, and regretted the fact that about 1894 the benchers had abandoned a system of obliging students to report on cases before the courts. Then in 1906 the lecturing arrangements at King's Inns were subjected to a critical commentary by Brougham Leech, professor of law at Trinity College Dublin. He submitted a statement to the Fry Commission, which had been appointed to consider the future of the University of Dublin, in which he depicted barristers scrambling to line up for the three-year teaching contracts at King's Inns, so that no individual could settle into the job whatever his merit. He said that an attempt to change the rule by renewing the contract of some professors had failed because of this pressure from expectant members of the bar. He also pointed out that the timing of classes was fixed for

25. Kennedy, *The state and the benchers*, passim; Littledale, *King's Inns*, passim.
26. *Ormrod Report*, p.12.

the convenience of teachers rather than students. He mocked the method of lecturing, or reading from a manuscript as he preferred to describe it. He declared to the commission that it was his 'duty' to make a bare statement of facts,

which, however notorious, would otherwise be likely to escape the notice of the commissioners. When men pay for instruction they ought to be provided with the best that can be secured, and further, care should be taken in the arrangements that this instruction should be as effective as possible. It is well-known that as regards the King's Inns professorships, neither of these considerations has ever had its rightful influence; and that it has not been the practice to appoint on the ground of merit alone.

But Brougham Leech may have been smarting from certain criticisms which had been made by practising lawyers about Trinity's law school and his observations of 1906 rebounded only on himself, leaving the benchers unscathed. This was a mark of their success in deflating the pressure for educational reform.[27]

UNIVERSITIES

The Wyse committee of 1846 had referred to the fact that the law schools of continental universities had far more staff than those of Britain and Ireland. Where Trinity had but two professors, some other European colleges had as many as fourteen. Even Longfield, notwithstanding his taste for reform, was in no hurry to recruit new professors, preferring to 'feel our way, and begin with the principle that so much must be taught, and then make further improvements from time to time as they are found practicable'. It was not until 1877 that Trinity added a third professor to its staff, this time devoted to jurisprudence and international law. In 1888 private munificence procured the foundation of the Reid professorship of penal legislation. But if this was expected to bring to four the number of professors, it did not do so because the university reorganised its affairs in such a way that there were still

---

27. *L.I.B.B.*, v, lviii, 262–65; Anon., 'Legal education in England and Ireland' (Feb. 1896), 75–76; *Royal commission on Trinity College Dublin and the University of Dublin . . . 1907* [Fry Commission]; McDowell and Webb, *Trinity College*, pp.321, 413–14. The law school at Trinity was not above criticism when it came to scheduling lectures to suit the demands of part-time professors. Thus, a committee of 1901–02 suggested that 'the honour lectures should be delivered at hours suitable to the students, and not necessarily at the hour of 9 o'clock' (Board register (TCD MS, mun. v/5/17, pp.335, 336, 344)).

only three chairs in law. At no point was any of these professors full-time and Longfield himself, when appointed to judicial office, even took to discharging his part-time duties through a deputy.[28]

A decision by the catholic hierarchy to establish a university specifically for catholics might have led to improved facilities for legal training had the initiative been officially welcomed. In 1851 John Henry Newman was appointed rector by the hierarchy to help make the necessary preparatory arrangements for the university. He told the catholics of Dublin that he saw a place for law in the curriculum, although he cautioned that 'law or medicine is not the end of a university course'. In 1854 the Catholic University opened at Saint Stephen's Green in Dublin, but it had no charter and, therefore, its graduates did not enjoy a status equivalent to those of the chartered institutions. Its school of medicine was recognised by medical authorities, but throughout its life the faculties of engineering and law 'were mere shadows'. The unofficial status of the college made it impossible to insist that its students and graduates enjoy the same relationship with King's Inns as did those of Trinity and, to a lesser extent, of the Queen's Colleges.[29]

In an angry article published anonymously in 1856 the catholic grievance concerning Trinity's privileged position was articulated. It has been indicated by Paul O'Higgins that the author of this piece was Patrick MacMahon, presumably the catholic member of parliament for Wexford who was also a solicitor and journalist. The author had been provoked by the fact that Joseph Napier and George Hamilton, on behalf of Trinity College Dublin, were moving a bill in the house of commons to repeal the Statute of Jeofailles and were basing their argument on the sufficiency of the special relationship between that college and King's Inns, an arrangement which they considered to constitute 'a complete school of law'. The author complained that there was no intrinsic reason why Trinity should enjoy this position, and objected particularly to the fact that graduates of chartered universities, in arts or law,

---

28. *Sel. comm. leg. ed.*, pp.iii–iv, qq. 2979–82; *Royal commission on Trinity College Dublin and the University of Dublin . . . 1906* [Fry Commission], p.75, for a statement from Trinity's law school registrar outlining the school's history from 1858; Board register, 1877 (TCD MS, mun. v/12/358–64); McDowell and Webb, *Trinity College*, pp.169, 330–31. In 1895 David R. Pigot complains that 'under the existing arrangements . . . it is impossible that the subject of International Law can be satisfactorily taught in our law school' (TCD MS, mun. p/1/2516).

29. Society of Jesus (ed.), *A page of Irish history: the story of University College, Dublin, 1883–1909*, p.182; Newman, *The idea of a university*, p.166; Dowling, *Irish education*, pp.167–69; *NHI*, v, 396–98; McRedmond, *Thrown among strangers: John Henry Newman in Ireland*, passim.

could have their period of training reduced while those of other colleges could not – 'thus the one must spend in the pursuit five years, and attend four courses of lectures, and the other spend only three years and attend two courses of lectures'. Acknowledging that the Catholic University was unlikely to be granted a charter, 'the protestant prejudices of England [having been] lashed to fury by the Maynooth cry', the author called for 'free-trade in education', and argued that the cause of legal education would be better served if the benchers of King's Inns were 'kept in fear of competition, by allowing all persons called to the bar in England to practise here on producing a certificate of their call, just as is done in the colonies'. It was the case at this time that Irish medical students were opting for educational institutions in London instead of for the College of Surgeons in Dublin. So the author suggested that if the Catholic University was not to be put on an equal footing with Trinity in relation to King's Inns, at least catholics might be given the option of being called in England where the inns were no longer hostile to them. A similar proposal by Sir Valentine Blake of Galway had been rejected seventeen years earlier. On this occasion, too, the author's suggestion was not taken up and, in any event, Napier's bill lapsed.[30]

But in 1859 McMahon himself, as member of parliament for Wexford, brought forward another bill which proposed that the benchers of King's Inns admit students to the Irish bar on the same terms as students were admitted to the English bar. McMahon pointed out that 'for the last twenty years the benchers in England had admitted students to the bar in three years, whether they were graduates or not; but in Ireland a student could not be called to the bar in less than five years after his name had been entered in the books unless he was a graduate of the university'. However, as shall be seen in the next chapter, McMahon's measure was coupled with a demand to repeal the Statute of Jeofailles, and the whole bill ultimately failed. That same year of 1859 a report of a sub-committee of the senate of the Catholic University recommended to the bishops, among other things, the establishment of an actual law school. But the bishops did not act on this suggestion.[31]

Although the students of the Queen's Colleges did benefit from the benchers' concession to graduates of the chartered universities,

30. [MacMahon], 'The Catholic University and legal education', 226–46; O'Higgins, *Bibliography*; *Hansard, 3*, cxlii, col. 588 (23 May 1856).
31. [MacMahon], 'The Catholic University and legal education', passim; *Saunders's News-letter*, 23 April 1842; *Hansard, 3*, lxi, col.1294 and lxii, col. 894 (20 April 1842); *Hansard, 3*, clv, col. 81f. (19 July 1859); McGrath, *Newman's University: idea and reality*, passim.

their teachers, too, were complaining of the injustice of Trinity's special position when it came to combining law courses at the inns and at a college in order to qualify as a barrister. In 1858 the commissioners appointed to examine the progress and conditions of the three new Queen's Colleges regretted the fact that a full legal education was not required for admission to practice, and said that this was one of the chief causes of the small numbers in the law schools of the Queen's Colleges. Since 1852 the average attendance per year across the colleges in Belfast, Cork and Galway had been just twenty. In 1872 O'Shaughnessy returned to the fray in a speech already quoted above. He explained at length to the Statistical Society how the rules of King's Inns resulted unfairly in practical advantages for the students of Trinity College over those of the Queen's Colleges, in that the latter were obliged to spend three years on a diet of legal instruction which could be ingested at Trinity in just two. In this and in other ways, the benchers had equated courses which were not equivalent and discounted what O'Shaughnessy clearly considered to be the superior and more complete lectures of the Queen's Colleges. The Queen's professors did not enjoy the special relationship with the benchers which those of Trinity did, and O'Shaughnessy could see no good reason for this.[32]

But the arrangement for legal education was by no means the only aspect of university education regarded by critics as being unsatisfactory. In 1873 Gladstone attempted to answer continuing complaints about the whole system by bringing forward a university bill centred on the concept of a great new University of Dublin, with many colleges and associated institutions throughout the country. Theo Moody has described the scheme as 'bold, ingenious and far-sighted'. But, in practice, it antagonised both catholic and protestant interests and the bill was soon abandoned. However, parliament did in 1873 pass another bill, opening up Trinity to catholics by the removal of all remaining religious tests. The catholic bishops were unimpressed, believing that the possibility of catholics being appointed to the board of Trinity was remote in practice, and many supporters of this bill indeed saw it largely as a means of pre-empting further interference with the college.[33] Every office and emolument in Trinity, outside of the Divinity School, had now in theory been opened to catholics and one of

32. *Report of commissioners on the Queen's Colleges, 1857–58*, pp.27–29, 97–101 (Molyneux and Leslie); above, note 24.
33. Atkinson, *Irish education*, pp.137–39; Dowling, *Irish education*, pp.170–71; Moody and Martin, *The course of Irish history*, p.281; Burke, 'Trinity College and the religious problem', 102–03.

those invited to apply for one was John Naish, the future chancellor of Ireland. A former student of the college, Naish was a senior moderator in mathematics and science and it was his old professor in mathematics, Richard Townsend, who recommended him to colleagues. Townsend wrote that

> of all the Roman catholics who passed through my hands during my long lectureship, the one, after Casey, I would most wish to see connected with us permanently, – as a man of high ability and distinction, but of right mind and proper feeling, – is Naish.[34]

Although Naish had been called to the bar in 1865 and although Townsend described the law school as being of all the schools 'that considered outside college the least efficient as at present conducted', it was neither to law nor to mathematics but to the chair of modern history that he suggested Naish be appointed. Naish declined on the grounds that he was too busy. But, in doing so, he passed a few remarks about the law school, supporting the teaching of civil law on the basis that 'no lawyer could be said to be fully educated who had not a reasonable acquaintanceship with it', and observing that the law of property and the law of equity ought to be taught by two separate professors, instead of one. He ended by referring to the fact that there were five lectureships at the inns of court in London. Whatever others might think, Naish in 1873 did not then see great pedagogic benefits in the connection between King's Inns and Trinity College, remarking to Townsend that

> the benchers, as you are aware, have a series of lectures delivered at King's Inns. It is certainly somewhat of a pity that some arrangement for a systematic teaching of law could not be arrived at between the university and the benchers. It would be a great advantage to law students.[35]

But such practical reforms were overlooked while the debate on the nature of university education continued. In 1879, in another attempt to create a university system which might command widespread support, parliament dissolved the Queen's University and established the Royal University of Ireland. This was purely

34. Townsend to Carson, 7 Nov. 1873 (TCD MS, mun. p/1/2203–04).
35. ibid., Naish to Townsend, 14 Nov. 1873 (TCD, MS, mun. p/1/2220). In 1873 the bursar and historian of T.C.D., John W. Stubbs was more concerned about the timing than the quality of legal education. He complained that lectures at King's Inns did not actually begin until 5 o'clock and that this 'seriously interfered' with students dining in commons at Trinity (TCD MS, mun. p/1/2198).

an examining body, intended both to encompass existing courses at the Queen's Colleges and to meet some of the claims of the Catholic University. But the new arrangement was unsatisfactory and a decade later Archbishop Walsh still found it necessary to defend himself against those who believed that catholics might yet make do with Trinity College:

I may be told that individuals have passed, not only in safety, but in honourable fidelity to every catholic principle, through Trinity College and other colleges of mixed education in the country. Yes. And there were survivors of the charge of the six hundred at Balaklava. And men have passed with their lives through the rapids of Niagara.[36]

In 1901 certain catholic law students complained to the royal commission on university education in Ireland (the Robertson Commission) that young men registering at University College Dublin had not had extended to them the same opportunity to study law as had the students of the Queen's Colleges, Trinity and the University of London. The complainants were contemporaries of James Joyce, who apparently attended as a spectator the law students' debating society at King's Inns and later in the pages of *Ulysses* made creative use of what he had heard there. Discussing their predicament amongst themselves at their college on St Stephen's Green, perhaps as Joyce jousted verbally with them on his way to some meeting or lecture, the catholic law students agreed that they were disadvantaged by the current arrangements:

all efforts, however, which have been made to secure similar privileges for the catholic law students attending University College, Dublin, have failed. A projected law school was refused recognition on the ground of the unofficial character of the college. Hence all catholic law students residing in Dublin are obliged to attend lectures at Trinity College, though they are not members of it. This necessity of attendance is, naturally, objected to by students who do not feel themselves justified in otherwise attending the college.[37]

36. Walsh, *The Irish university question*, p.157.
37. *Royal commission on university education in Ireland, second report . . . 1902* [Robertson Commission], p.328. The law students who signed the memorial were Arthur Clery, Hugh Kennedy (later first chief justice of the Irish Free State), James A. Murnaghan (later of the supreme court), Cornelius Lehane, William Barrett and Vincent Rice; Eugene Sheehy, *May it please the court* (Dublin, 1951), pp.12–20; *Royal commission on university education in Ireland, final report . . . 1903* [Robertson Commission], p.14, for a thumbnail history of U.C.D. From 1883 the running of U.C.D. had been entrusted to the jesuits, whose philosophical speculations stimulated their most famous graduate, James Joyce, to ruminate on college life. It appears

But the Robertson Commission proceeded to ignore the whole question of legal education, and there is no entry listing the King's Inns in the index to its four volumes of evidence and reports. Five years later, the Fry Commission was more interested in the subject, winning from the benchers a concession which vindicated Naish's suggestion of 1873 that the linkage between King's Inns and Trinity College had not worked efficiently in practice. Notwithstanding the self-complacency of their own education committee in 1876, the Irish benchers now admitted to Fry in 1906 that 'no adequate attempt was made to arrange the curriculum of the King's Inns and that of any collegiate law school so that the former would be supplementary to the latter, and so that the two taken together would provide a complete and consistent course of legal study'.[38]

Finally, in 1908, the government came up with an acceptable compromise on the university question. The Royal University was dissolved and parliament created instead the present National University of Ireland and the Queen's University of Belfast. U.C.D. soon had its own active law school but there were still those who resented its very existence. Speaking at a meeting in the college on 12 November 1911, the chancellor of the new N.U.I., Archbishop Walsh, remarked that,

I took it for granted, when our National University of Ireland was established, with its university college here in Dublin, and in this college a fully equipped law school, that this particular feature of our old university grievance was at an end. I was, however, speedily undeceived. When one or two of our students went over to the King's Inns, and claimed the benefit of what was known as 'the exemption clause', – the clause exempting students of a chartered university with a duly constituted school of law from the necessity of attending lectures in Trinity College Dublin, – the curious point was raised that the university of which they were members, the N.U.I., was not in existence when the exemption clause in favour of university students was made by the benchers many years ago, and that, therefore, it was not clear that students of the new university of ours could claim any benefit under that clause.

Dr Walsh noted that the problem had been solved subsequently and said that the N.U.I. was particularly indebted to Chief Baron Palles and to Judge Barton for the benchers having agreed to certain changes in the rules of King's Inns which resulted in

that 'Hugh Boylan' of *A portrait* is based on the 'prim and proper' Kennedy (Ellmann, *James Joyce*, pp.57–75, 91; Joyce, *A portrait of the artist as a young man*, pp.177–257).

38. *Royal commission on Trinity College Dublin and the University of Dublin . . . 1907* [Fry Commission], p.389.

U.C.D. being put on exactly the same footing as Trinity College as regards legal education.[39]

The story of the creation of a full-scale law faculty at U.C.D. lies outside the scope of this work. It also appears to have lain outside the scope of Delany's 'History of legal education in Ireland', for, in his article published in 1960 in the United States, the Trinity professor ignored University College Dublin and made only passing reference to any events in the twentieth century. Moreover, his statement that the law school at Trinity 'continued to flourish' from the introduction of an honours degree in 1903 disregarded the bitter contemporary attack by Brougham Leech on that particular reorganisation of legal education. Brougham Leech, part-time professor of feudal and English law and busy registrar of deeds, claimed that the reorganisation had actually made matters worse and had placed the King's Inns in a stronger position in its relationship with the college.[40]

But whatever shortcomings there might be in the system as it existed by the end of the first decade of the twentieth century, the years between 1850 and 1873 had witnessed a revival of legal

39. Benchers' minute book, 1901–17 (King's Inns MS, p.277: 8 June 1911); *Irish Times*, 13 Nov. 1911; *Freeman's Journal*, 13 Nov. 1911; *ILT & SJ*, xlv, 280 (18 Nov. 1911). Palles had been a member of the Fry Commission and was subsequently appointed chairman of a special commission to oversee the creation of the N.U.I. Walsh, too, was a member of this body and it was assisted in its work by the young barrister, James A. Murnaghan, one of those catholic law students who had earlier protested about their lot to the Roberston Commission. When Palles died, Walsh bought his library for U.C.D. (Delany, *Christopher Palles*, pp.134–37). Dunbar Plunket Barton was co-author of an account of the English inns of court and of a biography of Tim Healy which includes a chapter on the Irish bar (Barton et al., *The story of our inns of court*; Barton, *Timothy Healy*).

40. Delany, 'Legal studies in T.C.D. since the foundation', 3–16; Delany, 'The history of legal education in Ireland', 405–06; *Royal commission on TCD and the University of Dublin, final report . . . 1907* [Robertson Commission], pp.61–63, 388–90; ibid., evidence, qq. 2312–17, 2484–85, 3202–358. Although Brougham Leech was a vigorous and active unionist, it is said that 'in university politics he was an iconoclastic radical'. However, his criticisms of King's Inns may have been coloured by the fact that the committee which was formed by the board of T.C.D. in 1901 to report on the law school was dominated by practising lawyers and was critical of the courses there (Delany, 'Legal training and the universities', 201–02, 207–08, 217–19, 223–24, 237–38; McDowell and Webb, *Trinity College*, pp.321, 413–14). For legal education in the first-half of the twentieth century see Duncan, 'The law school during the last half-century', passim; Johnston, 'Legal education in Ireland', 182, 187–88, 193–94; Moran, 'Legal education in Eire', 213–15; Binchy, 'The law and the universities', with 'comments on the foregoing article' by Tierney, Gavan Duffy, O'Keeffe and O'Sullivan, passim; Osborough, 'Review of McDowell and Webb', passim.

training on both sides of the Irish Sea. This could only be considered a great advance, given the absence of educational facilities for lawyers in the preceding period. However, change was slowed by the conservatism of English and Irish benchers whose attitude during the nineteenth century is reminiscent of Shakespeare's 'whining schoolboy . . . creeping like snail unwillingly to school'.[41]

A further factor restraining more extensive reform in Ireland before 1885 was the requirement that anyone who wished to practise as a barrister had first to spend time at one of the London inns. Such a person, in the words of O'Shaughnessy,

> neither studies, nor practises, nor endeavours to come to a knowledge of law, in his hurried visits; but 'as in duty bound' tries the cellar, in wine and beer, of the society which he selects to receive his fees, and dines upon the venerable oak of Gray's Inn or the Middle Temple, or amidst the newer pomp of the halls of Lincoln's Inn or the Inner Temple.[42]

But the requirement was not only educationally inefficient on a personal level: it also obstructed the development of a comprehensive system of legal training generally in Ireland. To this requirement and to the attempts to repeal it we now turn.

---

41. *As you like it*, act 2, scene 7, lines 146–47.
42. O'Shaughnessy, 'Legal education', 145.

CHAPTER NINE

'So many legs of mutton': Irishmen forced to the English inns, 1542–1885

MANY IRISH LAW STUDENTS who were required to spend time and money at the English inns of court were contemptuous of the statutory provision which, from 1542 to 1885, obliged them to 'keep terms' in London. At a meeting called by law students in 1841 to consider this obligation, it was observed that

> most of us . . . may readily recollect that the first words which we heard, or ourselves used, on entering the King's Inns, Dublin, or any of the inns of court in London, contained reflections on the absurdity of the present system, the necessity for its abolition, and the substitution of some other in its place. If we were to go to the oldest standing of the bar, and even trace these opinions still further, we would find that the sentiments in circulation during our own times, are but the thoughts re-echoed from a period almost contemporaneous with the passing of the [statute].[1]

Had the English inns trained their young members in law and practice then Irish sentiments might have been different. But it is widely accepted that the inns of court in London provided no significant educational service from the seventeenth century onwards.[2] So why then was the Tudor statute not repealed until 1885? The explanation lies in factors which were principally cultural and ideological rather than pedagogic.

Although it was the parliament of Ireland which in 1542 passed the Statute of Jeofailles, thereby obliging the Irish to reside for a period at the inns of court in London, there is little doubt that the provision was forced upon it by royal officials in London. There were new political and ideological realities emerging and, as Patterson has pointed out in regard to the period generally,

1. *Saunders's News-letter*, 16 Nov. 1841; *Sel. comm. leg. ed.*, pp.341f. The students referred to the statute of '5th Eliz', intending presumably to refer to 11 Eliz., sess.1, c.5 which perpetuated 33 Hen VIII, sess.2, c.3 (Statute of Jeofailles, below).
2. Kenny, *King's Inns and the kingdom of Ireland*, pp.6–10, pp.160–62.

the impersonality of law in the centralising nation-states became the jural ideal of modern legal systems: law emanated from outside the local community, and equity was now thought to reside not in sensitive interpretation of norms in the light of contingencies, but in uniformity, precision, clarity and 'certainty'.

So, forcing the Irish to attend London may have seemed like a way of ensuring their conformity in legal matters. But the results were less than satisfactory. Before long the Irish who travelled over to England in accordance with the requirement were being accused by Fynes Moryson of 'lurking' at the inns just long enough to get 'a smack of the grounds of our law'. It was hardly surprising that this was so. In the past the inns had evinced a chauvinistic hostility to the Irish, and the Reformation ensured that such xenophobic suspicion and antagonism would be reinforced by religious prejudice. Thus, from a very early stage, London had been an uncongenial climate for many law students from Ireland and it long remained so. By the time such hostility towards the Irish had waned the standard of education at the inns had long fallen from its zenith. The fact that by the seventeenth century educational exercises were at best reduced to a series of mere formalities meant that no amount of subsequent good-fellowship could compensate for the lack of professional benefits to Irish law students under the arrangement.[3]

Whatever humiliations the students from Ireland had to suffer in London by virtue of the act of 1542, suffer these they did for the first hundred years without any great recorded protest. The list of proposed reforms which Hugh O'Neill, earl of Tyrone, presented to the government in 1599 included some demands for educational changes generally. But he sought no specific measures in relation to legal training, demanding neither an Irish inn of court nor the repeal of the Statute of Jeofailles. Perhaps the Irish were more worried about simply being permitted as catholics or 'recusants' to practise law than about the details of the qualifying procedures. It was certainly to the practice of law, and not training in it, that Sir John Bath gave priority in the 1620s.[4]

However, with Irish confidence in full spate during the rebellion of the 1640s, the representative catholic assembly known as the Confederation of Kilkenny sought and secured assurances

---

3. ibid., pp.13–20, pp.40–53; *Stat.Ire.*, 33 Hen VIII, sess.2 (1541–42), c.3; Moryson, 'The commonwealth of Ireland', 278, 317; Patterson, 'Brehon law in late medieval Ireland', 61.
4. *Cal.S.P.Ire., 1599–1600*, pp.279–80; Corcoran, *State policy in Irish education*, p.58; Kenny, *King's Inns and the kingdom of Ireland*, pp.95–98.

that a new inn of court might be created in Ireland and that 'such students, natives of the kingdom, as shall be therein may take and receive the usual degrees accustomed in any inns of court'. In effect, such a concession would have meant the repeal of the Statute of Jeofailles, with its requirement for residency in England, and would have allowed the new inn to develop as the King's Inns never had.[5]

While the concession of the 1640s was soon to be overtaken by political events, the prospects of a new and native inn elicited a riposte from the Irish protestants which is worth repeating because it is a clear exposition of one rationale for the requirement that Irish law students reside for a period in England. Whatever about the original Tudor 'jural ideals' which may have lain behind the Statute of Jeofailles, there was a simpler cultural reason why many of those who supported the connection with England continued to defend the measure. They believed that exposure to the metropolis might overawe or civilise the Irish. Thus, in 1644, the agents of the protestants who had been greatly frightened by the recent rebellion in Ireland, asserted that the laws and statutes of Ireland were similar in general to those of England and argued that

the inns of court in England are sufficient, and the protestants come thither without grudging, and that is a means to civilize them after the English customs, to make them familiar and in love with the language and nation, to preserve law in the purity, when the professors of it shall draw from the original fountain, and see the manner of the practice of that in the same great channels where his majesties courts of justice of England do flow most clearly, whereas by separation of the kingdoms in that place of their principal instruction where their foundations in learning are to be laid, a degenerate corruption in religion and justice may haply be introduced and spread with much more difficulty to be corrected and restrained afterwards by any discipline to be used in Ireland. . . .[6]

Implicit in this statement was a suggestion that catholic begrudgers were unenthusiastic about going to London. The civilising and professional value of such visits appears to have been less evident to them than to their protestant colleagues. For centuries efforts had been made to induce the inhabitants of

5. Paul Cullen, 'On protestant ascendancy and catholic education in Ireland', 510; Kenny, *King's Inns and the kingdom of Ireland*, pp.118–24.
6. Borlase, *The reduction of Ireland*, pp.69–70, citing 'The propositions of the Roman Catholics of ireland . . . with the humble answers of the agents for the Protestants of Ireland . . . made in pursuance of Your Majesties directions of 9 May 1644'.

Ireland to adopt English ways. A notable example was the passage in 1536 by the Irish Reformation parliament of 'an act for the English order, habit and language'. In 1541, the judges and law officers of Ireland assured the English privy council that one of the functions of the recently established King's Inns was, in fact, 'the bringing up of gentlemen's sons within the realm in the English tongue, habit and manner'. Complaints about the reliability and competence of the legal profession in Ireland were a recurrent feature of English official discourse, a distrust reflected in the petition from the protestants of 1644.[7]

The protestants of 1644 gave priority to cultural considerations, referring in their petition to the need to civilize law students 'after the English customs' and 'to make them familiar and in love with the language and nation'. Only subsequently in the text did they refer to the law. There was an implicit endorsement of the pedagogic value of a visit to London, although how and where the visitors were supposed to 'draw from the original fountain' was not explained. Apparently, students were expected to attend the courts. There is little evidence that the inns of court were then providing comprehensive or valuable training even to English students. In their petition, the protestants also asserted that as between England and Ireland there existed a close affinity in both common law and statute law. They echoed the most likely Tudor rationale for the statute by suggesting that the law requiring residency in London was intended to ensure that divergence was avoided. But even here cultural considerations were again given priority, with a reference being made specifically to the danger of 'a degenerate corruption in religion and justice'. Overall, the petition of 1644 is the most comprehensive extant argument in favour of the residency requirement. It reveals a high ideological factor in the reasoning of those who continued to support the measure. Such supporters included the benchers who, in 1779, restated the rule and announced that they did 'highly approve of such regulations as contributing much to preserve the honour and credit of the bar',[8] this notwithstanding the fact that the English inns had reached their educational nadir by the late eighteenth century. As late as the second half of the nineteenth century the provision still had its defenders.

7. *Stat.Ire.*, 28 Hen VIII, c.15, esp. ss.1, 3, 19; Corcoran, *Irish education*, pp.15–17; Kenny, *King's Inns and the kingdom of Ireland*, pp.23–27, 30–40, app. 1; ibid., p.14, n.38 for references to the alleged venality and ignorance of Irish lawyers.

8. Admission of benchers, 1741–92 (King's Inns MS, p.147); Kenny, *King's Inns and the kingdom of Ireland*, p.179.

No doubt many of the students who went to London by force of the Statute of Jeofailles were influenced by the dominant values and practices of the city. Whatever about their legal education, there was plenty to see and do there, and a young man might enjoy the opportunity of coming to terms with himself in an environment free of homely constraints, just as students today take advantage of 'Erasmus' exchanges or postgraduate courses to reside temporarily in other countries. Thus, in the 'enlightened' second half of the eighteenth century, Irishmen such as John Philpot Curran, Robert Day and Theobald Wolfe Tone went as required to the English inns and proceeded to devote a great deal of their time to debating, literature, and socialising. If Day's biographer is to be believed 'these were formative years for the student, and Day's attitude towards social life, politics, travel and his literary tastes were strongly influenced by these five years spent in English surroundings at the Middle Temple'.[9] The framers of the Statute of Jeofailles and the protestants of 1644 might have been well-pleased by such civilizing results. Even Daniel O'Connell, who is said to have dismissed the requirement to attend the inns as just 'so many legs of mutton', acknowledged that his time in London might be used fruitfully for 'the acquisition of all those qualities that constitute the polite gentleman . . . the latter serves as a first passport or recommendation'.[10] But the future activities of law students such as Wolfe Tone and Daniel O'Connell were to belie any crude or mechanical connection between residency in England and a yearning for close affinity with her political or legal system. Indeed, the Irish lawyers as a body opposed the Act of Union of 1800. Of course, circumstances had changed considerably since the sixteenth and seventeenth centuries. There had never been any guarantee that Irishmen would be so overawed by imperial thinking that they would meekly adopt English perspectives. But, in any

9. Kenny, *King's Inns and the kingdom of Ireland*, pp.180–81; Day, *Day of Kerry*, p.52. But Curran's biographer hastens to assure us that the man 'rose very early and studied till he was exhausted', before going out on the town, and that 'during second year he spent a considerable portion of his time in the courts of law' (Curran, *Life of John Philpot Curran*, p.57); Elliott, *Wolfe Tone*, pp.43–61.
10. Houston, *Daniel O'Connell*, pp.124–26; O'Faolain, *King of the beggars*, p.62, citing a letter of 10 Dec. 1795. There is an apocryphal story that O'Connell 'rose superior to national prejudice' and refused to move to have the Statute of Jeofailles repealed, saying supposedly that 'it did a young Irishman good to come and eat dinners in an inn of court before he was called to the Irish bar'. But if he ever made such a remark, and it is possible that he felt that a period in the metropolis might broaden the mind, it seems unlikely to have been his considered opinion. For the story see Blackham, *Wig and gown*, p.69.

event, by the late eighteenth century there was such a variety of political views being expressed in London that young men were at least as likely to be influenced by liberal and revolutionary ideas as by tory tenets.

One of Day's close companions in London was Henry Grattan. In 1767 Grattan entered the Middle Temple, but a biographer of his early life notes that

> he looked with contempt upon the absurd 'qualification', then . . . the only one necessary for admission to the Bar, namely that he should eat a certain number of 'contract' dinners. He also felt the degradation of being compelled to complete the number at one of the English Inns of Court. There was little to excite enthusiasm for the profession in Ireland at the time; certainly Grattan troubled himself very little about it. But he obtained [while in London] admission into the society of prominent politicians and traced the opinions of Fox, and Burke, and the Earl of Chatham, from the drawing-room to the House of Commons . . . . Henceforward he took to ruminating deeply over the melancholy subjection of his country, wandering in the gardens and through the moonlit forests of Windsor, and indulging his vein of spontaneous eloquence – habits which often led him into ludicrous situations, but which undoubtedly preserved him from demoralising indulgences of every kind.[11]

One wonders had the English inns of court been more active educationally, would the course of Irish history have run differently. Burdened by legal reading and examinations, might the minds of Wolfe Tone and Henry Grattan have been confined to points of law and their careers to a life at the bar? For their part, other students such as William Conyngham Plunket, Thomas Lefroy and Francis Blackburne sought to avoid 'demoralising indulgences' in London by a solitary commitment to learning the law.[12] But it was quite a challenge. Thomas Ruggles commented in 1791 that while in pursuit of his legal education,

> especially that part of it which passed at the Temple, the writer experienced the want of a monitor to teach him the best method of employing his time; to point out to him the shoals and quick-sands, which he should endeavour to avoid, and to show him the fair passage to honourable success in the profession.[13]

---

11. [Plunkett]. *The early life of Henry Grattan*, pp.7–8. A copy of this pamphlet, signed in 1943 by V.T.H. Delany, was bought in 1993 by this author in an Edinburgh bookshop.
12. Plunket, *Life, letters and speeches of Lord Plunket*, i, 39; Lefroy, *Memoir of Chief Justice Lefroy*, p.20; Blackburne, *Life of Francis Blackburne*, pp.21–23.
13. [Ruggles], *The barrister: or strictures on the education proper for the bar*, p.iii.

Between 1803 and 1805, Blackburne experienced 'what is probably felt by most men who enter on such a study unaided (as I was) – a great degree of disappointment'. He later wrote that

> no matter what the amount of time or attention devoted to it, there was scarcely a sense of progress; there were no tests to try what degree of knowledge was acquired, or the power of applying any that was to any practical use.

Dismissing the possibility of entering the chambers of a conveyancer or special pleader as too expensive, Blackburne found that

> the only insight into the great machinery of the law was that of attendance in the King's Bench in England; and after spending the vacation of the year 1804 at Broadstairs, and labouring incessantly to make some impression on 'Coke', 'Blackstone' and 'Fearne', the three following terms were usefully employed in reading assiduously and attending that court.[14]

Blackburne subsequently became in 1839 one of the first lawyers to join the council of the Dublin Law Institute. Another Irishman, recalling his days in London between 1814 and 1816 and how he had applied himself, 'with great ardour', to the acquisition of general knowledge, whilst 'deferring for the present a regular course of legal reading', remarked that

> it may appear somewhat singular, but so it was, that previous to the day of my call, I was never inside an Irish court of justice. When at the Temple, I had occasionally attended the proceedings at Westminster Hall, where a common topic of remark among my fellow students was the vast superiority of our Bar in grace of manner and classical propriety of diction.[15]

Irish students were certainly to have plenty of time to develop their manners and diction over dinner, because from the last decade of the eighteenth century they were expected also to 'keep terms' at King's Inns, which had built for itself a fine new dining hall designed by James Gandon. The fact that keeping terms essentially meant nothing more than eating was underlined by one author in 1827, who wrote that

> gentlemen, who intend to be called to the bar in Ireland, must keep nine terms in the King's Inns, Dublin, and eight terms in one of the inns of court in London. The sum required on admission to the King's Inns is

---

14. Blackburne, *Life of Francis Blackburne*, pp.21–24.
15. Anon., 'Confessions of a junior barrister' [1825], 238.

£45. The mode of keeping a term there is by attending in the hall, at dinner hour, one, or any number of days, in each of two separate half days.

Noting that it was not always convenient for Irish students to keep their eight terms successively in London, the author added that the 'student may keep terms in London and Dublin alternately, or in any other order that he may think proper'.[16]

In 1834, a nice statement of the supposed benefits of obliging law students from England and Ireland to eat dinners at the inns in London was advanced by the commissioners appointed to inquire into the practice and proceedings of the Superior Courts in England, namely

its making known the person of the student, and exposing him, if his character be disreputable, to more easy detection by the society, before the period of his application to be called to the bar. It also gives an opportunity of attending the courts, and of associating with students and other members of the profession.[17]

---

16. Kenny, *King's Inns and the kingdom of Ireland*, pp.185–86, 248–49, 254; [Lee], *The law student's guide*, pp.107–08. The latter also states (p.108) that 'the generality of Irish students resort to Gray's Inn, it being by far the most convenient, not only on account of the facility of keeping terms there, but also that of admission, for they are not required at the inn to have the entrance document signed by two barristers, or to procure two housekeepers to join in a bond. It will suffice if any other student or member of the inn do sign both'. He also adds that it is the least expensive inn and that there is no charge for absent commons, a good thing because 'it is not always convenient for Irish students to keep the eight terms successively'. Throughout the centuries Irish students favoured different inns at different times, but Hogan's research confirms that more Irish students were at Gray's Inn than at any other single inn in the period from 1820 to 1840. Joseph Napier, for example, entered in 1828 and would later, in the house of commons, relate his experiences as an Irish student arriving in London at that time. Before 1825 the rules of Gray's Inn appear to have required 'Irish gentlemen' not only to lodge special securities but also to take a sacramental test. That the society's rules may have been relaxed even earlier is suggested by the fact that in 1796 Daniel O'Connell transferred his membership from Lincoln's Inn to Gray's Inn in order to be called one half year earlier than otherwise. Thus, having 'kept terms' at two English and one Irish inn before being called, he could joke later of his 'threefold apprenticeship to the law' (*Hansard*, 3, cxxxi, col.151 (1 March 1854); *Statement of the regulations of the four inns of court as to the admission of students, etc.* . . . 1846; *L.I. adm. reg.*, i, 549; *L.I.B.B.*, iv, 68; *Pension Book of Gray's Inn, 1669–1800*, p.371; Houston, *O'Connell*, p.125 n. f; O'Connell, *Correspondence*, i, 14, 23–25; Hogan, *Legal profession*, pp.32–33, 39).
17. *Sixth report of the commission on the practice and procedure of the superior courts in England . . . 1834*, p.9.

But the courts might also be attended in Dublin, and there were other ways of associating with like-minded individuals. As regards exposing their character to scrutiny, no doubt just such inspection by the English rankled many Irishmen. Moreover, to their native sense of humiliation at having to eat pie at the London inns, was added a self-conscious awareness of the inadequacy of educational facilities when it came to the teaching of law in Dublin. This was especially so as the need for formal professional training became generally better appreciated from the second quarter of the nineteenth century onwards. Although Henry Grattan forsook a career at the bar upon qualification, his son could not resist a savage attack on the system which had seen his father and himself forced to attend the Middle Temple. In 1839, the younger Grattan wrote that

the absurd and useless form of sending Irishmen to London in order to qualify them to practise at the bar in Ireland is one of the badges of servitude long worn by the people of the country. It has no recommendation in point of principle, and is only to be excused inasmuch as it takes the young mind from a narrow and prejudiced locality, and tends to make it expand in a freer region, where liberty is more prevalent, and where the doctrines enforced in a colony cease to contaminate. Yet the practice is not without its dangerous concomitants. Youth, at its most vigorous and tempting period, is left to range in the greatest capital in the world, free from restraint, and amidst pleasures and allurements of every kind; for as to studying law at the age of twenty-one in London, that seldom seriously occupies the mind or the time of any Templar.[18]

It was also in 1839, the year of Grattan's critique, that the Dublin Law Institute opened its doors. This was further grist to the mill of those who wished to break any connection with the English inns. One observer who was highly supportive of the new institute saw its existence as tending to secure the abolition of what was termed 'the gross injustice inflicted upon law students, by compelling them "to serve terms" in London':

the latter is a compulsion which can only be justified upon the principle that they have there an opportunity of receiving a superior legal education, to what they can obtain at home. This, if it ever were, at all events, can be no longer the case; and we protest against the continuance of a system which would be ludicrous for its absurdity, if it were not a monstrous inconvenience and expense, an irreparable loss of valuable time, and a badge of subjection insufferably offensive.[19]

18. Grattan [jnr.], *Memoirs of the life and times of Henry Grattan*, p.113.
19. Anon., 'The Dublin Law Institute' (Nov. 1840), 431.

If the requirement to eat dinners in London appeared absurd to Irish protestants such as Grattan and Curran, how much more offensive it must have been to Irish catholics. From 1792 these had been permitted to practise at the bar, and from 1829 were eligible to be appointed king's counsel or judges. The first catholic to sit on the Irish bench since the battle of the Boyne was Michael O'Loghlen, who became master of the rolls in 1836. Speaking at a dinner in the Dublin Law Institute in January 1841, as we saw in chapter 5, he was reported to have observed that 'the difficulties which he had himself experienced in the direction of his own course of study, on entering the legal profession, were too deeply impressed on his mind to be easily forgotten'. He added that 'the ordinary obstacles to which all men were exposed who made the law their study induced him to hail with extreme satisfaction the foundation of this institution in Ireland'.[20]

As praise was lavished on the Law Institute, so mounted frustration at the deficiencies in Irish legal training. One author wrote of 'the sense of weariness and disappointment which arises from the obscurity and uncertainty that attend the unaided efforts of the student to acquire a competent degree of legal knowledge', and pointed out that 'the professorship of Feudal and English Law in Trinity College . . . has been found of very little practical utility to the student . . . notwithstanding the learning and ability of the present occupant of that chair, Dr. Longfield'.[21]

With the solicitors and attorneys at this time also stepping up the pressure for educational reforms on their side of the profession, a number of bar students mounted a campaign to have the Statute of Jeofailles repealed, as a step towards the provision of better training for the bar. In November 1841, in a memorial which they adopted for despatch to the benchers of King's Inns, the students pointed out that the existing training of future barristers merely required the eating of dinners and not the study of law. They added that 'even if the system were acted on, as originally designed . . . such system would be inadquate'. For the sake of argument, the students appear to have been prepared to accept that the original objective of the Statute of Jeofailles had been educational and that English and Irish law were very similar at the time of the statute's adoption. However, they claimed, that was no longer the case. There were discrepancies in statute law, common law and practice: 'the numerous and important differences in the law

20. Anon., 'Recollections of the late Sir Michael O'Loghlen', 95–98; *Hansard*, 3, lxxxv, col. 680 (7 April 1846); *Sel. comm. leg. ed.*, pp.358–59.
21. Anon, 'On the study of the law in Ireland: The Dublin Law Institute' (July-Dec. 1842), 305–07.

and practice of the English and Irish courts rendering it essentially necessary that a system should be established which would have, for its actual as well as declared object, the study of those differences'. They cited an instance where one young barrister had relied upon his training in London chambers only to find his case struck out because certain English rules had not been adopted in Irish courts. Item by item, the students addressed those arguments which had long been used to prop up the requirement, rejecting in turn any suggestion that attending the courts at Westminster or debates in the house of commons brought with it some special or useful insights which might not otherwise be equally well obtained in Dublin, and ridiculing the notion that the system was justified because students might, while in London, attend 'splendid institutions and galleries of the several arts and sciences . . . the previous study of which is essential to the formation of that liberality of mind so necessary to all who aim at eminence at the bar'. If the object was really to broaden the mind, then other European capitals ought to be included in a general requirement to travel – 'the expense of going . . . would be more than amply covered by the appropriation for that purpose of those fees which we pay on entering inns of court, fees for dinners, etc'. Complaining about the expense of repeated visits to London, the students pleaded in vain that the benchers 'take into consideration the abolition of the present system and the substitution of such other (adopted to the wants of your petitioners and more likely than the present to fulfil its declared purposes) as to your honorable society shall seem fit'. It was claimed that the whole system was just another ruse to drain Irish resources, and that it accounted for up to £20,000 each year flowing out of Ireland, the students describing it as

a hypocritical scheme of impudent impositions, extorting from each student, either directly or by contingent expenses, between £300 and £400, and proffering as an equivalent some dozen or so dinners, in value about 10d a piece.[22]

22. *Saunders's News-letter*, 16 Nov. 1841; *Legal Reporter*, ii, no.2, p.22; *Sel. comm. leg. ed.*, p.339. Sir William Wilde believed that travelling fellowships ought to be established at Trinity College Dublin for the benefit of all students intent on a profession. In 1840, he also wrote: 'I know of no profession in this country that gives a proper *preliminary* education to its students. This is a truth that I think few will deny, and it is one felt by all who enter these professions, at some one period of their course through life'. He noted that the Dublin Law Institute had recently been set up in the light of the deficiency and he wished it every success (Wilde, *Narrative of a voyage to Madeira, Tenerife and along the shores of the Mediterranean*, p.418).

In 1841, Hercules Ellis, chairman of a committee of Irish barristers which was pressing for the appointment of an Irish lawyer to the vacant Irish chancellorship, described the provision for residency in London as 'an unequal and insulting law, which brands an Irish legal education as insufficient or worthless'.[23]

In 1842, the first parliamentary effort to overturn the requirement for residency in London was made, exactly three hundred years after the passage of the Statute of Jeofailles. Sir Valentine Blake of Galway moved the bill, arguing that there may have been a time when such a regulation was necessary, but that that time had passed. He asserted that 'Irish lawyers were considered of equal authority with English lawyers, and the student had such means of obtaining a knowledge of his profession in Dublin, that it was unnecessary for him to come to London'. But the bill fatally complicated the question and split potential support by proposing that those qualified to be called to the bar in England ought also to be entitled by right to be called in Ireland.[24] Such a measure would later be promoted publicly by Irish catholics as a means of encouraging young men to avoid Trinity College by studying in England. But Blake did not dare to propose reciprocal rights for Irish barristers at the English bar, something which would have been utterly unacceptable to the English legal profession. Thus, his bill both offended the benchers and alarmed not only those disturbed by the implications of catholic emancipation, but also those who feared the arrival of English barristers in Dublin. The number of barristers in practice in England had more than tripled between 1800 and 1840, and the prospect of hungry young English barristers coming over to Dublin alienated many Irish law students who might otherwise have supported a bill intended simply to reverse the effects of the Statute of Jeofailles. On 16 April 1842, these agreed to communicate their strong views on the proposal to members of the house of commons. Their opposition to the bill was later misunderstood or misrepresented as disagreement with those law students who had earlier petitioned the benchers to change the requirement for residency in London, and who had recently asked the benchers in vain to reconsider that memorial. Whether the bill might have passed had it been confined to the issue of residency is a matter for speculation. Hansard records only a short debate on the motion of 1842. Serjeant Devonsher Jackson, a conservative member for

23. Anon., *Memoranda by obscure men*, p.75.
24. Benchers' minute book, 1835–44 (King's Inns MS, pp.182–83: 15 April 1842); *Hansard*, 3, lxi, col. 1294 and lxii, col. 894 (20 April 1842); *Saunders's News-letter*, 23 April 1842.

Trinity College, opposed the proposal to abolish attendance in London, suggesting idiosyncratically that English students should likewise be compelled to go to Dublin. Given that one argument occasionally advanced to justify the provision was that it created a community of feeling between the English and Irish bars, there was at least some logic to Jackson's position. The serjeant also spoke of the 'incalculable' benefits derived by Irish students from having to travel to London, adverting to the fact that 'he could attend the courts of law, and obtain much information in the conveyancers and special pleaders office'. John O'Connell also contributed a few words to the debate, but Hansard does not record what these were. The opponents of change succeeded in their motion that the second reading be put off for six months, thus effectively killing the bill.[25]

That the opposition had been led by the representative for Dublin University was significant. Between 1842 and 1885, as will be seen, a succession of lawyers who were also parliamentary representatives for the university were relied on by the benchers to provide information from Westminster and to oppose proposed changes in the requirement for residency in London when these were being debated in the house of commons. The lawyers included a future lord chief justice and a future lord chancellor who, perhaps partly in expectation of advancement, were willing to voice the concerns of their future colleagues on the bench.

Yet, those who defended existing practice were hard-pressed for pedagogic arguments. Writing in the English *Law Times* in 1846, one observer claimed that

> there are advantages in fixing the Irish student in London, which would make it undesirable to dispense with that portion of his apprenticeship. It must tend greatly to the removal of prejudices of nation, sect, and party, enlarge the sympathies, widen the experience and assist mightily in preparing him for the duties of an advocate, so infinitely varied in their demands.

But, conceded the author, 'something should be done to teach him a little *law*, either at home, or here, or both'.[26]

---

25. Above, pp.126–27; Duman, 'Pathway to professionalism', 619; Letter from J.C. Coffey and J.E. Piggot [law students' spokesmen] to members of parliament, 18 April 1842, in William Smith O'Brien papers (NLI MS). Some students did oppose the abolition of the residential requirement itself, the student body being split on this as late as 1885 (Benchers' minute book, 1870–85 (King's Inns MS, pp.474–75: 22 April 1885)).
26. Anon., 'Legal education in Ireland', in *Law Times,* vii (11 April 1846).

Moreover, such defenders of the existing law had to contend with the complaint of Grattan and others that there were 'demoralising indulgences' to which those young men going to 'widen their experience' might fall victim. The law students who wished to end the requirement for residency made sensational claims about such dangers:

We see London; it is said we see life; if by seeing life (and we fear it is the intended sense) is to be understood life in its well-known meaning, i.e. a commingling with all the depravaties which the evil disposition of our nature is capable of inventing, then indeed has London been well selected for the school of our initiation, since every street in the metropolis presents us with the open, the notorious haunts of the most abandoned profligacy; haunts, any one of which alone is sufficient to make the mind not altogether divested of sensibility to turn aside with disgust and abhorrence. It may be said that we are not obliged to frequent these, and it is easy for us to avoid them. They who attempt to make that reply know but little of natural bias and the force of example; those who had first avoided are in the end induced readily to frequent the most revolting of those scenes. And this is not an empty allusion, since the fact is too well-known to be for a moment controverted, that of the number of Irish law students who enter their names at the inns of court, more than one third of these have fallen victims to English dissipation; a broken constitution having sunk them into a premature grave, and over many of whom it closed even months before they were to be called to the bar.[27]

Here is an image of Irish students in London given over to debauchery, drinking themselves into obliteration, perhaps contracting venereal disease from prostitutes and others of lax sexual behaviour, gambling and besmirching their family honour by sinking into debt. It is hard to believe that had the situation been as extreme as that depicted by the students, Irish parents would have continued to allow their children to register at the inns of court. That there was some concern there can be no doubt, as there always is when the young leave home. It found expression in 1846 during evidence given to the select committee on legal education when Michael Barry, a barrister who had been partly responsible for the course in criminal law at the Dublin Law Institute, pointed out that 'there is a great and obvious danger in exposing young men at that very early age and at a season of the year, in the height of what is termed the London season, to all the allurements of pleasure and dissipation, without the constraint or control of their parents or guardians'. But such protective sentiments were not shared by the 'incorrigible' Pierce Mahony, a solicitor in Ireland of thirty-two

27. *Saunders's News-letter*, 16 Nov. 1841.

years standing who had been agent to the Catholic Association in the year of Emancipation. He approved of the regulation requiring students to go to London and he told the select committee at Westminster:

MAHONY: Yes; I should be very sorry to see a man brought into practice in Ireland, who had not had an opportunity of spending some time in this country as well as in Ireland; I think it is of great value to him, and I think it is of greater value to the Empire.
WYSE: Do you attach much importance to the apprehensions entertained of their being affected by the immorality of a large capital?
MAHONY: I do not know any greater degree of immorality existing in London, than is to be found at Dublin, Limerick, Cork, Waterford, or elsewhere. I think, on the contrary, a well-regulated young man would have his time better filled up in London in acquiring knowledge, than it would be in Dublin; and that, therefore, if he thinks fit to employ his time usefully, he will have less temptation to go into dissipation in London than in Dublin.[28]

The existing requirement was also defended by Brougham. The latter, an English bencher and former lord chancellor, had fallen out with the liberals and from 1839 had opposed their Irish policy. He had a reputation in England as an educational progressive, and in 1845 had chaired joint meetings of benchers of the four London inns who met to consider the reform of legal training. But even amongst his admirers Brougham's intellectual strengths were considered to be of a general rather than of a specifically legal nature. Indeed, it was said that 'if he had known a little law he would have known a little of everything'.[29] Perhaps it was personal insecurity which made him so scathing about the standards of Irish lawyers. In 1839, he had attacked Sir Michael O'Loghlen, claiming him to be 'grossly ignorant of the law and to have betrayed his trust when attorney general by defeating the administration of justice in Ireland to gratify his fellow catholics and political friends'. Brougham was the latest in a long line of English observers who regarded the Irish legal profession as inferior to, and more ignorant and untrustworthy than, that of England. In

28. *Sel. comm. leg. ed.*, qq.1635–36, 2514. The description of Mahony as 'incorrigible' is that of Joseph Lee (Lee, 'The social and economic ideas of O'Connell', 80). The relative levels of dissipation in London and Dublin were a matter of opinion. William Conyngham Plunket had been in no doubt earlier that when it came to drunkenness, Irish barristers could leave their English colleagues standing, or not standing as the case may be (Plunket, *Life, letters and speeches of Lord Plunket*, i, 46–47).
29. Duman, 'The judicial bench in England', p.153; *DNB*, s.v. Brougham and Vaux.

1841, when forced to support a measure which made Irishmen eligible to hold the two new vice-chancellorships of England, Brougham assured parliament that 'there was no intention of appointing an Irish barrister to such a situation'.[30] In these circumstances, his views on the requirement that Irish law students attend the London inns hardly come as any surprise. Asked was it of advantage, he replied,

> I should say certainly, on this account, that though there are very many most eminent and learned lawyers at the Irish bar, as well as upon the Irish bench, yet it is impossible to deny that the legal business of Ireland is carried on in a less accurate and more slovenly manner than here. We have frequent instances of that in our appeals, of things being taken for granted, being assumed, which are not so, and steps being omitted which are essential, and steps being multiplied in discussion; but above all, of carelessness and inaccuracy, apparently showing a defect of that rigorous attention to what is laid down, and proved, and established in the case, which distinguishes, no doubt, the practice of the law in this country; and therefore I consider that very great benefit arises from the attendance of the Irish barrister for a certain period of time in this country. It will also be of advantage by the intercourse between the two nations being beneficial to each other, on the footing upon which the Union has placed the inhabitants of each.[31]

Brougham's imperious assertion of the purported benefits of the residency requirement did not address the question of how, after three centuries, such exposure to the London inns had failed to remedy the alleged defects in Irish practice which he felt that the Statute of Jeofailles was ideally suited to correct. Clearly, on his own evidence, the requirement which he supported failed to achieve the objective to which he felt it was suited, namely that of making the Irish more precise. He boasted later in his evidence that there was 'much greater exactness' amongst members of the legal profession in England than 'in the sister kingdom', oblivious to his own inexactitude in describing Ireland as a discrete kingdom almost half a century after the passing of the Act of Union. He also ignored the gritty reality of how in fact his inn and others allowed the Irish students to make a mockery of the requirement

---

30. Anon., 'Recollections of the late Sir Michael O'Loghlen', 168; *Hansard*, 3, lix, col. 497 (7 Sept. 1841). Irishmen, tory and nationalist, were also prepared to criticise the profession, although in whose pocket you thought the lawyers were, depended on your politics. See, for example, [Madden], *The voice of the bar: no.1. The reign of mediocrity*, passim; Stradling [Mahony?], *The bar sinister*, passim.
31. *Sel. comm. leg. ed.*, q.3805.

to keep terms. Evidence given to the select committee by other witnesses indicated that the requirement was not adequately policed, especially as the bars of both countries burgeoned. The benchers of King's Inns had in the past tried to ensure that students might not speed up their dining by keeping the same terms in London and Dublin. Mistakes made in the certificates from London inns or made by students themselves in computing their dinners were looked upon unsympathetically by the benchers, although terms might be allowed occasionally for medical reasons or, for example, because snow had prevented the completion of the requisite number of dinners or 'in consequence of the cholera then prevalent in Dublin'.[32] In January 1840, the under-treasurer at King's Inns had written somewhat desperately to the four inns of court in London that,

as the facility is now so great in being admitted to the Irish bar, and as some gentlemen keep the same term here and in one of the inns of court in London, which is contrary to the rules of this society, and as I have no means of discovering it, I shall be much obliged if you will in future when giving a certificate, note in the margin of the certificate, the name of each particular term kept that I may compare them with my books and put a stop to this practice.[33]

Later that same year, one writer indicated that while the benchers could stop students from keeping double terms, they might not be able to prevent other practices, such as that of staying in London for 'very few days indeed, usually comprising the last three days of Easter, and the three first days of Trinity terms, upon which they present themselves in the Hall of the Honorable Society of Gray's Inn, frequently by proxies, and thus render a suitable obedience to the statute'. According to Mountifort Longfield, this latter practice allowed a young man to 'eat his mutton or beef by deputy'. Longfield made this observation in 1846 in the course of his evidence before the Wyse committee on legal education, where he also expressed concern about the fact that the requirement for residency in London interefered with the study of law in Dublin. Longfield said that the provision took men out of Ireland at the very time they would be inclined to study law, that is 'the two years previous to their being called to the bar'. While some of

32. Benchers' minute book, 1819–30 (King's Inns MS, pp.46, 153, 193, 212); Benchers' minute book, 1830–35 (King's Inns MS, pp.33, 63, 137); Benchers' minute book, 1835–44 (King's Inns MS, pp.17, 56, 68, 231, 233); Benchers' minute book, 1844–49 (King's Inns MS, pp.11–12).
33. Letterbook, 1836–69 (King's Inns MS, p.36: 24 Jan. 1840).

the Irish stayed as short a time as possible in London, others actually chose to live in the city during their period at the English inns in order to save the expenses of going backwards and forwards: 'The additional expense of living in London is very little', thought Longfield. But whether they stayed long or made repeated shorter visits, they were distracted from a steady programme of studies. Longfield attributed to 'men's natural indolence' the tendency to delay studying until it was too late to benefit fully from any courses at the university. Eighty years earlier his predecessor in the chair, Francis Stoughton Sullivan, had complained that the provision requiring attendance at the London inns effectively confined him to supervising students of little more than two years' standing, 'making it highly improper for him to enter minutely into those parts of the law his audience have not yet had time to apply to'. Asked by Wyse if he thought that there was no advantage deriving from young men becoming acquainted with the practice of the English courts, Longfield replied tersely, 'None'.[34]

Longfield was soon presented with an opportunity to amplify his concern about the fact that dinners in London distracted from studies in Dublin. In 1851 he was appointed one of the royal commissioners to inquire into the state, discipline, studies and revenues of the University of Dublin or Trinity College. Among a number of matters in relation to which the commissioners invited submissions was 'the means of rendering the Law School more efficient for the professional education of barristers and solicitors'. At the time, it had been less than a year since a pioneering joint scheme of legal lectures had been introduced at Trinity College and the King's Inns, and there was widespread agreement that this ought to be given a chance to work before other changes might be introduced. However, the commissioners did direct their attention to the effects on lectures in the law school of the requirement that students for the bar attend the inns in London. The provost of Trinity took a lonely stand in defending the tradition, writing that he would 'deprecate' any change making professional legal education in Ireland independent of attendance at the English inns: 'Such a measure', claimed Provost Richard MacDonnell, 'would tend most seriously to *keep* the two countries apart'. But the vice-provost and senior fellows made it clear that they disagreed with the requirement, and the commissioners in the end

---

34. *The Citizen*, ii, no. 13 (Nov. 1840), p.431; *Sel. comm. leg. ed.*, qq. 3013–14, 3019–22. Longfield's allegation was backed by Michael Barry, who believed that some students had kept terms solely by proxy (q.1600); Sullivan, *An historical treatise*, lecture 2. Tristram Kennedy thought that only two or three persons had attended Sullivan's lectures (*Sel. comm. leg. ed.*, q.1035).

were adamant that the practice of forcing law students to London was undesirable. Mountifort Longfield, whose attendance record at sessions of the commission was excellent and who himself gave written evidence as the professor of feudal and English law, may well have been instrumental in framing the withering finding of the commission in relation to 'the necessity imposed on students preparing for the bar in Ireland, to keep some of their terms at the inns of court in England':[35]

This subject is referred to by both the law professors and also by the senior fellows.

Thus Dr. Anster says – 'The fact of the graduates of the Dublin University having to attend terms in England, does, I think, very materially intereferes with "the complete development of a Law School in the university", or in Ireland at all. In my own class of last year, some of the students had to go over to England to keep a term, during a period when the lectures were going on, which interfered materially with the instruction of the class, as some of the students went over just to keep the terms, and returned after a few days, in time to attend enough of lectures to entitle them to my certificate, but compelling me to vary a good deal the plan I had endeavoured to adopt of strictly systematic teaching. I had to change my days of lectures more than once, for the purpose of enabling such students to keep the English terms without losing the class lectures'.

Again, he says – 'If the question is to be regarded as confined by the inquiry to the mere fact, of whether the present mode of keeping terms interferes with the effectiveness of our law school, in the university, I have no hesitation in saying, that it does most injuriously interfere with it, and that (unless where students are engaged in learning their profession, in conveyancers' or pleaders' offices, which is altogether optional to them, and which, from the expense of it, is a course not often adopted, and which is not made a condition precedent to being called to the bar either in England or Ireland), there is no compensating advantage whatever for the interruption created by this attendance on terms in England'.

Dr Longfield, also, says – 'I am of opinion that the necessity of keeping terms in England does interfere with the complete development of a law school in the university. It is obviously the interest of the student to postpone his visit to London (which occasions expense and trouble) as long as he can; and they generally postpone to the same period the commencement of their study of the law. They argue, that they need not commence their studies until they go to London, where there are more and better opportunities of learning law than in Ireland. The student naturally will pay more undivided attention to the study of law as the time approaches for his being called to the bar, and commencing to practise: and this period is spent in England. I do not give an opinion

35. *Dub. Univ. comm . . . 1853*, pp.28-32, 43, 96-97, 284, 298.

whether the present system is unfavourable to the study of law, but merely that it is unfavourable to the success of the school of law in Ireland'.

Then the committee of the Board [of T.C.D.], in their report, say – 'Arrangements have recently been made, in conjunction with the benchers, for the establishment of an efficient law school. Until we see how these regulations will work, we are not prepared to say whether any or what further institutions may be necessary. But it is our present impression, that so long as the rule exists which requires law students to keep terms by residence in London, no really efficient law school can be established in this country. If we were permitted to add the same time and expense to the studies of a law student, which he must now spend in London, it would be very easy to render the law school of the university more efficient'.

This suggestion of the committee of the board has received the approval of the Right Honourable Francis Blackburne, the vice-chancellor of the university. He says – 'The proposition or suggestion of the vice-provost and six of the senior fellows for devoting to the establishment of a law school the money which it costs the law students to keep terms in London, and the dedication of the time now spent there to attendance on the schools at home, deserves most serious consideration. Though I agree with the provost, for the reason he states, in assigning some value to the residence of the Irish law student in England, the great increase of intercourse between the two countries, the power of easily evading that residence, and other causes, make this now of little comparative importance; while, on the other hand, it seems to me self-evident, that the compulsory attendance on public lectures, and on private ones in small classes, with catechetical examination, will impart and fix the principles of law much more effectually than attendance on the courts at Westminster, or in the offices of a special pleader or conveyancer. This attendance, it will be remembered, is not obligatory, and therefore no certain benefit, no actual proficiency, is insured by the residence in London. But should importance be attached to the peculiar means of instruction accessible there, a student will be eminently qualified to derive the utmost advantage of them from his previous studies and knowledge acquired in the university'.

The next two paragraphs of the report were devoted to reviewing the statutory and other bases for the requirement that students go to London, the commissioners pointing out that no attempt was ever made by the benchers to ensure that the time spent by Irish students in England was used for studying. The commissioners concluded:

Under these circumstances, we think that the provisions of this ancient statute, passed before the foundation of Trinity College, which are not, at the present day, carried out in any respect but as a mere form, should not be allowed to stand in the way of the development of a complete law school in the university of Dublin. And we are of opinion, therefore, that the provision in the Statute of Henry VIII, to which we have referred, should be repealed; and that the rules with respect to admission to the bar in Ireland, should be left entirely with the benchers of the King's Inns, in the same manner as the rules with respect to admission to the bar in England are entirely intrusted to the benchers of the inns of court there.

From the position of the university of Dublin in the metropolis of Ireland, where the law courts are situate, and from the connexion already established between the college and the benchers of the King's Inns, a complete law school might well be developed under their joint superintendence.

But the legal profession kept a stony silence on the whole matter. Prior to the presentation of the report in 1853, letters inviting comment on a range of matters under consideration had gone out to a number of leading lawyers including the chief justice in common pleas, James Monahan, Chief Baron Pigot, Judge Crampton, Judge Perrin and Joseph Napier, who in 1852 had become the attorney general. But none of them replied. For his part, Blackburne gave his opinion as vice-provost rather than as a member of the bench. Thomas Lefroy did answer in his capacity as chief justice in queen's bench, but merely to say that the only question in relation to which he felt in any degree competent to form an opinion was that relating to religious restrictions imposed on the candidates for endowments and scholarships. These he supported as tending to encourage the established religion.[36]

While Joseph Napier did not respond to the commissioners, it was not long before he was speaking in the house of commons and urging parliament to give effect to their recommendation on attendance at the London inns. In 1856, in what was the first serious parliamentary attempt since 1842 to change the law, he and George Hamilton brought in a bill to repeal the Statute of Jeofailles. They recited the improvements in legal education in Ireland and referred particularly to the arrangement between Trinity College and the King's Inns. Napier noted that the compulsory attendance of students at one of the inns of court in London was 'inconvenient and calculated to interfere with the freedom of such arrangements as may from time to time be made

---

36. ibid., pp.284, 293; Acheson Lyle, chief remembrancer and bencher, who had welcomed the Dublin Law Institute, said in 1846 that he personally supported the requirement for attendance in London and that 'a large majority of benchers also do so' (*Sel. comm. leg. ed.*, q. 2390).

for the systematic teaching of the School of Law in Ireland'. He suggested that the board of Trinity College and the benchers had effectively created in Ireland a 'complete School of Law'. Although parliament on 23 May 1856 ordered the bill to be printed, the proposals did not win sufficient support to become law. The following year the lord chancellor himself, Maziere Brady, took a personal initiative by proposing that the benchers vote for not only the abolition of the requirement that students eat dinners in London but also the abolition of all dining in Dublin. Brady, as attorney general in 1839, had been quick to join the council of the Dublin Law Institute, and he now wished King's Inns to concentrate its resources on the provision of legal education. His colleagues devoted 'considerable discussion' to their chairman's idea, and then tossed it out by a hefty majority.[37]

The report from the Dublin University commissioners, presented in 1853, was a strong indictment of the requirement for residency, but their pleas for reform fell on deaf ears. Nevertheless, as law courses in Ireland grew, at King's Inns and Trinity and the Queen's Colleges, the rationale for getting young men to cross the Irish Sea weakened. Yet those who wished to change the law continued to find that their opponents on the bench and elsewhere were able to defeat them. One incentive for those who opposed change was that the requirement kept down the numbers at the bar, doing so by means of a financial burden which tended to discriminate against the less well-off. In 1846, the Irish barrister, Michael Barry, had been asked by George Hamilton, a member of the select committee on legal education and himself a member of the Irish bar, if, 'taking into account the class from which Irish barristers usually come, . . . the extra expense incurred in travelling and residing in London constitutes an obstacle to many persons, who would otherwise be desirous of going to the Irish bar, doing so?' Barry replied, 'A very serious obstacle'. Keeping down numbers in this way put off the day when examinations, a more democratic mechanism for restricting entry, might be made compulsory and the sons of those currently enjoying prominence in the profession might find themselves having to compete with the rising, and predominantly catholic, middle classes for a place at the bar. The high number at the bar was causing great anxiety to some existing members of the legal profession, and James Whiteside reflected this when, in 1859, he rose to oppose a bill introduced by two Irish liberals, Patrick MacMahon

37. [MacMahon], 'The Catholic University and legal education', 227, 230–31; *Hansard*, 3, cxlii, col. 588 (23 May 1856); Benchers' minute book, 1856–69 (King's Inns MS, p.26: 26 Nov. 1857).

of Wexford and Francis William Brady of Dublin. The bill was the third attempt in seventeen years to repeal the statute requiring Irishmen to attend the London inns. MacMahon was one of the remnants of the Independent Party, to which Tristram Kennedy also belonged but which was in shreds by July 1859. A catholic solicitor and journalist, he was 'a ready speaker with a knowledge of a wide assortment of subjects'. Had he and Brady confined their bill of 1859 to a proposal that the Statute of Jeofailles be repealed they might have succeeded, although the fate of the simple bill introduced three years earlier by Napier and Hamilton meant that nothing was assured. In any event, MacMahon complicated matters, as had Valentine Blake in 1842, by coupling the main objective of repealing the Statute of Jeofailles with a secondary one intended to circumvent the dominant position of Dublin University in Irish legal education. He proposed, as we saw in the previous chapter, that the benchers of King's Inns admit students to the Irish bar on the same terms that the benchers in London now admitted students to the English bar, namely after three years in all cases and not only in the case of graduates of Dublin University. This argument was the cue for Whiteside to rise with a 'very great objection'. A queen's counsel, who six years later would be appointed lord chief justice in Ireland, he held a parliamentary seat for Dublin University. His politics now took precedence over any earlier enthusiasm for educational reform. A tory, who has been described as 'authentically reactionary', Whiteside argued that the effect of the measure proposed by MacMahon would be greatly to increase the number of barristers and that this was not sought by the Irish bar. But Whiteside moved on swiftly to address the primary question of the statutory requirement for attendance in London, and he then expressed an opinion which he can scarcely have believed, namely that 'no complaint had been made of that law'. One of the leading supporters and professors of the Dublin Law Institute in its day, he now defended the practice of forcing young men to London: 'It had the sanction of antiquity, and he believed that it was attended with beneficial results . . . The Irish students who came over enjoyed themselves very much'. Brady immediately contested Whiteside's claim that there was no dissatisfaction with the requirement. With the solicitor general for Ireland supporting the bill, the house of commons voted to allow it to go forward.[38]

38. *Sel. comm. leg. ed.*, q. 1648; Whyte, *Independent party*, pp.90, 139, 183; Hansard, 3, clv, col. 81f. (19 July 1859); Hoppen, *Elections in Ireland*, p.279; Hogan, 'Judicial appointments in Ireland, 1866–67', 212.

However, neither this bill of 1859 nor yet others proposed in 1872, 1874 and 1878 were ultimately passed. They appear to have been sidelined by a combination of procedural mechanisms and, in one case, a general election. The benchers delegated the lord chancellor to express to the government their 'strong disapproval' of such proposals. The government of the day had no reason to face down its leading Irish judges and law officers in the absence of any political imperative. A number of the proposals appear to have been tentative, with little or no debate taking place, and it was not until Irish representatives at Westminster arose from three decades of confusion and frustration to assert themselves in the cause of Home Rule that the objections of the benchers were finally brushed aside.[39]

The leading light in the final campaign to have the Statute of Jeofailles repealed was a controversial politician and member of the bar. In 1865, at the age of twenty-eight, Philip Callan had acted for the liberals as electoral barrister to both Tristram Kennedy and Chichester Fortescue in County Louth. Nine years later, he and A.M. Sullivan were returned for the same county as home rulers. Callan has been included by Cruise O'Brien in that small force of members 'which prided itself on its activity and its contempt for English institutions' and which by 1877 was supporting Parnell against Butt within the Irish party at Westminster. But Callan was a maverick, noted in particular for his outstanding work on behalf of the drink lobby at a time when temperance was a political issue throughout the United Kingdom. He so disgusted his Home Rule colleague, A. M. Sullivan, that when the two men were re-elected for the same constituency in 1880, Sullivan refused to sit for Louth, and had to be found instead a safe vacancy elsewhere. Apparently, the publicans had 'organised attacks on the water-drinking Sullivan, and helped, by means of £500 cheques and personal canvassing, to keep the bilbous Philip Callan afloat, despite the fierce opposition of Parnell'. It is said that on occasion Callan actually appeared drunk in the house of commons. Parnell

39. *Hansard, 3*, ccix, col. 649 (19 Feb. 1872); ibid., ccxiii, col. 642 (7 Aug. 1872); ibid., ccxxviii, col. 709 (17 April 1874); ibid., ccxxi, index under 'Barristers (Ireland) Bill'; ibid., cclvii, cols. 1586 f. (27 Jan. 1881); Benchers' minute book, 1870–85 (King's Inns MS, pp. 115–16: 22 April 1872, p.191: 29 April 1874, p.297: 24 April 1878, p.374: 20 April 1881). On 11 May 1872 the *Irish Law Times and Solicitors' Journal* described the requirement as 'utterly indefensible in principle and barely tolerable in practice' (*ILT & SJ*, vi, 249). The benchers may have been willing to countenance a change in the law in 1860, provided they themselves had been left free to insist on students keeping terms in London (Benchers' minute book, 1856–69 (King's Inns MS, p.79: 19 Jan. 1860)).

came to regard him as politically and personally untrustworthy, and later managed to have him defeated at the general election in 1885. By that stage, however, Callan had succeeded in his efforts to rescind the requirement that Irish law students travel to London. There is considerable irony in the fact that a provision which had long seen Irishmen resort to the inns of court in London for little more than substantial quantities of food and drink should finally be revoked through the efforts of a man who was a leading parliamentary mouthpiece for Irish inn-keepers. That Callan achieved his objective with the active support of both Sullivan and Parnell reflects the strength of feeling about the matter throughout the body of home rulers.[40]

Callan brought forward a bill in April 1874, not long after he was first elected. His motion was also signed by the home rulers McCarthy Downing of Cork, Richard O'Shaughnessy of Limerick and Sir John Gray of Kilkenny. But then, and apparently again in 1878, his efforts were opposed by the benchers and were frustrated by notice of motion under the 'half-past twelve rule', and there was no debate. However, in January 1881, he came forward again with the backing of O'Shaughnessy and Gray, and this time the matter was given an immediate airing. The government was extremely sensitive to contemporary Irish demands, with the Land War waging and with Chief Secretary Forster on 24 January introducing an unpopular coercion measure, the Protection of Person and Property (Ireland) Bill. During the last week of the month Parnell and his supporters mounted the greatest obstructionist campaign ever seen in parliament. This was also the week that Callan's Barristers' Admission (Ireland) Bill was given a second reading and debated. Perhaps anxious to placate the Irish representatives, the chief secretary supported Callan's measure and disregarded the views of the Irish benchers, much to the chagrin of those who opposed change.[41] Most prominent amongst the latter was once again a tory member for Dublin University, this time

40. Kenny, 'Honest Tristram Kennedy', 24, 32, 35; O'Brien, *Parnell and his party 1880–90*, p.23, nn. 1 and 2; Malcolm, *'Ireland sober, Ireland free': drink and temperance in nineteenth-century Ireland*, pp.223, 233, 251, 255, 258–59; Kee, *The laurel and the ivy*, p.494; Hoppen, *Elections in Ireland*, p.53. As may be seen from a note on the Hall sketch in the National Library, Callan was even suspected at one point of forging letters which ostensibly linked Parnell to 'the Phoenix Park murders'. In 1889, it turned out that the letters had in fact been forged by a Dublin journalist, Richard Pigott (Lyons, *Ireland since the famine*, p.192). That Hall's sketch is of Callan may be seen by comparing it with the group sketch and key in the *Illustrated London News*, 9 March 1889, reproduced at Kissane, *Parnell*, pp.74–75 (no.7).
41. Note 39 above; O'Brien, *Parnell*, pp.57–59; *Freeman's Journal*, 28 Jan. 1881.

David Plunket. He told the house that he had received a letter from the benchers of King's Inns requesting him to oppose the bill. This he was ready to do for

he had practised for some time at the Irish bar and he never heard the system complained of. It had been found most useful for the younger men preparing for the Irish bar to come and spend some time in London. They only came for four terms out of twelve; and it had been found that, among other advantages, it had led to valuable study in London, where it was very desirable that the students should have an opportunity of studying the English law as it was taught there.

Plunket himself had written how his own grandfather, William Conyngham Plunket, had found student life in London to consist at times of 'cheerless days of struggle, privation and study', and how, during the summer of 1785, wealthier colleagues went elsewhere and left him 'feeding on the rust of Coke's reports and talking metaphysics with the curate'.[42] The younger Plunket must also have known that many did indeed oppose the requirement for residency, even if contemporary custom and communications meant that the amount of time actually spent in England by students might be less than in earlier centuries. But in the legal circle in which he moved it was clearly not a matter for discussion, scarcely surprising if the benchers were solidly in favour of it and one had ambitions to join them on the bench. Plunket claimed that the benchers were 'the custodians of the interests of the bar in Ireland' and that they were 'unanimous . . . that the bill would be very injurious if it became law'. The solicitor general for Ireland, W.M. Johnson, told the house that he found the resolutions of the benchers in the matter to be 'of the most absolute character'. He added that 'they are a repetition of what has been resolved by them over and over again, and laid before the house in 1872, 1874 and 1878'. Johnson himself was a bencher, but was at pains to point out that he had not formally communicated with the benchers. He did not give their stance a ringing endorsement.

Foremost amongst those who backed Callan's motion in 1881 was his party colleague and, as we have seen, bitter personal opponent, A.M. Sullivan. Described by Cruise O'Brien as 'a really fine debater, with great inventiveness and spontaneity as well as tenacity', Sullivan ridiculed the provision:

42. *Hansard*, 3, cclvii, cols.1586 f. (27 Jan. 1881); Plunket, *Life of Lord Plunket*, pp.39–41. Plunket was to be appointed the chief commissioner of works in 1885 (Walker, *Parliamentary elections in Ireland*, p.275).

there was nothing more enjoyable than a good dinner in London unless it was a good dinner in Dublin; but the right honorable and learned gentleman spoke as if by the consumption of beef and mutton there was to be swallowed a vast amount of legal lore. If the Irish students were asked to attend lectures in London, he could understand and might even support the opposition; but what advantage was there to a student coming to London by the night-mail, going through his dinners as fast as he could and speeding back to Dublin? The reason for this practice was the idea of training Irish barbarism to learn the manner and dress of the English people.

Sullivan knew about dinners. A leading nationalist journalist, he had been persuaded to enter King's Inns shortly after being first elected to parliament in 1873. In December 1875, he submitted a memorial to King's Inns to remit certain of his terms in consideration of his having been obliged to serve in parliament while they were going on, 'stating that as to the lectures he had thus missed he had got notes of them taken and forwarded to him and had otherwise studied the subjects of which they had treated'. The case which he made appears rather unconvincing, and the benchers seem to have acted quite generously in the circumstances by showing some leniency. But Sullivan did not think so and believed that their refusal to concede all of his demands was influenced by the fact that there was 'scarcely a man of them who had not at one time or another come under his editorial lash'. Subsequently called to the Irish bar and, in special circumstances, to the English bar at the Inner Temple, A.M. Sullivan could now enjoy making his views on the imposition of compulsory dining known to the house. A fellow home-ruler, T.D. Sullivan, said that the requirement was 'regarded by a very large number of people in his country as an insult to the Irish nation', and referred to the schools of law in Ireland which were 'at the present moment perfectly capable of preparing students for the profession'. Another member 'believed that the great majority of Irish members would vote for the bill'. There seemed little reason why the bill would not pass into law but Callan seems to have held back at the last moment. He was clearly stung by the continuing campaign by the benchers to retain the measure and may have wished to avoid a humiliation of the Irish bench, either for personal professional reasons or because it could rebound against those charged in connection with their activities in the Land War at home in Ireland. 'Looking at the spirit in which his proposal had been received', Callan announced petulantly that 'he was sorry that he had made it'. The house agreed to a second reading only when Chief Secretary Forster suggested that 'a sufficient interval should be allowed for the collection of Irish opinion before the committee stage was taken'. It is difficult to see what additional opinions needed to be collected and the effect of this decision was to put back the bill indefinitely.[43]

However, Callan did not let the matter drop. Four years later, in the final months of the same parliament, he once more brought forward a bill relating to the admission of barristers to practice in Ireland, and was 'received with Irish cheers on rising to move the second reading'. This time a truly formidable group of home rulers had signed his motion. Notwithstanding any personal animosity between the two men, Parnell seconded Callan. Then followed the signatures of Justin McCarthy, Tim Healy, Edmund Leamy and M.J. Kenny. Shortly before this bill came to be debated in April 1885, Edward Sullivan, the lord chancellor of Ireland, died and, as a mark of respect, the benchers adjourned the meeting at which they were due to decide their position on the renewed proposal. An attempt was then made in parliament to use their adjournment as a device to defer a vote in the matter, but to little or no avail. Making the case for the benchers of King's Inns was once again a tory representative for the University of Dublin, this time Edward Gibson Q.C. Later in 1885 Gibson would be created Lord Ashbourne and appointed lord chancellor of Ireland. But in April he was batting for the Irish benchers at Westminster, fearing

that if the measure were passed without reservation or qualification it might be regarded by some as lowering of the character of the Irish Bar. [*Laughter from Irish members below the gangway*]. He meant that with some the Irish Bar might afterwards be viewed as a provincial bar instead of as part of the bar of the United Kingdom.[44]

To place his observations in context it is worth noting that following the establishment of county courts in England in 1847, but especially after the reform of the assize system subsequent to the passing of the Judicature Act 1873 and its amendment of 1875, provincial bars had developed rapidly in cities such as Liverpool and Manchester. The members of these bars were permanently

43. *Hansard*, 3, cclvii, cols. 1586f. (27 Jan. 1881); King's Inns, *Report of the education committee* (Dublin, 1876), pp.12–14; T.D. Sullivan, *A.M. Sullivan: a memoir*, p.128; *D.N.B*, s.v. Sullivan; O'Brien, *Parnell*, p.58. T.D. Sullivan's son was to become president of the high court of the Irish Free State, 1924–1936.
44. *Hansard*, 3, ccxcvii, col. 418 f. (22 April 1885); *Freeman's Journal*, 23 April 1885; Benchers' minute book, 1885–1901 (King's Inns MS, p.475: 22 April 1885).

resident in the provinces and rarely if ever practised in the metropolis.[45] Perhaps Gibson believed that they had some inferior status when it came to promotions. But did he seriously think that the Irish bar was more favoured than these, that because students ate dinners at the English inns they were more likely to succeed professionally? If anything the requirement that students go to London could be regarded as *undermining* the standing of the Irish bar, a point made by Edward Carson, the future unionist leader, who was a law student himself in the 1870s and who is also said to have described the requirement, as had others before, as 'one of the badges of servitude of the Irish nation'. Carson resented the fact that, before being admitted to the Middle Temple, he and other Irish students had to obtain the signature of two English barristers as guarantors to vouch for his personal honour, 'lest he might steal the silver spoons'.[46]

But Gibson was not alone in opposing change in 1885. On this occasion, the chief secretary sided with the benchers; thus Campbell-Bannerman did not follow in his predecessor's footsteps. Once more Plunket too spoke, claiming that the benchers 'know the practice and working of the bar in Ireland, and he was quite sure that they enjoyed the confidence and represented the general opinion of the bar [*Cries* of "No!"]'. Earlier in the debate Callan had impugned Plunket's motives by suggesting that the latter wanted the old statute continued because he was a director of the London and North Western Railway Company 'and perhaps the existing system . . . promoted the interests of that company'. To which Plunket might have riposted that Callan's position was dictated to him by his publican backers who yearned for the custom currently lost in the inns of London.

Two key contributions reflect the determination of those proposing change to see the matter through on this occasion. Mitchell Henry, a home ruler from Galway, claimed that

the opposition to this bill had always been in inverse ratio to the social and legal position of those who had spoken about it. The people who felt the grievance were the students, who had to go to the expense of coming to England. The judges and benchers did not feel the grievance, because they had obtained rank and emoluments and did not wish to make admission to the bar too easy.

45. Duman, 'Pathway to professionalism', 620.
46. Marjoribanks, *The life of Lord Carson*, i, 17. In later days, Carson became treasurer at the Middle Temple. The Middle Temple had become the most popular inn among Irish students after 1850 (Hogan, *Legal profession*, p.39).

For his part, Tim Healy, sometime treasurer of Gray's Inn and the future first governor-general of the Irish Free State, was dismissive of the benchers and claimed that the law was not theirs to decide: 'It was of importance to the people of Ireland, who were prevented by the present mediaeval arrangements from going into the profession in large numbers, that this bill should be passed'. Callan himself pointed out that students preparing for the Irish bar were now compelled to attend lectures and to pass an examination in Ireland and that the requirement for a trip to London 'involved an interruption of the studies of the person whom it affected, and also entailed on them a useless expenditure of time and money'.

With parliamentary criticism of the old requirement growing, and with the prospects of home rule seeming high at the time, the benchers finally decided to throw in the towel and to accept defeat. But to the bitter end they were reluctant to do so, voting amongst themselves as late as 22 April 1885 to advise 'no change' in the law. At the same meeting the Prince of Wales, then visiting Ireland, was elected a bencher. However, not entirely overcome by loyalist zeal, the council of King's Inns did refer the bill for further consideration by one of the society's sub-committees and it counselled surrender. When parliament resumed its debate on the question on 8 May 1885, Lord Fitzgerald rose to inform the house that 'the benchers of King's Inns do not object to the bill, provided that in place of repealing the Statute of Henry VIII, it is made merely a permissive measure'. No member of parliament appears to have objected to this face-saving device. All that was left was for the house to hear from the new chancellor, the catholic John Naish. Naish was to hold the great seal for just a few months, until a change of government saw Gibson appointed to the position. He now got to his feet to make a simple acknowledgment which had long been resisted by the benchers: 'I only rise to say that I see no objection to the bill, which is desired by the bar of Ireland'. On 21 May 1885 the measure received the royal assent.[47]

47. *Hansard, 3*, ccxcviii, cols. 2–4 (8 May 1885); Ball, *Judges*, ii, 376; Barristers' Admission (Ireland) Act 1885 (48 & 49 Vict, c.20); Benchers' minute book, 1870–85 (King's Inns MS, pp.470–75: 15 and 22 April); Benchers' minute book, 1885–1901 (King's Inns MS, p.3: 2 Nov. 1885). On the first day on which the barristers' bill was debated (23 April), the *Freeman's Journal* devoted a long editorial to calling for the appointment of a catholic chancellor. Naish became the second catholic to be appointed to the position since the reign of James II, the first being Thomas O'Hagan (1868–74, 1880–81). Naish resumed office briefly during 1886, only to be superseded once more by Gibson (1886–92).

One English contributor to the debate of 1885 had claimed that 'the dinners in the English inns of court would lose all their charm if Irish students were not present at them'. But with the number of barristers living in England said to have risen by almost 300% between 1835 and 1885 it may be that the absence of Irishmen was barely noticed. In any event, there would always be some Irish preparing for the English bar, while those intent on the Irish bar were still permitted to dine in London if they wished. Relatively few of the latter seem to have considered it a choice worth making and nearly all kept their terms exclusively in Dublin, where the King's Inns continued to require the consumption of food and drink as a condition precedent of admission to the practice of law. In the past, there had been complaints about the quality of food at King's Inns, with a suggestion that, from time to time, meat and fowl which had been dressed for dinner on a previous day was reheated and sent to table again.[48] But, overall, the food appears to have been quite adequate, if unimaginative. In 1906, Arthur Houston wrote that

> a curious regulation existed until very recently as regards the bill of fare at dinner at the King's Inns. It probably existed in O'Connell's time. It was this. The bill of fare was a fixed thing for every day in every term. Thus, in Michaelmas and Hilary terms the student or the barrister, if he chose to dine, was regaled with boiled beef, mashed parsnip and boiled fowl or turkey, on every Monday; while on the same day in Easter and Trinity terms he dined off boiled chicken, pig's cheek, or bacon, spinach, parsley or plain sauce, and roast mutton. The menu varied each day in the week, vegetable soup and fish, as well as flesh meat, being provided on Fridays and some other days, to meet the wants of catholics.

Houston also commented upon 'the erroneous assumption that law students discuss jurisprudence over their wine, of which, as well as of beer, they get an adequate allowance from the cellar of the inn, English or Irish, to which they happen to belong'.[49]

Yet the King's Inns has felt no obligation to justify the practice of requiring students to eat dinners in Dublin. The keeping of terms is still compulsory today, and no rationale is offered to students for the requirement. In the early 1970s, when this author

---

48. Benchers' minute book, 1844–49 (King's Inns MS, p.111); ibid., p.96 records that in October 1846, as famine stalked Ireland, the caterer was granted permission to discontinue for the time being the use of scarce potatoes in the dining-room.
49. Houston, *O'Connell*, pp.124–26. There was an old rule, presumably to avoid contention, that 'no healths shall be drank in the dining hall' (Benchers' minute book, 1835–44 (King's Inns MS, p.194: 11 Jan. 1843)).

was a law student, it was sometimes said by members of the bar that dinners were a way of teaching lawyers how to hold their alcohol. The illusion that one can function competently while inebriated has since been discredited. Another reason advanced over dinner for the requirement was that it provided a means of meeting colleagues and of making contacts within the profession. Perhaps there were those who found that dinners at the King's Inns had such an indispensable utilitarian value but they never said so in this author's presence. What dining in common undoubtedly provided was an opportunity to congregate with other law students and perhaps to enjoy an evening socially with them, attending the debating society or going later to some pub. The accents of some people one knew changed perceptibly in this milieu, tending to become standardised to the familiar tones of the Law Library. Few students seemed to be either aware or concerned that the cost of dinners might be a burden on families or to have thought that dinners constituted a social occasion which ought to have been optional rather than compulsory. A recently published anecdote encapsulates the bewildering futility of the requirement.[50]

More than a century after the repeal of the Statute of Jeofailles, the King's Inns continues to perpetuate that process of socialisation through which Irish law students were so long obliged to pass at the London inns. Like the framers of the Statute of Jeofailles, the benchers appear to have confidence in the civilising or conforming influence of such practices. Forced in 1885 to yield to national and professional objections to the requirement that law students also eat dinners in London, the council of King's Inns continues to ensure that they will partake of their share of mutton in Dublin.

---

50. J. Ardle McArdle, 'Nothing changed', in *Books Ireland* (summer 1993), p.130.

CHAPTER TEN

'No memory of the past': King's Inns and Queen's Inns Chambers

IN THE HUSTLE AND BUSTLE of the Law Library at Dublin's Four Courts Irish barristers daily conduct their legal business. Between home and court, the members of Ireland's noisiest library find a small niche whence they may be summoned at any moment to huddle in conference with solicitors and clients. The members' professional routine is quite different from that of the bar in London. There a private system of chamber practice has long been in existence. It is found useful not only by established practitioners but also by those who are still learning about law and legal procedures. In Ireland the young barrister is left to take her or his chances as a 'devil', hitched to the coat-tails of an individual practitioner for a short period after being called, and then abandoned to fortune.

The merits or demerits of the chamber system will not be argued here. If it leads to specialisation at the expense of general ability, it may also ensure continuity and consistency. The fact is that the chamber system never caught on in Ireland, although for much of the nineteenth century there was some indication that it might do so. At first, the benchers of King's Inns themselves planned to erect chambers for the profession. Given the failure of their ambitions, it was left to individual lawyers to develop a rudimentary private system of chambers in the houses which lay just outside the gates of King's Inns, along Henrietta Street. Foremost amongst those individuals was Tristram Kennedy.

Henrietta Street today is a sorry sight. Although listed by the corporation for preservation, most of its fine Georgian buildings appear unkempt and neglected. There is, perhaps, still time to save them from destruction, and the recent decision by Dublin Corporation to replace the tarmac surface of the street with cobblestones signals on the part of the city authorities a certain awareness of the area's historical and architectural value.

For almost two centuries, lawyers have walked up Henrietta Street on their way to the King's Inns and the Registry of Deeds. Ascending the hill from Bolton Street, their gaze has been drawn since 1821 to a great gateway surmounted by lion, unicorn and royal arms in Portland stone.[1] This arched gate closes Henrietta Street at the top of the hill, and through it one enters a narrow courtyard lying between the dining hall of the inns and the registry. Here, originally, in the early eighteenth century Henrietta Street opened onto a meadow known as the Plover Field.

The street was laid out in the 1720s by Luke Gardiner, being the earliest of a number of important streets which he contributed to the city. Known also as 'Primate's Hill', because a number of prominent bishops lived along it, Henrietta Street is believed to have been given its present name in honour of the wife of the duke of Grafton, who was lord lieutenant from 1724 to 1727. It appeared in outline on Charles Brooking's map of Dublin, published in 1728, and again on Rocque's plan of the city in 1756. The three earliest houses stood at the top of Henrietta Street on the site of the present King's Inns library. These were leased in 1724 by the archbishop of Armagh, Hugh Boulter, and one of them became his official Dublin residence. Here the prerogative court sat. Opposite the archbishop's property Luke Gardiner built himself a residence known successively as 'The Manor House', 'Mountjoy House' and 'Blessington House'. This later became home to the Dublin Law Institute and Tristram Kennedy's 'Queen's Inns Chambers'. Today it is occupied by an order of nuns.[2]

Throughout the eighteenth century Henrietta Street remained a very attractive place to live, with not only bishops but also peers and senior members of parliament residing next door to one another. According to Maurice Craig, the Dublin historian, 'though it contains only some sixteen houses, they are so palatial a cast that one easily understands how it remained the most fashionable single street in Dublin till the Union, long after many rival centres of social attraction had been created'.[3]

It was to this distinguished neighbourhood that the benchers came at the end of the eighteenth-century to build a new home

1. New entrance and gateway: architect's certificates, builder's bond and articles of agreement, tradesmen's bills and requests for payment, 1819–21 (King's Inns MSS); King's Arms over gateway: John Smyth, sculptor: bill and request for payment, 1820–21 (King's Inns MSS).
2. Wright, *A historical guide to ancient and modern Dublin*, pp.293–94; Anon., 'Blessingon House'; Anon., 'Henrietta Street' in *Irish Builder*, 15 Jun.–15 Aug. 1893. For a synopsis of the latter articles see O'Mahony, 'Some Henrietta Street residents'; Anon., 'Henrietta Street' in *Irish Times*, 19 Nov. 1896; Green Book: admission of benchers, 1712–41 (King's Inns MS, p.216, where it is recorded that in 1730 Luke Gardiner, then deputy vice-treasurer of Ireland, was admitted a bencher of King's Inns).
3. Craig, *Dublin 1660–1860*, p.103.

for their society. For over two hundred years the inns had been located on the banks of the River Liffey, the premises there including a small number of chambers. But from the early eighteenth century the old inns fell into disrepair and were eventually abandoned. That site was then taken for the erection of courts of law and the benchers acquired their present property between Henrietta Street and Constitution Hill. The conveyance under which this came about may have involved a breach of trust on the part of one of the benchers. A late effort by the benchers to extricate themselves from certain expensive and complex leases failed, and it finally took a special act of parliament in 1798 to pass the title to the society of King's Inns.[4]

As early as 1793, the benchers had decided not only to undertake the construction of a new dining-hall and library, but also to have chambers built, both by the society directly and by members who were expected to lease from the benchers ground for the purpose. From that year deposits for chambers were levied annually from new barristers and attorneys, 'the deposit for chambers to be allowed when the gentleman shall purchase from the society chambers or ground to build chambers on'. Rules were even agreed concerning the regulation of tenancies in chambers. The erection of chambers was mentioned in the statute of 1798 as being one of the objectives of the society.[5] But the architect James Gandon baulked at starting to construct chambers while work on the main building was in progress. He pointed to

> many inconveniences likely to arise from the workmen of different employers working at the same time within the gates and the danger of encouraging combination and rise of wages by setting so much building on foot at once.[6]

In fact, chambers were never afterwards erected by the society, a sore point for the members of King's Inns who were being levied specifically for the cost of erecting them. The attorneys would later make much of this imposition.

4. Kenny, *King's Inns and the kingdom of Ireland*, pp.169–74, 229–39; Littledale, *The society of King's Inns*, pp.24–27; *Stat.Ire.*, 38 Geo.III, c.49 (1798), 'An act to enable the dean and chapter of Christ Church, Dublin, and other persons therein named to grant certain grounds in the city of Dublin, to the society of King's Inns'.
5. 'King's Inns General Rules, 1794', nos. xxxii-xlvi, included at Duhigg, *History of the King's Inns*, pp.596–605. For printed copies of the rules, see King's Inns MSS A. 2/1–3; *Stat.Ire.*, 38 Geo.III, c.49 (1798).
6. Benchers' minutes, 1792–1803 (King's Inns MS, ff. 47,133v, 159v, 162, 181, 197, 200v).

That slow progress was made in completing the main building at King's Inns allowed the benchers to defer a final decision in the matter of chambers. In 1812, one visitor to Ireland welcomed their absence, suggesting that the Irish lawyer was, in consequence of not being so confined, 'a more agreeable companion in private life'. A sketch of the King's Inns site which was drawn in 1813 suggests that it was intended then that chambers would face the new building on Constitution Hill, 'the intended line of buildings by the society' being traced in a bow approximately where the front railings of the King's Inns stand today.[7]

The benchers' ambitions for the new site were further complicated in 1814 when the government took possession of the unfinished south wing for a repository for public records. This was already being used for sittings of the prerogative court, although originally intended for a new King's Inns library. The statute passed by the government to enable them to acquire this wing in 1814 restricted the freedom of the benchers to erect buildings anywhere on that part of their land lying to the south of the new registry of deeds. The reason for this restriction was a recurrent fear about the security of Irish records in the event of fire.[8] With the benchers apparently intending to build chambers to the west of their dining-hall, such a restriction was not objectionable, but when they later changed their plan, the statutory provision proved to be a hindrance.

A more immediate priority than the provision of chambers was the erection of a new library building. This was commenced in 1825 on the site of Archbishop Boulter's former property at the top of Henrietta Street. Littledale has written that this site was chosen by the society because it stood exactly opposite the residence of an eminent judge and bencher who was exceedingly displeased at a proposal that the archbishop's old large house be converted into a mendicity institute. But it is also likely that the benchers wished to keep their existing property as free as possible for the erection of chambers, for these might be a means of generating income for the society.[9]

7. Wakefield, *An account of Ireland*, ii, 341; *Rec. comm. Ire. reps*, fold-out; McParland, *James Gandon*, pp.165–71. McParland suggests that Gandon never intended to interrupt passage from Henrietta Street to the inns courtyard by erecting a gateway between them.
8. 54 Geo. III (1814), c.113, 'An act to vest in his majesty, his heirs and successors, for ever, part of the ground and buildings now belonging to the society of King's Inns, Dublin, for the erecting thereon a repository for public records in Ireland'; Wright, *Ancient and modern Dublin*, pp.293–94.
9. Littledale, *King's Inns*, p.27. It was said that, in digging the foundation of the new library, workmen came on a brick-vaulted wine-cellar with old bottles of wine still in it, but the wine had turned into water (*Irish Times*, 30 Aug. 1886).

The society was spending money not only at the King's Inns itself but also at the Four Courts, where it felt obliged to pay for the wages of tipstaffs and other attendants, as well as funding in 1825 the construction of a new library for the bar and a chamber under it for officials of the rolls court. This commitment to the bar prompted a response from some of the attorneys and solicitors, who wrote to the benchers, 'respectfully to request the accommodation of a chamber in such building for the members of their profession and which they claim with greater confidence having contributed the greater part of the funds of the society'.[10] The benchers were being called upon to make up their minds about how to dispose of the deposits collected for chambers from new barristers and attorneys since 1794. But, rather than responding directly to the request of the attorneys and solicitors for accommodation at the Four Courts, the benchers' standing committee forthwith agreed unanimously, in relation to their property at Henrietta Street, that

it would be manifestly just, and highly expedient for the interests of the society to erect two buildings consisting of six sets of chambers each, as delineated in the plan annexed, as a commencement of a general plan of building chambers to be realised.[11]

The committee calculated that it had about £15,000 in hand to pay for the two buildings, having liberally allowed some of the accumulated deposits against the cost of other construction to date. The report of the committee bemoaned the head rent of £1,120 per annum paid by the society under the unhappy terms of its holding between Henrietta Street and Constitution Hill, and noted

that while the society is subject to this heavy outgoing rent, all the rest of the ground unoccupied by the hall and the Prerogative Court and Record Offices is waste and not merely unproductive, but in such a state of disorder and neglect, as to be disgraceful to a public body having funds properly applicable to make and keep it in public order.

So the proposal of the committee was that the society would build two sets of chambers and that other sites would then be let

10. Law Library, Four Courts: builders' estimates, bond and articles of agreement; architect's accounts, builder's accounts; thanks of members of the bar, 1825–26 (King's Inns MSS); Solicitors' memorial for a chamber at the Four Courts, 1826, with subsequent related materials (King's Inns MSS).
11. Proposals for building chambers: report of the standing committee, estimates, etc., 1826–27 (King's Inns MSS).

'to persons disposed to invest their capitals in continuing similar buildings, to be erected and built according to these two model buildings, so as to render the line of these buildings, which would have the newly-projected line of a new street in front of them, similar and uniform'. The committee had before it plans drawn up by Frederick Darley, jnr. These colour sketches have survived and show the outline of the proposed new thoroughfare. It was intended to branch off to the south at right angles from Henrietta Street, between the present library and the registry of deeds. Then, some distance beyond the corner of the registry, the street was to turn west at right angles, leading in a straight line thence to Constitution Hill.[12] Had it ever been laid out, it would have passed through the location of the present King's Inns car-park. Facing this street, along the side furthest from the registry, would have stood all of the planned chambers. The committee of 1826 concluded

> that considering the subject, abstracted from mere pecuniary view, the adoption of such a plan of buildings appears to the committee as likely to produce much convenience to the members of both professions, and as probably conducive to the advancement of professional knowledge and regular habits of business.

But the benchers identified an obstacle to their ambitions. The statute of 1814, as noted earlier, prohibited the erection of any buildings to the south of the registry. Accordingly, an amendment was now drafted and parliament persuaded to pass it. This act of April 1826 acknowledged that the extent of the restriction was 'unnecessary and useless', and that the society of King's Inns might need to use part of the ground to the south of the registry ' . . . in laying out sites for chambers and in building thereon, if they shall proceed to build chambers . . . '.[13]

Although the benchers adopted the report of 1826 and agreed to place advertisements inviting proposals to undertake the building

---

12. Survey of the ground belonging to King's Inns, with a design of a new street leading from Henrietta St. to the Four Courts [and] design for the new gateway to [its] entrance, by Frederick Darley, jnr. (King's Inns MSS). The 'Plan, sections and elevation of the proposed chambers to be erected for King's Inns, by Frederick Darley jnr., 1827' (King's Inns MSS) appear to have been for the proposed chambers at the Four Courts, and were drawn up by Darley at the behest of the attorneys.
13. 7 Geo.IV (1826), c.13, 'An act to alter and amend an act passed in the fifty-fourth year of the reign of his late majesty, King George the Third, for vesting in his majesty, his heirs and successors, for ever, part of the ground and buildings now belonging to the society of King's Inns, Dublin, for the erecting thereon a repository for public records in Ireland'.

of chambers, such proposals to be submitted by Easter 1827, still the chambers did not appear. Given the continuing absence of such accommodation, some attorneys and solicitors in 1830 made an application to the benchers which echoed that of their brethren in 1826 by shifting the focus away from the question of private chambers at King's Inns and onto a demand for rooms at the Four Courts. In pursuit of this objective, the recently formed Irish Law Society sent a memorial to the benchers, noting that,

> with a view to the speedy attainment of this important object, they . . . find that a space, sufficient for the purpose, may be obtained at the rere of the Four Courts, the eligibility of which, (in every point of view), surpasses that of any other situation.

Asking the benchers to purchase this site and 'to erect sufficient and convenient chambers', the application of 1830 set in train the process which led eventually to the erection behind the Four Courts of the Solicitors' Building, containing arbitration chambers and a library. The Law Society itself had offices there for many years until it moved to Blackhall Place in 1978.[14]

In pressing for rooms at the Four Courts, it would later be said by parliamentary commissioners that

> the attorneys and solicitors . . . seemed to prefer the erection of buildings which would benefit the whole body, rather than that of chambers which could accommodate a limited number of their profession. We are, therefore, of opinion that the benchers have substantially . . . performed what was incumbent on them towards the attorney branch of the profession.[15]

With the Law Society demanding space at the Four Courts from 1830, there was less reason for the benchers to incline towards providing accommodation for them at King's Inns, and this decreased the likelihood of the benchers actually beginning to build chambers there. But there were other reasons, too, why the society hesitated. For one thing, the location of the King's Inns was commented upon unfavourably by a number of observers in the nineteenth century. Some lawyers found it just too far away from the Four Courts for their professional convenience.[16]

14. Benchers' minute book, 1819–30 (King's Inns MS, pp.197, 200, 208); Memorial of the committee of the Irish Law Society relating to chambers, 1830 (King's Inns MS); O'Reilly and Robinson, *New lease of life*, pp.37–48.
15. *Report of the King's Inns, Dublin, inquiry commission in respect of sums received on the admission of attorneys and solicitors as 'deposits for chambers' and other matters . . . 1872*, p.7.
16. Duhigg, *History of King's Inns*, pp.480–81; Littledale, *King's Inns*, pp.27–28.

More convenient would have been chambers erected in accordance with a plan promoted about 1831 by William Carroll, one of the founders of the Law Society. He wished to see erected at the rear of the Four Courts, 'from which it should be separated only by a handsome palisade', a complex of buildings to be known as King's Inns Square. This was intended to consist of 'nine hundred college-like chambers . . . commodious and permanently built, on the plan of the flats of Edinburgh chambers', with a single meeting room capable of holding six hundred members of the profession at one time. Had his proposal been accepted, the manner in which Irish lawyers organised their daily business and their consultations with colleagues might have changed radically. But it came to nothing.[17]

It should also be said that there were certain principled objections to chambers from some benchers who were afraid that an English style of chamber life in Dublin would have undesirable consequences for young lawyers, and the reservations of these faint hearts may have been the last straw in tipping the scales against proceeding with chambers at King's Inns. The reservations came to light in 1846 when Acheson Lyle appeared before the select committee on legal education. The sole Irish bencher to give evidence, Lyle admitted that a system of chambers was something that had been frequently talked about:

Some of the benchers are much disposed for it; but there is a very great difference of opinion prevailing. . . . Some of the benchers I have heard express opinions adverse to it, from the facility that it gives to young men, by separating them from their families, of contracting habits leading to immorality and licentiousness.

Openly admitting that finance had not been in fact a major obstacle to the building of chambers, Lyle reiterated this other reason for the delay. Some people, he said, believed that the chamber system in England 'leads to habits of life . . . which they would not desire to introduce into Ireland'.[18]

While the Irish were obliged to attend the inns of court in London, they were not compelled to enter chambers in that city, and most chose not to do so. Enrolling in chambers was expensive and there were variations between English and Irish law, in relation to the details of which most English barristers were presumably unable to give advice. One Irishman who did enter chambers

17. Suggestions for building chambers, from William H. Carroll, [1830–31] (King's Inns MS).
18. *Sel. comm. leg. ed.*, qq. 2234–40.

was, as we have seen, Michael Barry, a student at Gray's Inns in 1830. He went first to an equity barrister and conveyancer, subsequently to a special pleader. He later stressed that such a course of action for an Irishman was 'an exception, it is not usual'. Furthermore, those who chose it stayed only a short time, 'sometimes but for six months'. Moreover, Barry believed that even when a student managed to stay a whole year in chambers in London ' . . . he really learns nothing, and he is about to leave the chambers just as his eyes, as it were, are about to open upon the subject of real property and conveyancing'.[19] Perhaps Barry was also the anonymous writer who complained in an article in 1841 that the young man who entered chambers while resident in London returned 'as innocent of both law and practice as he was when he left'. The author added that English law students 'never think of approaching the bar until after several years attendance in the chambers of a barrister', whereas, in Ireland, this practice 'is almost a rarity. It is quite a novelty . . . '.[20]

That there was such a 'novelty' at all arose largely from the initiative of Tristram Kennedy in acquiring Luke Gardiner's former home in Henrietta Street in 1837 and converting it into what he dubbed 'Queen's Inns Chambers'. There Kennedy located from 1839 his new Dublin Law Institute and recruited rising and talented barristers as part-time lecturers. According to that same anonymous writer in 1841,

we understand that numerous applications have been made to the professors of the Law Institute, since its commencement, to receive private pupils into their chambers, and that several of them have done so, under the sanction and approbation of some of the leading members of the bar. . . .[21]

With Kennedy in 1841 buying the house next to Gardiner's former home, the scope for such arrangements increased. In March of that year, he wrote to William Napier,

I had it not in my power to do anything for your son John with respect to a residence for him in our Dublin chambers; however, next month my premises will be considerably extended and he can have chambers if he wished and upon terms to suit him.

I have had a good deal of conversation with one of the professors in our Law Institute and we agree in thinking, if John has any taste for

19. ibid., qq. 1579–82, 1595, 1599, 1647, 1651, 3022–24; above pp.150–51.
20. Anon., 'Legal education in Ireland', i, 138–39 (27 Feb. 1841).
21. ibid., 141–42.

study, that there would be no difficulty whatever in his being a good conveyancer and this you are aware is one of the most profitable branches of the barristers' profession, – his course of study would not necessarily interfere with his present engagements. I should like to know what you think on this subject as I could obtain considerable advantages for John through the professors in our Institute if he were disposed to attempt the undertaking.[22]

Insofar as practitioners in Dublin had an office in their own home or at some other address for purposes connected with their profession, it could be said that there were indeed chambers in Dublin. But these offices were sprinkled around the city, and lacked the distinctive features of the London system. Like their American colleagues, Irish lawyers generally rated as low the advantages to be gained from reading in chambers. The Irish bar found more attractive its centralised Law Library. With the early collapse of the Dublin Law Institute, which had been dogged by professional jealousies, Kennedy's personal ambitions for a more coherent pupillage system in Ireland were dealt a severe blow. In 1846 he was forced to admit to the select committee on legal education that such a system had only been ' . . . to a slight degree carried out within the last ten years . . . There are very few people who do take pupils, and they for the most part are in general practice'. Michael Barry told the committee that he knew of only three conveyancers who took pupils, and they were not exclusive conveyancers. This was a reference to an opinion that the benefits of pupillage were in direct proportion to the degree of specialisation involved, a view which Kennedy did not share. Kennedy told the committee that Irish students could derive as much advantage from being placed in chambers in Dublin as could English students 'under the present system'.[23]

In acquiring in the late 1830s the former 'Mountjoy House' at the top of Henrietta Street and turning it and some other property there into his 'Queen's Inns Chambers', Kennedy was encouraging his colleagues to make Henrietta Street an annexe of King's Inns. In fact, as the prospect of the society itself building chambers receded, some lawyers did indeed seem to rally to the street to create an informal collegiate network. The fact that the King's Inns library opened there in the early 1830s was an inducement to them.

22. Kennedy to Napier (Bodl. MS, f.97).
23. Dicey, 'The teaching of English law at Harvard', 748; *Sel. comm. leg. ed.*, qq. 1064–69, 1652–55, 2397.

The benchers did not formally agree to change the society's name to 'Queen's Inns' during Victoria's long reign from 1837 to 1901, as they had during that of Anne, but there were many who referred to it as such during that period. The young Victoria was a favourite of liberals like Kennedy, and it is not surprising that by 1838 he had chosen to name his recently acquired property in her honour. In February 1840, he threw a party at his 'Queen's Inns Chambers' to celebrate the queen's marriage to Prince Albert. Members of Kennedy's family and his professional colleagues attended. According to one account,

> the building was tastefully illuminated and the several transparencies with which it was decorated were much admired for their elegance. The large centre figure of the queen, surrounded by the allegorical emblems of the arts and sciences, was beautiful in the extreme, and the judicious application of the gas-light tended much to heighten the effect.[24]

In this illuminated spectacle, was there perhaps a flickering shadow of the macabre and extravagant wake which just a few years earlier had been held in this house by Luke Gardiner's great-grandson, Viscount Mountjoy, on the occasion of his first wife's death? In funereal splendour, the event eclipsed even the departure of Archbishop Boulter, who had been waked in state at his house across the road. A catholic married woman with whom the viscount had eloped just six years before her death, her obsequies in 1814 were estimated to have cost nearly £4,000:

> The body placed in a coffin, sumptuously decorated, had been conveyed to Dublin by a London undertaker of eminence in the performance of state funerals, attended by six professional female mourners, suitably attired in mourning garments, and was laid out in a spacious room hung with black cloth, on an elevated catafalque covered with a velvet pall of the finest texture, embroidered in gold and silver, which had been purchased in France for the occasion, and had recently been used at a public funeral in Paris of great pomp and splendour, that of Marshal Duroc. A large number of wax tapers were ranged around the catafalque, and the six professional female mutes remained in attendance in the chamber in becoming attitudes, admirably regulated; while the London undertaker . . . expressed a hope that the arrangements were to the satisfaction of the visitor.[25]

---

24. *Evening Packet*, 11 Feb. 1840. Gaslight came to Henrietta Street in 1825, the year King's Inns library was commenced (Benchers' minute book, 1819–30 (King's Inns MS, pp.146, 158, 171, 174)).
25. Madden, *The literary life and correspondence of the countess of Blessington*, i, 55. The scale of this public event may have exceeded that of her spouse's

It is a twist of fate that the room in which this very ornate ceremony was staged for the deceased convert to protestantism, replete with its funeral pall from Paris, would later serve as a chapel for a French order of catholic nuns who at the turn of the century acquired the house for a convent. But as Kennedy's guests danced around the gas-lit ballroom in 1840, they were less likely to be haunted by such images than to be delighted by the distinguished company. Kennedy's Dublin Law Institute seemed set to achieve great things and his confidence was reflected in the acquisition of his houses. He would later be accused of 'spoiling one of the finest dining-rooms ever designed' by making the present hall-door in the middle of the mansion about 1860. It was he too, apparently, who closed the covered carriage entry, or porte-cochère, between his house and the King's Inns.[26]

When Kennedy purchased Blessington House in 1837, it was listed as 'no.9' Henrietta Street. But eight years later, the street was renumbered due to the addition of a residence on the east side of Henrietta Lane, so that from 1845 Gardiner's old home became 'no.10'. By that date Kennedy had also acquired the house next door, formerly belonging to Judge Arthur Moore, making nos. 9 and 10 together 'Queen's Inns Chambers Upper'. The adjective distinguished these from no.3, the first house in the terrace, which he had purchased by 1842, and which was dubbed 'Queen's Inns Chambers Lower'. By the time of Kennedy's death in 1885, as will be seen, he had gradually come to own most of the houses in Henrietta Street, including the entire terrace, from no.3 to no.10. Kennedy wished to secure the street for the continuing enjoyment of members of the legal profession, with whom it was popular before he came to live in it himself in the 1830s. But he was fighting against the tide. He himself had not enough money to restore the houses to their former splendour, and the north side of the city generally continued to decline.[27]

grief for within a year he was throwing a party at the same house and, in 1818, recently created earl of Blessington, brought his second wife there to meet friends.
26. [Prendergast], 'Blessington House' in *Irish Times*, 30 August 1886. The attribution to Prendergast is at Harrison, *Memorable Dublin houses: a handy guide, illustrated*, p.114; Crimmins, 'Henrietta Street: a conservation study', pp.28, 48. For an illustration of the house before Kennedy changed it, see *Dublin Penny Journal*, 13 Feb. 1836 (reproduced above).
27. Thom's *Dublin directory*, passim, esp. 1837–38, 1841–42, 1845; *Irish Builder*, 1 July and 15 Aug. 1893, where it is said that, on 29 Nov. 1892, nos.3–10 were sold by Kennedy's representatives to Alderman Joseph Meade LL.D. for £4,000. Kennedy also appears to have owned no.11 (see note 34 below), and Thom's *Dublin directory* for 1881 gives him also at no.13 in that year.

That there was extreme poverty in Dublin at the beginning of the twentieth century, especially just north of the river, is well-known. But what has not been so widely noticed is that Henrietta Street so long continued to be a respectable centre of legal business throughout the nineteenth century. It is clear from Dublin directories that proctors, attorneys and barristers lived or worked there in substantial numbers during the reign of Victoria.

In 1851, the newly appointed commissioners for the sale of encumbered estates (encumbered estates court) opened their offices at no.14 Henrietta Street and some civil engineers and surveyors were attracted to the street, moving in beside the lawyers. But when the landed estates court (the encumbered estates court's successor) subsequently vacated its premises, less welcome neighbours arrived in the early 1860s, in the form of two regiments of militia which were quartered at nos. 12 and 14. The benchers were alarmed by this decline in the fortunes of the street which, insofar as it served as chambers for lawyers, disguised their failure to build accommodation within their own grounds. This failure still irked 'the lower branch' of the profession, but in 1872 a parliamentary enquiry into the matter disappointed the attorneys and solicitors who, having left the society of King's Inns in 1866, had hoped to receive some compensation for the deposits for chambers which their branch had paid to the benchers since 1794. At least the enquiry appears to have spurred the benchers into considering one last time the possible advantages for aspiring lawyers of an Irish chamber system. In 1873, they adopted a motion proposed by Chief Justice Whiteside, one of the former professors at the Dublin Law Institute and a conservative politically,

That having regard to the rules which now regulate the admission of students and call to the bar, it be referred to a committee to consider and suggest such plans as might be judiciously adopted for promoting the establishment or extension of chambers, to meet the requirements of those entering upon, or engaged in, legal study, in both branches of the legal profession.[28]

The committee members acknowledged that many houses along Henrietta Street had already been privately converted into chambers, these being the ones owned by Kennedy. The committee did so in a petition which, in April 1873, was addressed to Earl Spencer, lord lieutenant of Ireland. This petition ranged over

28. *Report of the King's Inns, Dublin, inquiry commission in respect of sums received on the admission of attorneys and solicitors as 'deposits for chambers' and other matters . . . 1872*, p.7; Kennedy, *The state and the benchers*, p.16.

a number of matters, and is worth reproducing in full, because of the clear picture it conveys of life in Henrietta Street at the end of the third quarter of the nineteenth century, and of the central position occupied there by lawyers in chambers:

The members of a special select committee of the benchers of the honourable society of the King's Inns most respectfully beg leave to submit to the consideration of your Excellency the following statement of facts on the necessity existing for removing from Henrietta Street the two depots of Militia regiments now quartered there, namely, the staff of the County Dublin Militia and the staff of the City Artillery.

1st. – That the main portion of the street consists of the King's Inns Law Library, and fourteen houses formerly occupied by nobility and gentry. Ten of those are now for the most part converted into law chambers for the accommodation of members of the legal profession, and law students desirous of availing themselves of the King's Inns Law Library, long established in the street.

Of the remaining four houses, two are occupied by the staff of the Militia regiments referred to, and the two others are used as common lodging houses, in which six of the Militia staff, with their families, reside, in consequence of the insufficient accommodation which the barracks depots afford. Besides, some others are resident in the immediate locality.

2nd. – That at the head of the street stands the King's Inns Building, the Offices for Registry of Wills and Deeds of Title to Property in Ireland, and the offices of the Probate Court, and a gate has long stood there, preventing ordinary thoroughfare.

3rd. – That the Law Library of the Society of the King's Inns is the only place in Dublin to which those studying for the Bar can have recourse for the advantages which an extensive library affords, and an orderly quiet street is essential to admit of their prosecuting their studies.

4th. – That since the staff of the Militia, with their numerous families, came to reside in the street, there has long been an absence of all order and quiet; and the nuisance resulting from the street being made the resort of recruits and their followers, has become so intolerable as to be incapable of any control even by the police, who consider themselves exonerated from interference whilst the barracks remain.

Besides, the street, being a cul de sac and consequently having little carriage traffic, is made a perpetual playground by the children of the Militia, and those of the surrounding district, to the great annoyance of the inhabitants and the numerous persons having business to transact daily in the several public offices referred to.

5th. – We have, therefore, most earnestly to urge, for the consideration of your Excellency, the necessity of such steps being taken by the Government and other authorities concerned, to secure the earliest possible withdrawal of the two Militia depots from Henrietta Street, in which they are now stationed, both to the serious prejudice of the interests of private property, and the peaceful enjoyment by the legal profession of their library and chambers.

But above all, this appeal is made for your Excellency's consideration on behalf of the Law Students, as on the benchers devolves the duty of securing such necessary facilities for study as are now sought to be obtained by the removal of the barracks.[29]

Notwithstanding the heartfelt nature of this detailed plea, the benchers' request did not elicit an immediately enthusiastic response from government. Any official familiar with the history of the benchers' abdication of responsibility over three centuries in the matter of legal education must have regarded with some derision a petition which appeared to reduce the 'duty of securing necessary facilities for study' to allowing students access to a library and chasing noisy little girls and boys out of their way. Nor might the benchers take any credit for the existence of chambers in Henrietta Street, however valid their objections to the nuisance being caused by the militia and their families. But the lawyers found the editor of the *Irish Times* to be sympathetic. In August 1874, he turned his attention to Henrietta Street:

When the Act of Union was passed the glory of this street as of others collapsed. The nobility departed, the gentry followed. It resembled a silent street in the city of the dead. The child who wandered into it fled in terror, affrighted by the echo of his own footsteps.

Then the inns of court, known as the King's Inns, were raised on a vacant space of ground at the top of the street. Here is the provincial court of the archdiocese of Dublin; the registry of deeds; the benchers' hall; the extensive law library, &c. The place had the air of a law university where the silence which prevailed aided the student at his work.

Very soon ten of the fourteen houses were converted into law chambers for the accommodation of members of the legal profession and students. Two other houses were let in lodgings and the other two make the place a pandemonium. For here in these houses are quartered the staff of two militia regiments who create a never-ending din. The Tyro musician bleats through a gigantic trombone, or tortures the flute, or toot-toots through a squeaking fife, or belabours a drum. There is shouting, there is singing of war songs, voices of angry women, squalling of quarrelling children. The quiet street roars with discordant noises, and students in distraction close their books in despair.

The editor noted that the benchers had appealed to Lord Spencer to remove the militia to the Linen Hall barracks, but that Spencer had merely referred the matter to the War Office which was unsympathetic. A subsequent change of government had not altered the attitude of the War Office.[30]

29. Kennedy, *The state and the benchers*, pp.16–17.
30. *Irish Times*, 7 Aug. 1874.

It was in this context that Tristram Kennedy, by then owner of most of the property along Henrietta Street, published his proposal that the benchers acquire every house in the street and erect a gateway near the bottom of the hill to encompass it into the inns. He claimed that both the benchers and the state had failed to discharge their obligations to the society of King's Inns in general, and to the law student in particular. To convince readers that his plan was feasible, Kennedy explored the finances of King's Inns, arguing that the society was owed compensation by the state for various dealings relating to its former and present properties and for certain services provided at the Four Courts out of the funds of King's Inns. Once such debts were paid to it, he suggested,

The simple course for carrying out the plan proposed would be under an Act of Parliament, to be obtained for effecting the sale and purchase, on jury valuation, of all property not now belonging to the society in that portion of Henrietta Street extending from the repository of deeds' gate-entrance to Henrietta-place on the one side, and to Henrietta-lane on the other side, where a gate should then be placed. This course, if taken, would meet with the sanction and support of the proprietor of three-fourths of the premises required for the purpose, leaving but three persons' interests in the remaining one-fourth part of the premises in the street to be acquired in like manner.[31]

Kennedy was not the first person to recognise the potential value to the profession of Henrietta Street. In 1806, Bartholomew Duhigg, the first historian of the King's Inns, had criticised the benchers for squandering money in the confusion surrounding their acquisition of the site at Constitution Hill, and had observed that 'Henrietta Street itself might by this time be purchased, and the present ground form a cheap garden annexed thereto'.[32]

Kennedy's plan was not adopted but the government did eventually pull out the militia. Unfortunately, their departure did not have the desired effect of returning the houses to better order. The owners of no.12 refused to take responsibility for it and, according to one account, 'the upshot of the affair was that, in some time after the War Office abandoned the premises, the landlord did not take them up, and the old noble mansion was left tenantless and derelict . . . the hall-door left standing wide open. The result may be imagined. There was not a whole pane of glass left'. By 1893 both no.12 and no.14 were in tenements.[33]

31. Kennedy, *The state and the benchers*, p.14.
32. Duhigg, *History of the King's Inns*, p.538.
33. Kennedy, *The state and the benchers*, p.17; *Irish Builder*, 1 July and 15 Aug. 1893.

As the quality of the street declined, the benchers failed either to intervene or to build chambers of their own. But they did acquire title to the house which stood next door to their library and which once had belonged to the earls of Shannon and to Tristram Kennedy,

for finding that Henry Monck Mason, their former librarian, about forty years ago, then dwelling in the library, had some very fine girls for daughters, they thought their beauty troubled the studies of the young barristers, and for the future (after his demise) they required the librarian to dwell in the adjacent house, taken by them for that purpose.[34]

In 1885 Tristram Kennedy died, and in 1892 the sale of that part of Henrietta Street which had belonged to him marked the end of an era. Already more than two decades had passed since nos. 9 and 10 had last been listed as 'Queen's Inns Chambers' in the annual *Dublin Directory*. Yet up to a dozen barristers had chambers there and elsewhere in the street right into the 1890s. Only as the twentieth century dawned did the full extent of dereliction become apparent. In 1900, all of the houses in the street were in tenements, bar two, and not one lawyer remained. The houses not in tenements were those which had together constituted Queen's Inns Chambers Upper. At no.9, generally regarded as the finest architectural specimen in the street, was to be found a house and estate agent. At no.10 was the Discharged Female Prisoners' Aid Society. Into this environment, out of the registry of deeds, stepped 'Thomas Malone Chandler', one of James Joyce's *Dubliners*:

When his hour had struck he stood up and took leave of his desk and of his fellow-clerks punctiliously. He emerged from under the feudal arch of the King's Inns, a neat modest figure, and walked swiftly down Henrietta Street. The golden sunset was waning and the air had grown sharp. A horde of grimy children populated the street. They stood or ran in the roadway or crawled up the steps before the gaping doors or squatted like mice upon the thresholds. Little Chandler gave them no thought. He picked his way deftly through all that minute vermin-like life and under the shadow of the gaunt spectral mansions in which the old nobility of Dublin had roistered. No memory of the past touched him, for his mind was full of a present joy.[35]

---

34. Anon., 'Henrietta Street', in *Irish Times*, 19 Nov. 1896. In 1865, Tristram Kennedy appears to have acquired a title to this house (no.11) from the landed estates court (deeds at King's Inns MS G.3/2-2). It has been used in the twentieth century as a residence for the under-treasurer of King's Inns.
35. Joyce, *Dubliners*, p.77.

In 1910, the Georgian Society had some photographs of the street taken and one, of the side once owned entirely by Kennedy, is reproduced above. In 1952, Maurice Craig, in his history of the city of Dublin, maintained that Henrietta Street 'still contains the oldest and grandest houses on the North Side'. But since then too little has been done to stop most of the buildings from simply rotting away. Fortunately, the Daughters of Charity have, at great cost to their order, preserved nos. 9 and 10, Kennedy's old Queen's Inns Chambers. In 1994, the Irish Legal History Society was permitted by the sisters to hold its annual general meeting in the parlour of no.10 and a talk was also given by this author.[36]

At least the street did not fall victim to the craze for demolition which swept Dublin in the 1960s and 1970s. It survived to serve only too well as a set for tenement scenes in RTE's *Strumpet City*, the television version of James Plunkett's novel about Dublin at the turn of the century. In 1987, a conservation study pointed out how the street could be revitalised, and in recent years some individuals have done what they could personally to preserve bits of it. The area has even begun to acquire a certain cachet among the fashionably artistic, but not yet sufficient to inspire some city planner or politician to advance it as a northside equivalent of the Temple Bar area. Too many appear to share with 'Thomas Malone Chandler' of *Dubliners* 'no memory of the past'. The street was once a powerhouse of Irish politics and later served as an embryonic legal quarter. It would be a great loss to the city were it finally to disappear.[37]

---

36. Craig, *Dublin 1660–1860*, p.102; Kenny, 'Irish ambition and English preference in chancery appointments, 1827–41: the fate of William Conyngham Plunket'. An expanded version of this talk is at Osborough (ed.), *Explorations in law and history*, pp.133–76.
37. *Georgian Society records of domestic architecture*, ii, 10–13; Crimmins, 'Henrietta Street: a conservation study', passim; Fitzgerald, 'The Caseys of Henrietta Street, Dublin', 87–89; McLaughlin, 'Living among the ghosts of old grandeur' in *Sunday Independent*, 27 June 1993; O'Brien and Guinness, *Dublin: a grand tour*, pp.70–73, where Henrietta Street is described as 'a prince among streets'. In 1994, Dublin Corporation became involved in a dispute over the closure, and filling by it, of cellars or basements under the newly cobbled Henrietta Street. At this time, Ms Carmencita Hederman (independent community councillor) described the street as 'the city's finest' (*Irish Times*, 24 May 1994).

Epilogue

THE EDITOR of the *Irish Times* was not simply being nostalgic in recalling in 1874 the short period when Henrietta Street had had about it 'the air of a legal university'. He was also touching a raw nerve in the debate about the future of legal education. For in 1855, as we have seen, the commission enquiring into the English inns of court, set up on foot of a motion from Joseph Napier, had recommended that the London inns establish a legal university with power to grant degrees in law. While the benchers in London chose to disregard this proposal, others such as the English attorney general, Richard Bethell, supported it enthusiastically. Then, in 1870, the Legal Education Association was formed in London to press for reforms, and in particular for the establishment of a 'General School of Law' based on the inns. From the following year, the issue was raised in the house of commons by Sir Roundell Palmer, whose efforts evoked a sympathetic response in Dublin. In 1872, the editor of the *Irish Law Times and Solicitors' Journal* recommended that what Ireland needed was 'some scheme like Sir Roundell Palmer's for the institution of a legal university'.[1]

But the Irish benchers saw no reason for such an initiative. They had in 1850 decided against the insular approach of the English inns, and had created instead a unique hybrid system involving the University of Dublin and, later, the Queen's Colleges. This system might be developed, as it was by the new rules which came into effect from 1873, but the benchers were unwilling to overthrow it and to assume complete responsibility for the provision of law courses. As it was, they effectively controlled the system while not being obliged to fund it fully.

Nor were the benchers inclined to be tempted into the acquisition of new property for any purpose. The history of their dealings in land and buildings, both at their former site on the banks of the Liffey in the eighteenth century and when acquiring the ground at Constitution Hill later, had been lamentable and involved gross negligence or, possibly, even fraud. For them to have accepted

---

1. *Irish Times*, 7 Aug. 1874; *Ormrod Report*, pp.9–10; *ILT & SJ*, vi, 249 (11 May 1872).

Kennedy's proposal that they purchase Henrietta Street would have meant speculating on the chances of lawyers being tempted to an area which was generally regarded as somewhat inconvenient to the courts and already in a state of decline. So Kennedy's dream of the hill behind King's Inns becoming a centre for professional activity was not realised. He died without having disposed of his houses there. Perhaps to the end he hoped that the benchers might change their minds but they disappointed him, as they had done more than forty years earlier when they refused to continue their support for the law school which he had tucked under the wing of King's Inns.

Kennedy lived just long enough to see abolished the provision which for over three hundred years had required Irishmen to attend the inns of court in London. While he himself always appears publicly to have exercised restraint in supporting its repeal, his reserve being born in the days when he feared that his law school might be damaged by being too closely associated with nationalist sentiments, it is clear from a consideration of his life's work that he could only have welcomed the act of 1885. For it finally left the King's Inns and the universities free to provide legal education in a manner appropriate for Ireland.

As he approached his death, which occurred on 20 November 1885, Kennedy is said to have been in weak health. But he suffered no bodily pain. Even on the day before he passed away he was well enough to be engaged in making arrangements for a visit to Dublin on business.[2] While he did so, perhaps his thoughts turned back over the years to the day in 1834 when he was called to the Irish bar. He will have recalled his early enthusiasm for the profession and his fateful decision to establish the Dublin Law Institute. He had risen above the political and religious sectarianism of the time to create a law school which commanded widespread support. As any reader of this book will surely have discovered, Kennedy had reason to feel satisfied that his initiative had been at the very least a catalyst for changes long overdue at the inns of court. In the short term, the campaign which he launched in 1839 was frustrating and disappointing. But, in the long term, with the support of Thomas Wyse in particular, he had an impact on legal training in England and Ireland which has continued to be felt to the present day. He might with some justification claim credit for the appointment of Wyse's committee of 1846 and for Napier having had such an intense interest in the subject that the latter moved, successfully, for the appointment of a special enquiry into

---

2. Unidentified press obituary (Stack MS).

the English inns in 1854. Kennedy, as we have seen, continued into his old age to press the case for reform on both the benchers and the state. His 'Queen's Inns Chambers' ensured that Henrietta Street was frequented by lawyers in greater numbers and for longer than would otherwise have been the case.

No single person was responsible for the changes which took place in legal education in the nineteenth century. Many individuals sensed that the time had come for reform, with social and economic factors creating conditions in which the process of professionalisation was bound to take a certain direction.

But in shaping the course of events and in welcoming the opportunity for improvement which the times provided, Tristram Kennedy stands out as a very special lawyer. The diversity of his activities was remarkable: as a land agent dispensing rough economic justice to tenants, as an innovator creating the Carrickmacross lace industry, as a parliamentarian keeping alive the ideal of independence and national pride and as a practising lawyer and teacher. In his own way, Kennedy was as multi-faceted as any brehon and as successful as any attorney or barrister solely and single-mindedly devoted to a legal career.

It is said that up to the moment of Tristram Kennedy's death 'he never complained' about his health and that 'his spirit passed away without leaving the slightest trace of a struggle in a single feature of his countenance'.[3] He surely deserved a peaceful death after his eighty years of professional and personal efforts on behalf of his country.

3. ibid.

APPENDIX

Letters of Tristram Kennedy, MP, to Sir William Napier, 1841

There follow transcriptions of English letters C251, ff. 97–108, Department of Western Manuscripts, Bodleian Library, Oxford. It should be noted that where the letters are underlined below, they are underlined on the originals.

William Napier's brother, Charles, was both the commanding officer and an old friend of Tristram's brother, John Pitt Kennedy. For Napier see Bruce, *Life of General Sir William Napier*.

---

f. 97   59 South Molton Street,
                                        London.
                                        29 March 1841.

My Dear Colonel,

Whenever you can dedicate a few hours to the Dublin Law Institute do not forget to throw together your ideas on any subject connected with International Law likely to interest our society in Dublin. The general who is to give me a paper on Military Law suggested that I should call your attention to a subject you have already given your consideration, 'American slavery and the power given thereby to our country over theirs in case of war'. This would be a matter of interest; perhaps in the course of three weeks you could let me have something on this or any other subject you may select which will occupy in reading not less than half an hour and as much longer as you please.

I had it not in my power to do anything for your son John with respect to a residence for him in our Dublin chambers. However, next month my premises will be considerably extended and he can have chambers if he wished and upon terms to suit him.

f.97v

I have had a good deal of conversation with one of the professors in our law institute and we agree in thinking, if John has any taste for study, that there would be no difficulty whatever in his being a good conveyancer and this you are aware is one of the most profitable branches of the barristers' profession; his course of study would not of necessity interfere with his present engagements.

I should like to know what you think on this subject as I could obtain considerable advantages for John through the professors in our Institute if he were disposed to attempt the undertaking,

Believe me my dear colonel,
yours very truly,
Tristram Kennedy.

---

f.98   Queen's Inns Chambers,
Dublin.
17 April 1841.

My Dear Colonel,

Your essay on the Poor Law has come safe to hand. I will attend to your <u>three directions,</u> in the meantime I am having a copy made, which I will send over, marking any portion which might not suit the taste of <u>some strange and mighty particular members in the society I have to work with</u>. Thanks for your kind licence in permitting me to do so,

Yours most sincerely obliged,
Tristram Kennedy.

ff. 98v–99v Blank.

Appendix

f.100

59 South Molton Street,
London.
29 March 1841.

My Dear Colonel,

I send a copy of the essay with a few red ink marks in the margin at those parts where the alteration of a word or two might make the subject more palatable to some who may hear or read it.

It is desirable our society should at this moment avoid making enemies of any party, of the <u>govnt</u>. as we are seeking both endowment and charter for the institute and in our own body we have a queer compound of individuals whose taste we must endeavour to consult. Thanks for all your kindness and trouble.

Yours very truly,
Tristram Kennedy.

ff.100v–101v Blank.

---

f.102

Queen's Inns Chambers,
Dublin,
29 May 1841.

My Dear Colonel,

By the same post which takes this I send you a number of the Dublin *Citizen* for June in which you will find a review or notice of your *Peninsular War* [*The Citizen*, iii, no.20 (June 1841), pp. 340–46]. The author is a great admirer of yourself and your works and will be delighted to correct any mistakes he may have made in fact or opinion

f.102v

which you are disposed to suggest, and in future reviews which he proposes giving of your works his attention will be directed to any portion or subject you may like the public mind brought to bear upon.

A line to me at any time will procure *The Citizen's* attention in the matter.

f.103

I got the Poor Law essay all safe and return *you* thanks for your alterations. It has, however, been decided that the meetings of our society for the reading of papers do not commence until November next. I therefore think it a pity so valuable a paper should remain so long dormant and if you allow me I will get it a place in the next number of *The Citizen* or one of our other periodicals.

Whatever you dictate me I will do, publish it now or keep it until November for

f.103v

our society.

Yours very truly,
Tristram Kennedy.

[See *The Citizen*, iv, no.21 (July 1841), pp.73–80 for a piece by Napier on the Poor Laws.]

f.104   [1841]

My Dear Colonel,

Two copies of the Poor Law essay came to hand this day but I do not forward them to you as a letter by the same post informs me that several copies have been forwarded to you also.

I leave for London tomorrow and if there is anything I can do there calculated to direct attention to the subject, a line to 59 South Molton Street will find me.

f.104v

No rational jury will give a verdict against you for anything but nominal damages in the hustings case; were I upon the jury my verdict would be 'served him damned right'. He left you no alternative but to treat him

f.105

as you did.

Yours very truly,
Tristram Kennedy.
Harrowgate,
Wednesday.

P.S. I have got and will take care of your Bath speech.

[Further note written up margin of letter]. I enclose by this day's post a copy of the essay to my friend the editor of one of the legal periodicals in London. I am directing his attention to the subject.

f.105v Blank.

---

f.106 Liverpool,
16 October 1841.

My Dear Colonel,

The accompanying letter I received on my return from Scotland to London the other day in reply to the communication forwarded the editor of *The Citizen* in relation to *The Star and Vindicator*. McCullagh's letter is the best explanation of the obligation he feels for your kindness in the matter.

The Citizen is the only liberal periodical we have in Dublin of any

f.106v

stamp, in it you will find space at all times for the investigation of any subject worthy your consideration. I will send the editor on my return to Dublin a copy of your paper to Lord Ashbury on the Corn Laws [see Bruce, *Life of Napier*, ii, 77–78 and 568–71]; I read it once and must read it

f.107

again, the subject is one I have not considered; the anecdote of the censusman in the west of Ireland is not a bad one.

I got to London in time to shake hands with Sir Charles the day before his departure,

Most sincerely yours,
Tristram Kennedy.

f.107v Blank

f.108

    Colonel Napier C.B.,
    Freshford,
    Bath.

[written up the side] Tristram Kennedy and *Citizen*.

Bibliography

MANUSCRIPT SOURCES

Bodleian Library, Oxford
Kennedy (Tristram) MP. Letters to Sir William Napier. English letters MS C.251. A transcript of these has been lodged by this author with the National Library of Ireland. See also Appendix, above.

British Library
Kennedy to Gladstone, 22 Feb.1866. Add. MS 44,409, ff. 213–18.

King's Inns, Dublin
The Green Book: admission of benchers, 1741–92. MS B.1/3–1.
Benchers' minute books: council meetings, 1792–1901. MSS B.1/5.
New entrance and gateway: architect's certificates, builder's bond and articles of agreement, tradesmen's bills and requests for payment, 1819–21. MS H.2/2–1.
King's arms over gateway: John Smyth, sculptor: bill and request for payment, 1820–21. MS H.2/2–2.
Admission papers: Tristram Kennedy, 1821–34.
Law Library, Four Courts: builders' estimates, bond and articles of agreement; architect's accounts, builder's accounts; thanks of members of the bar, 1825–26. MSS H.1/3–1 and 2.
Solicitors' memorial for a chamber at the Four Courts, 1826: with subsequent related materials. MSS H.1/5–1 to 5–6.
Proposals for building chambers: report of the standing committee, estimates, etc., 1826–27. MS H. 2/4.
Survey of the ground belonging to King's Inns, with a design of a new street leading from Henrietta St. to the Four Courts [and] design for the new gateway to [its] entrance, by Frederick Darley, jnr. MSS H.4/3–6 and 7.
Plan, sections and elevation of the proposed chambers to be erected for King's Inns, by Frederick Darley, jnr., 1827. MSS H.4/3–2, 3, 4, 5.
Memorial of the committee of the Irish Law Society relating to chambers, 1830. MS H.1/5–2.
Suggestions for building chambers: from William H. Carroll [1830–31]. MS H.1/5–2.
Law Students Debating Society secretary's book, 1830–33. MS K.1/1.
Letterbook, 1836–69. MS C.2/1–1.
Bills for the better regulation of the profession, prepared by Mr O'Connell, 1838–39. MSS J.3/3–1 and 3.

Bill for the incorporation of King's Inns, prepared by Mr O'Connell, 1839. MS J.3/3–2.
Scrapbook (The Dublin Law Institute: scrapbook of news cuttings, correspondence, etc. 1839–42 – donated to King's Inns by Tristram's son in 1935). MS L.3/1, unpaginated.
Dublin Law Institute: rules and bye-laws, 1841. MS L.3/2.
Building, Standing, Education and Library Committees, 1844–52. MS B.2/1–1.
Standing and Education Committees, 1846–73. MS B.2/1–3.
Charter and rules of the Incorporated Society of the Attorneys and Solicitors of Ireland, 1852. MSS J.1/2 and 3.
List of candidates [professorships]. MS, printed and dated 1853. No MS number, cannot currently be located.
Title deeds for no.11 Henrietta Street in 1865. MS G.3/2–2.

Londonderry Council
Minutes, 1824 and 1827.

Longleat House, Wiltshire
Bath papers, Irish box.

National Library of Ireland
Dublin Law Institute papers. MS 2987.
Johnston family, Stranorlar diary, 1846–53. MS 3463.
William Smith O'Brien papers. MS 22,393.

Public Record Office, London
Kennedy to Normanby, 2 April 1840. PRO. Home Office, vol. 263, pp. 235 ff. Micro-copy at NLI n.4562, p.4528.

Public Record Office of Northern Ireland
Lease for three lives, Marquis of Donegal to T. Kennedy, Shandy Hall, Co. Donegal. D. 652/1066.

Registry of Deeds, Dublin
Deeds, nos. 1835/7/166–67, 1837/5/221, 1837/7/283, 1840/13/219, 1845/17/158, 1846/4/47–48, 1844/1/236, 1882/35/124.

Stack papers, Taunton, Somerset
(in the possession of Tristram Kennedy's grandson, Mr T.L. Stack)

Letter from Edward B. Sugden to Tristram Kennedy, 16 July 1840.
Letter from Gavan Duffy to Pitt Kennedy, 28 Nov. 1885.
Printed obituary, Tristram Kennedy. Unidentified newspaper.

University of Dublin (TCD)
Board registers. Mun. v/5/8, 9, 12, 17.
Mountifort Longfield on law school, 30 June 1849. Mun. p/1/1799.

Townsend to Carson, 7 Nov. 1873. Mun. p/1/2203–04.
Naish to Townsend, 14 Nov.1873. Mun. p/1/2220.
Complaint of John W.Stubbs concerning time of King's Inns lectures, 1873. Mun. p/1/2198.
Observations of David R. Pigot on the teaching of international law, 1895. Mun. p/1/2516.

PARLIAMENTARY PAPERS, JOURNALS AND REPORTS

Rec. comm. Ire. reps. Reports of the commissioners appointed by his majesty . . . respecting the public records. 3 vols. London. 1815–25.
Report from the select committee on admission of attorneys and solicitors in England . . . 5 March 1821. H.C. 1821 (137), iv. 325.
Sixth report of the commissioners appointed to inquire into the practice and proceedings of the superior courts of common law in England . . . 1834. H.C.1834 (263), xxvi. 1.
Report from the select committee on foundation schools and education in Ireland . . . 1838. H.C. 1838 (701), vii. 345.
Petition of Tristram Kennedy presented in the House of Commons, 22 May 1843 by T.Wyse Esq., chairman of the select committee on education, on the state of legal education in Ireland. Printed copies at NLI P 1044 and P 2443; in [Kennedy], *Legal education in Ireland*; at *Report on legal education, 1846,* app. iv, p.356.
[Devon] *Report from the commissioners of inquiry into the state of the law and practice in respect of the occupation of land in Ireland, evidence . . . 1845.* H.C.1845 (606), xix. 57.
[Devon] (Kennedy, John Pitt). *Digest of evidence taken before Her Majesty's commissioners of inquiry into the state of the law and practice in respect to the occupation of land in Ireland.* 2 vols. London and Dublin, 1847–48.
Statement of the regulations of the four [English] inns of court as to the admission of students, etc. . . . 1846. H.C. 1846 (134), xxxiii. 1.
Sel. comm. leg. ed. [Wyse] *Report from the select committee on legal education, together with the minutes of evidence . . . 1846.* H.C. 1846 (686), x. 1.
Fourth report from the select committee on the Poor Laws (Ireland). H.L. 1849 (365), xvi. 543.
Report of the commissioners of national education in Ireland, xv. H.C. 1849 (1066) (1066 – II), xxiii. 91. 101.
Report of the commissioners of national education in Ireland, xvi. H.C. 1850 (1231) (1231-II), xxv. 121. 141.
Dub. Univ. comm. Report of her majesty's commissioners appointed to inquire into the state, discipline, studies and revenues of the University of Dublin and of Trinity College . . . 1852–53. H.C.1853 (1637), xlv.1.
Report of the royal commission on the arrangements in the [English] inns of court, and inns of chancery for promoting the study of the law and jurisprudence . . . 1855. H.C.1855 (1988), xviii. 345.
Return of the amount of all moneys received by the Hon. Society of King's Inns, Dublin, in each year since 30 June 1839 to the present time . . . with

a statement of the expenditure of the same . . . 1856. H.C. 1856 (360), liii. 441.
Report of commissioners on the Queen's Colleges, 1857–58, H.C.1858 (2413), xxi. 53.
Report from the select committee of the house of lords on the Tenure (Ireland) Bill . . . 1867. H.C. 1867 (518), xiv. 423.
Report of the King's Inns, Dublin, inquiry commission in respect of sums received on the admission of attorneys and solicitors as 'deposits for chambers' and other matters . . . 1872. H.L. 1872 (c.486), xx. 739.
[Robertson] Royal commission on university education in Ireland, second report . . . 1902. H.C. 1902 (899–900), xxxi. 459.
[Robertson] Royal commission on university education in Ireland, final report . . . 1903. H.C. 1903 (1483–4), xxxii.1.
[Fry] Royal commission on Trinity College and the University of Dublin, first report . . . 1906. H.C. 1906 (3174), lvi. 601.
[Fry] Royal commission on Trinity College and the University of Dublin, final report . . . 1907. H.C. 1907 (3311–2), lxi. 1.
Ormrod report. [Ormrod] Report of the committee on legal education [in England and Wales] . . . March 1971. H.C. 1971 (4595).
Commons' jn.
Hansard, 3.
Stat. Ire.
Stat. parl. U.K.

SOURCE COMPILATIONS AND REFERENCE WORKS

Cal. S. P. Ire.
Correspondence of Daniel O'Connell. O'Connell, Maurice (ed.). The correspondence of Daniel O'Connell. 8 vols. Dublin, 1972–80.
DNB. Dictionary of national biography.
Dod's parliamentary companion.
Foster, Joseph. Men-at-the-bar: a biographical hand-list of the members of the various inns of court. London, 1885.
Georgian Society records of domestic architecture.
G.I.P.B. Fletcher, R.J. (ed.). The pension book of Gray's Inn, 1669–1800. 2 vols. London, 1901–10.
King's Inns adm. Keane, E., Phair, P.B., and Sadleir, T.U. (ed.). King's Inns admission papers, 1607–1867. Dublin, 1982.
L.I. adm. reg., i. Foster, Joseph (ed.). The records of the honourable society of Lincoln's Inn, vol. 1: admissions . . . 1420–1799. London, 1896.
L.I. adm. reg., ii. Foster, Joseph (ed.). The records of the honourable society of Lincoln's Inn, vol. 2: admissions . . . 1800–1893. London, 1896.
L.I.B.B. Baildon, W.P. and Roxburgh, R.F. (ed.). The records of the honourable society of Lincoln's Inn: The Black Books. 5 vols. London, 1897–1969.
O'Higgins, Paul. A legal bibliography of periodical literature relating to Irish law. Belfast, 1967. First supplement, Belfast, 1973. Second supplement, Belfast, 1983.

Thom's *Dublin directory*. Annual.
Walker, *Parliamentary elections*. Walker, B.M. (ed.). *Parliamentary election results in Ireland, 1801–1922*. Dublin, 1978.
Waterloo directory. North, John. *Waterloo directory of Irish newspapers and periodicals 1800–1900*. Waterloo [Ontario], 1986.

BOOKS, ARTICLES AND THESES

Abel, R.L. *The legal profession in England and Wales*. Oxford, 1988.
Abel-Smith, Brian and Stevens, Robert. *Lawyers and the courts: a sociological study of the English legal system 1750–1965*. London, 1967.
Akenson, D.A. *A protestant in purgatory: Richard Whately, archbishop of Dublin*. Connecticut, 1981.
Anon., 'Confessions of a junior barrister' [1825]. In Curran, *Sketches of the Irish bar*.
Anon. 'The Dublin Law Institute'. In *The Citizen*, ii (June, 1840).
Anon. 'The Dublin Law Institute'. In *The Citizen*, xiii (Nov. 1840).
Anon. 'Henrietta Street'. In *Irish Builder* (15 Jun.–15 Aug. 1893).
Anon. 'Henrietta Street'. In *Irish Times* (19 Nov. 1896).
Anon. 'Law School of the Dublin University'. In *Dub. Univ. Mag.*, i (Jan. 1833).
Anon. 'Legal education in England and Ireland'. In *ILT&SJ*, xxx (Feb. 1896).
Anon. 'Legal education'. In *Dublin University Mag.* (July 1847).
Anon. 'Legal education in Ireland'. In *The Legal Reporter*, i (27 Feb. 1841).
Anon. 'Legal education in Ireland'. In *Law Times*, vii (11 April 1846).
Anon. *Memories of Father Healy of Little Bray*. London, 1899.
Anon. 'On the study of the law in Ireland: The Dublin Law Institute'. In *Dublin Monthly Magazine* (July–Dec. 1842).
Anon. *Memoranda of Irish matters by obscure men, of good intention. Part 1: the rules of Irish promotion*. Dublin, 1844.
Anon. 'The present condition and future prospects of the Irish bar'. In *Irish Quarterly Review*, i (1851).
Anon. 'Recollections of the late Sir Michael O'Loghlen'. In *Dublin Magazine* (1843).
Atkinson, Norman. *Irish education: a history of educational institutions*. Dublin, 1969.
Ball, F.E. *The judges in Ireland 1221–1921*. 2 vols. London, 1926.
Barry, Michael. 'Legal calculation and the division of time'. In Dublin Law Institute, *Papers*.
Barton, Dunbar Plunket, Benham, Charles and Watt, Francis (ed.). *The story of our inns of court*. Boston and New York, 1928.
Barton, Dunbar Plunket. *Timothy Healy*. London, 1933.
Bateman, J. *The great landowners of Great Britain and Ireland*. 4th ed., London, 1883. Reprinted Leicester, 1971.
Beasley, Thomas J. *Lectures delivered at the Dublin Law Institute*. Dublin, 1841.

Beckett, J.C. *The making of modern Ireland*. London and Boston, new ed.,1981.
Bellot, H. Hale. *University College London, 1826–1926*. London, 1929.
——. *The University of London*. Bristol, 1969.
Berry, H.F. *A history of the Royal Dublin Society*. London, 1915.
Binchy, D.A. et al. 'The law and the universities' (together with 'Comments on the foregoing article' by Michael Tierney, George Gavan Duffy, Denis Canon O'Keeffe and Richard O'Sullivan). In *Studies*, xxxviii (1949).
Binchy, D.A. 'Lawyers and chroniclers'. In O'Cuiv, *Seven centuries of Irish learning, 1000–1700*.
Birks, Peter (ed.). *The life of the law: proceedings of the British legal history conference, 1991*. London, 1993.
Black, R.D. Collison. *Statistical and Social Inquiry Society of Ireland: centenary volume 1847–1947*. Dublin, 1947.
——. 'Mountifort Longfield: his economic thought and writings reviewed in relation to the theories of his time and of the present day'. Ph.D thesis, University of Dublin, 1954.
——. *Economic thought and the Irish question*. Cambridge, 1960.
Blackburne, Edward. *Life of the Right Hon. Francis Blackburne, late lord chancellor of Ireland*. London, 1874.
Blackham, Robert. *Wig and gown, the story of the Temple, Gray's and Lincoln's Inn*. London, n.d. [but c.1937].
Borlase, Edmund. *The reduction of Ireland to the crown of England*. London, 1675.
Bowen, Desmond. *The protestant crusade, 1800–1870*. Dublin, 1978.
Boyle, Elizabeth. *The Irish flowerers*. Belfast, 1971.
Breatnach, Liam. 'Lawyers in early Ireland'. In Hogan and Osborough, *Brehons, serjeants and attorneys*.
Bruce, H.A. (ed.). *Life of General Sir William Napier*. 2 vols. London, 1864.
Burke, Andrew. 'Trinity College and the religious problem in Irish education'. In Kelly and Mac Gearailt (ed.), *Dublin and Dubliners*.
Burke, O.J. *History of the lord chancellors*. Dublin, 1879.
Burrage, Michael and Torstendahl, Rolf (ed.). *Professions in sociology and history: rethinking the study of the professions*. London, 1990.
Cameron, Charles. *A history of the Royal College of Surgeons in Ireland*. 2nd ed., Dublin, 1916.
Carlyle, Thomas. *Reminiscences of my Irish journey in 1849*. London, 1882.
Connell, K.H. *Irish peasant society*. Oxford, 1968.
Corcoran, Timothy (ed.). *State policy in Irish education, 1536–1816, exemplified in documents*. Dublin, 1916.
Craig, Maurice. *Dublin 1660-1860*. Dublin, ed. 1969.
Cregan, Donal F. 'Irish catholic admissions to the English inns of court 1558–1625'. In *Ir. Jurist*, v (1970).
Crimmins, Cathal. 'Henrietta Street: a conservation study'. M.Arch.Sc. thesis, University College Dublin, 1987.
Cullen, Paul. 'On protestant ascendancy and catholic education in Ireland'. In *Irish Ecclesiastical Record* (n.s.), v (Aug. 1869).

Curran, John Adye. *Reminiscences*. London, 1915.
Curran, W. H. *Life of John Philpot Curran*. 2 vols. Edinburgh, 1822.
——. *Sketches of the Irish bar*. 2 vols. London, 1855.
Daly, Mary. *The famine in Ireland*. Dundalk, 1986.
Day, Ella B. *Mr Justice Day of Kerry, 1745–1841: a discursive memoir*. Exeter, 1938.
Delany, V.T.H. 'A note on the history of legal education in Ireland'. In *N.I.L.Q.*, xi (1954–56).
——. 'Legal studies in Trinity College, Dublin, since the foundation'. In *Hermathena*, lxxxix, no.3 (May 1957).
——. 'The history of legal education in Ireland'. In *Jn of Legal Education*, xii (1960).
——. *Christopher Palles: his life and times*. Dublin, 1960.
——. 'Legal training and the universities'. In *ILT&SJ*, xcvii (July–Aug. 1963).
Dicey, A.V. 'The teaching of English law at Harvard'. In *The Contemporary Review*, lxxvi (Nov. 1899).
Dowling, P.J. *History of Irish education: a study in conflicting loyalties*. Cork, 1971.
Dublin Law Institute. *Papers*. Dublin, 1846 (NLI pamphlets IR 308 P.11 and 799 Law no.10).
Dublin Law School. *Proceedings of the Dublin Law School comprising the four introductory lectures of the several professors and a prospectus of the plans of instruction to be adopted in the several departments of the institution*. Dublin, 1840.
Duhigg, Bartholomew. *History of the King's Inns*. Dublin, 1806.
Duman, Daniel. *The judicial bench in England 1727–1875: the reshaping of a professional elite*. Royal Historical Society. London, 1982.
——. 'Pathway to professionalism: the English bar in the eighteenth and nineteenth centuries'. In *Journal of Social History*, xiii (1982).
Dun, Finlay. *Landlords and tenants in Ireland*. London, 1881.
Duncan, G.A. 'The law school during the last half-century'. In *Hermathena*, lviii (Nov. 1941).
Edwards, R.D. and Williams, T.D. (ed.). *The Great Famine: studies in Irish history, 1845–52*. Dublin, 1956.
Elliott, Marianne. *Wolfe Tone: prophet of Irish independence*. New Haven and London, 1989.
Ellmann, Richard. *James Joyce*. Oxford, new ed., 1983
Ferriman, Z.D. *Some English philhellenes*. London, 1918.
Fitzgerald, Olda. 'The Caseys of Henrietta Street, Dublin'. In *Apollo: The International Magazine of the Arts*, cxxix, no. 324 (n.s.) (Feb. 1989).
Fortescue, John. *De laudibus legum Angliae*. London, various editions with translations, first published *c*.1468.
Foster, R.F. *Charles Stewart Parnell: the man and his family*. Sussex, 1976.
Gavan Duffy, Charles. *The league of north and south: an episode in Irish history 1850–4*. London, 1886.
——. *My life in two hemispheres*. 2 vols. London, 1898.
Gerard, Frances. *Picturesque Dublin, old and new*. London, 1898.

Goldstrom, J.M. and Clarkson, L.A. (ed.). *Essays in honour of the late K.H. Connell.* Oxford, 1981.
Grant, James. 'The great famine and the poor law in Ulster: the rate-in-aid issue of 1849'. In *IHS*, xxvii, no. 105 (May 1990).
Grattan, Henry [jnr.]. *Memoirs of the life and times of the right honorable Henry Grattan.* London, 1839.
Hanbury, H.G. *The Vinerian chair and legal education.* Oxford, 1958.
Hancock, W. Neilson. *The tenant-right of Ulster considered economically.* Dublin, 1845.
Hanham, H.J. *Elections and party management: politics in the time of Disraeli and Gladstone.* London, 1959.
Harrison, Wilmot. *Memorable Dublin houses: a handy guide, illustrated.* Dublin, 1890.
Hempton, John (ed.). *The siege and history of Londonderry.* Londonderry, Dublin and London, 1861.
Hickie, D.B. (ed.). *The satires of Juvenal.* Dublin, 1820.
Hogan, Daire. *The legal profession in Ireland 1789–1922.* Dublin, 1986.
——. 'Judicial appointments in Ireland, 1866–67'. In Hogan and Osborough, *Brehons, serjeants and attorneys.*
—— and Osborough, W.N. (ed.). *Brehons, serjeants and attorneys: studies in the history of the Irish legal profession.* Dublin, 1990.
Holdsworth, W.S. *History of English law.* 3rd ed., 16 vols. London, 1923–66.
Hoppen, K. Theo. *Elections, politics and society in Ireland, 1832–85.* Oxford, 1984.
——. 'Landlords, society and electoral politics in mid-nineteenth century Ireland'. In Philpin (ed.), *Nationalism and popular protest in Ireland.*
Horgan, John. *Dublin City University: context and concept.* Dublin, 1989.
Houston, Arthur. *Daniel O'Connell: his early life and journal, 1795–1802.* London, 1906.
Howard, G.E. *A compendious treatise of the rules and practice of the pleas side of the exchequer in Ireland.* 2 vols. Dublin, 1759.
Hurst, Michael. 'Ireland and the Ballot Act of 1872'. In *Hist Jn*, viii (1965).
Johnston, R.W.R. 'Legal education in Ireland'. In *ILT&SJ*, lxxvi (July–Aug. 1942).
Joy, Henry H. *Letters on the present state of legal education in England and Ireland.* Dublin and London, 1847.
Joyce, James. *Dubliners.* London, 1991.
——. *A portrait of the artist as a young man.* London, 1991.
Kee, Robert. *The laurel and the ivy: the story of Charles Stuart Parnell and Irish nationalism.* London, 1993.
Kelly, Fergus. *A guide to early Irish law.* Dublin, 1988.
Kelly, James and Mac Gearailt, Uaitear (ed.). *Dublin and Dubliners.* Dublin, 1990.
Kennedy, David. 'Captain Pitt Kennedy's plan for Irish agriculture, 1835–45'. In *Ir Comm Hist Sc Bull*, no. 32 (1944).

Kennedy, Evory. *Observations on obstetric ausculation with an analysis of the evidences of pregnancy and an inquiry into the proofs of the life and death of the foetus in utero: with an appendix containing legal notes by John Smith esq., barrister-at-law.* Dublin and London, 1833.

——. *On the principles and uses of alliteration in poetry.* London and Dublin, 1866.

Kennedy, F.M.E. *A family of Kennedy of Clogher and Londonderry c.1600–1938.* Taunton, 1938.

Kennedy, John Pitt. *Instruct; employ; don't hang them; or Ireland tranquilised without soldiers and enriched without capital.* London, 1835.

——. *Digest of evidence taken before Her Majesty's commissioners of inquiry into the state of the law and practice in respect to the occupation of land in Ireland.* 2 vols. London and Dublin, 1847–48.

Kennedy, Liam. 'Regional specialisation, railway development and Irish agriculture in the nineteenth century'. In Goldstrom and Clarkson, *Essays.*

—— and Ollerenshaw, Philip. *An economic history of Ulster 1820–1940.* Manchester, 1985.

Kennedy, Tristram. *First report on the progress of legal education in Ireland, 22 October 1840.* Dublin, 1840.

——. *Opening address to the Dublin Law Institute, 31 January 1842.* Dublin, 1842. (Copy of full address at RIA Hal. 1834).

——. *Petition of Tristram Kennedy presented in the House of Commons, 22 May 1843 by T. Wyse Esq., chairman of the select committee on education, on the state of legal education in Ireland.* Printed copies at NLI, P 1044, P 2443; in [Kennedy], *Legal education in Ireland*; at *Report on legal education, 1846.* app.iv, p.356.

[Kennedy, Tristram]. *Legal education in Ireland.* London, 1843.

Kennedy, Tristram. *The patient, the physician and the fee: a law tract for the times by a student of fifty years standing.* Revised ed., London and Dublin, 1877.

——. *The state and the benchers, – being an account of undischarged obligations on the part of both to the law student and the society of King's Inns, with annals and incidents on the origin of, and progress made in, systematic legal education in Ireland during the reign of Queen Victoria.* Dublin, 1878.

—— and Sullivan, W.K. *On the industrial training institutions of Belgium, and on the possibility of organising an analogous system in connection with the national schools of Ireland.* Dublin, 1855.

Kenny, Colum. 'Counsellor Duhigg – antiquarian and activist'. In *Ir Jur*, xxi (winter, 1986).

——. 'The exclusion of catholics from the legal profession in Ireland'. In *IHS*, xxv, no. 100 (Nov. 1987).

——. 'Paradox or pragmatist? "Honest Tristram Kennedy" (1805–85): lawyer, educationalist, land agent and member of parliament'. In *RIA Proc.* xcii (1992), sect. c.

——. *King's Inns and the kingdom of Ireland: the Irish 'inn of court', 1541–1800.* Dublin, 1992.

──. 'Irish ambition and English preference in chancery appointments, 1827–1841: the fate of William Conyngham Plunket'. In Osborough (ed.), *Explorations in law and history.*
King's Inns, *General rules.* Dublin, 1794.
King's Inns. *Report of the education committee, King's Inns.* Dublin, 1876. Printed copy bound with the benchers' minute book, 1870–85.
Kissane, Noel. *Parnell: a documentary history.* Dublin, 1991.
Larkin, Emmet. *The consolidation of the Roman Catholic Church in Ireland 1860–1870.* Dublin, 1987.
Lawson, James A. 'Law as it relates to the economic condition of a people'. In Dublin Law Institute, *Papers.*
──. 'The Landed Estates Court: its history and prospects'. In *Transactions of the National Association for the Promotion of Social Science.* London, 1862.
Lee, Joseph. 'The social and economic ideas of O'Connell'. In Nowlan and O'Connell, *Daniel O'Connell.*
[Lee, P.B.]. *The law student's guide. By a member of Gray's Inn.* London, 1827.
Lefroy, Thomas. *Memoir of Chief Justice Lefroy, by his son.* Dublin, 1871.
Leighton, C.D.A. *The Irish manufacture movement 1840–1843.* Maynooth, 1987.
Littledale, William F. *The society of King's Inns, Dublin, its origin and progress, and the present results of its assumed control over the legal profession in Ireland.* Dublin, 1859.
Livingstone, Peadar. *The Monaghan story.* Enniskillen, 1980.
[Londonderry]. *The Londonderry discussion; or a statement of an agreement between six R.C. priests and six Protestant clergymen to discuss the points at issue between both churches in which the former failed!; the speeches of the latter.* Dublin. 1827.
[Londonderry]. *Authenticated report of the discussion which took place at Londonderry between six Roman Catholic priests and six clergymen of the Established Church in the diocese of Derry, March 1828.* Dublin, 1828.
Longfield, Elizabeth Conner, 'Visits to Longueville c.1805–1815'. In *Ir Georgian Soc Bull*, iii, no.3 (July–Sept., 1960).
Longfield, Mountifort. 'Address by the president at the opening of the eighteenth session of the society'. In *JSSISI*, iv (Jan. 1865).
[Louth]. *An analysis of the parliamentary register of voters for the county of Louth with the names of the landlords and their tenants on the register of voters, shewing the candidate for whom they voted at the election in April 1865.* Dublin, 1865.
Lyons, F.S.L. *Ireland since the famine.* London, 1971.
MacDonagh, Oliver. *The hereditary bondsman: Daniel O'Connell, 1775–1829.* London, 1988.
──. *The emancipist: Daniel O'Connell, 1830–1847.* London, 1989.
[MacMahon, P]. 'The Catholic University and legal education'. In *Dublin Review*, xli (1856).
[Madden, D.O.?]. *The reign of mediocrity.* Dublin, 1850.

Madden, R.R. *The literary life and correspondence of the countess of Blessington*. 3 vols. London. 1855.
Malcolm, Elizabeth. *'Ireland sober, Ireland free': drink and temperance in nineteenth-century Ireland*. Dublin, 1986.
Manchester, A.H. *Modern legal history of England and Wales 1750–1950*. London, 1980.
———. *Sources of English legal history: law, history and society in England and Wales 1750–1950*. London, 1984.
Marjoribanks, Edward. *The life of Lord Carson*, i. London, 1932.
Matthew, H.C.G. (ed.). *The Gladstone diaries, vi*. Oxford, 1978.
McArdle, J. Ardle. 'Nothing changed'. In *Books Ireland* (summer 1993).
McDowell, R.B. *Irish public opinion, 1750–1800*. London, 1944.
———. *Public opinion and government policy in Ireland 1801–46: studies in Irish history, v*. London, 1952.
———. and Webb, D.A. *Trinity College, Dublin, 1592–1952, an academic history*. Cambridge, 1982.
McEldowney, J. and O'Higgins, P. 'Irish legal history and the nineteenth century'. In McEldowney and O'Higgins, *The Common Law tradition*.
McEldowney, J. and O'Higgins, P. (ed.). *The Common Law tradition: essays in Irish legal history*. Dublin, 1990.
McGee, Thomas D'Arcy. *A life of the right rev. Edward Maginn, co-adjutor bishop of Derry*. 2nd ed., New York, 1863.
McGrath, Fergal. *Newman's University: idea and reality*. London, 1951.
McLaughlin, Brighid. 'Living among the ghosts of old grandeur'. In *Sunday Independent* (27 June 1993).
McParland, Edward. *James Gandon: Vitruvius Hibernicus*. London, 1985.
McRedmond, Louis. *Thrown among strangers: John Henry Newman in Ireland*. Dublin, 1990.
Moran, Frances. 'Legal education in Eire'. In *ILT&SJ*, lxxvi (Aug. 1942).
Molyneux, Echlin. *Dublin Law School: part of an introductory lecture on equity delivered in the theatre of the Royal Dublin Society, 23 November 1839* (copy at TCD OLS 188q.54, no.11).
Moody, T.W. and Martin, F.X. *The course of Irish history*. Dublin, rev. ed.1984.
Moryson, Fynes. 'The commonwealth of Ireland.' In Falkiner, C. Litton. *Illustrations of Irish history and topography, mainly of the seventeenth century*. London, 1904.
Moss, Laurence S. *Mountifort Longfield: Ireland's first professor of political economy*. Ottawa, Illinois, 1976.
Murnane, James. 'The national school system in County Monaghan'. In *Clogher Record*, xii (1986).
Napier, Charles. *An essay on the present state of Ireland, dedicated to the Irish absentee landed proprietors*. London, 1839.
Napier, Joseph. *Introductory lecture on the study of the common law*. Dublin, 1839.
Napier, William. *History of the war in the peninsula and in the south of France, from . . . 1807 to . . . 1814*. 6 vols. London, 1828–40.

———. *Life and opinions of General Sir Charles James Napier.* 4 vols. London, 1857.
Newman, Henry Cardinal. *The idea of a university.* London, 1912.
Ní Dhonnchadha, Maírín. 'An address to a student of law'. In Ó Corráin et al. *Sages, saints and storytellers.*
Norman, E.R. *The Catholic Church and Ireland in the age of rebellion 1859–73.* Southampton, 1965.
Nowlan, K.B. and O'Connell, M.R. (ed.). *Daniel O'Connell: portrait of a radical.* New York, 1985.
O'Boyle, Lenore. 'The problem of an excess of educated men in Western Europe, 1800–1850'. In *Jn of Mod Hist*, xlii (Dec. 1970).
O'Brien, Conor Cruise. *Parnell and his party 1880–90.* Oxford, 1957.
O'Brien, Jacqueline, with Desmond Guinness. *Dublin: a grand tour.* London, 1994.
O'Brien, R. Barry. *Thomas Drummond, life and letters.* London, 1889.
O'Brien, W.P. *The Great Famine in Ireland and a retrospect of the fifty years, 1845–95.* London, 1896.
O'Cathaoir, Brendan. *John Blake Dillon, Young Irelander.* Dublin, 1990.
O'Connell, Maurice R. 'O'Connell: lawyer and landlord'. In Nowlan and O'Connell, *Daniel O'Connell.*
Ó Corráin, D., Breatnach, L., McCone, K. (ed.). *Sages, saints and storytellers: Celtic studies in honour of Professor James Carney.* Maynooth, 1989.
O'Cuiv, Brian. *Seven centuries of Irish learning, 1000–1700.* Cork, 1971.
O'Faolain, Seán. *King of the beggars.* London, 1938.
O'Flanagan, J.K. *Lives of the lord chancellors of Ireland.* 2 vols. London, 1870.
O'Hegarty, P.S. *A history of Ireland under the Union, 1801 to 1922.* London, 1952.
O'Higgins, Paul. 'Arthur Browne (1756–1805): an Irish civilian'. In *NILQ*, xx (1969).
O'Mahony, Eoin. 'Some Henrietta Street residents'. In *Ir. Georgian Soc. Bull.*, ii, no. 2 (April–June 1959).
Ó Mórdha, Brian. 'The Great Famine in Monaghan: a coroner's account'. In *Clogher Record*, iv (1960–61).
O'Rahilly, Thomas. 'Irish poets, historians and judges in English documents, 1538–1615'. In *RIA Proc.*, xxxvi (1922), sect. c.
O'Reilly, Bernard. *John MacHale: his life, times and correspondence.* 2 vols. New York and Cincinnati, 1890.
O'Reilly, Seán and Robinson, Nicholas. *New lease of life: the Law Society's building at Blackhall Place.* Dublin, 1990.
Osborough, W.N. 'Review of McDowell and Webb, *Trinity College Dublin*'. In *Ir Jur*, xviii (1983).
———. 'The regulation of the admission of attorneys and solicitors in Ireland, 1600–1866'. In Hogan and Osborough, *Brehons, serjeants and attorneys.*
———. 'Puzzles from Irish law reporting history'. In Birks, *The life of the law.*

——. (ed.). *Explorations in law and history*. Dublin, 1995.
O'Shaughnessy, Mark. 'On legal education in Ireland'. In *JSSISI*, vi (1876).
Ó Tuathaigh, Gearóid. *Ireland before the Famine, 1798–1848*. Dublin, 1972.
——. *Thomas Drummond and the government of Ireland, 1835–41*. O'Donnell lecture, N.U.I., 1977.
Pakenham, Thomas and Valerie (ed.). *Dublin: a traveller's companion*. London, 1988.
Patterson, Nerys. 'Brehon law in late medieval Ireland: "antiquarian and obsolete" or "traditional and functional"'. In *Cambridge Medieval Celtic Studies*, xvii (summer, 1989).
——. 'Gaelic law and the Tudor conquest of Ireland: the social background of the sixteenth-century recensions of the pseudo-historical prologue to the *Senchas már*'. In *IHS*, xxvii, no.107 (May, 1991).
Perkin, Harold. *Origins of modern English society*. Reprint, London and New York, 1991.
Philpin, C.H.E. (ed.). *Nationalism and popular protest in Ireland*. Cambridge, 1987.
Pinkerton, J.H.M. 'Evory Kennedy: a master controversial'. In *Ir Medical Jn*, 77, no.3 (March 1984).
Plunket, David. *Life, letters and speeches of Lord Plunket*. 2 vols. London, 1867.
Plunkett, Eric A. 'Attorneys and solicitors in Ireland'. In *Record of the centenary of the charter of the Incorporated Law Society 1852–1952*. Dublin, 1953.
[Plunkett, G.N.]. *The early life of Henry Grattan*. Dublin, 1878.
[Prendergast, John]. 'Blessington House'. In *Irish Times*, 30 August 1886.
Reader, W.J. *Professional men: the rise of the professional classes in nineteenth-century England*. London, 1966.
[Ruggles, Thomas]. *The barrister: or strictures on the education proper for the bar*. Dublin ed., 1792.
Ryan-Smolin, Wanda. *King's Inns portraits*. Dublin, 1992.
Sanderson, Michael. *The universities in the nineteenth century*. London, 1975.
Sheehy, Eugene. *May it please the court*. Dublin, 1951.
Simms, Katharine. 'The brehons of later medieval Ireland'. In Hogan and Osborough (ed.), *Brehons, serjeants and attorneys*.
Society of Attorneys and Solicitors. *First report of the Society of Attorneys and Solicitors of Ireland, with appendix*. Dublin, 1841.
——. *Report of the committee of the Society of the Attorneys and Solicitors of Ireland, 10 May 1842*. Dublin, 1842.
Society of Jesus (ed.). *A page of Irish history: the story of University College, Dublin, 1883–1909*. Dublin and Cork, 1930.
Solow, B.L. *The land question and the Irish economy*. Harvard, 1971.
Steele, E.D. 'Gladstone and Ireland'. In *IHS*, xvii (1970–71).
——. *Irish land and British politics: tenant right and nationality 1865–70*. Cambridge, 1974.

Stradling, Matthew [pseud. Martin Francis Mahony?]. *The bar sinister*. Dublin, 1871.
Sullivan, Francis Stoughton. *An historical treatise on the feudal law and the constitution and laws of England.* London, 1772.
Sullivan, T.D. *A.M. Sullivan: a memoir.* Dublin, 1885.
Thomas, David J. *Universities.* Essex, 1973.
Thornley, David. *Isaac Butt and Home Rule.* London and Belfast, 1964.
Trench, W. Steuart. *Realities of Irish life.* London, 1868.
[Trench, W. Steuart]. *On 'tenant right' or 'good-will' within the barony of Farney and county of Monaghan in Ireland.* London, 1874.
Vaughan, W.E. (ed.). *A new history of Ireland, vol.v: Ireland under the Union, 1, 1801–70.* Oxford, 1989.
deVere, Aubrey. *Recollections.* New York and London, 1897.
Wakefield, Edward. *An account of Ireland, statistical and political.* 2 vols. London, 1812.
Walker, B.M. (ed.). *Parliamentary election results in Ireland, 1801–1922.* Dublin, 1978.
Walsh, William J. *The Irish University question: the catholic case.* Dublin 1897.
Watt, J.A. *The church and the two nations in medieval Ireland.* Cambridge, 1970.
White, Terence de Vere. *The story of the Royal Dublin Society.* Tralee [1955].
Whiteside, James. *Introductory lecture on the law of nisi prius.* Dublin, 1840.
———. 'The Landed Estates Court'. In *Transactions of the National Association for the Promotion of Social Science.* London, 1862.
Whyte, J.H. *The Independent Irish Party, 1850–59.* Oxford, 1958.
———. 'The influence of the catholic clergy in elections in nineteenth-century Ireland'. In *Eng Hist Rev*, lxxv (1960).
Wilde, William. *Narrative of a voyage to Madeira, Tenerife and along the shores of the Mediterranean.* 2 vols. Dublin, 1840.
Woodham-Smith, C. *The Great Hunger: Ireland 1845–9.* London, 1962.
Wright, G.N. *A historical guide to ancient and modern Dublin.* London, 1821.
Wright, Thomas. 'The duties and licence of counsel'. In Dublin Law Institute, *Papers*.
Wyse, Winifrede. *Notes on education reform in Ireland . . . compiled from speeches, letters, etc., contained in the unpublished memoirs of Thomas Wyse.* Waterford, 1901.

NEWSPAPERS AND GENERAL PERIODICALS

Anglo-Celt
Citizen
Dublin Evening Post
Dublin Magazine
Dublin Monitor
Dublin Monthly Magazine
Dublin Penny Journal
Dundalk Democrat
Evening Packet
Freeman's Journal

Illustrated London News
Irish People
Irish Times
King's County Chronicle
Londonderry Journal
Londonderry Standard
Morning Register

Nation
Newry Examiner and Louth Advertiser
Northern Whig
Saunders's News-letter
Times
Ulster Examiner

Index

Act of Union, 11, 59, 68, 72, 190
Albert College, Glasnevin, 23
Alcock, John Beresford, 122
Amos, Andrew, 14, 127, 141, 142, 148, 150
Anster, John, 167, 204
apprentices, 76, 80–1, 84, 148, 154–5, 168–9
   number of, 71
attorneys, 12, 62
   and Dublin Law Institute, 83–4
   and King's Inns, 73–7
   training of, 154–7, 168–71
   see also solicitors

Ball, Judge John, 165n
Bannon, Fr, 37–8, 39, 42, 46
Bar Council, 77
Baring, Henry Bingham, 138–9
Barnewall, Patrick, 7
Barrett, William, 182n
barristers, 6, 76, 77, 84, 126
   bills to repeal residency in London etc.,
      1842, 126–4
      1856, 178–9, 207
      1859, 179, 207–8
      1881, 210–13
      1885 (passed), 213–15
      see also Statute of Jeofailles, 1542
   and Campbell appointment, 122–3
   training of, 149–54, 171–7
Barry, Michael, 124, 129, 142, 150–1, 199, 207, 226, 227
Barton, Judge Dunbar Plunket, 183
Bath, Lady, 1849–51, 33, 34, 42
Bath, Lord, 1849–51, 34
Bath, Sir John, 1627–28, 10, 187
Bath estate, Monaghan, 26–35, 57
Beasley, Thomas, 120–1, 122, 123, 129
Bell, George J., 133, 136

Bellew, Hon Edward, 40
Bellew, Richard Montesquieu, 37, 38, 43–4, 45, 51
Bellew family, 40, 54
benchers. *see* King's Inns
Bennett, George, 112, 118, 130
Betham, William, 94
Bethell, Richard, 141, 236
Billing, Mr, 124
Blackburne, Francis, 64, 118, 130, 191, 192, 205, 206
Blackhall Place, 224
Blackstone, William, 78, 148
Blake, Sir Valentine, 126, 127, 179, 197, 208
Blakesley, Rev. J.W., 140
Blessington House, 229
Bliss, Philip, 141
Board of Works, 33
Boulter, Hugh, archbishop of Armagh, 219, 221, 228
Brady, Francis William, 207–8
Brady, Maziere, 207
Brady, Thomas, 89, 90, 96, 99
brehon law, 3–9, 7. *see also* Gaelic law schools
Brougham, Henry Lord, 14, 142, 145, 148–50, 200–2
Browne, Arthur, 158
Bushe, Lord Chief Justice, 100
Butt, Isaac, 209

Callan, Philip, MP, 47, 58, 61, 209–17
Cambridge, university of, 159
Campbell, John, lord chancellor, 67, 142, 143, 147, 148, 149
   appointment opposed, 87, 101, 122–3, 130–1
Campbell, Revd Mr, 38
Campbell-Bannerman, Sir Henry, 214
Carlyle, Thomas, 22, 25, 57

Carrickmacross lace, 17, 28, 30–2, 41, 45
Carroll, William, 225
Carson, Edward, 12, 153n, 214
Cary, George, 17
Cary, Mary, 17–18
Catholic Association, 200
catholic emancipation, 10, 12, 65
catholic hierarchy, 46, 53, 178
Catholic Relief Act, 1829, 65
Catholic University, 52–3, 168, 178–9
Cavan, County, 54
chambers, 2, 149–50, 174, 218
  Kennedy encourages, 15–16, 152, 175–6
Chitty, Joseph, 147
Christie, William, 138, 139
church law, 3, 7
Citizen, 100–1, 115, 120, 123
Clery, Arthur, 182n
Clogher, bishop of, 26
Clontarf repeal meeting, 67
codification, 59
Coffey, James, 127
common law, 1–2, 4, 6, 9, 14, 148, 189
Confederation of Kilkenny, 9, 187–8
constabulary, 51
Constitution Hill, 220–3, 233, 236
Council of Legal Education, 161
'counsellor', 6
Crampton, Judge Philip, 94, 117, 118, 158, 206
Crawford, Sharman, 36, 37, 38
Creasy, Edward Shepherd, 140, 141
Crookshank, Alexander, 18, 58
Cullen, Paul, archbishop of Dublin, 37, 43, 45–6, 48–9, 52, 56
Curran, John Adye, 153
Curran, John Philpot, 190, 195
Curry, William, 105, 118
D'Alton, John, 79–80
Darcy, William, 2, 4, 8
Darley, Frederick, jnr, 223
Daughters of Charity, 235
Davies, Sir John, 13
Davis, Thomas, 130
Day, Robert, 190, 191

Dease, Matthew O'Reilly, 54, 55–6, 58
debating society, 127
Delany, V.T.H, 9, 184
Denver, Mr, 54
devilling, 3, 153n, 175–6, 218
Devon, earl of, 1843, 25
Dillon, John Blake, 49–50, 130
disestablishment, 45, 50–1, 53, 56
Disraeli, Benjamin, 52
Dixon, Joseph, archbishop of Armagh, 46, 47, 48, 56
Doherty, Chief Justice John, 64, 100
Donegal, County, 22–3, 25, 27–8, 29, 56–7
Donegal, marquis of, 26
Downing, McCarthy, 210
Drainage Commissioners, 33
Drummond, Thomas, 65, 66, 75, 109
Drury, William, 167n
Dublin Castle, 114
Dublin Evening Post, 93
Dublin Law Institute, 12–13, 17, 58–9, 149, 152, 219, 226–7, 237
  and attorneys, 155
  calendar of events, 93–131
    1839, 93–102
    1840, 102–15
    1841, 115–24
    1842, 124–31
  council of, 97–100, 192, 207
  curriculum, 89–90
  deputation to Morpeth, 105–6
  history of, 83–92
  in Kennedy petition, 132–4
  King's Inns and, 84–6, 88–9, 115, 118–19, 121, 128–31, 143, 162–3
  lecturers, 14, 89–90, 175, 199, 208
  name adopted, 102
  numbers attending, 90–2
  opened, 1, 10, 23, 78, 82
  prospectus, 93–4
  publications, 70, 114, 136
  revived, 1845–6, 92, 135–7
  staff, 25
  Sugden and, 66–8, 85–9, 166

support for, 35, 53, 62–3, 69, 160, 171–2, 194, 195
Wyse Committee, 140, 143
Dublin Monitor, 108
Dublin Statistical Society, 41
Dublin University Commission, 168, 171
Dublin University Magazine, 163–4
Duffy, Charles Gavan, 130
Duhigg, Bartholomew, 58, 59, 233
Dunbar, George, 105
Dundalk Democrat, 47, 53–4
Dunleer, Co. Louth, 40, 54

East India Company, 78, 139
Ecclesiastical Titles Act, 36, 37, 39, 41
education, 52
  select committee on, 79–81
Edward, Prince of Wales, 215
Ejectments Suspension (Ireland) Bill, 52
Eliot, Lord, 126
Ellis, Hercules, 197
Elphinstone, Sir Howard, 138, 139
emigration, 33, 34
Empson, William, 108, 109, 115, 140–1
encumbered estates court, 167n, 230
Estrete, John, 2
Evening Packet, 95–6, 97, 99, 101–2, 103–4, 109–10
Ewart, William, 138, 139
examinations, 11, 12, 156
  compulsory, 173, 174–5
  optional, 79, 89, 137, 166
  refused, 169
  in Wyse Report, 145
Famine Relief Committee, 26
Fenians, 45, 49
Ferguson, Mr, 124
Fitzgerald, Lord, 215
Forster, Chief Secretary, 210, 212–13
Fortescue, Sir John, 8, 9
Fortescue, Chichester, 50, 209
  chief secretary, 56
  Louth elections, 37–40, 43–4, 46–7, 49, 58

Foster, Vere, 53
Four Courts, 68, 76, 101, 120, 128, 151, 152. *see also* Law Library
  expenses of, 222, 233
  in relation to King's Inns, 224–5
Fowler, Villiers, 74, 75
Foyle Diocesan College, 18, 21
Freeman's Journal, 37, 40, 46, 59, 95, 96–7, 103
French, Fitzstephen, 105
Fry Commission, 176–7, 183

Gaelic law schools, 1, 3–9, 14, 147
  families, 8
  training methods, 5–7
Gandon, James, 15, 192, 220
Gardiner, Luke, 219, 226, 228
Gartlan, Thomas McEvoy, 39
Gavan Duffy, Charles, 22, 33, 35, 36, 42, 43, 60
General Council of the Bar, 77
Geoghegan, Thomas, 153
Georgian Society, 235
Gibson, Edward, 213–14, 215
Gladstone, W.E., 46, 50, 51, 52–3, 56, 180
Godson, Richard, 138, 139
Goold, Thomas, 118n
Grafton, duke of, 219
Graham, Sarah, 45
Grattan, Henry, 15, 191, 194, 195, 199
Graves, John Thomas, 141
Gray, John, 36, 37, 42, 46, 47
Gray, Sir John, 210
Gray's Inn, 7, 125, 185, 226
  Irish students in, 171–2, 193n, 202
Great Famine, 12, 26, 61, 143–4
Greece, 22, 51, 53
Greenleaf, Professor Simon, 133, 136
Grey, Earl, 64

Hamilton, George, 138, 139, 140, 152–3, 163, 178, 206–8
Hardey, James, 89, 90, 102, 108, 127

Hardey, James *contd.*
  forgery, 88, 130
  introductory lecture, 98–9
Hayes, Edmund, 138, 139, 166
Hayter, Mr (MP), 134
Healy, Fr James, 54
Healy, T.M., 213, 215
Hennessy, John Pope, 44–5
Henrietta Street, 15–16, 55, 82–3, 103–4, 117, 218–20, 237
Henry, Mitchell, 214
Heron, Denis Caulfield, 167n
Hickson, William, 170
historians, 8
Holmes, Robert, 112, 118, 118n, 130
home rule movement, 12, 57–8, 209
Houston, Arthur, 216
Hutton, Robert, 105

income tax, 42
Incorporated Law Society, 154, 169
  bill, 170–1
Independent Party, 43, 208
industrial schools, 41
Inner Temple, London, 79, 153, 185
inns of court, London, 3, 147, 165
  commission, 1855, 172–3
  examinations, 175
  Irish students in, 1, 11–12, 14–16, 62–3, 78, 87, 119–20, 150–2, 154, 171–2, 186–217
  students' memorial, 123, 124–5, 195–6
  training, 7, 8, 135
International Statistical Congress, 1852, 41
Irish Law Times, 236
Irish Legal History Society, 235
Irish Parliamentary Party, 61, 209–10
Irish Party, 46, 49
Irish People, The, 49, 53
Irish Society, 56
Irish Times, 232, 236

Jackson, Judge Joseph, 164
Jackson, Serjeant Devonsher, 127, 197–8

Johnson, W.M., 211
Joy, Chief Baron Henry, 64
Joy, Henry H., 163–4
Joyce, James, 182, 234
Judicature Act (England), 1873, 213
Judicature Act (England), 1875, 213
Judicature Act (Ireland), 1877, 12

Kelly, Bishop, 39
Kelly, Mr, 124
Kennedy, Caroline, 60
Kennedy, Charles, 18n, 25, 26, 35, 104n
Kennedy, Charles R., 104n
Kennedy, Evory, 18, 21–2, 23, 36, 57, 60
Kennedy, Henry, 18n, 19
Kennedy, Horas, 17
Kennedy, Hugh, 182n
Kennedy, John Pitt, 17, 18, 19, 22, 25, 28, 30, 39, 41, 53, 60
  agricultural improvement, 23–4, 27
  famine relief, 26
  in India, 35–6
  and poor law, 66, 117, 125
Kennedy, John Pitt jnr, 26n
Kennedy, Mary, 28, 30
Kennedy, Pitt, 60
Kennedy, Sarah, 45, 60
Kennedy, Thomas, 18n, 19, 20, 26n
Kennedy, Tristram, 140, 146, 149, 162–3, 166, 173, 208, 209, 219. *see also* Dublin Law Institute
  Campbell appointment protest, 87, 122–3, 130–1
  death of, 237–8
  encourages chambers, 15–16, 152, 175–6
  famine relief, 26
  on King's Inns, 72–3, 175–6
  land agent, 24–35
  late years, 56–61
  legislator, 35–56
  life of, 17–61
  marriage, 45, 55

petition to parliament, 132–3, 136
Queen's Inns Chambers, 219, 227–34
reform campaign, 10–14
sheriff of Londonderry, 19–21
and Wyse Committee, 141–2, 143
Kennedy, William, 19
Kennedy, William Pitt, 18
Kenny, M.J., 213
Kent, Thomas, 2, 4, 8
Kenyon, John Robert, 141
Keogh, William, 124
Kieran, Michael, archbishop of Armagh, 46, 47, 56
King's College, London, 78, 99, 107
King's County, 44–5
King's Inns, 14–15, 18, 62, 72, 82, 86, 188
   attorneys revolt, 73–7
   authority of, 12
   benchers' committee, 117–19, 121
   bill on English practititioners, 126
   chambers, 15–16, 152, 220–3
   criticisms of, 137
   and Dublin Law Institute, 84–6, 88–9, 115, 118–19, 121, 128–31, 143, 162–3
   eating dinners, 192–3, 202, 207, 212, 216–17
   established, 4
   finances, 76, 134
   functions of, 189
   history of, 71–3, 170
   innovation, 1846–76, 161–85
   Kennedy enters, 21
   Kennedy pamphlet, 58–9, 175–6
   and legal education, 154–7, 164
   links with London, 9–10
   number of students, 71, 90
   petition on chambers, 230–2
   and Queen's Inns Chambers, 218–35
   role of lord chancellor, 66
   solicitors leave, 12
   and Statute of Jeofailles, 211, 213–17
   students protest, 119–20, 123, 124–5, 195–6
   and TCD, 162–8, 206–7, 236
   training, 1–3, 7, 9–10
   and universities, 177–85
   and Wyse Committee, 139–40
   in Wyse Report, 145–6
Knox, Dominick, 19

La Touche, Theophilus Digges, 74, 76, 140, 142
Labouchère letter, 30
Lamb, quaker, 33
Land War, 210, 212
landed estates court, 167n, 230
Law Library, 77, 115, 151, 169, 216, 218, 221–2, 227, 231
Law Society, Irish, 73, 74, 83, 108, 121, 128, 155, 156, 224
   charter of incorporation, 1852, 169
   and Dublin Law Institute, 84, 102, 109, 113
Law Society, London, 10, 11, 72, 75, 79, 89, 154
   charter of incorporation, 1831, 154
Law Times, 136–7, 198
Lawson, James A., 76–7, 117, 128, 140–1, 152–3, 155, 175
Leamy, Edmund, 213
Leech, Brougham, 176–7, 184
Lefroy, Thomas, 112, 130–1, 191, 206
legal education, 62–3, 78–81. *see also* Statute of Jeofailles
   barristers, 126, 149–54
   for catholics, 178–9, 195
   Kennedy petition, 132–3, 136
   London domicile, 11–12, 14–16, 62–3, 78, 87, 119–20, 150–2, 154, 171–2, 186–217
   number of terms, 148–9
   patronage, 63–6
   position in 1846, 147–60
   reform campaign, 11–13, 24, 58–9, 66, 72, 73–7
   in universities, 177–85

legal education, select committee on. *see* Wyse Committee
Legal Education Association, 236
Legal Observer, 104
legal profession
  barriers to entry, 70–1
  catholics in, 77, 84–5, 195, 215
  political patronage, 63–6
  in 1830s, 77–8
  status of, 67–71
Legal Reporter, 69, 131
Lehane, Cornelius, 182n
Ley, Sir James, 14
Liberal Party, 46, 48, 58
Liberal Registry Association, 23
Lichfield House compact, 12–13
Lincoln's Inn, 21, 108–9, 125, 147, 153, 162, 185, 193n
Littledale, William, 170, 173, 176, 221
London inns. *see* inns of court, London
Londonderry, 56, 60–1
  reform society debate, 20–1, 38
  siege of, 17
Longfield, Mountifort, 124, 158, 159, 164, 167, 195
  evidence to Wyse Committee, 103, 140–1, 202–3
  lecture, 89
  president, SSIS, 175
  on Statute of Jeofailles, 204–5
Lough Swilly, 22–3
Loughash estate, 22, 27–8
Louth, County, 15, 29, 61, 209
  banquet for Kennedy, 42–3
  by-election, 1865, 46–9
  election, 1852, 38–40
  election, 1857, 43–4
  election, 1865, 49
  election, 1868, 53–6
  election, 1874, 58
  Kennedy as MP, 35–56
Loyal National Repeal Association, 109
Lucas, Frederick, 36, 41, 42, 43
Lyle, Acheson, 94, 114, 152, 206n
  evidence to Wyse Committee, 128–9, 140, 142, 162, 225
Lynch, A.H., 105

McCarthy, Alexander, 138, 139
McCarthy, Justin, 213
McCausland, Richard Bolton, 167n
McClintock, John, 40, 44, 49
MacDonnell, Richard, 203
MacHale, John, archbishop of Tuam, 37, 114
Mackintosh, James, 147
MacMahon, Patrick, 178–9, 207–8
MacManus, Henry, 59
Maconochie, Allan, 141
Maginn, Edward, bishop of Derry, 21, 26–7
magistrates, 65, 67
Mahony, Pierce, 140, 142, 156, 157, 199–200
Manchester Law Association, 141
Manufacture Movement, 31
Mason, Henry Monck, 234
Maugham, Robert, 142
Maynooth College, 42
Meath, County, 58
medical education, select committee on, 68
Melbourne, Lord, 64, 122, 133
Mercer's Hospital, 84, 107
Middle Temple, London, 153, 185, 191, 194, 214
militia, 232, 233
Milnes, Richard, 138, 139
Mitchell, John, 95
Molyneux, Echlin, 89, 90, 99
  introductory lecture, 96–7
Monaghan, County, 39, 51, 57
  Kennedy as land agent, 26–35
Monahan, James, 206
Moore, Judge Arthur, 229
Moore, Richard, 112, 118n, 130–1
Moriarty, Edward, 140, 141
Morning Register, 96, 104
Morpeth, Lord, 65, 83–4, 85–6, 101, 108, 109
  deputation to, 105–6
  receives form of charter, 111–12
Moryson, Fynes, 187
Mountjoy, Viscount, 228–9
Mountjoy House, 227
Municipal Reform Act, 1840, 113–14

Murnaghan, James A., 182n, 184n
Murphy, Mr, 127

Naish, John, 181, 183, 215
Napier, Admiral Charles, 42
Napier, Sir Charles, 19, 22, 25, 28, 35, 117
Napier, John, 226–7
Napier, Joseph, 85, 87, 99, 130, 171–2, 193n, 236, 237
   attorney general, 206
   bill for Statute of Jeofailles repeal, 178, 179, 208
   debating society, 127
   lectures, 14, 89, 94–5, 102–3, 129, 135, 136
   lord chancellor, 90, 173
   portrait of, 58–9
Napier, General Sir William, 117–18, 120, 123, 226–7
Nation, The, 130
National Association, 45–6, 47, 48, 49, 52, 53, 109
national schools, 25, 30–2, 53, 81
National University of Ireland, 183
Newman, John Henry, 178
Nolan, Michael, 147
Normanby, Marquis of, 84, 107
Norton, Thomas, 140, 142

O'Brien, William Smith, 127
O'Connell, Daniel, 17, 64, 106, 151
   bill on legal profession, 74, 76
   'counsellor', 6
   and Dublin Law Institute, 112
   king's counsel, 65
   mayor of Dublin, 113–14, 124
   and O'Loghlen, 153–4
   and Queen's Colleges, 160
   repeal movement, 12, 67, 86–7, 109, 116
   studies in London, 15, 190, 193n
   on Sugden, 67
   Wyse Committee, 69, 138, 139
O'Connell, John, 105, 106, 198
O'Doran family, 4
O'Hagan, Thomas, 215n
O'Loghlen, Michael, 100, 116, 137, 155, 200
   and Dublin Law Institute, 84–5, 88, 117–18, 130
   master of the rolls, 65, 195
   and O'Connell, 153–4
O'Neill, Hugh, earl of Tyrone, 187
Orange Order, 39
Ormrod committee, 11, 145–6, 176
O'Shaughnessy, Mark, 171, 175, 180, 185
O'Shaughnessy, Richard, 210
Otway, John Hastings, 166
Oxford, University of, 11, 78, 111
Oxford University, 148, 159

Palles, Andrew, 129–30, 183, 184n
Palmer, Sir Roundell, 236
Park, Professor, 99
Parnell, Charles S., 17, 49, 58, 61, 209–10, 213
Parnell, John, 61
Payne, Edward Turner, 142
Peel, Sir Robert, 10, 26, 50, 123, 132–3, 139
Perrin, Judge Louis, 118n, 206
Phillimore, Joseph, 111, 141
Phillipps, Mr, 108, 109
Pigot, Chief Baron David, 127, 206
Pigot, John, 127, 198n
Pilot, 106
Plunket, David, 211, 214
Plunket, William Conyngham, 67, 68, 87, 100–1, 122, 191, 200n, 211
Plunkett, James, 236
poets, 8
poor law, 45, 66, 117, 118, 120, 125
   Napier attack, 123
Poor Law Act, 1838, 27
presbyterian church, 51
Protection of Person and Property (Ireland) Bill, 1881, 210
Provincial Colleges Committee, Cork, 134
pupillage, 2–3, 153n, 174

Queen's College, Cork, 171
Queen's College, Galway, 167n
Queen's Colleges, 12, 81, 134–5, 136, 178, 236

Queen's Colleges *contd.*
  legal education, 90, 159–60, 162, 168, 170, 179–80, 182, 207
  Wyse and, 53
Queen's Inns Chambers, 15–16, 97, 104, 219, 227–34
Queen's University, 181,
Queen's University, Belfast, 183

Radley's Commercial Rooms, 124
'reading', 7
Reformation Society, Londonderry, 20–1
Reid professorship, 177
repeal movement, 12, 61, 67, 86–7, 109, 116
Rice, Vincent, 182n
Richards, Baron John, 165n
Richmond Hospital School, 23
Robertson Commission, 182
Robinson, Sir John, 46
Rotunda hospital, 21, 23
Royal College of Physicians of Ireland, 57, 90, 96
Royal College of Surgeons, 69, 179
Royal Dublin Society, 66, 82, 83, 94, 129
Royal Irish Academy, 59
Royal University, 181–2, 183
Ruggles, Thomas, 191
Russell, Lord John, 37, 139
Rutherford, Andrew, 138, 139

Sadlier, John, 38
St Lawrence, Viscount, 55
Saunders's News-letter, 95, 102, 106, 111, 122, 131
sectarianism, 37–8, 54–5
Shirley estate, 34
Sir Patrick Dun's hospital, 163
Smith, Thomas, master of the rolls, 165n
Society of Attorneys and Solicitors of Ireland, 121, 128, 157
Society of King's Inns. *see* King's Inns
solicitors, 12, 62
  accommodation at Four Courts, 120, 224
  and Dublin Law Institute, 83–4
  and King's Inns, 73–7
  training of, 122, 154–7, 168–71
Solicitors (Ireland) Act, 1866, 170
Solicitors (Ireland) Act 1898, 171
Somerville, Sir William, 138, 139
Spencer, Earl, 230–2
Staples, Thomas, 165n
Starkie, Thomas, 140, 141
Statistical and Social Inquiry Society, 58, 153n, 170, 175, 180
Statute of Jeofailles, 1542, 2, 9, 14–15, 162, 186, 187, 201, 217
  bills for repeal, 178–9, 197–8, 206–13
  repeal sought, 87, 188, 195–6
  repealed, 13, 16, 213–17
Stephen, Sir George, 142
Stewart, James, 142
Stewart, W.V., 105
Story, Judge Joseph, 134, 136
Stubbs, John W., 181n
Style, Sir Charles, 22, 27
Style estate, 25, 27–8
Sugden, Edward, 13, 90, 123, 129, 130, 166
  and Dublin Law Institute, 66–8, 85–9, 131, 166
  letter from Kennedy, 107
  letter to Kennedy, 113
Sullivan, A.M., 58, 209–10, 211
Sullivan, Edward, 213
Sullivan, Francis Stoughton, 78, 158, 203
Sullivan, T.D., 212
Sullivan, William, 41

Taylor, Thomas, 141
Tenant League, 36, 37, 39
tenant right movement, 29, 36–7, 40–1, 45, 50, 51–2, 54, 56
Tennent, J.E., 105
The Temple, London, 153, 192
Times, The, 47, 48, 53
tories, 64–6, 87
Torrens, Judge Robert, 117, 118, 165n
Townsend, Richard, 181

Trench, William Steuart, 34
Trinity College, Dublin, 11, 12, 76–7, 79, 89, 90, 131, 170, 182, 184, 208
  chairs in law, 78, 177–8
  and Dublin Law Institute, 84
  Fry Commission, 176–7, 183
  and King's Inns, 162–8, 171, 183, 206–7, 236
  legal education, 9, 103, 148, 158–9, 160, 195
  numbers attending, 91–2
  opened to catholics, 180–1, 182
  political economy chair, 117
  royal commission, 172, 203–6, 207
  staff, 94, 117, 128
  and Statute of Jeofailles, 197–8, 210–11
Tudor, Richard, 108
Tyrone, County, 29

Ulster custom, 29, 36, 51
Ulster Examiner, 53
Ulster Tenant Right Association, 36
Ulster Times, 94
United States, 151–2
  legal education, 133, 134, 175
university bill, 1873, 180
University College, Dublin, 182, 183–4
University College, London, 78, 105, 159
University of London, 10–11, 72, 91, 127, 141, 148, 182
  and Dublin Law Institute, 84, 106–8, 109, 115

Victoria, Queen, 15, 45n, 83, 103–4, 228
Vigors, N.A., 105

Walpole, Spencer Horatio, 138, 139

Walsh, William, archbishop of Dublin, 182, 183
War Office, 232
Warren, Samuel, 135
Watson, William, 138, 139
Whately, Richard, archbishop of Dublin, 66, 89, 117, 125, 158
whigs, 64–6, 87, 113–14
Whiteside, James, 89, 90, 127, 135–6, 175, 207–8, 230
  lectures, 102, 103
Wilde, Sir Thomas, 138, 139
Wilde, Sir William, 196n
Wolfe Tone, Theobald, 15, 190, 191
workhouses, 27
Woulfe, Chief Baron Stephen, 100
Wright, Thomas, 128
Wylie, James, 162
Wyse, Thomas, 10–11, 13, 53, 79–81, 83–4, 89, 109, 114, 160, 237
  banquet for, 84, 116–17
  committee on legal education, 132, 135, 136–46
  on Institute's aims, 110–11
  Morpeth deputation, 105–6
Wyse Committee, 11, 14, 69, 75–6, 80–1, 103, 129, 132, 135, 136–46, 162–3, 172, 175, 237
  chambers discussed, 225, 227
  members of, 138–9
  report of, 143–6, 161
  on solicitors, 156–7
  on students in London, 202–3, 207
  on universities, 159–60
  witnesses, 140–3, 152–3, 155, 200
Wyse report, 14

Yates, J.A., 105
Yeo, Mr, 124
Young Ireland, 35, 49

The Irish Legal History Society

Established in 1988 to encourage the study and advance the knowledge of the history of Irish law, especially by the publication of original documents and of works relating to the history of Irish law, including its institutions, doctrines and personalities, and the reprinting or editing of works of sufficient rarity or importance.

PATRONS

The Hon. Mr Justice Liam Hamilton

Rt. Hon. Sir Brian Hutton

LIFE MEMBERS

Rt. Hon. Lord Lowry

The Hon. T.A. Finlay

COUNCIL, 1994

PRESIDENT

His Honour Judge Hart, Q.C.

VICE-PRESIDENTS

Professor G.J. Hand

Professor D.S. Greer

SECRETARIES

Professor W.N. Osborough
Dr. A. Dowling

TREASURERS

Daire Hogan, esq.
J. Leckey, esq.

ORDINARY MEMBERS

The Hon. Mr Justice Costello

J.F. Larkin, esq.

J.I. McGuire, esq.

J.A.L. McLean, esq., Q.C.

R. O'Hanlon, esq.